THE BYZANTINE DIVINE LITURGY

MELETIUS MICHAEL SOLOVEY, O.S.B.M.

The Byzantine
Divine Liturgy

HISTORY AND COMMENTARY

Translated by

DEMETRIUS EMIL WYSOCHANSKY, O.S.B.M.

THE CATHOLIC UNIVERSITY OF AMERICA PRESS, INC.

WASHINGTON, D.C. 20017

1970

Nihil obstat: Basilius Wawryk, OSBM, Censor Deputatus

Imprimi potest: Nicholas M. Kohut, OSBM, Provincial,
                   American Province of the Order of St.
                   Basil the Great
                   LONG ISLAND CITY, N.Y.
                   Nr 131/68, August 3, 1968

Nihil obstat: Rev. William M. Bilinsky, Censor Deputatus

Imprimatur: Jaroslav GABRO, D.D., Bishop of St. Nicholas
                   Diocese of Chicago, Illinois,
                   2238 West Rice Street,
                   Nr. 547/68, September 24, 1968

TRANSLATOR'S NOTE

The book of which this is a translation, entitled BOZHESTVENNA LITURGHIA or THE DIVINE LITURGY was written in the Ukrainian language by Fr. Meletius Michael Solovey, O.S.B.M., and was published by the "ANALECTA" of the Basilian Fathers in Rome in 1964. This work, the product of five years of study and research (1947-1952), is a comprehensive study on the Byzantine Divine Liturgy (of St. John Chrysostom). In reading the book one can note that every possible aspect of the Divine Liturgy of the Byzantine Rite has been extensively treated. Father Solovey considers the subject of the Liturgy from the dogmatic, historical, homiletic, scriptural, philological and symbolic viewpoints. The result of this intensive research is a veritable encyclopedia.

The book is also a critique. The author criticizes the method of interpretation used in the past, namely, the symbolic method. The author himself prefers to use the historical-genetic method of interpretation, although he does admit the symbolic interpretation when there is sufficient evidence to confirm the method as sound and veritable. Father Solovey shows clearly whether a rite of the Divine Liturgy was purely utilitarian in origin, esthetic, objectively symbolic or subjectively symbolic. He traces the origins of rites pointing out the weakness in the interpretations of earlier commentators who leaned too heavily on imagination. His commentary on the Divine Liturgy of the Byzantine Rite strives to avoid purely symbolic interpretations and attempts to arrive at the essential meaning of the prayers and rites of the Eucharistic Sacrifice.

We hope that this book will be welcomed not only by those who belong to the various branches of the Byzantine Rite, but also by those of the Roman Rite of the Catholic Church. The Eastern Churches and their Liturgies are gaining more recognition today because they have retained the ancient and original forms of worship to a purer degree. Since this is the age of ecumenism and a period of "awareness," people everywhere are becoming more and more interested in the various ways the Church expresses her faith.

This book has been long awaited by those of the Eastern Church—both Catholic and Orthodox. It is our sincere hope that the fruit of the labor shall be understanding. With a deep understanding, it is our wish that many more people may come to appreciate the Divine Liturgy and its significance in the life of the individual. But before one can appreciate, one must first come to know; may this book be effective in planting the seeds of knowledge.

The translator of this book wishes to express his profound gratitude to the Father Basil Wawryk, O.S.B.M., Mundare, Alberta, Canada, for his sustained and kindly interest in the progress of this endeavor, for his encouragement and his valuable suggestions. The deepest appreciation is also expressed to the Very Reverend Michael Skrincosky, Dean and Rector of St. Basil's College in Stamford, Connecticut, who took the time and care to read my translation and offer constructive criticism on the text, and to the Father James Enright, OSB, Catholic Central High School English Department, Detroit, Michigan, for his assistance. To Miss Sonia Peczeniuk and Mrs. Olga Wojtyshyn, sincere gratitude is offered for the tireless and invaluable assistance in correcting and typing the manuscript of my English translation.

Finally, sincere thanks is expressed to any and all those persons who helped in any manner or form to make this translation a reality.

May 28-th, 1969

Fr. Demetrius Emil Wysochansky,
O.S.B.M.
Basilian Fathers, Hamtramck,
Michigan.

AUTHOR'S PREFACE

Among the various riches of the Christian religion, the first place is, without question, occupied by the Divine Liturgy, which was instituted by Christ Himself and left to us as an everlasting "remembrance," a precious inheritance.

The very dignity and meaning of the Liturgy as the unbloody sacrifice of the New Law demands that Christians esteem, honor and love it. But before one can appreciate the Liturgy, one must understand the meaning of the prayers and ceremonial actions that go to form it. This is why an explanation of the Liturgy is so important. It would be a mistake to think that it requires no interpretation, for just as Sacred Scripture requires a thorough exegesis, so does the Liturgy. Without such exegesis many of the ceremonies and prayers, and indeed the very internal structure of the Divine Liturgy itself would be difficult to understand.

During the past several decades the Catholic world has become greatly interested in liturgics. Both in Europe and here in the Americas the liturgical movement has as its goal a better understanding of the Divine Liturgy and other liturgical services. Historians and liturgists alike are studying ancient liturgical documents in order to gain a deeper insight into the texts and correctly to explain them together with the ceremonies, rites, practices and customs which accompany them. Besides systematic investigation of the Liturgy and the publication of the results, the liturgical movement is concerned with making the Liturgy more meaningful for the largest possible number of Christians. Sermons, studies, conferences, lectures and translations of texts beyond numbering aim at giving the Christian world a more profound interest in the liturgical life of the Church, and at bringing Christians to take an active part in their liturgical worship so that they may receive more benefit from it—in a word, to make them live the liturgical life.

In the Western Church one basic motive for the liturgical movement lay in the fact that the services are in Latin, a language which most people do not understand. But in the past few decades this difficulty has been largely overcome, and the increased use of the vernacular has made the Liturgy more meaningful for the faithful.

Is such a movement needed in the Eastern Churches where the Liturgy is already in the vernacular? Some—perhaps not a few—are convinced that there is no such need. Yet, Eastern Christians do not always understand the meaning of the prayers and ceremonies of the Liturgy despite the fact that it is celebrated in the vernacular or in a liturgical language (e.g., Church Slavonic) which closely resembles the vernacular and poses no problem for the understanding of the texts.

Beginning with the nineteenth century, the literature on the Eastern liturgies, and especially that on the Byzantine-Slavonic Rite, became the subject of special study of both Western (Catholic) and Eastern (Catholic and Orthodox) students. Many excellent works on the Liturgy appeared and helped spread interest in the liturgical life. The results of scientific investigations of the Liturgy, created the need for new explanations, especially of the Divine Liturgy—historical-scientific explanations which would correspond to the present state of liturgical studies.

This work is divided into two parts. In Part I we treat of the origin of the Divine Liturgy, its historical development and the factors which caused this development. In Part II we give a systematic treatment of the prayers and ceremonies of the Divine Liturgy, based not only on the traditional explanation, but on the results of more recent studies. In this Part we have tried to benefit from as wide a selection of material as possible.

Actually, the present book was written ten years before the Vaticanum II, and its publishing was completed in the year 1963, when the *"Constitution on the Sacred Liturgy"* was solemnly promulgated. These facts contributed much in arousing interest in the aforesaid work, mainly amongst the clergy, regular and secular, nuns, seminarians, candidates for the Holy Priesthood and for the religious life. After the work was published in Ukrainian, it was suggested by some of my friends that a translation be made into the English language. This difficult task was undertaken by my Confrater, the Reverend Father Demetrius Emil Wysochansky, O.S.B.M. It took him two years to complete the translation. I hereby wish to express my gratitude to him for this difficult undertaking.

Likewise I wish to thank sincerely the Very Reverend Father Redmond A. Burke, C.S.V., Associate Director of the Catholic University of America Press, for his interest in the said translation and for presenting it to the Committee of the same Press for publication. Finally, I am grateful to all concerned in giving me help in regard to translation, technical form and printing of my book in English, especially to Mr. Aloysius Croft of Wauwatosa, Wisconsin, for the final revision and correction of this English edition of my work.

If it be permitted the Author to express any wish on the occasion of this edition of his work, it would be simply this: that his work would contribute something to a better knowledge and deeper understanding of our beautiful Liturgy. If this wish is realized, the purpose of the book will be accomplished, and the author's labors will be more than amply rewarded.

July 28-th, 1969

Meletius Michael Solovey,
O.S.B.M.
St. Paul University,
Ottawa, Ontario, CANADA

CONTENTS

PART TWO

COMMENTARY OF THE PRAYERS AND RITES OF THE DIVINE LITURGY

Section 1. The Proskomide

Section 3. The Liturgy of the Faithful

PART ONE

HISTORICAL INTRODUCTION
TO THE
DIVINE LITURGY

Chapter I

GENERAL NOTIONS REGARDING
THE DIVINE LITURGY

Catholic doctrine regarding the Divine Liturgy is best embodied and summarized in the definitions and canons of the Council of Trent [1] which developed the doctrine in concise but clear terms to counteract the teachings of Protestantism.

The whole teaching can be reduced to two fundamental concepts: that of sacrifice and that of sacrament. It is not the aim of this chapter to examine the entire Catholic dogma on the Divine Liturgy, but only the most important truths that touch upon its nature, character, object and author. This chapter will help us form an adequate idea of the Divine Liturgy, thus enabling us to undertake a proper exegesis or interpretation of its text and rites.

1. The Term "Divine Liturgy"

Very often, the name of a thing expresses its nature and essence. This is so with the term *Divine Liturgy*.

The expression *Divine Liturgy* [2] is derived from the Greek words *theia*, meaning "of or pertaining to God," hence "divine," and *leiturghia*, meaning "public service." Together they mean "divine public service." We first come across the word *leiturghia* in the Greek classics. The ancient Greeks understood this word to denote any service to the state undertaken by a citizen for the general welfare of the people or public. The first part of the word *leiturghia* etymologically comes from *leitos*, meaning "public" and the second part stems from *ergon*, meaning "duty, deed, act, function or service." The word, then, referred to all those acts or services which were performed for the benefit or welfare of the general public, as for example, military service, services of public officials and all other services carried out in the common interest of the state. It also implied such things as the paying of taxes, the defending of the state against enemy attack, as well as services offered to the gods, especially in the form of sacrifice.

---

[1] H. Denzinger-Umberg, *Enchiridion Symbolorum* (Freiburg in Br: 1937), nos. 937a–956 (De sanctissimo Missae sacrificio), nos. 873a–893 (Decretum de SS. Eucharistia).

[2] The Old-Slavonic term for Divine Liturgy is *Bozhestvenna Liturghia* and the Ukrainian colloquial term is *Sluzjba Bozha*. Since this book deals with the Byzantine (Greek)-Slavonic Liturgy (Liturgy celebrated on Slavic soil especially in Ukraine), for consistency in the use of terminology we shall give first the Greek word then the Slavonic term and finally here and there the Ukrainian colloquial equivalents. This is to acquaint the reader with the liturgical nomenclature peculiar to each Rite (Greek and Slavonic-Ukrainian).

It was in this last meaning that the word found its way into the Christian vocabulary. Even in the Old Testament, the services or functions of the priest in the temple were termed liturgies.[3] The word "liturgy" retained this meaning in the New Testament writings (Heb 8:6; 9:21). It meant the offering up of sacrifices. Again we find the word being used in a religious sense in the works of the Fathers and in the documents of the Church. By the fourth century, the word "liturgy" had become the technical term for the Eucharistic Sacrifice or the Divine Liturgy.[4]

But why is the Divine Liturgy called "divine"? In what sense is the Divine Liturgy a *"divine service"—the service of God* or *God's service*? Is it the people's service to God or is it God's service to the people? It is, in fact both, but predominantly it is service rendered to God. The Divine Liturgy is a service rendered to God by the people because the "whole community"—priest and faithful —takes part in it. The Divine Liturgy, then, is a community or public service by means of which God is paid supreme homage through a variety of prayers, songs and hymns, but above all in the offering of the Unbloody Sacrifice of the New Testament. The Divine Liturgy is also to an extent "God's service to the people," because it is a sacrifice, an offering up of the God-Man, Jesus Christ, in reparation for the sins of mankind.

There are also other names for the Divine Liturgy, as the "Table of the Lord," "Breaking of the Bread," "The Lord's Supper," the "Holy Eucharist," etc. This latter name usually and popularly refers only to Holy Communion and, as a result, the "Divine Liturgy" in this usage is seen as a sacrament rather than as a sacrifice. Other designations have only historical value [5] since they have now fallen into disuse.

There is a marked difference between the words "liturgy" and "Divine Liturgy."[6] Although they are really related in meaning, current textbooks on liturics use the two terms indiscriminately and, as a result, create confusion.

Liturgists understand the word "liturgy' to mean not only the Eucharistic Sacrifice, that is, the Divine Liturgy, but also any kind of sacred service performed in the Church such as vespers, matins and, of course, the sacraments. In this general sense, "liturgy" encompasses the totality of official ecclesiastical observances: all rites, ceremonies, prayers and sacraments of the Church. But in the less extended sense, "liturgy" is restricted to the Eucharistic Sacrifice, or the "Divine Liturgy." Although we may use the term "Eucharistic Sacrifice," we will generally use the term "Divine Liturgy" because this is the correct term used in

---

[3] See the Greek translation of the Bible, the Septuagint (LXX) for the ancient usage of this word.

[4] P. Oppenheim, *Institutiones systematico-historicae in sacram liturgiam,* Vol. VI: Notiones liturgicae fundamentales (Taurini-Romae: 1941), pp. 1–16.

[5] J. M. Hanssens, *Institutiones liturgicae de ritibus orientalibus* (Romae: 1930), Vol. II, pp. 21–41 (De liturgico Missae nomine in ritibus orientalibus).

[6] It must be noted that the word "liturgy" spelled with a capital "L" and preceded by the definite article "the" is the equivalent of the Latin Rite word "Mass." The word "liturgy" spelled with a small "l" and used as a common noun means any official public service of the Church.

the Byzantine Rite, and because it applies exclusively to the Unbloody Sacrifice and not to other services of the Church.

2. Institution of the Divine Liturgy

The first and most important teaching of our faith concerning the Divine Liturgy is that it is of divine institution. It was not instituted by man nor by the Church nor by the Apostles, but by Jesus Christ Himself. This can be determined from the Gospels and from the letters of St. Paul where we read that, on the eve of the Jewish Passover, Christ, shortly before His passion and death on the cross, sat with His Apostles for the last time at the Last Supper. We read how Jesus took bread, blessed and broke it, gave it to His disciples, and said, "Take ye, and eat. This is my body." (Mt 26:26) Then Christ added these memorable words, "Do this in commemoration of Me." (Lk 22:19)

With these words Christ established the Divine Liturgy which He gave to the Apostles and to the Church with the express command that it be offered in His memory. The Divine Liturgy, therefore, was the last will and testament of our Lord. He left to the Church an invaluable inheritance, for in the Divine Liturgy we have our Lord Himself, His most holy Body and Blood. That is why Christians consider the Divine Liturgy to be, after Christ Himself, their most priceless treasure.

The motive underlying the establishment or institution of the Divine Liturgy was Christ's desire to remain with man here on earth to the end of time and to leave mankind a memorial of the redemption. The Egyptian Pharaohs left lasting memorials in their pyramids. Poets, writers, scholars, artists and musicians immortalize themselves by creating masterpieces. But even these remarkable memorials are insignificant when compared with the Divine Liturgy in which Christ perpetuates the memory of His redemption. This means of perpetuation could have stemmed only from the wisdom, omnipotence and love of God. In instituting the Divine Liturgy, Christ showed that "He loved His own, to the end He loved them." (Jn 13:1) The Divine Liturgy was to remind man constantly of what Christ did for his salvation and of His endless, mysterious love for mankind.

3. Essence of the Divine Liturgy

Christ instituted the Divine Liturgy as an Unbloody Sacrifice of the New Testament. It is a true sacrifice offered to God. The sacrificial gifts are the Body and Blood of Jesus Christ under the appearances of bread and wine. To understand better this significant truth of our faith, we must know what *sacrifice* means in general and how it applies to the Divine Liturgy.

Catholic theologians tell us that sacrifice involves three essential conditions: 1) a sacrificial gift, i.e. something material and visible; 2) a sacrificial act by which the gift is offered to God; and 3) the intention of paying supreme homage to God with the gift offered. These three conditions must be present to constitute a true sacrifice, and they are found in all sacrifices of every religion, both primitive and civilized.

The history of religions shows that sacrifice was a universal phenomenon among all peoples, even the most savage. No man of science has ever disproved this fact or discovered a people with a religion whose supreme act of worship was not sacrifice. The universality and ubiquity of offering sacrifices prove that the need to offer them is natural to man. Man everywhere and always instinctively has worshipped a Supreme Being, and no matter how distorted some ideas of the Supreme Being may have been, it still remains true that a Supreme Being was worshipped and that the highest act performed in that worship was the offering of gifts. Man by his very nature has arrived at the notion of sacrifice. By use of his reason, man concludes that God is the First Cause, the Supreme Being, the Supreme Judge, the Supreme Good. Man then perceives, and naturally expresses, his inferiority and dependence by paying due homage. One cannot believe in God, the Lord and Master, and still deny the obligation of paying Him due homage. *God* and *worship* are two inseparable ideas. One suggests the other. Sacrifice means an act of worship It implies active faith in God. Through sacrifice man expresses his faith in God, acknowledges His supremacy; and gives Him due homage. This act of paying homage to God is the most important and most essential condition of sacrifice.

In the Old Testament God Himself gave the Chosen People fundamental rules for offering sacrifice to Him, thus shielding them against the errors and aberrations of the pagan sacrifices in which even human beings, including children, were offered as burnt offerings. The Old Testament sacrifices which were offered only in the temple, the center of the religious life of the Chosen People, were types or forerunners of the New Testament sacrifice. The offering of sacrifices consisted in the priest officially taking the gift presented to him by the people, and offering it up, to be burned or destroyed in some manner. Gifts such as fruit and bread which were not destroyed or burned, became the property of the temple or the priest.

Applying the notion of sacrifice together with its essential characteristics to the Divine Liturgy, we see that the Divine Liturgy possesses all the constituent elements necessary for a sacrifice.

First of all, we have in the sacrifice of the Divine Liturgy a physical, material, visible gift or offering, which, in this case, is not the fruits of the earth, an animal, or something similar, but Jesus Christ Himself. In the Divine Liturgy, His Body and Blood is offered under the appearances of bread and wine. Secondly, this gift is offered by an officially authorized person called a *priest*, who, in the act of sacrificing, takes the place of Jesus Christ. Finally, the purpose of offering the Body and Blood of Jesus Christ is to offer supreme worship to God. Compared to the Old Testament sacrifices which were only weak symbols of the Divine Liturgy, we find that the sacrifice of the New Testament is far superior and that it is a true sacrifice having all the essential sacrificial elements. It is the greatest and most perfect of sacrifices ever offered by man. It is the highest act of worship by which man renders the greatest homage and honor possible to God. The Divine Liturgy is, as we have mentioned, the service of God Himself, and not only a service rendered by people to God. It is the sacrifice of the God-Man for His people.

4. The Character of the Divine Liturgy

Another fundamental teaching of the Catholic faith relating to the Divine Liturgy is that it is essentially one and the same sacrifice as that of Jesus Christ on the cross. This teaching identifies the character of the Divine Liturgy. Like other mystical teachings of our faith, this doctrine may seem contradictory and abstruse. At first sight, a comparison of the two sacrifices—the sacrifice of the cross and the Eucharistic Sacrifice—seems to point up a distinction between them rather than an absolute identity. On the cross, our Lord suffered excruciating pain; He shed His blood and died. In the Divine Liturgy He does *not* suffer, die nor shed His blood. How, then, are these two sacrifices one and the same? In what does their identity consist?

According to the teaching of the Church, the identity lies in the fact that both sacrifices have the same sacrificial minister, the same purpose and the same gift. The minister in both sacrifices is Christ Himself. The sacrificial purpose is the redemption of mankind and the rendering to God of the highest act of worship. The sacrificial gift is also the same Body and Blood of Jesus Christ. This same Christ, shortly before He offered up His Body and Blood on the cross, in anticipation, gave this same Body and Blood to His Apostles at the Last Supper.

The only difference existing between these two sacrifices is the manner in which the gifts are offered. On the cross Christ offered Himself up; in the Divine Liturgy He offers Himself through the priest who represents Him. Then, He offered Himself only once; now He offers Himself more than once. Then, He offerd Himself physically in a bloody manner; now He does so sacramentally and mystically. Then, He offered Himself in His own person; now He offers Himself under the appearances of bread and wine. It follows, therefore, that it is one and the same sacrifice, the identical Body and Blood of Christ which Christ gave to His Apostles at the Last Supper. (Mt. 26:26–28; Lk 22:19)

The Divine Liturgy is a representation, a memorial, an application and a renewal of the sacrifice of the cross. St. Paul clearly emphasizes this fact when he says: "For as often as you shall eat this bread and drink the cup, you proclaim the death of the Lord, until He comes." (1 Cor 11:26) Looked at from this point of view, it is much more than any human drama. In a drama, a historical event is reproduced in an artificial manner, whereas in the Divine Liturgy the work of salvation, which reached its fulfillment in Golgotha, is *really*, and *truly* reproduced and represented. It is a Divine Drama—a drama of the redemption of mankind.

5. Purpose of the Divine Liturgy

Ordinarily, we distinguish four main purposes and four corresponding manners of sacrifice. The first and primary purpose for offering sacrifice is to acknowledge God's supreme dominion over His creatures. As a result we offer Him adoration. All other reasons for offering sacrifice can be reduced to this one purpose. Just as the aim of man on earth is the glorification of God, so too, the purpose of sacrifice is the *glorification of God.* This type of sacrifice is called the sacrifice of praise or adoration (latreutic purpose).

The second end of sacrifice is *to express our gratitude to God* for the benefits He has bestowed upon us (eucharistic purpose). This flows from the first, but there is a slight difference in motive. The first motive for sacrifice, that of adoration, is "unselfish"; its end is God Himself. In the second motive, that of thanksgiving, man offers sacrifices because of personal, selfish reasons, i.e., he thanks God for the benefits he has received from Him.

The third motive for sacrifice, called the sacrifice of *propitiation,* is also personal (expiatory end). The object of this sacrifice is *to placate God's anger, and to make amends,* in a spirit of sorrow, for the sins man has committed. History shows that the majority of sacrifices were offered to obtain pardon for sins and to appease God's anger. Sin was considered the cause of all calamities and misfortunes: floods, drought, plague, sickness and enemy attack. Thus, man offered sacrifices of reconciliation and reparation to God.

The final purpose of sacrifice is *to ask God for help* (impetratory end). This motive springs from man's belief that everything is subject to the Providence of God, and that man is incapable of doing anything without His divine help and blessing. This is why sacrifices of petition are offered before any public or private undertaking.

These four objects of sacrifice are fulfilled ideally in the Divine Liturgy which is the most perfect sacrifice of adoration, thanksgiving, propitiation and petition.

First of all, the Divine Liturgy is the perfect sacrifice of adoration. In the Divine Liturgy we glorify and adore God, through His Only-begotten Son, Jesus Christ. It is not we alone who praise God, but Christ prays with us and for us, since we are offering His prayers, merits, suffering and death to God. No human adoration, not even that of the saints, will ever equal this act of adoration performed in the Divine Liturgy.

The same can be said of the sacrifice of thanksgiving. In the Divine Liturgy we do not ourselves alone offer thanks to God but Christ does so with us. What more perfect way is there to express thanks to God for His countless benefits than to offer up the Unbloody Sacrifice of the Mass? We are incapable of thanking God for all the benfits He has conferred upon us; so, in the Divine Liturgy, we offer to God all the merits of Christ in order to repay our debt of gratitude.

And what can we say about the Divine Liturgy as a sacrifice of reconciliation? Has there ever been, or is there now, a sacrifice that would or could surpass the Divine Liturgy in reconciling mankind with God? In this respect all sacrifices have been less than perfect because they were too weak to merit God's pardon and too weak to remove the great gulf that separated God from mankind. The Divine Liturgy is a sacrifice of peace and reconciliation—a sacrifice that has become the source of God's grace, salvation and blessing. Never again need we offer the blood of animals to make ourselves pleasing to the Deity; in the sacrifice of the Holy Eucharist we have the most perfect and most effective means of obtaining pardon for our sins.

Finally, if the object of sacrifice is to obtain help from God, is there a better and more effective means of obtaining it than through the Divine Liturgy? In the Divine Liturgy not we alone, but Christ with us, pray to God. Christ's infinite merits give our prayers infinite value.

6. The Divine Liturgy—A Sacrament of the New Testment

Our concept of the Divine Liturgy would be incomplete were we to overlook still another important aspect of its nature. So far we have considered the Divine Liturgy as a sacrifice, but the content of the Divine Liturgy is not exhausted when looked upon from this viewpoint, for it is not only a sacrifice, but also a sacrament of the New Testament.

Christ wished to establish the Divine Liturgy as the Unbloody Sacrifice of the New Testament and also as a sacrament which was to be an endless source of God's grace, help and consolation. The most holy Body and Blood of Jesus Christ are not only elements of sacrifice but also nourishment and food for the soul. This spiritual food is given to the Christian at Holy Communion where the sacrificial gifts are distributed to the communicant. In this manner, Christ unites Himself with His chosen one, gives Himself entirely to him and permits him to share in His divine life.

The Holy Eucharist, like the other sacraments, is an outward sign of invisible grace; it is the fountain and storehouse of God's grace which is supernatural life—the life of God. It is above all other sacraments in every respect. Other sacraments either confer grace upon the soul, restore it or increase it. Baptism, for instance, confers the grace that makes us adopted children of God and removes original sin. The sacrament of Penance restores grace which has been forfeited by the soul. The sacraments of Holy Orders and Matrimony bestow upon those who receive them the grace and help to fulfill the duties of their respective states. The sacrament of Last Anointing increases grace and gives strength to the soul. All sacraments, therefore, are sources and channels of the supernatural life which is the life of God.

In Holy Communion, however, we receive not only the particular graces of that sacrament, but also the Giver of all graces, our Lord Jesus Christ Himself. At Holy Communion He comes to dwell within us and to unite Himself with us in order to make us partakers of His divine life. Holy Communion is a spiritual banquet wher the spiritual food in the Body and Blood of Jesus Christ. It draws us into a very close and intimate union with God, a union scarcely conceivable.

Human reason cannot plumb the depth of this divine mystery; it stands powerless before it. God's wisdom, omnipotence and love could not have done more. It is small wonder that this sacrament was considered by the Jews as "a stumbling block." Christ, long before the establishment of the Holy Eucharist, promised to give His Body and Blood to the world, and the people upon hearing this departure from Him murmuring that His words were hard. (Jn 6:10;) But Christ did not recall His words. On the contrary, at the Last Supper He fulfilled this promise and gave the Apostles His Body and Blood with the explicit command that they do likewise in His memory by renewing and repeating this Divine Banquet.

Long ago people dreamed of union with God, and expressed this desire through sacrifice. Externally this union with the divinity was expressed by the consumption of the victim (the Paschal Lamb among the Jews). The sacrifice of the Divine Liturgy answers the craving of the human heart for union with the divinity. At Holy Communion this union is achieved. Holy Communion is the re-enactment of Christ's coming into the world, for the God-Man, Jesus Christ, is born again in the hearts of men at Holy Communion. He comes to the soul and repeats and renews the mission which he has already fulfilled on earth. He comes with His teaching, enlightening the minds of men and performing those same miracles He once performed while in this world. He cures sicknesses, opens the eyes of sinners, strengthens the weak, raises the dead to a new life and sends the Holy Spirit with graces and assistance. In short, at Holy Communion we receive every grace necessary for our salvation.

7. The Excellence and Value of the Divine Liturgy

In light of the previous observations on the nature of the Divine Liturgy, we can see clearly its great significance and infinite value. In all respects it is superior to all the other sacrifices mankind had ever offered, whether of pagan or of Jewish (Old Testament) origin.

Jewish sacrificial offerings were not only a natural expression of the worship rendered by the Jewish people, but they were also more perfect than pagan sacrifices. The Jews, who possessed the true faith, sacrificed to the true God and not to false gods as the pagans did. Of all the nations then existing, they were the ones chosen to be the bearers of true faith in God, of the first revelations of God and of the promise of a redeemer of the world—the Messiah.

Some sacrifices, such as the paschal sacrifice, were prescribed by God Himself and, therefore, carried the seal of divine approval. In the divine plan the Paschal Lamb was a forerunner, although a weak one, of the Unbloody Sacrifice. For this reason, Jewish sacrifices were far more perfect than all pagan sacrifices. Yet, they were at the same time imperfect since they were only figures and shadows of the Divine Liturgy and did not completely fulfill the ends or purposes of sacrifice. In themselves, they were incapable of reconciling mankind with God or of restoring the union with God which had been destroyed by sin.

All these imperfect, temporary and weak sacrifices have been replaced by the Bloody Sacrifice of the God-Man on the cross and the unbloody renewal of this same sacrifice in the Divine Liturgy. St. Paul clearly demonstrates the real emptiness and incomplete nature of all sacrifices offered before Christ: "For it is impossible that sins should be taken away with the blood of bulls and of goats." (Heb 10:4) He adds that Christ had to come in order to obtain the remission of sins by offering up His Body and Blood as a sacrifice: "Therefore, in coming into the world, he says, 'Sacrifice and oblation Thou wouldst not, but a body Thou hast fitted to me: in holocausts and sin-offerings Thou hast had no pleasure.' Then said I, 'Behold I come—(in the head of the book it is written of me)—,' to do Thy will, O God.'" (Heb 10:5–7) Fulfilling the wish of His Heavenly Father, He died on the cross, thus offering Himself as a sacrifice for the sins of the world.

By dying on the cross, Christ nullified all sacrifices that had been thus far offered, and in their place He inaugurated a new sacrifice, a "pure offering" of which the Prophet Malachias spoke: "I have no pleasure in you, saith the Lord of hosts: and I will not receive a gift of your hand. For from the rising of the sun even to the going down, my name is great among the Gentiles, and in every place there is sacrifice, and there is offered to my name a clean oblation: for my name is great among the Gentiles, saith the Lord of hosts." (Mal 1:10–11)

These prophetic words found their fulfillment in the sacrifice of the Divine Liturgy. The Divine Liturgy is, therefore, that new, perfect, holy, universal and pure offering.

From all that has been said of the Divine Liturgy, we may conclude, first of all, that we Christians have no greater nor more precious treasure than the Divine Liturgy which is a memorial of our salvation. In the Divine Liturgy, God continues to manifest His love for us. He left us a unique memorial of His death—a memorial "more lasting and durable than bronze," the only memorial of its kind, a memorial immortal, imperishable and unforgettable. In it He perpetuates His death on the cross for the salvation of mankind and He demonstrates, over and over again, His endless love for us.

Secondly, if the Divine Liturgy is our greatest treasure, it follows that we should cherish it. The Divine Liturgy, as the sacrifice *par excellence* and the highest act of divine worship should be the heart and soul of our Christian religion. It must cease to be merely an ordinary Sunday formality, a spiritless and monotonous ritual. A more intimate knowledge of its nature, its rites, its prayers and its symbolism will help us to appreciate the Divine Liturgy more, for it is only by knowing and understanding that we can truly and sincerely appreciate and cherish it, and derive spiritual benefit from it.

SELECT BIBLIOGRAPHY

Batiffol, P. *Leçons sur la Messe.* Paris: 1919.

Fillograssi, J. De Sanctissima Eucharistia. 3d ed. Roma: 1940.

Gihr, N. *Das heilige Messopfer.* Freiburg: 1922.

Kramp, J., S.J. *Eucharistia—Von ihrem Wesen und ihrem Kult.* Freiburg: 1926.

Levynsky, A. *Nauka o Sluzhbi Bozhiy.* Lviv: 1906.

Chapter II

THE HISTORICAL DEVELOPMENT OF THE DIVINE LITURGY IN THE FIRST CENTURIES

In the first chapter we examined the nature of the Divine Liturgy. Now we shall consider the Divine Liturgy from the viewpoint of its historical setting and development.

Historical knowledge of the Divine Liturgy, at least in its general aspects, is necessary not only for experts, but also for those who wish to derive benefit from its prayers and rites. Without such knowledge, the present-day form of the Divine Liturgy cannot be adequately understood.

The Divine Liturgy as we know it today, besides being a divine institution, is also the product of many centuries of evolution. Like the Bible, it is the work of both God and man. Jesus Christ is its true author, but its *external form* is the work of the Church.

In the Old Testament God gave Moses a plan for the making of the tabernacle and minute prescriptions regarding the place, time and manner of offering sacrifice. Christ could have done likewise: He could have arranged and formulated the words, prayers, hymns, rites and ceremonies of the Divine Liturgy. But instead, Jesus Christ gave the Church a "free hand" in determining the vehicle of the Divine Liturgy, in selecting prayers and in formulating detailed prescriptions governing the various rites.

The Divine Liturgy can be truly compared to the mustard seed which Christ spoke about in His parable of the Kingdom of Heaven. Christ planted this seed at the Last Supper and from it sprung an enormous tree adorned with liturgical prayers, rites, customs and symbolism.

Documents still extant help us to trace development of this "seed" through the centuries. We shall especially consider, in general, the first centuries of the Christian era, the most important period in this long development.

1. The Last Supper—The First Divine Liturgy

In treating the development of the Divine Liturgy, we must begin with the Last Supper, for it was then that the first Divine Liturgy was celebrated by our Lord.

How was this first Divine Liturgy celebrated? In what form did our Lord institute it? The Evangelists did not leave us any detailed description of the course or text of the Divine Liturgy. Nevertheless, we can, from their scant accounts of the Last Supper, form a fairly good, though incomplete, picture of the manner of celebration. In reading the Gospel accounts we note only the

27

most essential elements of the Divine Liturgy: the rite of consecrating and the rite of consuming the bread and wine. We read in the Gospels that Christ first blessed the bread and wine and then gave it to the Apostles as food. (Mt 26:26–28) We also note some non-essential rites which were later incorporated in the Divine Liturgy. For instance, we read that Christ washed the feet of His Apostles. This rite of washing or cleansing was retained in all the Liturgies. The priest, at the beginning of the Liturgy, performs the same rite; however, instead of his feet, he washes his hands to symbolize the necessity of spiritual purification when offering the unbloody Sacrifice. The Evangelists further relate that Christ delivered a touching farewell speech. (Jn 14:17) From this developed the custom of preaching the Word of God at the Divine Liturgy. The Evangelists also tell us that, at the end of the Last Supper, Christ sang with the Apostles a hymn of praise composed of Psalms (Mt 26:80), a practice which is common to all Liturgies.

Another important fact worth noting and emphasizing is that Christ instituted and celebrated the Divine Liturgy in a manner parallel to the Paschal sacrifice of the Old Testament. This fact is very important both from the doctrinal and developmental point of view.

From the doctrinal point of view, in instituting the Divine Liturgy within the framework of the Passover sacrifice of the Old Testament, Christ revealed its redemptive character. The Divine Liturgy is the New Testament sacrifice which was prefigured by the Old Testament Paschal offering. The sacrifice and the consumption of the Paschal Lamb were instituted by God through Moses to remind the Jewish people of God's beneficence shown in delivering the Jews from Egyptian bondage. The Divine Liturgy likewise is a commemoration of the work of redemption which was accomplished by the "Lamb of God," Jesus Christ Himself, who voluntarily assumed the role of the sacrificial Lamb to atone for the transgressions of mankind. (Jn 1:29)

From the developmental point of view, the Old Testament Paschal sacrifice and other Old Testament rites exerted considerable influence upon the structure of the Divine Liturgy. Certain rites, customs and even prayers in our modern Liturgy found their way into the Divine Liturgy according to the pattern of the Old Testament sacrifices and other Old Testament services. Christ did not form a new or special rite; however, the fact that He modelled the Divine Liturgy on the Old Testament Paschal sacrifice gave His Apostles the opportunity and occasion to borrow from the Old Testament forms of divine worship. We shall say more about this later. Here, we only wish to show what influence the Last Supper had on the further development of the Divine Liturgy.[1]

---

[1] Select Bibliography: A. Arnold, *Der Ursprung des christlichen Abendmahles* (Freiburg: 1937); M. Barth, *Das Abendmahl—Paschamahl, Bundesmahl und Messiasmahl*, "Theol. Studien, Heft 18", (Zurich: 1945); W. Berning, *Die Einsetzung der heiligen Eucharistie* (Munster: 1901); G. Bickell, *Messe und Pascha.* Der apostolische Ursprung der Messliturgie und ihr genauer Anschluss an die Einsetzungsfeier der hl. Eucharistie durch Christus aus dem Pascharitus nachgewiesen (Mainz: 1872); K. G. Goetz, *"Die Entstehung der Liturgie aus der Einsetzungs-*

2. The Divine Liturgy in Apostolic Times

(First Century)

The Last Supper was the beginning of the gradual development of all other Liturgies. The first stage or phase of development dates back to the Apostolic Period. What did the Divine Liturgy look like in this period?

We have two sources of information concerning the Apostolic Divine Liturgy: the *Acts of the Apostles* and the *Epistles of St. Paul.*

In the Acts of the Apostles, the Divine Liturgy is called the "breaking of bread." We read "And they were persevering in the doctrine of the apostles, and in the communication of the breaking of bread, and in prayers. . . .And continuing daily with one accord in the temple, and breaking bread from house to house, they took their meat with gladness and simplicity of heart." (Acts 2:42–46)

Unfortunately, we are unable to ascertain from Acts the details and sequence of this *"breaking of bread."* We can, however, say that the "breaking of bread" was somewhat reminiscent of the Last Supper which served as a model for the Apostles. It was a very simple ritual. Since the Jews persecuted the first Christians and forced them to meet in the evenings in private homes to celebrate the "breaking of bread" in secret, the Divine Liturgy had to remain short and simple in form.

The Liturgy of the Apostles was of a domestic nature not only because it was celebrated in private homes, but primarily because it was like a family affair. The Acts tell us of a Divine Liturgy celebrated by St. Paul in Troas (Asia Minor) during his third mission. "And on the first day of the week, when we were assembled to break bread, Paul discoursed with them, being to depart on the morrow. . . .Then going up, and breaking bread and tasting, and having talked a long time to them, until daylight, so he departed." (Acts 20:7–11) From this we learn that the "breaking of bread" took place in the evening, in the presence of all the congregation and during the community supper. As an introduction to the "breaking of bread," a sermon on the Gospel was usually delivered and the Apostles or their immediate successors in the priesthood explained the Holy Scripture to the assembly, recalling especially the death of Christ. After the explanation of the Scriptures they recalled the words of Christ's command: "Do this as a memorial to me." Then bringing the bread and wine they began the "breaking of bread" or the Eucharistic Sacrifice. It is very probable that the course of this sacrifice was similar to that of the Last Supper and that it contained all the essential elements of the Last Supper: the rites of consecrating the gifts and the consuming of these gifts.

---

feirer," Zeitschrift f. kath. Theologie, IV (1880); Fr. Hamm, *Die liturgischen Einsetzungsberichte* (Munster: 1928); J. M. Hanssens, *Ritus paschales et eucharistici in ultima coena,* "Periodica de re morali, liturgica et canonica", XVI (1927), pp 238–257; F. Dibelius, *Das Abendmahl* (Leipzig: 1926); H. Lietzmann, *Messe und Herrenmahl* (Bonn: 1926); E. Loymeyer, *Vom urchristlichen Abendmahl,* "Theol. Rundschau", Neue Folge, 1937, pp. 168–277; 273–314; 1938, pp. 81–99.

St. Paul, in his First Epistle to the Corinthians, informs us about the custom
of arranging the repast of love, the *agape*.[2] Some, especially the wealthier class of
Christians, who attended the meetings and took part in the "breaking of bread,"
brought bread, wine and other victuals, in order that in the spirit of Christian
love they could share it with others, especially the needy and poorer Christians.
The Acts allude to this great love of the first Christians. "And the multitude of
believers had but one heart and one soul: neither did any one say that aught of
the things which he possessed, was his own; but all things were common unto
them." (Acts 4:32) The repast of love, or the agape, which either followed
immediately or, more frequently, preceded the Eucharistic Sacrifice, was an
expression of this love and spiritual unity. In the course of time, however, these
love meals or banquets proved impractical, for they led to many abuses which
St. Paul vigorously decried.

In the same letter to the Corinthians, St. Paul rebukes them for the improper manner in which they conducted these love banquets. Some of the richer
class, instead of sharing their food with the poor, would eat it themselves. They
even ate and drank to excess. "For first of all I hear that when you come
together in the church, there are schisms among you; and in part I believe it.
For there must be also heresies: that they also, who are approved, may be made
manifest among you. When you come therefore together into one place, it is not
now to eat the Lord's supper. For every one taketh beforehand his own supper
to eat. And one indeed is hungry and another is drunk. What, have you not
houses to eat and to drink in? or despise ye the church of God; and put them to
shame that have not? What shall I say to you? Do I praise you? In this I praise
you not." (1 Cor 11:18–22)

These abuses of the *agape* must have crept into the other Christian communities as well for we read in the Epistle of St. Jude: "These men are stains on
their feasts, banqueting together without fear, feeding themselves; clouds without water, which are carried about by winds, trees of the autumn, unfruitful,
twice dead, plucked up by the roots." (Jude 1:12) Already in the first century we
discover that the *agape* was separated from the Eucharistic part and was held in
this manner until finally, in the later centuries, it ceased to be a custom and disappeared completely.

From what has been said we may conclude that in the Apostolic Period, the
Eucharistic Sacrifice in its external form and domestic nature was similar to that
of the Last Supper. Its characteristic features were simplicity and domestic inti-

---

2 Select Bibiography: P. Batiffol, *L'agape*, *"Etudes d'histoire et Theologie positive"* (Paris:
1926), pp. 283–325; —— *L'agape*, DTC, I (1930), cols. 551–556; Baumgarten, *Eucharistie und
Agape im Ur-Christentum*, (Solothurn: 1909); F. Cirlot, *The Early Eucharist* (London: 1939);
Ermoni, *L'Agape dans l'Eglise primitive* (Paris: 1907); J. M. Hanssens, *L'Agape et l'Eucharistie*,
"Ephemerides Liturgicae" (Roma: 1927), 525–548; 1928, 545–571; 1929, 177–198, 520–529; Keat-
ing, *The Agape and the Eucharist in the Early Church* (London: 1901); H. Leclercq, *L'Agape*,
DACL, I (1907) , col. 775–848; P. Sokolov, *Agapi ili vecheri lyubvi vo drevnekhristiyanskom
myerye*, Ser. (Posad: 1906) ; K. Völker, *Mysterium und Agape. Die gemeinsamen Mahlzeiten der
alten Kirche* (Gotha: 1927).

macy. Because of lack of documents, however, we have no complete or detailed knowledge of how the Liturgy was celebrated at that period.[3] Yet, we do know that the customs of the Jewish synagogue played a great role in the formation of the Divine Liturgy, a role which we will now investigate.[4]

When speaking of the services of the synagogue, we have in mind those services which were conducted on the Sabbath. The Apostles and the first Christian community, who were of Jewish extraction, still frequented the synagogue and participated in its services even after the descent of the Holy Spirit—the Pentecost. It was only for the "breaking of bread," or the Eucharistic Sacrifice, that they assembled in private homes. This state of affairs did not last long. The Jews began shunning the Christians whom they considered heretics and traitors and would not associate with them. As a result the Christians were forced to segregate themselves from the Jews and to meet in private homes. Even after this separation, however, they still adhered to the order of services observed in the synagogue: a community prayer, followed by readings from the Law of Moses and from the Prophets, which in turn were explained. These readings were interrupted with songs taken from the Psalms. After the explanation of the Old Testament selections, they again prayed in common, thus ending the services. Liturgists refer to this type of service as the homiletic-didactic service. Already in the Apostolic Period, this homiletic-didactic service was conducted in con-

---

[3] Select Bibiography: Andersen, *Das Abendmahl in den zwei ersten Jahrhunderten nach Christus* (Giessen: 1904); P. Cagin, *L'Eucharistia—Canon primitif de la messe* (Rome: 1912); —— *L'Anaphore apostolique et ses temoins*, (Paris: 1919); F. Cirlot, *The Early Eucharist* (London: 1939); O. Cullmann, *Urchristentum und Gottesdienst*, "Abhandlungen zur Theologie des Alten and Neuen Bundes," No. 3, 1944; M. Goguel, *L'Eucharistie des origines a Justin Martyr* (Paris: 1910); J. Hoffmann, *Das Abendmahl im Urchristentum*, "Zeitschrift f. neutest. Wissenschaft," V (1904); A. Golubtsov, *Liturghia v perviya vyeka khristiayanstva*, "Bog. Vyestnik," 1913, iyul, pp. 621–643, noyabr 332–356, dekabr 779–802; Juelicher, *Zur Geschichte der Abendmahlsfeier in der aeltesten Kirche* (Freiburg in Br.: 1892); H. Lietzmann, *Messe und Herrenmahl* (Bonn: 1926); A. Krasovsky, *Bogosluzheniye khristiyanskoye so vremeni apostolov do chetvertoho vyeka*, "Trudy Kiev. Dukh. Akad.," 1874, 11, pp. 155–230; 1875, 5, pp. 360–426, 7, pp. 42–106, 8, pp. 290–321, 11, pp. 169–201, 12, pp. 426–454; 1876, 2, pp. 330–358, 3, pp. 405–451, 4, pp. 92–142, 6, pp. 425–471; A. Petrovsky, *Apostolskiya liturghii vostochnoy Tserkvi* (Spb: 1897); F. Smirnov, *Bogosluzheniye apostolskaho vremeni*, "Trudy K. D. A.", 1873, pp. 493–560, 5, pp. 77–155; —— *Bogosluzheniye khristianskoye so vremeni apostolov do chetvertoho vyeka*, "Trudy K.D.A.", 1874, 4, pp. 155; Spitta, *Die urchristliche Tradition über den Ursprung des Abendmahles* (Goettingen: 1893).

[4] Information on the influence of the Jewish synagogue services on the development of Christian worship, especially on the liturgical-ritual development of the Divine Liturgy is copious. Here we give only select literature: A. Baumstark, *Das eucharistische Hochgebet und die Literatur des nachexilischen Judentums*, "Theologie und Glaube", II (1910), 353–370; G. Bickel, *Messe und Pascha* (Mainz: 1872); A. Dmitrievsky, *Drevne-Yudeyskaya synagoga i yeya bogosluzhebniya formi v otnosheniyu k drevne-khristianskomu khramu i yeho bogosluzhebnim formam* (Kazan: 1893); Drach, *Harmonie entre l'eglise et la synagogue* (Paris: 1844); Dugmore, *The Influence of the Synagogue upon the Divine Office* (London: 1945); F. Gavin, *The Jewish Antecedents of the Christian Sacraments* (London: 1928); J. Leitpold, *Der Gottesdienst der aeltesten Kirche juedisch, griechisch*, christlich (Leipzig: 1937); G. Loeschke, *Juedisches und Heidnisches im christlichen Kult* (1910); W. O. E. Oesterley, *The Jewish Background of the Christian Liturgy* (Oxford: 1925); W. F. Skene, *The Lord's Supper and the Passover Ritual* (Edinburgh: 1891). Gregory Dix, *The Shape of the Liturgy*, (London: 1964).

junction with the Eucharistic Sacrifice, and in the second century we find the
two services merging to form one liturgical whole.

We shall learn more about the influence of the synagogue services and other
Old Testament elements of divine worship on the Divine Liturgy, in the second
part of this book.

Another factor that affected the development of the Liturgy was the non-
Christian cultural atmosphere, which was that of Hellenism.[5] Even in the first
years of its existence the Church of Christ had spread beyond the boundaries of
Palestine into other areas of the world and had come into contact with the prevailing culture and thought. The Apostles and their followers had to adapt
Christian doctrine to the mentality of their new environment. St. Paul, the great
champion of Christian doctrine, said of himself: "To the weak I became weak,
that I might gain the weak. I became all things to all men, that I might save
all." (1 Cor 9:22) He did this in order to bring all to Christ and His doctrine.
He was a Greek to the Greeks and a Jew to the Jews. Undoubtedly, the other
Apostles and their followers who were converts had to adjust to the new circumstances and, in preaching the doctrine of Christ, had to take into consideration
the mentality and mores of non-Jewish peoples. The mentalities of the Jews and
the non-Christians were foreign to each other; hence, both had to be considered
and respected.

The influence of Hellenism can best be seen in the fact that the Greek language was used among non-Jewish Christians, since the Aramaic, spoken by the
Jews was not understood by the Greeks or Romans. We also find Hellenistic
thought expressed in the prayers and rites of the Divine Liturgy. In their studies
of the origin of each individual prayer, rite and symbolic action of the Divine
Liturgy and other Christian services, liturgists frequently detect the influence of
Hellenism and discover that many elements in the Christian cult were taken
from non-Christian religions and mysteries which had no small influence upon
the rites of the Christian Liturgy.

To a certain extent, the heresies of the first centuries also contributed to the
development of the rites and prayers of the Liturgy. To justify their erroneous
doctrines, the heretics did not hesitate to falsify the Scriptures. Even in their
cults they gave expression to their heretical convictions especially the Christological heresies of the fourth and fifth centuries: Arianism, which taught that
Christ was not God nor the eternal Son of God nor of the same substance; Nes-

---

[5] The following are the more important works dealing with the influence of Hellenism on
Christian services: A. Baumstark, *Vom geschichtlichen Werden der Liturgie* (Freiburg in Br.:
1923) ; Odo Casel, *Altchristliche Kult und Antike,* "Jahrbuch f. Liturgiewissenschaft", IV
(1923) , 1–7; G. Loeschke, *Juedisches und Heidnisches im christlichen Kult* (1910) ; A. Loisy,
Les Mysteres paiennes dans le culte juif et dans le culte chretien (Paris 1919) ; H. Platsch-
bacher, *Hellenismus und Christentum,* "Theologie und Glaube", 21 (1929) , 697-709; H. Pinard,
Infiltrations paiennes dans le culte chretien (Bruxelles: 1909); K. Schneider, *Studium zum
Ursprung liturgischer Einzelheiten oestlicher Liturgien,* "Kyrios, I (1936), 57–73; 3, (1938),
149–190, 239–311; ——— *Das Fortleben der Gesamtantike in den griechischen Liturgien,*
"Kyrios," 4, (1939) 185–221; P. Wendland, *Die hellenistisch-roemische Kultur und Christentum*
(Tübingen: 1907).

torianism, which said that in Jesus Christ there were two persons, a divine person and a human person joined in perfect harmony of action but not in the unity of a single individual; Monophysitism, which held that Christ had but a single nature which was composed of two natures, human and divine. These heretics introduced into the already-existing prayers of the Liturgy heretical innovations and distortions.

Hence, true Christians had to guard against and counteract these heretical falsifications and innovations by giving expression to the true faith in the prayers and rites of the Liturgy. Thus, new prayers of an antiheretical nature were formulated, prayers which contained in short but clear words the true Christian belief. An example of an antiheretical prayer is the *Monogenes* (The Hymn of the Incarnate Word) or the "Only-begotten Son" which is a refutation of the teachings of Arius, Nestorius and Eutychius.

The Divine Liturgy was also influenced by Neo-Platonic philosophy which manifested itself in the arrangement and style of certain prayers, especially in symbolism. Glancing back at the liturgical evolution throughout the centuries, we observe that each century, with its peculiar mentality and culture, left its mark on Christian services.[6]

It is now apparent why the Divine Liturgy is the work both of God and of man, for in essence it is of Divine origin while in its external form it is the work of man.

3. Development of the Divine Liturgy in the Second and Third Centuries

There is not much to be said about the historical development of the Divine Liturgy in the second and third centuries, the period of rigorous persecutions of the Christians. We have but few historical documents and testimonies regarding the form and course of the Divine Liturgy of that time, especially regarding the text of the Eucharistic Sacrifice. Because of the conditions of the times, the Eucharistic Sacrifice could not develop freely and normally.

The persecuted Christians were forced to safeguard their religious practices against the desecration of the pagans. This was particularly true of the Eucharistic Sacrifice which, after Christ Himself, was their most precious treasure. They used symbols to conceal their faith, practices and rites even from those who after long indoctrination proved themselves worthy to become members of the Christian community and mysteries. This use of symbolism was called the *Disciplina Arcani*—the Discipline of Secrecy.

This explains the relative lack of evidence regarding the external form of the Divine Liturgy. Besides, the Eucharistic Sacrifice, being by its very nature the most incomprehensible and inscrutable mystery of the Christian faith, was to pagans and Jews a "stumbling black"; so misunderstood and misinterpreted was it that the pagans accused the Christians of cannibalism.

---

[6] A. Baumstark, *Vom geschichtlichen Werden der Liturgie*, pp. 21–29 (Hellenistischer Einschlag).

However, on the basis of a few documents, we are able to reconstruct approximately the course of the Liturgy celebrated at that time. Pope St. Clement, in his letter to the Corinthians (*c.* 96 A.D.), mentions the gathering of the Christians for the Eucharistic Sacrifice, the sacrificial gifts that were offered, community prayer, and he even quotes an example of a lengthy prayer which, with a few small alterations, is found in an Egyptian Liturgy (St. Mark). According to certain liturgists this prayer is an excerpt from the original Liturgy.[7] The letters of St. Ignatius, Martyr (d. 107 A.D.),[8] provide us with some further allusions to the Eucharistic service. But neither St. Clement nor St. Ignatius gives us a full description, or still less, a text, of the Divine Liturgy of that time.

We do learn more, however, about the Divine Liturgy of the second century from an ancient Christian document, the *Didache* or "Doctrine of the Twelve Apostles," written, scholars believe, in the first half of the second century or toward the latter part of the same century. In the *Didache* we find some examples of the first eucharistic prayers. We also discover that a confession of sins preceded the Eucharistic Sacrifice, so that one could receive the Sacred Species with a clean conscience and in the spirit of true reconciliation and charity.[9]

A more detailed description of the Divine Liturgy in the first half of the second century was handed down to us by St. Justin (d. 165 A.D.) in his *Apologies* written about 155 A.D. Here he describes the structure and course of the second-century Divine Liturgy. It is the oldest description of the Divine Liturgy of the Post-Apostolic Period.[10]

---

[7] F. Probst, *Liturgie des vierten Jahrhunderts und deren Reform* (Muenster in W.: 1893), pp. 26–29. Cf. T. Schermann, *Griechische Zauberpapyri und das Gemeinde—und Dankgebet im l. Klemensbrief* (Leipzig: 1909).

[8] J. Migne, *Patrologia Graeca* (PG), Vol. 5, cols. 656, 700, 713. Cf. F. X. Funk, *Patres Apostolici*, 1–2 (Tubingae: 1901); K. Bihlmeyer, *Die Apostolischen Vaeter* (Tübingen: 1924), pp. 82–113.

[9] For the *Didache* see the following works: P. Batiffol, *L'Eucharistie dans Didache*, "Revue Biblique," I (1925), 58–67; L. Baumgartner, *Die Agapen in der Didache* (Freiburg in Schw.: 1909); F. X. Funk, *Die Didache*, "Kirchengeschichtlichen Abhandlungen und Untersuchungen", II, (Paderborn: 1899); P. Drews, *Untersuchungen zur Didache*, "Zeitschrift f. neutest. Wissenschaft", (1904), p. 74 ss.; E. Goltz, *Das Gebet in der aeltesten Christenbeit* (Leipzig 1901);—— *Tischgebete und Abendmahlsgebete in der altchristlichen und in der griechischen Kirche,* (Leipzig: 1905); A. Harnack, *Die Apostellehre und die Juedischen zwei Wege* (Leipzig: 1886); G. Klein, *Die Gebete in der Didache,* "Zeitschrift f. neutest. Wissenchaft", 9 (1908), 132–146; Ladeuze, *L'Eucharistie et les repas communs des fideles dans la Didache*, "*Revue de l'Orient chretien*", 1902, 339–359; G. Robinson, *The Problem of the Didache,* "Journal Theol. Stud.", 13 (1912), 339 ss.; P. Savi, *La dottrina degli Apostoli* (Roma: 1893); P. Tosti, *La Didache—Traduzione italiana e commento* (Roma: 1945); A. Seeberg, *Die Didache des Judentums und der Urchristenheit* (Leipzig: 1908); K. Popov, *Ucheniye dvanadtsyati Apostolov* (Novootkrytiy pamyatnik drevney tserkovnoy literaturi v perevodye s grecheskoho, s vvedeniyem i prymyechaniyami, (Kiev: 1885).

[10] Select Bibliography: O. Casel, *Die Eucharistielehre des hl. Justinus des Maertyrers,* " *Der Katholik,*" (1914); F. X. Funk, *Die Abendmahlselemente bei Justin,* "Theologische Quartalschrift," 74 (1892), 643–659; A. Harnack, *Brot und Wasser Die eucharistische Elemente bei Justin* "Texte und Untersuchungen," VII, 2, (Leipzig: 1891); K. Hubik, *Die Apologien des hl. Justinus* (1912); T. Otto, *Corpus apologetarum,* I (Jena: 1876); S. Salaville, *La liturgie décrite par S. Justin et épiclèse,* "Echos d'Orient," 12 (1909) 129 ss, 222 ss.

The Eucharist according to St. Justin is not ordinary food but the Body and Blood of Jesus Christ. According to his description, the Divine Liturgy began with selective readings from the Old and New Testaments which were followed by a sermon or homily delivered by the one presiding over the assembly. In his sermon, the preacher exhorted the faithful to lead a life in conformity with Christ's teachings. After the sermon the people all stood up for community prayer and greeted one another with the kiss of peace. The deacons then brought the bread and wine with water for the Eucharistic Sacrifice which followed immediately. The presiding minister pronounced the words of the Eucharistic Prayer (the Consecration) and the people responded with the word "Amen." The consecrated Gifts were then distributed to the faithful in Holy Communion.[11]

Thus, St. Justin describes the course of the Divine Liturgy. It can be remarked that in his description there is no mention of the agape or repast of love. From this we may infer that by his time this feature had disappeared from the Eucharistic Sacrifice and was held separately. In his description of the Divine Liturgy we have the first proof that, during his time, selective readings from the Scriptures and a sermon constituted the homiletic-didactic service, which was held in conjunction with the Eucharistic Sacrifice. These two services—the Eucharistic service and the homiletic-didactic service—formed a liturgical unit. Both of these, which in character, origin and object differ from each other, have been generally accepted by all the Liturgies up to the present day.

Although the Church writers, St. Irenaeus, (d. 202 A.D.),[12] St. Clement of Alexandria (d. 217 A.D.),[13] and Origen (d. 245 A.D.),[14] do not give us an accurate description of the Divine Liturgy, they do mention individual parts, as for example, the reading of the Scriptures, homilies, community prayer and eucharistic prayers. St. Irenaeus also mentions the epiklesis or the invocation of the Holy Spirit. If he is quoting a text from a liturgy of that time, then it would be the oldest record of the incorporation of the epiklesis.

The most valuable document of the third century regarding the Divine Liturgy is the *Apostolic Tradition* of St. Hippolytus of Rome (d. 234 A.D.).[15] This writing is very important not only because it gives us a description of the Divine

---

[11] J. Migne, PG, tome 6, cols. 427–430; T. Otto, *Corpus Apostolorum,* I, pp. 177–188.

[12] Migne, PG, tome 7, col. 1023–1024, 1077–1078.

[13] Migne, PG, tome 8, col. 240 (Protrept. XII); tome 9, col. 469 (Stromata, VII).

NOTE: Hereinafter Migne will be cited simply as Migne, PG (or PL—Patrologia Latina) 2, 167—the first figure referring to the tome or volume, the following figure or figures to the column or columns in which the cited material appears.

[14] Migne, PG, 11, 557–560; 12, 160, 551, 974; 14, 1282.

[15] Select Bibliography: A. Achelis, *Die ältesten Quellen des orientalischen Kirchentums*: Canones Hippolyti (Leipzig: 1891); B. Botte, *Hippolyte de Rome,* La Tradition Apostolique (texte latin, introduction, traduction et notes) (Paris: 1946); G. Dix, *The Treatise on the Apostolic Tradition of St. Hippolytus of Rome* (London: 1937); H. Connolly, *The so-called Egyptian Church Order and Derived Documents* (Cambridge: 1916); F. X. Funk, *Didascalia et Constitutiones Apostolorum,* II (Paderborn: 1905), cf. pp. 97–119; B. S. Easton, *The Apostolic Tradition of Hippolytus* (Cambridge: 1934); B. Haneberg, *Canones S. Hippolyti* (Muenchen:

Liturgy but also because it gives us the very text of the Liturgy used during his time.

The Divine Liturgy in this document appears under the name "Eucharist." It consists of only the Eucharistic-Sacrificial part or the Anaphora. Although we learn nothing about the homiletic-didactic service from the *Apostolic Tradition,* we must not conclude that, at the time when St. Hippolytus lived, there was no such service; for the testimonies of St. Justin, St. Irenaeus and Origen cited above testify to the reading of the Scriptures and the sermon before offering the Eucharist Sacrifice.

The *Apostolic Tradition* furnishes us with an accurate text of the Eucharistic-Sacrificial part of the Divine Liturgy. It begins with the kiss of peace, a symbol of Christian love and unity, in which all the faithful participate. After the kiss of peace, the bishop or minister greets the people with the words, "The Lord be with you," to which the congregation replies, "And with your spirit." Then he exhorts the faithful: "Lift up your hearts," and they in turn respond, "We have them lifted up to the Lord." Again the minister exhorts the people: "Let us thank the Lord," and the people respond, "It is just and meet, etc." After these exhortatory acclamations, come the prayer of "thanksgiving," Christ's words of institution (the words of Consecration) and the prayer of the epiklesis, i.e., a prayer invoking the Holy Spirit to descend upon the holy gifts to change them into the Body and Blood of Jesus Christ. These prayers prepare the faithful for a worthy reception of Holy Communion. Just prior to receiving Holy Communion, the faithful recite a beautiful prayer with bowed heads and the consecrated Gifts are then distributed to the faithful. When the minister exclaims, "Holy Gifts for the holy," the people respond, "One Father, One Son, One Holy Spirit." In the Anaphora of St. Hippolytus we find very beautiful prayers thanking God for the Holy Gifts just received. The priest then dismisses the faithful with the words: "Go in Peace."[16]

We can truly say that this liturgical formula of St. Hippolytus gives us a thorough account of the Eucharistic-Sacrificial part of the Divine Liturgy. It is very similar to the present canon of the Liturgy, although it was not completely developed. St. Hippolytus does not have the component elements of the present day Divine Liturgy in his Anaphora, as for example, the Hagiological Hymn, "Holy, Holy, Holy"; the Lord's prayer; and other hymns and prayers. However, the Anaphora of the *Apostolic Tradition,* in comparison with the Divine Liturgy of St. Justin, reveals considerable progress and enrichment.

There is no doubt that at the time St. Hippolytus wrote his Anaphora, there were other existing anaphoras, such as those of St. Mark or St. James. However, no documents containing a text, or even a description, of these anaphoras from

---

1870); E. Hauler, *Didascaliae Apostolorum fragmenta Veronensia latina* (Leipzig: 1906); E. Schwartz, *Ueber die Pseudo-apostolischen Kirchenordnung* (Strassburg: 1910); A. Wilmart, *Le texte latin de la Paradosis de S. Hippolyte,* "Recherches de sciences relig.", IX (1919), pp. 62–79. Gr. Dix, *The Shape of the Liturgy,* (London: 1964).

[16] The text is found in F. X. Funk, *op. cit.,* 97–119; cf. Hauler, *op. cit.,* 106–107.

the third century, have come down to us. We may assume that they were identical in form and internal structure.[17]

4. The Divine Liturgy in the Fourth Century

Finally in the fourth century, the Church obtained religious freedom after many long years of persecution. The Roman Emperor Constantine, who was sympathetic to the Christians, granted in his Decree of Milan (313 A.D.) religious freedom to all those who professed the Christian religion. As a result, Christianity and the Church began to spread and develop freely until it finally became the official religion of the Roman Empire. Thus the Decree of Milan ushered in a new era in the historical development of the Christian system of worship and the Divine Liturgy.

Once the Church was set free, magnificent churches and basilicas began to be built throughout the Empire, and the external form of the Liturgy assumed a character of beauty and splendor. A fourth-century document, *The Pilgrimage of Silvia Etheria* (c. 385 A.D.), describes this external beauty and splendor of Christian services.

In this document Sylvia Etheria, a pious noblewoman from Gaul (France) and a pilgrim in Jerusalem, describes with enthusiasm the divine rites and services in which she had participated in Jerusalem. From her descriptions we gain some insight into the form and structure of the Divine Liturgy and other divine services. According to the liturgists, the *Pilgrimage of Sylvia Etheria* is a document of primary importance.[18]

The fourth century furnishes us with still more documents and testimony regarding the Divine Liturgy—its form, course and text. After the Decree of Milan, Christian writers and the Fathers of the Church were able to write more

---

[17] The more important literature on the Divine Liturgy of the second and third centuries: A. Arndt, *O formye sv. Liturghiye v tryekh pershikh vyekakh, "Dushpastir"* XI (1895), pp. 7–10, 39–42, 103–105, 156–157, 209–211, 268–269, 301–303, 331–333; —— *O Yednosti bozhestvennoy Liturghii v tryekh pershikh vyekakh kristiyanstva, "Dushpastir,"* IV (1895), pp. 388...., 433......, 485......, 511; A. Baumstark, *Vom geschichtlichen Werden der Liturgie* (Freiburg in Br.: 1923); F. Cabrol, *Les origines liturgiques* (Paris: 1906); P. Gagin, *L'Eucharistia-Canon primitif de la messe* (Rome: 1912); —— *L'Anaphore apostolique et ses temoines* (Paris: 1919); L. Duchesne, *Origines du culte chretien* (Paris: 1909); W. H. Frere, *The Anaphora or Great Eucharistic Prayer* (London: 1938); A. Katansky, *Sobraniye drevnikh liturghiy* (Spb: 1874); A. Krasovsky, *Bogosluzheniye so vremeni apostolov do chetvertaho vyeka, "Trudy K.D.A."* (1874–1876); F. Probst, *Liturgie der drei ersten christlichen Jahrhunderte* (Tübingen: 1870); J. Quasten, *Monumenta eucharistica et liturgica vestustissima* (Bonn: 1935–1937); T. Schermann, *Fruehchristliche Liturgien* (Paderborn: 1915); F. Smirnov, *Bogosluzheniye Khristianskoye so vremeni apostolov do chetvertaho vyeka, "Trudy K.D.A."* (1874); J. H. Srawley, *The Early History of the Liturgy* (Cambridge: 1913); Warren, *The Liturgy and the Ritual of Antenicene Church* (London: 1904); G. P. Wetter, *Altchristliche Liturgien: Das christliche Mysterium* (Goettingen: 1921); —— *Das christliche Opfer,* (Goettingen: 1922); Wooley, *The Liturgy of the primitive Church* (Cambridge: 1910).

[18] The text of the *Pilgrimage* was discovered and first published by M. Gammurini. The more important works on the *Pilgrimage* are: A. Bladau, *Die Pilgerreise der Aetheria* (Paderborn: 1927); F. Cabrol, *Etude sur la Peregrinatio Silviae——Les Eglises de Jerusalem, la disci-*

freely about the practices and mysteries of Christian worship. The *Disciplina Arcani*,[19] "The Discipline of Secrecy," gave way to an outward expression of the Christian faith with its sacraments and mysteries. It is small wonder, then, that in fourth-century Christian literature we encounter more evidence and documents about the structure and texts of the Liturgy than in previous centuries. We can now follow the evolution of the Divine Liturgy more easily.

Of all the liturgical documents of the fourth century, the *Mystagogic Catecheses* of St. Cyril, Bishop of Jerusalem (315–386 A.D.),[20] commands our first interest. The *Mystagogic Catecheses* are teachings which St. Cyril explains to the neophytes or new members of the Church of Jerusalem. These contained teachings on the sacraments and the Divine Liturgy (5th catechesis). Cyril's explanation of the Divine Liturgy is of great importance to the liturgist because it is the first and oldest explanation of the Divine Liturgy of the Patristic Age or the age of the early Christian Fathers.[21]

This explanation is short, and, in its own right, traditional or classical. As the basis of his explanation, St. Cyril availed himself of the Liturgy of the Church of Jerusalem from which he quotes prayers and rites and then systematically explains them. He does not always quote the Jerusalem anaphora verbatim, though he frequently describes it, taking for granted that his listeners are acquainted with the text of this Liturgy.

St. Cyril begins his explanation with the canon or anaphora of the Divine Liturgy, namely, with the Eucharistic Sacrifice. He does not explain the homiletic-didactic part which preceded it. At the very beginning he explains the rites of washing of the hands and the kiss of peace symbolically, and then passes over to the eucharistic dialogue between the priest and the faithful ("Let us lift up our hearts . . ."). After explaining the contents of the eucharistic prayers preceding the Consecration and during the Consecration itself, St. Cyril gives an explana-

---

pline et la liturgie au 4-e siècle (Paris et Poitiers: 1895) ; L. Duchesne, *Les origines du culte chrétien* (Paris: 1920), pp. 512–542; (Paris: 1925), pp. 510–542; M. Gammurini, *Peregrinatio Aetheriae (Silviae) ad loca sancta*, (Roma: 1887–1888) ; P. Geyer, "*Itinera Hierosolymitana saeculi IV–VII,*" in *CSEL*, Vol. XXXIX, pp. 37–101 (Wien: 1898) ; W. Heraeus, *Silviae vel potius Aetheriae Peregrinatio ad loca sancta* (Heidelberg: 1908); N. Krasnoseltzev, *Bogosluzheniye Yerusalimskoy Tserkvi v kontzye IV vyeka*, "Pravoslavnij Sobesyednik" (1888), III, pp. 350–384; H. Richter, *Pilgerreise der Aetheria (oder Silvia) von Aquitanien nach Hierusalem und die heiligen Staetten* (Essen: 1919); E. Weigand, *Zur Datierung der Peregrinatio Aetheriae*, "Byzant. Zeitschrift," XX (1911), 1–26.

[19] During the persecutions of the early Christian Church some of its teachings and practices were kept secret from unbelievers, who parodied, misrepresented and made mockery of these most sacred "mysteries." (*Encyclopedia Americana*, Vol. 9, p. 152—see Disciplina Arcani or the Discipline of the Secret.)

[20] Migne, PG, 33, 1065–1128, especially the fifth cathechesis; pp. 1109–1128.

[21] In the opinion of some scholars, e.g., Swaans, the author of the "Mystagogical Catecheses" was not St. Cyril, but his immediate successor in the See of Jerusalem, Bishop John (d. 417). Select bibliography: F. Probst, *Die Liturgie des vierten Jahrhunderts und deren Reform*, 77–106 (Die Messe von Jerusalem nach den Schriften des hl. Cyrillus) ; S. Salaville, *Une question de critique litteraire: les catecheses de Saint Cyrill de Jerusalem*, "Echos d'Orient," XVII (1915) 531–537; W. J. Swaans, *A própos des catecheéses mystagogiques attribuees a S. Cyrille de Jerusalem*, "Le Museon", 55 (1942) , 1–43.

tion of the epiklesis. He then proceeds to explain the Our Father, the rite of Holy Communion, and the reason for commemorating the saints, the living and the dead. St. Cyril gives a detailed account of how the first Christians received Holy Communion, and from his catecheses we first learn that the "Our Father" was a component part of the Divine Liturgy.

In the same period, other Fathers of the Church mention the Divine Liturgy in their works. In their writings we encounter many allusions to, descriptions of, and other evidence regarding the structure, prayers and course of the Divine Liturgy. We have the testimony of Eusebius, Bishop of Caesarea (d. 338 A.D.) [22] and the first Church historian, regarding the Palestinian Divine Liturgy. Testimony concerning the Alexandrine-Egyptian Liturgy are given to us by St. Athanasius the Great (d. 373 A.D.), Bishop of Alexandria,[23] and those concerning the Liturgy of the ecclesiastical province of Cappodocia by St. Basil the Great (d. 379 A.D.), St. Gregory the Theologian (d. 390 A.D.), and St. Gregory of Nyssa (d. 395 A.D.), brother of St. Basil.[24] From the works of St. John Chrysostom (d. 407 A.D.,) we are able to reconstruct the Liturgy of Antioch (where he was a priest and the Liturgy of Byzantium where he was a bishop).[25] Other similar evidence is found in the works of St. Ephrem (d. 397 A.D.) where we learn of the Liturgy of Mesopotamia;[26] the works of St. Ambrose (d. 397 A.D.) [27] where we learn of the Liturgy of Milan; and of St. Augustine (d. 430 A.D.) where we are informed about the African Liturgy.[28]

There are also extant some formularies of the Divine Liturgy from the fourth century. Compared with the texts or formularies of the *Apostolic Tradition* of St. Hippolytus, they reveal additions and enrichments not evident in previous centuries. Among the more important innovations or interpolations are the Lord's Prayer, the Hymn of the Seraphim "Holy, Holy, Holy," the commemoration of the saints, the commemoration of the living and the dead in the Canon and the introduction of the ektenes or litanies, etc.

What claims our special interest here is the fourth-century liturgical formula of the *Apostolic Constitutions*. The authorship of this work was once ascribed to St. Clement of Rome (d. 96 A.D.); however, some scholars affirm that it is of the fourth century and most likely originated in Syria. In the sev-

---

[22] F. Probst, *Liturgie des vierten Jahrhunderts und deren Reform*, (Muenster in W.: 1893), 38–77 (Die Messe nach Eusebius von Caesarea).

[23] F. Probst, *op. cit.*, 106–124 (Die alexandrinische Liturgie nach den Schriften des hl. Athanasius).

[24] F. Probst, *op cit.*, 125–156 (Die cappadocische Messe nach den Schriften des Basilius, Gregor von Nazianz und Gregor von Nissa).

[25] F. Probst, *op. cit.*, 156–202 (Die antiochenische Messe nach den Schriften des hl. Johannes Chrysostomus), 202–226 (Die Liturgie von Constantinopel nach den Schriften von Gregor v. Nazianz und Chrysostomus).

[26] F. Probst, *op. cit.*, 308–318 (Die Ostsyrische Liturgie nach Ephraem).

[27] F. Probst, *op. cit.*, 226–277 (Die Mailaendische Messe nach den Schriften des hl. Ambrosius).

[28] F. Probst, *op. cit.*, 272–307 (Die afrikanische Liturgie, hauptsaechlich nach den Schriften des hl. Augustinus).

enth book of the *Apostolic Constitutions,* a liturgical text, commonly called the "Divine Liturgy of St. Clement," was inserted.[29] This text is of great significance mainly because it is a complete formula of the Divine Liturgy, i.e., it contains both the homiletic-didactic and eucharistic parts.

In the first part, the homiletic-didactic part, the Liturgy of the Catechumens is included. Here we have long prayers recited over the catechumens and penitents, who according to the prescription of the Church of that time, were not yet eligible to take part in the offering of the Body and Blood of Jesus Christ. At the end of the homiletic-didactic services, they were dismissed from the church, and as they were leaving, the faithful offered prayers to God in their behalf. It should not surprise us that the dismissal of the catechumens played a very important role in the *Apostolic Constitutions,* since it was in the fourth century that the catechumenate flourished. Owing to the mass influx of non-Christians into the Church, the Church was compelled to devote more time to the indoctrination of the catechumens. This consequently affected the structure of the Divine Liturgy.

The Divine Liturgy of St. Clement is very important because it is similar in structure to that of St. John Chrysostom. Indeed, so pronounced is this similarity, especially in the eucharistic part of the Liturgy, that liturgists consider St. John Chrysostom's Liturgy the sister to the Liturgy of St. Clement.

Another important Anaphora of the fourth century is that of the *Eucologion of Serapion,* Bishop of Thmuis, Egypt. It reflects the fourth-century Divine Liturgy prevalent in lower Egypt (Nile Delta).[30]

Toward the close of the fourth century, the evolution of the Divine Liturgy reaches its zenith. In fact the fourth century concludes the principal phase of liturgical development. It was in this century that the structure of the Divine Liturgy became fixed and stabilized. The modifications and additions that

---

[29] The liturgical text of the "Apostolic Constitutions" is found in Migne, PG I, 995–1156, and Funk. The more important literature on the subject: S. J. Drey, *Neue Untersuchungen ueber die Konstitutionen und Kanones der Apostel* (Tübingen: 1832) ; P. Drews, *Untersuchungen ueber die sogenannte clementinische Liturgie im VII Buch der apostolischen Konstitutionen* (Tübingen: 1906) ; F. X. Funk, *Didascalia et constitutiones Apostolorum,* I–II (Paderborn: 1905) ; —— *Die Apostolischen Konstitutionen. Eine literarhistorische Untersuchung* (Rottenburg: 1891) ; —— *Das achte Buch der Apostolischen Konstitutionen und die verwandten Schriften neu untersucht,* "Theol. Quartalschrift" (1893), 605–666; O, Krabbe, *Ueber den Ursprung und den Inhalt der Apostolischen Konstitutionen des Clemens Romanus* (Hamburg: 1829); H. Leclerq, *La liturgie des constitutions apostoliques.* DACL, III, 1914 2748–2795; H. Lietzmann, *Klementinische Liturgie,* Kleine Texte (Bonn: 1910) ; Th. Shermann, *Die allgemeine Kirchenordnung des zweiten Jahrhunderts* (Paderborn: 1914) ; —— *Fruehchristliche Liturgien* (Paderborn: 1915); —— *Die Kirchliche Ueberlieferung des zweiten Jahrhunderts* (1916); E. Schwartz, *Ueber die Pseudo-apostolischen Kirchenordnung* (Strassburg: 1910).

[30] Select Bibliography on the "Euchologion of Serapion": A. Baumstark, *Die Anaphora von Thmuis und ihre Ueberarbeitung durch den hl. Serapion,* "Roemische Quartalschrift" (1904), 123–142; F. E. Brightman, *The Sacramentary of Serapion of Thmuis* "Journal Theol. Stud." (1899) , 88–113, (1900) , 247–277; A. Dmitrievsky, *Euchologion IV v. Serapiona Tmuitskaho,* "*Trudy K.D.A.*" (1894), II, pp. 212–274; Wobbermin, *Altchristliche liturgische Stuecke aus der Kirche Aegyptens nebst einem dogmatischen Brief des Bischofs Serapion v. Thmuis* (Leipzig: 1898); Wordsworth, *Bishop Serapion's Prayerbooks* (London: 1910).

appeared afterward did not affect the fundamental plan and arrangement but only the nonessential elements. However, it does not follow that uniformity prevailed then; on the contrary, absolute and perfect uniformity never existed either in the fourth century or in the centuries that followed. The fourth century was, in fact, distinguished for its great freedom in the development of the Divine Liturgy. This freedom is the reason for the lack of uniformity that exists today; it only produced more liturgical-ritual types.[31]

5. Liturgical Types or Rites

From the various documents of the first centuries liturgists conclude that there was no liturgical-ritual uniformity in the Church from the very beginning of its growth and expansion but that there existed a variety of liturgical-ritual types. After the fourth century, this liturgical-ritual variety becomes increasingly crystallized and evident, so much so, that liturgists point to this period as the era of the origin of various Christian rites as we know them today.

We have explained how the diversity of liturgical forms arose in the first centuries. It has already been noted that this variety can be attributed to the fact that Jesus Christ, in instituting the Divine Liturgy, did not give the Apostles any detailed set of rules for celebrating the Divine Liturgy, but rather a general plan and a free choice in developing the manner of offering the Eucharistic Sacrifice in accordance with the circumstances of time and the needs of the Church.

In other words, this diversity in celebrating the Divine Liturgy and other divine services originated with the early Christians and Apostles. The first Christian communities founded by the Apostles did not celebrate the divine services in one and the same manner. Although there was one faith, one love and one head that united all Christian communities scattered over the wide territories of the Roman Empire, these communities lived a separate and even independent life. All indeed had the same divine service, but the manner in which they conducted this service varied. Ancient Christian documents, e.g., the *Didache*, the *Apologies* of St. Justine, and others, confirm that in the first centuries the minister recited the prayers from memory or improvised them as he

---

[31] Select Bibliography: A. Arndt, *O reformye sv. Liturghii v IV stolyetyu*, "Dushpastir" IX (1895), pp. 532....., 560....., 578...., 609......; A. Baumstark, *Die Liturgie des sog. Eusebius von Alexandria*, "Jahrbuch f. Liturgiewissenschaft," II (1922), 91–92; ——— *Die Messe im Morgenland* (Kempten-Muenchen: 1906); F. Cabrol, *Les origines liturgiques* (Paris: 1906); L. Duchesne, *Origines du culte chrétien* (Paris: 1909); H. Lietzmann, *Liturgische Texte zur Geschichte der orientalischen Taufe und Messe im II und IV Jahrhunderten* (Bonn: 1923); N. Krasnoseltsev, *Bogosluzheniye Yerusalimskoy Tserkvi v kontsye IV vyeka*, "Pravoslav. Sobes." (1888), III, pp. 350–384; B. Mercier, *La Liturgie de saint Jaques*, (Edition critique du texte grec avec la traduction latine) in "Patrol. Orient." Vol. XXVI, fasc. 2 (Paris: 1946); A. Rueker, *Die syrishe Jakobusanaphora nach der Rezension des Ja'quobh von Edessa* (Muenster: 1923); F. Probst, *Liturgie des vierten Jahrhunderts und deren Reform* (Muenster: 1893); T. Shermann, *Der liturgishe Papyrus von Der—Balizeh*, (Texte u. Untersuchungen, XXXVI, 1.), (Leipzig: 1910); ——— *Aegyptische Abendmahlsliturgien des ersten Jahrtausends* (Paderborn: 1912).

went along. Written texts or formulas of the Divine Liturgy did not exist at that time: the manner of celebrating, of distributing Holy Communion, and other Church practices, prayers, and rites were handed down in each Christian community by oral tradition. This ancient Christian custom gave rise to diversified forms of worship and was responsible for the division of the liturgical services into various types.

Another factor accounting for liturgical-ritual diversity was the persecutions launched against the Christians in the first centuries. During the persecutions, contact between the various communities was very often severed. Only after the Decree of Milan, which granted religious freedom to all Christians, do we note attempts to introduce uniformity in the celebration of the divine services.

The division of Christian communities into ecclesiastical provinces was one factor that helped to establish uniformity. Already in Apostolic times, we find certain Christian communities assuming leading positions and becoming prominent centers, such as Jerusalem, Antioch, Alexandria, Rome, Ephesus and others that were established by the Apostles, and which became, in relation to other churches, mother-churches. It was natural that the mother-churches came to exercise their influence upon the smaller and newly-established churches. This influence affected not only the juridical life of the Church but also its liturgical-ritual life. The manner of celebrating the Divine Liturgy and other divine services in the mother churches was frequently adopted by the smaller churches under their jurisdiction. This is how the various liturgical centers and liturgical-ritual types originated and were stabilized.

With the growth and expansion of Christianity, the external organization of the Church grew in strength and power. The first Church centers which were founded by the Apostles became outstanding centers of the great Church provinces. The external organization of the Roman Empire also had great influence on the division and fixing of the boundaries of these provinces. The vast territories of the Empire were divided into administrative and military provinces, called eparchies or dioceses, with their seats in the larger cities. Certain autonomous eparchies of the Roman Empire were so vast that they had their own emperors. The Church patterned her external organization after that of the Empire and in this way she consolidated her provinces, especially in the fourth century, when the Church centers were Rome, Alexandria, Antioch, Jerusalem, Caesarea (Asia Minor), Ephesus and finally Constantinople (the "New Rome").

These ecclesiastical centers not only became the See Cities of the hierarchy (patriarchs, archbishops, metropolitans, bishops) but also the centers of the religious and spiritual life of the Church. They, among other things, represented the law and served as a model of liturgical-ritual practices for the communities within their own ecclesiastical province. The minor Church communities, which perhaps had their own liturgical-ritual customs and usages, fell under the influence of their Church centers and endeavored to conform their liturgical practices to those of the centers.

It would be erroneous to think that this process of ritual adaptation and adjustment was always spontaneous and natural. There were cases when individual churches adhered obstinately to their local customs and practices and showed no desire to repudiate them. We know from Church History that there was a long dispute concerning the time when Easter should be celebrated. In certain churches of Asia Minor, Christians celebrated Easter at the same time the Jews celebrated the eve of the Passover, the 14th day of Nisan (April), with no regard as to whether the Christian Easter would fall on a Sunday or not. In other communities in the East as well as in the West, the Christians were accustomed to celebrate Easter always on Sunday, and avoided celebrating it with the Jewish Passover. When the dispute arose and some of the Popes expressed their desire to introduce into the whole Church the practice of celebrating Easter on Sunday, the churches in Asia Minor protested and in defense of their practice appealed to Apostolic tradition, i.e., that tradition handed down to them by St. John, the founder of various churches in Asia Minor. At the first Ecumenical Council of Nicaea (325 A.D.) this dispute was finally settled, and Easter was to be observed on Sunday.

This was only one of the numerous examples which show that the attempt to achieve liturgical-ritual uniformity was not an easy task. Not infrequently were provincial synods called to pass resolutions and decisions in the hope that each local church would accept the liturgical-ritual practices and usages of its See. The history of liturgy recounts instances where even the state authorities meddled in liturgical affairs in order to abolish certain local practices, or to spread and impose the practices and usages of the Metropolitan See upon other individual churches or entire Church centers. Examples of such intrusion into the liturgical life of the Church were Charlemagne in the West (d. 814 A.D.) and a score of Byzantine emperors in the East. Their motives for seeking liturgical uniformity were neither ecclesiastical nor religious, but political. They were motivated by the ideal of one nation, with one emperor or head, as well as one Church with one faith and one common rite. Charlemagne, influenced by such an ideal, endeavored to introduce the rite of the Roman Church into his empire and to banish from use other rites (e.g. Gallic) to which certain local churches in France, Germany and Northern Italy adhere even today. The Byzantine rulers did likewise through administrative decrees, enforcing upon all nations and ecclesiastical provinces of the Eastern Roman Empire the liturgy and rites of its capital city—Constantinople.

In the West, for many reasons, the Rite of the Roman Church did eventually gain supremacy, even in those provinces which had their own particular Rites, such as the Gallic, Mozarabic, Celtic and Ambrosian Rites. The Rite called the "Roman Rite," after the place in which it originated and from which it spread abroad, is also called "Latin Rite," after the language used in this rite.

Liturgical-ritual diversity is more evident in the East than in the West. From the manifold Rites that prevailed in the first Church communities of the ecclesiastical provinces in the East, the following important Rites evolved: (1)

the Byzantine, so called because of the city in which it was celebrated (Byzantium-Constantinople); (2) the Armenian, (3) the Syrian-Antiochian, (4) the Chaldean, (5) the Alexandrine-Coptic, and (6) the Ethiopian. Other related Rites are the Maronite, Malabar, and other forms of the Byzantine Rite. Each of these is a compound of ritual customs, practices and liturgical texts, each possessing its own particular characteristics in celebrating the Divine Liturgy, in distributing Holy Communion, and in celebrating holydays. Each has its own church architecture, vestments and vessels. In almost every Rite listed above, one may observe a common tendency to attribute liturgical formulas or texts to some Apostle, or to some distinguished bishop of a given Church with which the Rite was associated. For example, there are the Liturgies of St. James, St. Matthew, St. John, St. Peter, St. Clement of Rome, St. Ignatius the Martyr, St. Gregory, St. Basil, St. John Chrysostom, St. Athanasius, St. Thaddeus, St. Cyril and others.

Not all these Rites enjoyed the same popularity or rank. Just as in the West, the Latin Rite prevailed, so too in the East, the Byzantine Rite was predominant over all others. Most of the Eastern Rites are limited both in number and territory because they are celebrated by a small number of Christians. The majority of Christians in the East are affiliated with the Byzantine Rite whose wide popularity and precedence over all other Eastern Rites can be attributed to many ecclesiastical and political factors, especially the powerful influence of the Eastern Roman Empire, which promoted this Rite as the Rite of the capital, state and empire. A far more important factor in the dissemination of the Byzantine Rite, however, was the missionary work carried on by the Byzantine Patriarchate in neighboring countries and territories including Bulgaria, Serbia, Rumania, the Caucasus, Georgia and ancient Rus.

6. The Liturgy of the Byzantine Rite

The Byzantine Rite and the Byzantine type of Divine Liturgy did not originate in the city of Byzantium nor in the general political division known as Byzantium. Liturgists confirm that the Byzantine Rite owes its origin to Antioch, the most renowned center of Christianity in the Apostolic Era. It was in Antioch that the name "Christian" was first used and where Saints Peter and Paul and their disciples preached (e.g. St. Ignatius Martyr). From Antioch, Christianity spread abroad to neighboring Asia Minor and Mesopotamia. Antioch, together with Rome and Alexandria, became the most outstanding center of the ancient Christian world. When the Church was divided into large ecclesiastical provinces in the fourth century, Antioch was considered, after Rome and Alexandria, the third largest center of Christian life and the See of the Eastern Patriarchate. Even Palestine, together with Jerusalem, was included as an ecclesiastical province in the See of Antioch. It was not until later, at the Ecumenical Council of Chalcedon (451 A.D.), that Jerusalem became a separate patriarchate together with the three ecclesiastical provinces of Palestine.

Byzantium, or Constantinople, was not, in the first three centuries, considered equal to Rome, Alexandria and Antioch. Only later when Constantine the Great chose Byzantium, an insignificant city on the Bosphorus, as the capital of the Eastern Roman Empire, did it begin to gain recognition in the Church. He called this city "New Rome." Being associated with the seat of a great empire and enjoying the strong support of the state authorities, the bishops of old Byzantium, now the powerful capital of New Rome, employed all means to secure power and prestige for this administrative department of the Church. They succeeded for at the first Ecumenical Council of Constantinople (381 A.D.) this city secured a higher position than Alexandria and Antioch.

After the Council of Chalcedon (451 A.D.), Byzantium had achieved undisputed leadership in the territories of Asia Minor, Pontus, Thrace, and at the time of the expansion of the Roman Eastern Empire in the Balkans, the Byzantine Patriarchate became the Mother Church of Bulgaria, Serbia and Rumania. With the conversion of Kiev-Rus to Christianity, the influence of the Byzantine Church spread and reached ancient Rus-Ukraine and the northern frontiers of the original nation of Rus. These nations embraced Christianity in the Byzantine Rite and, consequently, adopted the Divine Liturgy and other divine services of the Byzantine type.

As mentioned earlier, Byzantium had nothing to do with the origin of the Rite that bears its name. It was borrowed from Antioch but it was developed and perfected in Byzantium, and thus came to be known as the Byzantine Rite.[32]

Setting aside the interesting study of the origin of the Byzantine Rite, it would be well to make a few pertinent observations here on the Divine Liturgy of the Byzantine type, and to explain some terms and expressions by which the Byzantine Liturgy was known in the past and is known today.

First of all, it must be noted that the Byzantine Rite cannot be called the "Eastern Rite," for this term is too general and ambiguous. In reality, there is no single "Eastern" Rite but many Eastern Rites. By "Eastern Rite" we mean not only the Byzantine Rite but also the Armenian, Syrian, Chaldean, Coptic, and Ethiopian Rites, etc. The Byzantine Rite is only one of the Eastern Rites.

Another term quite generally and improperly used in past centuries is "Greek Rite." The term "Greek" is inappropriate because it restricts the Byzantine Rite to the practices of the Greek-speaking peoples who actually constitute only a minority, a very small part, of Eastern Christians who belong to the Byzantine Rite. Furthermore, the term is misleading because it confuses Rite with liturgical language. It is true that the original language was "Greek," and that it is still the liturgical language for the Greeks, but it is not the only one used in the Liturgy, nor is it exclusively the official liturgical language of the Byzantine Rite. In fact, an overwhelming majority of Christians did not use this language in the past, nor do they use it at present in their liturgical services. Finally, the expression "Greek Rite" is inadequate because this Rite did not originate in Greece, but in Syria.

---

[32] R. Vancourt, *Patriarcats*, in *Dict. de Th. Cath.*, XI, 2 pp. 2253–97.

For these reasons liturgical scholars, toward the close of the last century, introduced the term "Byzantine Rite." Probably the first to use this term was Francis E. Brightman, the English liturgist, in his work on the Eastern and Western Liturgies.[33] Other liturgists soon adopted it and began using it instead of "Greek Rite." Gradually this term was not only accepted by scholars who used it in various works on the Liturgy and the Eastern Rites, but it also found its way into official Church terminology.

The Byzantine Rite has its subdivisions or ramifications. The factors responsible for these subdivisions are language and other liturgical peculiarities of a given Rite. For this reason, liturgists divide the Byzantine Rite into Byzantine-Greek, Byzantine-Melchite, Byzantine-Albanian, Byzantine-Slavonic, Byzantine-Rumanian, Byzantine-Hungarian, and Pod-Carpathian, and Byzantine-Georgian. The Byzantine-Slavonic Rite is again a generic term which embraces the Byzantine-Ruthenians (Ukrainians, Byelorussians or White Russians), the Byzantine-Russians, Byzantine-Serbians and Byzantine-Bulgarians.

The Byzantine-Ruthenian Rite, as just noted, designates also the Rite of the Ukrainian people, who in the sixteenth century (1596) reunited with the Church of Rome and retained its Eastern "Greek" Rite traditions. The Ukrainians at that time were part of the Metropolitan See of Kiev, which besides the ethnographical eparchy of Ukraine embraced also the eparchy of Byelorus or White Russia. In ecclesiastical nomenclature, the Rite of Kiev was styled the "Ruthenian" or "Graeco-Ruthenian" Rite, and in the Latin ecclesiastical terminology of the Apostolic See, the phrases "Graeco-Ruthenian" and "Ruthenian" correspond with *Ritus Ruthenus* or *Ritus Graeco-Ruthenus*. It must be emphasized that the terms *Ritus Ruthenus* and *Rutheni* in the official language of the Church were rarely employed to denote nationality—Ruthenian-Ukrainian or Ruthenian-Byelorussian (White Russian), but almost exclusively to designate a common Rite to which belonged not only the Ukrainians but also the Byelorussians. Today, when the Apostolic See uses the term *Rutheni* or *Ritus Ruthenus*, it is not to be taken in its ethnographic sense, but in the liturgical-ritual sense.

In the present work the term "Byzantine Rite" will be employed when referring to the common traits which are shared by all the branches or variants of this Rite. When we wish to emphasize the peculiarities of the Rite of the Ukrainian Catholic Church, we shall simply use the expressions *"Ukrainian Rite"* or the *"Byzantine-Ukrainian Rite."*

It is important to note that the word "Rite" means an external form of worship embracing the sum total of liturgical texts, practices, usages, customs, rubrics, prescriptions, and as such has nothing to do with faith—be it Catholic, Orthodox, or Protestant.

The Byzantine Rite boasts of two liturgical formulas: the Liturgy of St. John Chrysostom and the Liturgy of St. Basil the Great. We shall discuss the liturgical formula of St. John Chrysostom more extensively in the following

---

[33] *Liturgies Eastern and Western*, I (Oxford: 1896).

chapter. With respect to the Liturgy of St. Basil, we note that it is celebrated only ten times during the year: on the Eve of the Nativity of Our Lord, the Feast Day of St. Basil, Eve of the Epiphany, on the five Sundays of Lent, Holy Thursday and Holy Saturday. However, we may infer from various liturgical documents existing prior to the ninth century that the Liturgy of St. Basil was used more frequently at that time; it was even considered to have been the first formula or text of the Divine Liturgy in the Byzantine Rite. It differs from the Byzantine Liturgy of St. John Chrysostom in that its prayers are longer, especially those in the Anaphora (Eucharistic Canon). However, at first glance one can hardly notice the differences because the ektenes, the invocations and the hymns in both Liturgies are identical.

Liturgists do not share the same opinion concerning the origin and authorship of the Liturgy of St. Basil. Although it is true that a few ancient documents clearly ascribe to St. Basil a separate formula written by him (e.g. the testimonies of Pseudo-Proclus, Peter the Deacon, Pseudo-Amphilochius, Leontius of Byzantium, St. John Damascene), we cannot interpret these as evidence that the present day Divine Liturgy of St. Basil was solely the work of St. Basil. Most likely, the majority of the very important prayers are his and written by him, but the complete formula as we have it today is a collective work of centuries.[34] Reference to the Liturgy of St. Basil, especially to the Anaphora will be made in the second part of this book.

Besides the Liturgies of St. Basil and St. John Chrysostom, the Byzantine Rite also has what is termed the "Liturgy of the Pre-sanctified Gifts." It is celebrated during Lent on certain non-liturgical days, i.e., on days when the Liturgies of St. Basil and of St. John Chrysostom are not celebrated. The Liturgy of the Pre-sanctified Gifts is not a Liturgy in the precise meaning of the term, since it does not have the Anaphora, the essential part of the Divine Liturgy. It is only a solemn rite of Holy Communion which, in its external form and structure, recalls the scheme and structure of the Liturgies of St. Basil and of St. John Chrysostom.

---

[34] Pl. De Meester, *Grecques liturgies,* in *Dict. d'Archeol. Chret. et de Liturgie,* VI, 2 pp. 1591–1662.

Chapter III

THE HISTORICAL DEVELOPMENT OF THE DIVINE LITURGY OF THE BYZANTINE-SLAVONIC RITE

Having viewed in general the historical development of the Divine Liturgy from the first centuries of Christianity to the liturgical-ritual divisions of the ancient Christian services into various types or Rites, we shall now consider in particular the historical evolution of the Byzantine Divine Liturgy.

This chapter offers a brief outline of that evolution. It deals with the authorship and the origin of the Liturgy of St. John Chrysostom; the historical development of its texts and rites in the written and printed Liturgikons and Sluzhebnyks;* and some reforms which aimed at establishing uniformity in the celebration of the Divine Liturgy in Byzantium, and especially in the Slav territories.

The development of the Byzantine-Slavonic Rite and, especially the Byzantine Divine Liturgy, has interested historians and liturgists since the nineteenth century. It was then that scholars began to make scientific inquiries into the history, art, laws, archeology, literature and liturgical-ritual matters in Byzantium and in the lands of the Slavs. Thus, a new science called "Byzantology" was born. The findings of this science shed much light on many obscure questions regarding the Liturgy and the ritual practices of the Byzantine-Slavonic Rite.

In this chapter, a report on the general findings of these studies will be presented, since individual phases of development of the Byzantine Liturgy, especially in the southern part of the Slav territories and in the Ukraine, are still left unexplored.

Although we are primarily concerned here with the historical development of the Liturgy of St. John Chrysostom, any information given on the development of this Liturgy may also apply to the other Byzantine liturgical formula, namely, the Liturgy of St. Basil, since from the viewpoint of ritual, both Liturgies have gone through similar stages of development.

---

* Throughout the whole book we use the Greek word "Liturgikon" when referring to the Greek missals and the Slavonic word "Sluzhebnyk" when referring to the Slavonic missals.

1. Authenticity and Origin of the Liturgy of St. John Chrysostom

Establishing the authenticity or authorship of the Liturgy of St. John Chrysostom is not an easy task because of the absence of reliable and trustworthy evidence. Tradition tells us that St. John Chrysostom was the author of the Liturgy which bears his name.

Before approaching the problem of authenticity, however, it must be first understood what is meant by the authorship of the Liturgy of St. John Chrysostom. The Byzantine Liturgy, as known today, undoubtedly cannot be ascribed to St. John Chrysostom, since its present form includes many modifications, interpolations and alterations both in text and ritual made in the centuries since the Saint's death. Some of these interpolations were the Antiphons, *Monogenes* ("The Only-begotten Son"), *Trisagion,* the Symbol of Faith, *Cherubikon,* and other hymns and prayers. It is apparent that St. John Chrysostom could not have been the author of these additions. In speaking of the authorship of the Liturgy of St. John Chrysostom, therefore, liturgists have in mind the authorship of the Eucharistic Anaphora, i.e. the formula of the eucharistic-sacrificial portion in the Liturgy of the Faithful.

The question now is whether St. John was actually the author of the Eucharistic Anaphora, prescinding from all the later interpolations and modifications. If not, what connection does he have with the Liturgy that bears his name?

The mere fact that the Byzantine Liturgy has appeared under his name throughout the centuries is definitely inadequate proof of his authorship. Liturgists are generally very critical in dealing with the traditional ascriptions of various Liturgies to individual Apostles or to the prominent Church Fathers. In the East, many Liturgies bear the names of the Fathers of the Church or other ecclesiastical writers as St. Clement, St. Basil, St. Gregory, St. Cyril, Nestorius, Theodore of Mopsuestia. But recent studies show that a Liturgy has rarely been composed by the person whose name it bears.

There is, in fact, only one bit of evidence in favor of ascribing to St. John Chrysostom the authorship of the Liturgy bearing his name, namely, the Pseudo-Proclus testimony. The document exists now in a brief fragment entitled, "A Treatise on the Tradition of the Divine Liturgy," which was falsely ascribed to St. Proclus (d. 446 A.D.), one of the immediate successors of St. John Chrysostom in the bishopric of Constantinople.[1] In this "Treatise" the author points out that there were many holy men, such as St. Clement and St. James, who wrote Liturgies. When the pristine zeal of the Church gradually began to lessen and Christians ceased to attend these Liturgies because they found them too long and boring, St. Basil decided to abbreviate the Liturgy. Later when St. John saw the continuing apathy and the reluctance of the faithful to attend the Divine Service, he abridged it once again. This latter abridged form is the present day Liturgy of St. John Chrysostom.[2]

---

[1] Migne, PG, 65, 849–852.
[2] *Ibid.*

According to the Pseudo-Proclus testimony, St. John did not actually compose a new liturgical formula, but only abbreviated one which already existed. This testimony does not tell us which Liturgy St. John Chrysostom is supposed to have shortened and revised, whether it was that of St. James, St. Clement or St. Basil.

Older liturgists such as Goar, David and Probst did attribute the revision of the Byzantine Liturgy to St. John Chrysostom on the basis of the Pseudo-Proclus testimony. The same opinion was held by Russian scholars, Philaret, Bishop of Kharkov, and N. Stenkovsky.[3] Recent research of patristic sources, however, which indicates that the "Treatise" is not of the fifth century but of a far later date, complicates matters and renders its testimony inconclusive.[4] For this reason, later liturgists, such as Baumstark and De Meester, do not attach much significance to the "Treatise," but seek other ways to solve the problem of authorship.

Not only do we lack conclusive evidence that St. John Chrysostom wrote a Liturgy, but certain facts make us strongly doubt his authorship or his contribution as a reformer of the Byzantine Liturgy. If St. John had written the Liturgy, or even if he had simply revised it, why do Byzantine historians and chroniclers pass over this fact in silence? Neither the contemporary historians—Socrates, Sozomenus, Theodoret—nor the author of the *Paschal Chronicle* of the seventh century, nor such later writers as George Syncellus, Theophanes, Hamartolos mention St. John Chrysostom's revision of the Liturgy. Even the biographers and panegyrists of the Saint—Palladius, Theodore of Tremithus, George of Alexandria—say nothing about his liturgical reform. Although the silence of these historians and chroniclers is strictly an argument *ex silentio,* nevertheless, it is quite eloquent and symptomatic.[5]

It seems strange also that even the Synod of Trullo (692 A.D.) does not ascribe the composition or the abridgement of the Liturgy of St. John Chrysostom to that saint. In condemning the Armenian practice of mixing water with wine (canon 32),[6] a rite which Chrysostom himself supposedly introduced and practiced, the Synod explicitly referred to the Liturgy of St. Basil and that of St. James wherein we find this same practice. If there then existed a Liturgy bearing the name of St. John Chrysostom, it seems strange that the Synod did not mention it together with the other two.

The name of St. John Chrysostom first appeared in an ancient manuscript, the "Barberini Codex," of the eighth century which contains all three Byzantine Liturgies. More will be said about this Codex later. For the present it is enough to point out that in it Chrysostom's name appears only in connection with cer-

---

[3] The research works of these authors are given in the list of literature at the end of the chapter.

[4] O. Bardenhewer, *Patrologie,* (Freiburg i. Br.: 1910), p. 239. Some even regard it as a forgery of a Greek plagiarist of the sixteenth century, K. Paleocappa.

[5] De Meester, *Les origines et developpements du texte grec de la liturgie de S. J. Chrysostome* (Chrysostomika: 1908), 255.

[6] Mansi, *Sacrorum Conciliorum nova et amplissima collectio,* 11, 956.

tain prayers—the prayers for the catechumens, the prayer of prothesis, the prayer before the Canon and the prayer behind the ambo—and not before the whole Liturgy. Some liturgists, among them Krasnoseltsev and Petrovsky, do ascribe the entire Liturgy to John Chrysostom, but it was not until the eleventh century that we find in the manuscripts his name placed at the beginning.

It is also interesting to note that in the earliest Greek manuscripts the Liturgy of St. Basil took precedence over that of St. John Chrysostom.[7] Only toward the end of the eleventh century and the beginning of the twelfth were the positions reversed.[8]

This accumulated evidence makes it clear that the basis on which one of the Byzantine Liturgies is traditionally ascribed to St. John Chrysostom is quite unstable.

Certain scholars and liturgists, as F. Probst in the West, the Russian Bishop Philaret, and N. Stenkovsky, attempting to prove the authorship of St. John Chrysostom, but realizing the lack of positive historical data substantiating this authorship, direct their attention mainly to the great likeness found in the Liturgy of St. John Chrysostom to the descriptions and allusions to the Liturgy contained in his works and homilies. These authors gathered all excerpts pertaining to the Liturgy from the various works of St. John Chrysostom. From these quotations one can reconstruct almost every essential part of the Liturgy ascribed to him. This fact does, undoubtedly, have some significance and provides matter for consideration. Yet such marked similarity proves only that this Liturgy was in use during the Saint's time and not that he was himself its author or reformer, since he could well have been describing an already existing Byzantine formula of the Divine Liturgy.

From all this we may conclude that the Liturgy of St. John originated prior to his own time, and therefore probing the question of St. John Chrysostom's authorship bears little result. The author of the Liturgy of St. John Chrysostom was not St. John Chrysostom for at the time he governed the Byzantine Church the Church already had a liturgical formula. St. John did not have to compose a new Liturgy. His role in the liturgical field could only have been restricted to certain revisions made in an already-existing Liturgy. However, the absence of positive historical data and testimonies does not permit us to determine precisely in what these reforms of St. John Chrysostom consisted. Moreover, even if he had nothing to do with the reform or abridgement of the Divine Liturgy, the fact that one of the Byzantine Anaphoras bears his name indicates that he was one of the most prominent personages in the Byzantine Church; and that, as later tradition has it, perhaps it was out of deference to this outstanding figure that his name was attached to the Liturgy, thus giving it added prestige and authority.

---

[7] De Meester, *op. cit.*, p. 275–276.

[8] *Ibid.*

[9] F. Probst, *Die Liturgie des 4 Jahrhunderts und deren Reform* (Muenster: 1893), 226–228.

Laying aside, then, the question of St. John Chrysostom's supposed connection with the Divine Liturgy, let us now consider the origin of this Liturgy. The general opinion of liturgists is that the Liturgy of St. John Chrysostom, as well as that of St. Basil, belongs to the Syrian type [10] as do the anaphoras of the *Apostolic Constitutions,* the so-called Liturgies of St. Clement, St. James, Nestorius, and the Liturgy of Theodore of Mopsuestia. In these anaphoras liturgists discern common characteristics in the composition of prayers and the intrinsic structure. The origin of these anaphoras can be traced to Antioch and Jerusalem, two cities that played prominent roles in the first centuries of Christianity. Friendly relations existed between Syria and Palestine and between the Churches of Asia Minor and Mesopotamia, thus enabling Syria to become a convenient cradle of missionary work in neighboring territories. From here Christianity spread to Mesopotamia, Cappadocia and all Asia Minor. From this point, the influence of liturgical forms also spread. The first to receive the Liturgy from Syria was Cilicia and Cappadocia, and then later, Pontus and Byzantium. The Syrian Liturgy came to Byzantium with the modifications of Asia Minor and here in Byzantium it evolved further.

At first the Liturgy of the Byzantine Rite was prevalent only in the Byzantine ecclesiastical provinces. However, with the growth of both the religious and political power of this capital on the Bosphorus (Byzantium), the Liturgy spread to other adjacent provinces. It is quite understandable that, in the course of time, the Byzantine Liturgy, should and did prevail over all other local Liturgies and that Byzantine liturgical-ritual practices became the most predominant in the Eastern Roman Empire.[11]

---

[10] A. Baumstark, *Zur Urgeschichte der Chrysostomusliturgie,* "Theologie und Glaube," 5 (1913), 229–313.

[11] Select Bibliography: A. Baumstark, *Die Messe im Morgenland* (Kempten-Muenchen: 1906, 60–66); ––––– *Zur Urgeschichte der Chrysostomusliturgie,* "*Theologie und Glaube*," 5 (1913) , 299–313; ––––– *Die Chrysostomusliturgie und die syrische Liturgie des Nestorius* (Chrysostomika; Roma: 1908), 771–857; R. Engdahl, *Beitraege zur byzantinischen Liturgie* (Berlin: 1908); J. M. Hanssens, *De formulariis in ecclesiis orientalibus adhibitis,* "Institutiones liturgicae de ritibus orientalibus," III, 578–584; P. De Meester, *Les Origines et les developpements du text grec de la liturgie de S. J. Chrysostome* (Chrysostomika: 1908), 245–357; (Grecques) Liturgies, *DACL,* VI, 1591–1662; F. Probst, *Die antiochenische Messe nach den Schriten des hl. Chrysostomus dargestellt,* "Zeitschrift f. kath. Theologie," 7 (1873) , 251–303; ––––– *Die Liturgie von Constantinopel nach den Schriften v. Gregor v. Nazianz und Chrysostomus,* "Liturgie des 4 Jahrhunderts und deren Reform" (Muenster i. W.: 1893) , 202–226; V. Vasylyk, *Pro liturhiu sv. I. Zolotoustoho,* "Bohoslovia," IV (1926), 283–295, 357–367; V (1927), 20–29, 197–230; A. Petrovsky, *Ioann Zolotoust i yeho litughiya,* "Prav. Bohosl. Ents.," VI (1905), 947–959; Ramensky, *Ocherk bogosluzheniya po sochineniyam sv. I. Zlatoustaho,* "Rukovodstvo dlya selskikh pastirey" (Kiev: 1874); Filaret (Gumilevsky), *Istorichesky obzor pyesnopyevtsev i pyesnopyeniya gr. Tserkvi,* SpB. 1902 (3 izd.); N. Stenkovsky, *Dokazatelstva podlynnosti liturghii sv. I. Zlatoustaho, nakhodyashchiyasya v yeho pisaniyakh,* "Trudy K.D.A." (1875), IV, 304–305 (Protokoli) Philaret ep., *O Trudakh sv. I. Zlatoustaho po ustroystvu obshchestvennoho bogosluzheniya,* "Kh. Chtenie," (1849) 1, 11–61.

2. Historical Development of the Divine Liturgy of St. John Chrysostom
(Fifth-Seventeenth Centuries)

Another question associated with the origin of the Liturgy of St. John Chrysostom is its historical evolution throughout the centuries. The Liturgy of St. John Chrysostom did not retain the original form it had in the fourth and fifth centuries, but underwent various alterations and additions in later years. Indeed, the Liturgy began to evolve as early as the fifth and sixth centuries. This process of change affected not only the original text, but also the rites in the Liturgy—a fact that should not surprise us since the Liturgy of St. John Chrysostom was used for many years by various nations. Since many long centuries separate us from the fourth and fifth centuries, it would be unlikely that the Liturgy of St. John Chrysostom would come down to us in its original form. It had to undergo an evolution in both text and ritual.

Liturgical-ritual life, which is an inseparable part of the intrinsic life of the Church, does not always permit fixed forms, since the very law of nature orders that all life be in perpetual movement, ever striving for greater perfection. The current needs of man, historical circumstances and the spirit of the times, all influence the formation of liturgical forms. Moreover, speaking of the development of the Divine Liturgy of St. John Chrysostom, we must keep in mind that there was in the East no centralized Church authority that would show concern about promoting liturgical uniformity. In the West, the Roman Popes, by virtue of their supreme authority, began gradually to introduce uniformity.[12] In the East, the absence of such authority made the realization of uniformity impossible. These circumstances explain the great diversity found not only in the liturgical manuscripts but also in the printed Liturgikons.

The historical development of the Liturgy of St. John Chrysostom can be divided into three periods: 1) the period of "the original or first edition"; 2) "the period of manuscripts"; 3) "the period of the printed Liturgikons." Let us examine briefly the evolution of the Liturgy during these three periods.

A. *The Period of the First Edition of the Divine Liturgy of St. John Chrysostom*
(Fifth-Eighth Centuries)

Our information regarding this period is very limited, since not one formula of the Liturgy from this time has been preserved. As a result, we cannot form an adequate concept of the nature of the texts or ritual practices of the original Liturgy of St. John Chrysostom.

---

[12] The final step towards uniformity in celebrating the Latin Rite Mass was the Rome edition of the Missal of 1570 edited by Pope Pius V. This became the typical edition for the Latin Rite and remained so until Vatican Council II.

A few limited testimonies concerning the original form of the Liturgy are found in the works of Church writers and historians.[13] In these documents one may discover some innovations introduced into the first edition of the Byzantine Liturgy. We find that in the fifth century the hymn *Trisagion* was introduced, and in the sixth century, the Liturgy was enriched with such new additions as the *Monogenes,* and *Cherubikon,* and the "Symbol of Faith." During the sixth through the eighth centuries, the antiphons were inserted and the Proskomide was transposed from the Liturgy of the Faithful to the very beginning of the Liturgy. The second part of this book will offer more detailed information concerning the history of these additions.

From this period, the first commentary on the Byzantine Liturgy, written by St. Maximos the Confessor (d. 662 A.D.), has been preserved. This commentary, however, is very brief, and merely gives us a general outline of the contemporary Byzantine Liturgy. St. Maximus comments solely on the most important rites or ceremonies. He does not go into detail nor does he quote any liturgical texts. Hence, his commentary contributes very little to our understanding of the Divine Liturgy of St. John Chrysostom. The nature of his commentary will be discussed further in Chapter IV which deals with commentaries on the Byzantine Liturgy.[14]

B. The Second Period

The Period of Written Liturgikons

(Eighth-Sixteenth Centuries)

The second period of the development of the Liturgy of St. John Chrysostom is the period of the handwritten Liturgikons. This period begins with the eighth century and continues to the sixteenth century when the first printed Liturgikons appeared. Some handwritten copies were still being used, of course, even after the first printed books were published.

Scientific research on liturgical manuscripts began in the second part of the nineteenth century. Through the efforts of such liturgists as Krasnoseltsev,[15]

[13] These texts were gleaned by: F. E. Brightman, *Liturgies Eastern and Western,* (Oxford: 1896), 527–539 (Appendix O: The Byzantine Liturgy before the seventh century,—Appendix P.: The Byzantine Liturgy of the seventh century).

[14] Select Bibliography: J. Botsyan, *Liturghiya na Skhodi, "Niva"* IV (1907), 102–108, 172–176, 264–267, 343–347, 488–495; A. Baumstark, *Die Messe im Morgenland* (Kempten-Muenchen: 1906); —— *Die konstantinopolitanische Messliturgie vor dem IX Jh.* (Bonn: 1909); —— *Denkmaeler der Entstehungsgeschichte des byz. Ritus,* "Oriens Christianus," Serie 3, II (1927), 1–32; N. Borgia, *Origine della liturgia byzantina* (Grottaferrata: 1933); M. Jugie, *La messe en Orient du IV-e s.,* DTS, X (1925), pp. 1317–1332; J. Moreau, *Les liturgies eucharistiques, Notes sur leur origines et leur développement* (Bruxelles: 1924); J. Pargoire, *L'Église byzantine de 527 à 847* (Paris: 1905).

[15] Krasnoseltsev, *Svyedyeniya o nyekotorikh liturghicheskikh rukopisyakh Vatikanskoy biblioteki* (Kazan: 1885); —— *Materialy dlya istorii chynoposlyedovaniya liturghii sv. I. Zlatoustaho,* I (Kazan: 1889).

Dmitrievsky,[16] Petrovsky,[17] Orlov,[18] Muretov,[19] Swainson,[20] Brightman,[21] De Meester [22] and others, research on liturgical manuscripts made considerable progress and has made possible further studies on the development of the Liturgy of St. John from the eighth through the sixteenth centuries. From these centuries we have preserved a large number of Greek and Slavonic handwritten Liturgikons and Sluzhebnyks which were either published in fragments or described by the authors just mentioned.

A very significant document on the development of the Liturgy of St. John Chrysostom is the so-called "Barberini Codex," which is the oldest liturgical manuscript available to us today. A product of the eighth century, it was written in Southern Italy between 788 A.D. and 789 A.D. At present this document is preserved in the Vatican Library.[23] The Barberini Codex contains the Greek texts of all three Byzantine Liturgies—those of St. Basil, of St. John Chrysostom and of the Presanctified Gifts—as well as the prayers of Vespers, Compline, Matins, the rite of Baptism, the Blessing of Water, of Chrism, of Churches, the rite of Ordination and of Monastic Tonsure, the rites of Engagement and Marriage, and many other prayers for various needs.[24]

What interests us most, however, is the text of St. John Chysostom's Liturgy. It is worth noting that the Saint's name appears only before three liturgical prayers, and that this Liturgy ranks second after the Liturgy of St. Basil. In the text of St. John Chrysostom's Liturgy only the prayers of the priest are given; none of the deacon's prayers. There are no ektenes, hymns, or antiphons. The Liturgy begins with the prayer of the Proskomide. The Proskomide, however, does not have the prayers of the present day Proskomide and has only a

16 A. Dmitrievsky, *Opisaniye liturghicheskikh rokopisey, khranyashchikhsya v bibliotekakh pravoslavnoho Vostoka*, II, Evkhologhiya (Kiev: 1911) ; ——— *Bogosluzhenie v ruskoy tserkvi v XVI v.* (Kazan: 1894).

17 A. Petrovsky, *Istoriya slavyanskoy redaktsii liturghii I. Zlatoustaho* (Chrysostomika, Rym: 1908), 859–928.

18 M. Orlov, *Liturghiya sv. Vasiliya V. Pervoye kriticheskoye izdanie s izobrazheniem sv. Vasiliya, s chetirmi snimkami s rukopisey* (Spb: 1905).

19 S. Muretov, *K materialam dlya istorii chinoposlyedovaniya Liturghii* (Serghiev Posad: 1895); ——— *Istoricheskiy obzor chinoposlyedovaniya prokomidii*, "Chteniya Obshchestva Lyubit. dukh. prosv." (1893), I, 520–528, 599–630, 740–752; II, 1–20, 209–254, 441–464, 586–644; ——— *Poslyedovanie prokomidii, V. Vkhoda i prichashcheniya v slavyanorusskikh sluzhebnikakh* XII–XIV vv., "Chteniya v Imp. Obshch. ist. i drevn. ross." (1897), 2, pp. 1–43; ——— *Ist. obzor chinoposlyedovaniya proskomidii do "Ustava liturghii"* (konst. patriarkha Filofeya, Moskva: 1895).

20 C. A. Swainson, *The greek liturgies chiefly from original authorities*, (Cambridge: 1884) .

21 F. E. Brightman, *Liturgies Eastern and Western* (Oxford: 1896).

22 P. De Meester, *Les origines et developpement* . . . (Chrysostomika, Roma: 1908), 245–357.

23 Here it is number 336 in a series of Greek liturgical manuscripts, collections of Cardinal F. Barberini.

24 The text of the liturgies contained in the Barberini Codex is given by the following: Swainson, *op. cit.*, pp. 76–98; Brightman, *op. cit.* 309–352; The Russian translation in "Khr. Chteniye," 1875, 2, pp. 120–132. Cf. also the text in GOAR, *Euchologion*, (Paris: 1647), pp. 98–100, and Chr. Bunsen, *Analecta antinicaena*, III (London: 1854), pp. 201–236.

few rubrics. Generally speaking, the Barberini Codix is noteworthy for its great simplicity and because it bears more likeness to the original edition of the Liturgy of St. John Chrysostom.

Besides the Barberini Codex, there are others as the Porphyrian Codex, probably of the ninth century,[25] and the Sevastianov Codex,[26] of the tenth century, which are very valuable to the liturgist. In addition to the above-mentioned handwritten Greek Liturgikons, there are the two oldest Slavonic handwritten Sluzhebnyks, namely, the Sluzhebnyk of Anthony the Roman (d. 1147 A.D.), and the Sluzhebnyk of Barlaam Khutynsky (d. 1192 A.D.).[27] These are of great importance. Although both of these Sluzhebnyks date from the twelfth century, they differ from each other. In view of this difference, liturgists infer that there existed at least two editions of the Liturgy of St. John Chrysostom during the times when Rus was being invaded by the Mongols, (1240 A.D.) and that there was no liturgical-ritual uniformity. The same can be said of the handwritten Sluzhebnyks of the thirteenth and fourteenth centuries.[28] Just as in the Slavonic, so too in the Greek manuscripts of the Byzantine Rite Liturgy, diversity reigns and a multitude of variations are indicated in some parts of the Liturgy as the Proskomide, the Great Entrance and the Rite of Holy Communion. It is difficult to find two manuscipts that contain identical texts and rites for the Great Entrance, Holy Communion and especially the Proskomide.

A very important period in the development of the Liturgy of St. John Chrysostom is the fourteenth century. In this century we witness the first attempts at those liturgical reforms directed at standardizing the texts and especially the rubrics. This reform has been associated with the name of Philotheus, Patriarch of Constantinople (1354-1376), whose desire it was to bring about liturgical-ritual uniformity in the various services of the Byzantine Rite. The great need for such reform was deeply felt since the liturgical-ritual life of the Byzantine Church showed obvious signs of increasing chaos, owing to the fact that there were two versions of the "Typikon" or *Order of Celebration* for the Byzantine Rite—the Jerusalem and the Studite Typikons; both reveal conspicuous differences.

The Studite Typikon, which originated in Constantinople and was generally used in the "Great Church" (i.e. the Church of Constantinople) since the

---

[25] This codex was discovered by Bishop Porphyrius (Uspensky) in 1850 in the Sinai monastery and was later donated to the Imperial Public Library in Petersburg. See the description of this manuscript in Krasnoseltsev's *Svyedyeniya......*, 210–212, and the text itself on pp. 283–295. He gives only the text of St. John Chrysostom's Liturgy; the text of St. Basil's Liturgy is given by Orlov.

[26] This codex is to be found in the Moscow Rumyantsev Museum, in a collection of manuscripts of Sevastiyanov, under the number 15-374. Krasnoseltsev describes it in his *Svyedyeniya.....*, 209–210, and the text is given on pp. 237–282. Beside the text of St. John Chrysostom's Liturgy he gives in a parallel column the text of St. Basil's Liturgy.

[27] See Gorsky-Nevostruev, *Opisanie slav. rukopisey Mosk. Synodalnoy Bibl.*, III, under No. 1: "Knighi bogosluzhebniya," M. 1869.

[28] See Petrovsky's, *Ist. slav. redaktsii.....*, 872–890 and his: *Ioann Zlatoust i yeho liturghiya*, "Pravo. Bogosl. Ents.", VI (1905), pp. 947–959.

ninth century, was by the twelfth century slowly being replaced by the Jerusalem Typikon, thus leaving but one norm of celebration. The Jerusalem Typikon gradually found its way into certain Byzantine monasteries, especially at Mt. Athos by way of Antioch, and here, in the course of time, replaced the Studite Typikon and extended its influence even over the "Great Church." [29]

The reason for the prominence and popularity of the Jerusalem Typikon was the fact that it contained by far more detailed rubrics describing the movements of each sacred function. The Jerusalem Typikon, however, did not entirely replace the Studite Typikon which had many years of tradition behind it. The rivalry for precedence between these two Typikons is clearly reflected in the handwritten liturgical codices of the twelfth and thirteenth centuries, some of which followed the Jerusalem Typicon, others the Studite, while still others were a synthesis of both. The lack of a single definitive Order of Celebration was most reflected in the celebration of the Divine Liturgy, especially in the Proskomide.

The Patriarch Philotheus wished to remedy this situation. To do away with these differences in celebrating the Liturgy, he published his renowned *Diataxis* [30] containing the rubrics the priest and deacon were to observe in conducting Vespers, Matins and the Liturgy.[31] Philotheus also formulated a detailed Typikon for the Divine Liturgy wherein he interspersed the text of the Liturgy of St. John Chrysostom with rubrics for priest and deacon. This last Typikon, which was exclusively prepared for the rite of the Divine Liturgy, came to be known in the history of Byzantine Liturgical services as the "*Diataxis* of Philotheus, Patriarch of Constantinople." [32]

With his *Diataxis*, Philotheus finally introduced the Jerusalem Typikon and did away with the Studite version. Although the Typikon of Philotheus was not immediately accepted, it nevertheless gradually became the prevailing book of reference for the order of celebration, not only in Byzantine-Greek Churches but also in the Byzantine-Slavonic Churches. The great merit of Philotheus' *Diataxis* consisted in its detailed prescriptions for the rite of Proskomide. Its second merit was the stabilization of the text of St. John Chrysostom's Liturgy. This text was generally accepted in the ensuing centuries (*textus receptus*), and, except for minor and insignificant modifications, the same text is used today in the Byzantine Rite and its branches. But, perhaps the outstanding achievement of the

[29] J. Mansvetov, *Tserk. Ustav.* (Moskva: 1885); M. Skaballanovich, *Tolkovyj Tipikon.* Obyasnitelnoye izlozhenie tipikona s ist. vvedeniem, ed. II (Kiev: 1910).

[30] Migne gives this text in his 154, 745–766.

[31] J. Goar, *Euchologion sive Rituale Graecorum* (Lutetiae Parisiorum: 1647), pp. 1–11: Ordo s. ministerii quomodo videlicet sacerdoti diaconus ministrat in celebribus Vesperis, Matutino, et Missa a sanctissimo et oecumenico Patriarcha Domino Philotheo compositus et ordinatus, p. 11–35: Notae in ordinem.

[32] Krasnoseltsev gives the Old-Slavonic text of this "Typikon" in his work: *Svyedyeniya*, pp. 171–194. The Greek text with a parallel Old-Slavonic text is given in his other work: *Materiali.....*, pp. 30–80; "Sviatyeyshaho i blazhennaho arkhiepiskopa Konstantinya hrada Novaho Rima i vselenskaho patriarkha Filofeya Ustav bozhestvenniya sluzhbi kako dostoit svyashcheniku s diyakonom slouzhiti."

Diataxis was the formulation of specific rubrics for the Divine Liturgy which later were printed in the Liturgikons and Sluzhebnyks of the sixteenth and seventeenth centuries.

In the same century (fourteenth), this *Diataxis* of the Patriarch Philotheus was also carried into, and partially accepted in, the Slav lands. The last Bulgarian Patriarch of Ternova, Euthymius (1360–1389), a contemporary of Philotheus,[33] introduced it into the lands of Bulgaria, and the Metropolitan of Kiev, Cyprian Tsamvlak (1381–1382, 1390–1406), introduced it in the territories of the Ukraine and Muscovy (present-day Russia). Cyprian himself was from Bulgaria and he was on friendly terms with the Patriarchs Euthymius and Philotheus. The *Diataxis* of the Divine Liturgy introduced by Cyprian, however, was not accepted in that same century, but only later during the period of the printed Sluzhebnyks (sixteenth-eighteenth centuries).[34] The *Diataxis* of Philotheus marked the most important period of growth for the Byzantine Liturgy. It contributed to the gradual stabilization of the text and rubrics of the Divine Liturgy, and became the model for the printed Sluzhebnyks of following centuries.

C. The Period of the Printed Sluzhebnyks

(Sixteenth-Eighteenth Centuries)

The final period of evolution for the Divine Liturgy of St. John Chrysostom began with the appearance of the printed Sluzhebnyks, i.e., at the beginning of the sixteenth century. This period shows almost no development of the text of the Liturgy, what development there was touched mostly upon the ritual-rubrical aspect. This last period can be characterized as bringing about the ultimate determination of the texts and rites in the Greek and two Slavonic editions of the Liturgy of St. John Chrysostom. As stated above, the first printed Sluzhebnyks belong to the earlier part of the sixteenth century. The first Slavonic edition, which came out in Venice in the year 1519, was published by the monk

---

[33] More important references (besides those given above): V. Vasylyk, *Pro liturhiu sv. I. Zolotoustoho,* "Bohoslovia," IV (1926), pp. 283–295, 357–367; F. Gumilevsky, *Bogosluzhenie Russkoy tserkvi do mongolskaho vremeni,* "Cht. Obshch. ist. i dr. russ.," II (1847), p. 42; N. Krasnoseltsev, *Patriarkh Fotiy i Vizantiyskoe bogosluzhenie yeho vremeni,* (Zap. Imp. Novoros. Univ., Odessa: 1892), Vol. 57, pp. 23–40; —— *Pamyatnik drevne-russ. pismennosti, otnosyashchiysya k ist. nasheho bogosluzheniya v XVI v.* (Prav. Sobesyednik: 1884), I, pp. 93–108; —— *K ist. pravosl. bogosluzheniya* (Kazan: 1889); N. Odintsov, *Poryadok obshchestvennaho i chastnaho bogosluzheniya v drevney Rossii do XVI v.* (Spb: 1881); V. Prilutskiy, *Chastnoe bogosluzhenie v russ. tserkvi v XVI i v pervoy pol. XVII v.* (Spb.: 1912); P. Sirku, *K ist. ispravleniya knig v Bolgarii v. XIV v.,* Vol. I, ed. II, "Liturgh. trudy patriarkha Evfimiya Ternovskaho" (Spb.: 1890); Vol. II, ed. I, "Vremya i zhizn patr. Evfimiya Ternovskaho" (Spb.: 1898); M. Jugie, *La Messe dans l'eglise byz. apres le IXe s.,* DTC, X, 1332–1346. O. Horbatsch, *De tribus textibus Liturgicis Linguae Ecclesiasticae Palaeo-Slavicae in Manuscriptis Vaticanis* (Roma: 1966), pp. 36–37 sqq.

[34] J. Mansvetov, *Mitr. Kipriyan v yeho liturghicheskoy dyeyatelnosti,* M. 1882. The Sluzhebnyk of Cyprian is in the Moscow. Syn. Library under the number 344 (601).

Pachomius at the request of the Serbian Duke Bozhydar Vukovich.[35] The first Greek edition was issued seven years later, having been prepared in Rome in 1526 by Demetrius Duka at the request of Pope Clement VII. These first editions were followed by other Greek [36] and Slavonic [37] editions in the same century. At first, the center of publication for the Slavonic editions was Venice,[38] while Venice [39] and Rome were the centers of publication for the Greek editions.[40] During the seventeenth century, the Slavonic editions were published mostly in the Ukraine and Muscovy (or Russia). The Slavonic edition of the Sluzhebnyk first appeared in the Ukrainian-Byelorussian territories, in Vilna (1583), Striatyn (1604), and in the territories of Muscovy, in Moscow (1602). The seventeenth and eighteenth centuries managed to produce even more. The Greek Liturgikons continued to be issued in Venice and Rome, and the Slavonic editions in Vilna,[41] Kiev,[42] Lviv,[43] Suprasl,[44] Univ,[45] Pochaiv,[46] Chernihiv,[47] Moscow[48] and other cities.[49]

The printed Sluzhebnyks did not, as we have seen, immediately replace the handwritten Sluzhebnyks. The latter were still used, not only in the sixteenth century, but well on into the seventeenth, when many churches lacked the printed books,[50] because the first editions were expensive and, since they were

---

[35] J. Karataev, *Opisanie Slav.-russ. knig* (Spb.: 1883), pp. 44–47.

[36] Venice, 1527, 1554, 1570, and Vilna, 1583.

[37] Venice, 1528, 1558, 1562, 1571; Paris, 1560; Antwerp, 1562.

[38] Venice, 1519, 1527, 1554, 1570.

[39] Venice, 1624, 1626, 1644, 1650, 1663, 1687, 1714, 1737, 1740, 1764, 1765, 1775, 1781, 1785, 1795, 1798, 1803, 1805, 1814, 1817.

[40] Rome, *Liturgikon*, 1601, 1683, 1839, 1925; *Euchologion*, 1754, 1872, 1873. Other publications worthy of mention are: Constantinople, *Euchologion*, 1803, *Liturgikon*, 1820, 1830, 1875; *Hieratikon*, 1895. Athens, *Hierodiakonikon*, 1766, *Liturgikon*, 1912, *Euchologion*, 1927. Tripolis, *Liturgikon*, 1892.

[41] Vilna, 1583, 1597, 1607, 1617 (L. Mamonich), 1617, (Monastery of the Holy Spirit), 1624, 1634, 1638, 1640, 1641, 1692, 1773.

[42] Kiev, 1620, 1629, 1638, 1639, 1653, 1692, 1708, 1735, 1736, 1737, 1740, 1746, 1762, 1785, 1803, 1805, 1806, 1822, 1838, 1840, 1846, 1876.

[43] Lviv, 1637, 1646, 1666, 1680, 1681, 1691, 1702, 1712, 1720, 1755, 1757, 1759, 1780, 1808, 1842, 1905, 1929, 1930.

[44] Suprasl, 1695, 1727, 1733, 1758, 1763, 1793.

[45] Univ, 1733, 1740, 1743, 1747.

[46] Pochaiv, 1735, 1744, 1755, 1765, 1778, 1788, 1791, 1809.

[47] Chernihiv, 1697, 1733, 1747, 1754, 1763.

[48] Moscow, 1602, 1605, 1615, 1616, 1617, 1620, 1623, 1626, 1627, 1630, 1632, 1633, 1635, 1637, 1639, 1640, 1641, 1646, 1647, 1650, 1651, 1652, 1655, 1656, 1658, 1667, 1668, 1670, 1676, 1677, 1684, 1688, 1693, 1699, 1705, 1707, 1708, 1709, 1717, 1723, 1732, 1734, 1739, 1756, 1767, 1770, 1777, 1783, 1785, 1789, 1792, 1793, 1797, 1803, 1804, 1834, 1846, 1850, 1851, 1854, 1860, 1901.

[49] Sluzhebnyks were printed also in other cities such as: Striatyn, 1604; Mohyliv, 1616, 1617; Yevye, 1638; Delsky Monastery, 1646; Kishinev, 1815; Petersburg, 1804, 1850; Peremyshl, 1840; Zhovkva, 1917, 1927; Beograd, 1928; Sophia, 1924; Varshava (Warsaw), 1926.

[50] E.g. in the Ukrainian Catholic Metropoly, because of the lack of printed Sluzhebnyks in the eighteenth century the handwritten ones were used instead. F. Dobryansky describes some of these handwritten Sluzhebnyks in his work: *"Opisanie rukopisey vilenskoy publichnoy biblioteki* (Vilna: 1882), PP. 301–310. These Sluzhebnyks described by him were the property of the Basilian monastery in Suprasl.

published in small shops in distant cities, were difficult to obtain. This was especially true of the Venetian publications.

The first editions, both Greek and Slavonic, still lacked uniformity. The publishers created this great diversity in texts and rubric by availing themselves of different codices. Furthermore, the Sluzhebnyks were printed without any prior examination or consent of Church authorities. At that time a critical and emended edition of the Sluzhebnyk was out of the question. Publishers had no interest whatsoever in correcting the books; their primary concern was for their own financial gain. Metropolitan Mohyla of Kiev complained bitterly about them, calling them "ignorant" and "corrupters." [51]

Actually, however, the principal reason for the continued diversity was the lack of a centralized ecclesiastical committee to supervise the correcting of all liturgical books. No such supervisory group existed in either the Greek or the Slavonic Church. Not until the seventeenth century do we find an attempt being made to control the printed editions and to arrange a revised edition of the Sluzhebnyks.

The printed Liturgikons and Sluzhebnyks can be divided into three editions: one Greek and two Slavonic. All three have their peculiarities and characteristics which deserve explanation.

The Greek Liturgikons form the first edition and although none of the three editions agree with one another, nevertheless they generally follow the same pattern. Basically they are modelled on the *Diataxis* of Philotheus. The Greek editions, in general, have a limited number of rubrics. Since it was always opposed to textual and rubrical innovations, the Greek edition was always considered the model. It served as the basic criterion for the liturgical revision of Peter Mohyla and the Patriarch Nikon.

Of the Greek editions of the Liturgikons, the Venetian publication took ascendancy. It enjoyed great prominence not only among the Greeks but also in Rus-Ukraine. These Greek editions were, however, not flawless for very often they were compiled from merely a few manuscripts, and sometimes even from only one which was used either in some monastery or on some island,[52] thus reflecting local practices and ritual peculiarities. The Greeks themselves complained about the many errors found in the Venetian publications. Nevertheless, these books, although they were not the official publications of the Greek Church, did eventually contribute to the establishing of liturgical-ritual prac-

---

[51] "We have today people in Lviv who have the audacity to print books filled with errors and to circulate them for the use of our spiritual flock without our knowledge, permission and blessing." They, "pursuing gain and not seeking Christ," have the audacity to "examine, amend, and correct" the sluzhebnyks. Cf. the foreword to Peter Mohyla's second edition of his Sluzhebnyk (Kiev: 1639). In another place Mohyla strongly denounces "the untutored and those present-day Lviv correctors or rather corruptors" (*ibid.*).

[52] De Meester, *Les Origines...*, 285. E. Legrand, gives a description of the Greek printed Liturgikons in his work: *"Bibliotheque hellenique des XVe et XVIIe siecles,* (3v.) (Paris: 1895).

tices. The first official Greek publication appeared in 1895. That same year, at the request of the Patriarch of Constantinople, the Greek priest Makarius Tantalides prepared a revised edition of the *Hieratikon,* in which the text of all three Byzantine Liturgies were corrected and compared with the ancient Greek codices or manuscripts.[53]

As for the Slavonic Sluzhebnyks, they were still less uniform than the Greek Liturgikons. Publishers in the sixteenth century were private individuals who cared little about correcting these publications. Thus, for example, Venetian publications of private individuals [54] issued in 1519, 1527, 1554 and 1570, mirrored the liturgical peculiarities or practices of the Serbian Church. In general, the publications of Leo Mamonich (Vilna, 1583, 1592, 1607 and 1617) imitated the Venetian publications, although they did not fully agree with the latter. The Striatyn publication of 1604, published by Bishop Gideon Balaban, holds a distinct place and is followed by the Vilna publication of 1617 (Typography of the Brotherhood of the Holy Spirit) and the Kievan publication of 1620, prepared by Archimandrite Elisey Pletenecky of the Kievan-Pecherska Lavra (Monastery of the Caves). All of these reveal pronounced differences, since they were arranged according to different manuscripts which the publishers selected according to their own liking.

This method of operation certainly did not promote uniformity. The published editions, so far as corrections were concerned, differed little from the manuscripts of the fourteenth-sixteenth centuries. Here and there we find the same errors, verbal distortions, occasional solecisms, defects and illogical structures. Some publishers (e.g., Bishop Balaban) assumed the task of correcting the liturgical text on their own, but they were not yet prepared for this endeavor. This project required a larger number of manuscripts, not only the Slavonic but also the Greek, for comparative study and analysis. The hierarchy, unquestionably, could have assumed the responsibility for supervising a liturgical reform, for the members were competent and they had the power to decide and determine how the reform was to be conducted. The task, however, was extremely complex and risky, since it involved elimination and correction of texts, rites and practices which had rooted themselves deeply in the individual Church centers.

In the seventeenth century two outstanding churchmen, the Metropolitan of Kiev, *Peter Mohyla* (d. 1647), and the Patriarch of Moscow, *Nikon* (1652–1667), sought to reform the liturgical rites. These two prominent ecclesiastical figures can be considered as the fathers of the two Slavonic editions of the liturgical books, especially the Sluzhebnyk. Mohyla was the father of the Rus-Ukrainian [55] edition and Nikon, of the Muscovite-Russian edition.[56]

---

[53] The Greeks were the first to eliminate from the service of the Liturgy the *troparion* in honor of the Holy Spirit in the epiklesis, arguing from the fact that they were a later interpolation unknown in the old Greek manuscripts. M. Tantalides also omitted them in the *Hieratikon* (Const. 1895) which he had issued.

[54] E.g. Vukovich (Venice, 1519, 1527, 1554) and E. Zahurovich (Venice, 1570).

[55] It is usually called: *recensio ruthena.*

[56] It is commonly called: "*synodal.*"

Peter Mohyla was not only a distinguished theologian and active church-man, but he was also an expert in liturgical matters. As Archimandrite of the Kievan-Pecherska Lavra, Mohyla took the responsibility of examining the liturgical books. During the previous century, prior to the signing of the Brest Union (1596), voices were heard clamoring for liturgical reform. In 1536, the Archimandrite of Suprasl, Sergius Kymbar, in his letter to the Kievan Metropolitan Makarius II (1534–1556), complained that in Lithuania and Rus divine services were not being conducted in the monasteries and churches "according to the prescription of the Holy Fathers, but according to one's own liking." The Archimandrite also complained of the many illegal interpolations and omissions that were being made in the services without the slightest reason.[57]

The liturgical-ritual chaos which prevailed in the churches of Old-Rus and Ukraine also attracted the attention of the Eastern Patriarchs who frequently visited these lands to collect alms. They sharply criticized the fact that the Slavonic churches differed from the Mother Church of Constantinople in liturgical practices, and they employed every means to bring order into the divine services.

Roman Catholic observers also made unfavorable comments on the disorder and chaos which was rampant in Rus at that time. This induced the Orthodox hierarchy to react and to attempt to bring order into Church services. Already before the Brest Union the bishops at the various councils sought to remove "divergency existing in liturgical functions." This was the sole topic of all their discussions. Finally it was decided that all liturgical books be carefully collated or compared, prior to publication, with the ancient Greek originals and the Slavonic manuscripts.[58]

A notable step toward liturgical reform was taken by Bishop Balaban. He sought, as we have mentioned previously, to amend the liturgical books. For example, his *Trebnyk** (Striatyn, 1606) had been compared to a certain degree with the ancient Slavonic manuscripts and with the Greek Euchologion which he had received from the Alexandrine Patriarch Meletius Pigas. However, it was due to the effort and initiative of Peter Mohyla that a definite and decisive step was taken to effect a comprehensive, wide-scale liturgical-ritual reform.

In the year 1629 Mohyla had his widely acclaimed "Liturgiarion," i.e. Sluzhebnyk, printed in the Kievan-Pecherska Lavra. This is the first revised Liturgikon or Sluzhebnyk that we find in the Slav lands. Based on the Greek original and on Slavonic manuscripts, this Liturgikon or Sluzhebnyk, before publication, was submitted for examination to the council of the Ukrainian Orthodox Bishops which convened in Kiev. The Ukrainian Orthodox bishops, under the guidance and direction of Metropolitan Job Boretsky, having examined it carefully and finding it "pure and flawless, unanimously accepted it, kissed it, extolled, praised, and sanctioned it."[59]

---

[57] S. Golubev, *Kievsky mitr. P. Mogila i yeho spodvizhniki*, I (Kiev: 1883), p. 371.

[58] Foreword to the Trebnyk of G. Balaban published at Striatyn in 1606. See also Golubev, *op. cit.*, 372.

[59] Foreword of Peter Mohyla to the Sluzhebnyk, 1629 edition.

* Trebnyk = Euchologion = Sacramentory or Ritual.

We shall not examine the Sluzhebnyk of 1629 in detail,[60] but we shall devote our attention to its characteristic traits. First of all, Peter Mohyla removed all orthographical errors. Afterwards, yielding to the wishes of the hierarchy and the lesser clergy, he inserted a number of rubrics accurately describing the liturgical movements. Besides the rubrics (which were printed in red), Mohyla added brief instructions covering the various circumstances that might confront a priest while celebrating the Divine Liturgy. Mohyla also prefaced the work with an excellent Forward or "Predyslovie" written by Taras Zemka, a monk-priest of the Pecherska Lavra. The Predyslovie contained a masterfully written summary of the most significant dogmatic and historical facts relating to the Divine Liturgy.

Peter Mohyla further enhanced his second edition of the Sluzhebnyk (Kiev 1638) by increasing the number of rubrics and adding a "Collection of Ektenes for various needs." The rubrics, especially the "Collection," were influenced by the Roman Rite Missal. Certain ektenes and improved prayers were also strongly influenced by the texts of the votive services of the Missal. Here we find Mohyla displaying a broad knowledge of Western theology. His Sluzhebnyk enjoyed great popularity not only among Orthodox but also among Catholics. Because of the technical care given to it and the precision of its rubrics, the Mohyla edition predominated over other editions throughout the seventeenth century, and even up to the first half of the eighteenth century. It has been reprinted frequently and at times without further alterations. It was reprinted, for example, during the seventeenth and eighteenth centuries in Kiev (1646, 1653, 1692, 1702) and in Lviv (1646, 1666, 1681, 1691, 1702, 1712).

The father of the Russian edition of the Sluzhebnyk was the Patriarch of Moscow, *Nikon*. Nikon and his liturgical-ritual reforms are better known than those of Mohyla because they brought about a split in the Muscovite Church and gave rise to the so-called "Raskol" (Schism).

The condition of liturgical-ritual observances in the Moscow Patriarchate preceding Nikon was no better than that in the Ukraine. Just as in the Kievan Metropolitan See, so also in the regions of the Patriarchate of Moscow, liturgical diversity and even a certain amount of liturgical anarchy prevailed. As long as the Church of Moscow was on friendly terms with the Church of Constantinople, it observed the liturgical-ritual customs of that Church. But after the close of the Florentine Union, especially after the seizure and capture of Constantinople by the Turks (1453), when the Metropolitan See of Moscow began to free itself more and more from the hegemony of Constantinople, the liturgical-ritual practices of Moscow began to incorporate local peculiarities. The reason for this diversity again was the use of different manuscripts which, especially in the fifteenth and sixteenth centuries, did not conform to the Greek types. Hence many errors, distortions, additions and omissions crept into Russian handwritten Sluzhebnyks.

---

[60] A. Raes, in his *"Le Liturgicon Ruthene depuis l'Union de Brest"* (Roma: 1942), pp. 96–98, gives a detailed analysis of the Mohyla Sluzhebnyk.

As early as one hundred years before Nikon, the so-called Stohlavy (Hundred Chapters Council, Moscow, 1551) had contemplated liturgical reforms and sought to eliminate "diversity in the church services," [61] but unfortunately did not succeed. The Council threatened to excommunicate all those who dared to alter in any way whatsoever the rite of the Church of Moscow. The Stohlavy Council, however, was very narrow in its views on liturgical-ritual matters for it completely ignored the practices of the Greek Church and recognized only local practices as legal.

The first attempts to revise the liturgical books date back to the time of the Patriarch Jonas (d. 1618), Patriarch Philaret (1619–1633) and the Patriarch Joseph (1642–1652). They, too, were not successful. By this time the attitude toward the Greek Rite had undergone substantial change. Patriarch Joseph, and especially his successor Nikon, were convinced that the only solution to the problem of revising the Sluzhebnyk was to use the Greek text and not exclusively the Moscow manuscripts. It was fortunate for Nikon that there was another champion of liturgical-ritual reform in the person of Czar Alexius himself (1645–1676) who was imbued with "Grecophile attitudes." [62] In 1651, he sent Arsenius Sukhanov to Greece to procure as many Greek manuscripts as possible and to act as an eyewitness to the practices of the Byzantine Greek Church.[63] After the death of Patriarch Joseph, Nikon took over the helm of the Church of Moscow and the liturgical-ritual reform advanced rapidly. The Synod of Moscow (1654) authorized the Patriarch to undertake the liturgical-ritual reform. He assumed the task enthusiastically and, although he himself had to resign, his reforms, notwithstanding the initial difficulties, were realized. They achieved their goal in full and brought about ritual uniformity. Liturgical-ritual practices in the Church of Moscow now harmonized with those of the Greek Rite. Thus a typical edition of the liturgical books was introduced. The Council of 1666–1667, which ratified Nikon's liturgical reform, became a milestone in the Muscovite Church, for it was then that ritual uniformity, which Metropolitan Cyprian had attempted to bring about in the fourteenth century, was truly initiated. All the Sluzhebnyks following 1666 adhere faithfully to Nikon's edition.

The reform of Nikon not only prevailed in the Moscow Patriarchate but was also imposed upon the Ukrainian Orthodox Church. In the year 1686, the Metropolitan of Kiev became subject to the Muscovite Patriarchate. Losing its ecclesiastical independence, the Ukrainian Orthodox Church was forced to accept the Muscovite ("Russian") edition of the liturgical books; the Ukrainian Rite was superseded by the Muscovite Rite. The Muscovite Church immediately opposed freedom of the press in the Ukraine and especially opposed the Kievan liturgical editions. The Patriarchs of Moscow, followed by the Synod of Moscow,

---

[61] A. Dmitrievsky, *"Bogosluzhenie v russ. Tserkvi za pervie pyat vyekov,"* in *Prav. Sobesyed.,* (1882), I, p. 157.

[62] P. Kaptyerev, *Patriarkh Nikon i tsar Aleksiy Mikhaylovich,* I, (Serg. Posad: 1909).

[63] S. Byelokurov, *Sobranie patr. Nikonom knig s vostoka,* *"Khr. Cht."* (1882), 2, pp. 444–494.

launched a formal proscription of all liturgical practices and customs of the Ukrainian Church which did not conform to the practices of Moscow. The Kievan-Pecherska printing presses were forbidden to publish any books without first obtaining approval of the Synod of Moscow. This restriction was directed especially against the Mohylian editions which were simply prohibited. The first restriction was issued by Peter the Great in 1720. In the middle of the century, Kiev and Chernihiv began reprinting the Moscow Synodal editions. Rigorous bans on printing anything without the approval of the Synod were again enforced in the years 1766, 1775 and 1786.[64]

By such means the Moscow Synodal editions achieved precedence in the Ukraine. In the eighteenth century the Ukrainian Orthodox Church lost its ritual individuality and became entirely Moscow-oriented.[65] The Mohyla edition was retained only by the Orthodox Eparchies which were under Polish occupation, i.e., the Eparchies of Galicia, Volhynia and the Ukraine on the Right Bank of the Dnieper (Pravoberezhna Ukraine). Here the Mohyla edition also had great influence on ritual development in the Ukrainian Catholic Church.

It has been observed that the dition of Nikon was also acknowledged in South Slav Orthodox Churches. The Serbian and Bulgarian Churches, freeing themselves from the hegemony of the Constantinople Patriarchate, accepted the liturgical books of Moscow, and together with these books the Muscovite-Russian Rite. This occurred in the seventeenth century and finally became established in the nineteenth century.[66]

While the Ukrainian Orthodox Church was being constrained to conform its Rite to that of Moscow, the Ukrainian Catholic Church partially preserved the Rite of the Metropolitan See of Kiev and partially yielded to the influence of the Latin Rite. Beginning with the second half of the seventeenth century, the Ukrainian Catholic Church pursued its own course of ritual development. Much could be said about the evolution of the Divine Liturgy according to the Rite of the Ukrainian Catholic Church, especially regarding the historic circumstances, causes and background of it. In the original text of this book there is complete chapter which expounds the history of the ritual differences and peculiarities in the celebration of the Divine Liturgy among the Ukrainian Catholics of the Byzantine-Ukrainian Rite, beginning with the Union of Brest (1596) to the present period. Because the said chapter deals primarily with the liturgical development of the Ukrainian Catholic Church, we deemed it proper to totally omit it in the English translation.

---

[64] I. Ohienko, *How Moscow destroyed the freedom of the press of the Kievo-Pecherska Lavra* (1921), pp. 10–15; ——— *The Ukrainian Church*, II (Prague: 1942), pp. 127–141, and *The History of the Ukrainian Press* (Lviv: 1925). All three are written in the Ukrainian language!

[65] I. Ohienko, *The Union of the Ukrainian Church with Moscow in 1686*, (1922); ——— *How Czarina Catherine russificated the Ukrainian Church* (1921). (All titles are translated).

[66] R. Rogosic, *Vicissitudines liturgiae slavicae in Jugoslavia et Bulgaria*, "Acta VII Conventus Velehradensis," (Olomouc: 1937), pp. 114–136.

SELECT BIBLIOGRAPHY

S. Byelokurov. *Sobranie patriarkhom Nikonom knig s vostoka*, "Khryst. Chtenie" (1882), 2, pp. 444–494.

—— *Arseniy Sukhanov*, Moskva: 1891.

Varlaam ihum. *Ob izmyeneniyakh v chinye liturghii Ioanna Zlatoustaho, Vasiliya Velikaho i Grigoriya Dvoyeslova, ukazannykh v Pomorskikh otvyetakh i Mechye dukhovnom, Kishinev:* 1860.

A. Gorsky. *Petr Mogila mitropolit Kievskiy: Pribavl. k tvor. sv. Otsov, IV* (1846), p. 40.

S. Golubev, *Kievsky mitropolit Petr Mogila i yeho spodvizhniki. Opit istoricheskaho izslyedovaniya,* I., Kiev: 1883. II, Kiev: 1898.

A. Dmitrievsky. *Bogosluzhenie v russkoy tserkvi za perviye pyat vyekov*, "Pravoslav. Sobyes" (1882), I, p. 138–166, 252–296; II, pp. 346–373; III, pp. 149–167, 372–394; 1883, II, pp. 345–374; III, pp. 198–229, 470–485.

—— *Bogosluzhenie v russkoy tserkvi v XVI v.*, Kazan: 1884.

N. Kapterev. *Patriarkh Nikon i tsar Aleksyey Michaylovich,* I, Sergiev Posad: 1909; II, Sergiev Posad: 1912.

—— *Patriarkh Nikon i yeho protivniki v dyelye ispravlyeniya tserkovnykh obryadov,* Sergiev Posad: 1913 (2 izd.).

N. Karatygin. *Obzor nyekotorykh osobennostey v chinoposlyedovaniyakh rukopisnykh trebnikov, prinadlezhashchikh rukop, bibliotekye Speterburgskoy Dukhovnoy Akademii,* "Khryst. Chtenie" (1877), I.

I. Karatayev. *Opisanie slavyanorusskikh knig,* Spb.: 1883.

A. Katanskiy. *Ocherk istorii liturghii nashey pravoslavnoy tserkvi,* "Khrist. Chtenie" (1868), II, pp. 345......, 525.......

N. Krasnoseltsev. *K istorii pravoslavnaho bogosluzheniya. Po povodu nyekotorykh tserkovnykh sluzhb i obryadov ninye ne upotreblyayushchikhsya,* Kazan: 1889.

E. Krizhanovsky. *Plvrezhdenie tserkovnoy obryadnosti i religioznykh obichayev v yuzhnorusskoy mitropolii:* "Rukovodstvo dlya selskikh pastirey," Kiev: 1860, 12.

M. Lisitsin. *Pervonachalnyj slavyano-russkiy tipikon,* Spb.: 1911.

A. Milovidov. *Staropechatnyya slavyano-russkiya izdaniya, vyshedshiya iz zapadno-russkikh tipografiy XVI–XVIII vv.,* "Chteniya Istor. i Drevn. Mosk." (1908), I, p. 27.

N. Mansvyetov. *Kak u nas pravilis tserkovniya knighi:* Pribavl. k tvor. sv. Otsov 1883, pp. 536–542, Prilozheniya: 1884, pp. 273–320.

K. Nikosky. *O sluzhbakh russkoj tserkvi, byvshikh v pervykh pechatnykh bogosluzhebnykh knigakh,* Spb.: 1885.

I. Ohienko. *The History of the Ukrainian Press,* written in the Ukrainian language, Lviv: 1925.

Makariy, mitr. *Patriarkh Nikon v dyelye ispravleniya tserkvonykh knig i obryadov:* Pribavl. k tvor. sv. Otsov: 1882, pp. 1–116.

I. Sakharov. *Obozryenie slavyano-russkoy bibliografii,* Spb.: 1849.

I. Svyentsitsky. *Katalog knig tserkovno slavyanskoy pechati,* Zhovkva: 1908.

T. Titov. *Tipografia Kievo-Pecherskoy Lavri,* Kiev: 1918.

V. Prilutsky. *Chastnoe bogoslyzhenie v russkoy tserkvi v XVI v. i v pervov polovinye XVII v.,* Kiev: 1912.

Undolskiy. *Ocherk slavyano-russkoy bibliografii,* Moskva: 1871.

Philaret. *Opit slicheniya chinoposlyedovaniy po izlozheniyu tserkovno-bogosluzhebnykh knig moskovskoy pechati, izdannykh pyervimi pyatiyu russkimi patriarkhami,* Bratskoe Slovo: 1875, 1–3.

—— *Chin liturghii Zlatousta po drevnym staropechatnym, novoispravlenomu l drevnepismennym sluzhebnikam,* Bratskoe Slovo: 1876,2–3.

Chapter IV

VARIOUS COMMENTARIES ON THE BYZANTINE-SLAVONIC LITURGY

Liturgical commentaries are very important sources for understanding the Divine Liturgy. It appears that, next to the Bible, there was no other subject writers were so fond of explaining or commenting on as the Divine Liturgy. Evidence of this is found in the numerous liturgical commentaries handed down to us from the Patristic Age to the present day.

Liturgical commentaries are valuable because they tell us how the various liturgical functions or rites were interpreted in former centuries. To-day they give us a better understanding of the Liturgy. Ancient manuscripts and printed Liturgikons and Sluzhebnyks provide us only with the texts and rubrics of the Divine Liturgy, but the liturgical commentaries describe the ritual forms of each part of the Liturgy and provide us with the meanings given them by the ancient Church writers and liturgists.

The Byzantine-Slavonic Liturgy has a great number of valuable commentaries, the authors of which have given us the traditional symbolic interpretations of the texts and rites of the Divine Liturgy, many of which are used even today. Scientific research, however, does not always confirm certain of these interpretations.

To date, we do not have a complete survey of the Byzantine-Slavonic commentaries on the Divine Liturgy although attempts at this have been made by the liturgists, Krasnoseltsev (Orthodox) and Salaville (Catholic).[1] In this chapter we shall present as complete a survey as possible of these commentaries, of which we shall later avail ourselves in our commentary on the texts and rites of the Divine Liturgy.

1. Liturgical Commentaries of the Patristic Age

(Fourth-Eighth Centuries)

The Patristic Age provides us with very few liturgical commentaries, and those few, predominantly brief and very general. They deal chiefly with the more important rites of the Divine Liturgy but do not give any detailed, systematic exposition of them. Nonetheless, they are still of great value for the litur-

---

[1] Kranoseltsev, N., *O drevnikh liturgicheskikh tolkovaniyakh*, (Odessa: 1894). Salaville S., *Indication sommaire des principales "Explications de la Messe orientale" anciennes et modernes* ("Liturgies Orientales," Appendix, pp. 135–148) (Paris: 1942).

gist, because they are documents that tell us how the Fathers of the Church understood the Liturgy and its sacred rites.

The oldest commentary on the Divine Liturgy is that of St. Cyril of Jerusalem (d. 386 A.D.), to which we referred in the second chapter of the historical introduction. It is an important document on the form of the Liturgy of the fourth century. In his commentary St. Cyril explains the Liturgy as it was celebrated in Jerusalem, most likely the Liturgy of St. James—not a Liturgy of the Byzantine type. But inasmuch as the Byzantine Liturgy is akin to the Jerusalem Liturgy, the explanations of St. Cyril contribute also to an understanding of the Byzantine Liturgy. St. Cyril's commentary is restricted only to the Liturgy of the Faithful. It is brief but clear. In it we encounter none of the symbolic interpretations which later prevailed in almost all the liturgical literature of the East and of the West. His interpretations are based on the literal sense. They delve into the essence of the liturgical rites. Symbolism appears only in those rites which have a truly symbolic character, e.g., the washing of the hands before offering the Eucharistic Sacrifice.[2]

After St. Cyril's liturgical commentary appeared the commentary of Pseudo-Dionysius.[3] This not too well-known author, writing under the pseudonym of St. Dionysius the Areopagite, disciple of St. Paul, most likely lived in the fifth century. His theological-mystical works, which were characterized by profound philosophical speculation, mysticism and an admirable logic, had an overwhelming influence on later Eastern and Western theological thought and actually formed a new school of theology. Later, the whole Byzantine Theology was based upon the principles of Pseudo-Dionysius. In his works we discern a fusion of the Platonic and Neo-Platonic philosophies with Christian philosophy. It was this fusion that was responsible for the wide acceptance of his works on Byzantine soil.

The liturgical commentary of Pseudo-Dionysius, which is part of his *Ecclesiastical Hierarchy,* is a systematic application of his whole theological system to the rites of the Liturgy. Hence the spirit and character of this commentary can be understood only in the light of his whole theological system.

Its essential characteristic lies in the principle that the visible and invisible worlds are a theophany, an emanation of the Supreme Being. The world is an emanation and imitation of God and its goal is God. This goal is achieved by stages. The lower and less perfect beings reach God through the higher and more perfect beings. The whole world is divided into the hierarchies, the celestial hierarchy and the terrestial hierarchy; both are a reflection of the beauty and perfection of God. Earthly existence has, therefore, a transitory and symbolic character rather than a true and genuine existence. Only God is true existence—true reality. He is Existence itself.

This Neo-Platonic concept of the world reduces reality to symbols, i.e., it can only lead to a symbolic understanding of things, especially those things

2 Migne, PG, 33, 1109.
3 Migne, PG, 3, 423–446.

which are connected with the cult of the Deity. For if the material world is a reflection and a symbol of the Supreme Being, then it follows that the sacraments, with all their rites, are also symbols of the Supreme Being because they are symbols of the divine supernatural Reality. Human reason must ascertain the meanings of these symbols; it must unveil what these symbols conceal and discover how they lead us to the True Reality—God. Pseudo-Dionysius is, therefore, the founder of the symbolic interpretation of the Liturgy. He was the first to apply systematically the symbolic concept which later was adopted and applied with varying success by the Byzantine liturgical commentators.[4]

The Pseudo-Dionysius liturgical commentary is remarkable for its speculative theological character. It is brief, but at times abstruse and unintelligible. Like the other sacraments, the Holy Eucharist, especially, possesses a host of symbolic actions. It is the queen of the sacraments, and its symbols and rites are designed to lead the faithful to God—the Prototype. The rites of the Liturgy are, therefore, stages leading to God. By passing through these stages, the Christian completes the cycle of his existence. With the help of symbols, the soul unites itself with the Deity Himself and becomes a partaker of God's life. An ascetical and mystical element, therefore, seems to pervade the symbolic commentary of Pseudo-Dionysius. The liturgical texts and rites on which this commentary is based were those contained in the Liturgy of the Syrian-Jerusalem type. Pseudo-Dionysius does not cite the text of the Liturgy but only alludes to its rites.

Another liturgical commentary written in the spirit of Pseudo-Dionysian symbolism was that of St. Maximos the Confessor (d. 662 A.D.). Its title itself suggests its character; St. Maximos called his commentary *Mystagogue*, i.e. an introduction into the mysteries and symbols of the Divine Liturgy.[5] He was a faithful disciple of Pseudo-Dionysius and his concept of the world was borrowed almost entirely from his master. Even in interpreting the rites of the Liturgy, he follows his teacher and is his commentator. Like Pseudo-Dionysius, he too at times looks for a deeper mystical meaning in the rites. His symbolism departs from that of Pseudo-Dionysius, but the same ascetical-mystical coloring still remains. The purpose of the Liturgy with all its concomitant rites is to elevate man from the mundane sphere to the heavenly sphere—to God. At times this interpretation is quite artificial and arbitrary. It is, indeed, very original but it is vaguely written. Perhaps this is why it soon slipped into oblivion and exerted only small influence upon later Byzantine liturgical commentaries.

Nonetheless, the commentary of St. Maximos is considered very important because it is the first and oldest commentary on the Byzantine Liturgy. The rites that he explains are those celebrated in the Byzantine Church, of which he was a member. Actually, then, he developed the symbolism of Pseudo-Dionysius and applied it to the rites of the Byzantine Liturgy.

---

[4] (Popov J., *Dioniziy Ar.*, "Prav. Bog. Ents.," IV, 903, p. 1080).

[5] Migne, PG, 91, 657–718 (Mistagogy). Cf. also "Scholia of St. Maximos to the works of Pseudo-Dionysius. Migne, PG, 4, 15–432, and 527–576.

The liturgical commentaries of the Patristic Age climax with the commentary of St. Maximos. Although some liturgists also attribute to this era the commentaries of the Patriarch John Postnyk (d. 595 A.D.), St. Sophronius (d. 638 A.D.), and St. Herman (d. 740 A.D.), they are not authentic and are of a post-Patristic period. For example, the commentary ascribed to John Postnyk [6] certainly is not of the sixth century, but of the tenth or eleventh century.[7] Proof of this later origin may be established by the allusion made to the use of the spoon in distributing Holy Communion. Research shows that the spoon was not used earlier than the eleventh century.[8] At any rate, this commentary with its symbolism and entire arrangement is typically Byzantine.

It may be in order to mention at least two more names connected with the Patristic Age and associated with the interpretation of the Byzantine Liturgy: St. Anastasius of Sinai (d. 700 A.D.) and St. Theodore Studite (d. 826 A.D.). St. Anastasius left a brief treatise on the Holy Liturgy [9] which contains moral-ascetical instructions rather than an interpretation of the Liturgy, and St. Theodore, a brief comment on the Liturgy of the Presanctified Gifts,[10] without any detailed interpretation of the rites.

2. Byzantine-Greek Commentaries on the Divine Liturgy

(Ninth-Nineteenth Centuries)

In contrast to the Patristic Age which provided us with very few commentaries, the Byzantine Period might well be called the "renaissance" of liturgical commentaries. This is the period during which the symbolic interpretation of rites flourished, but its symbolism indicates a striking departure from that of Pseudo-Dionysius and St. Maximos. The authors of the period discovered a new type of liturgical symbolism which almost forced that of the Patristic Age into the background.

The spirit of the age, which delighted in symbolic interpretation, contributed much to the development of symbolism. In this period we find the allegorical method of interpreting Sacred Scripture asserting itself in Byzantine liturgical commentaries. This method was the product of the Alexandrian School. The iconoclastic altercations of the eighth and ninth centuries also contributed to the symbolic interpretation of the Byzantine Liturgy. The iconoclasts opposed the veneration of holy pictures which they considered idolatry. They were actually religious rationalists who did not have the slightest concept of the

---

[6] Text: Pitra, J. *Specilegium Solesmense*, Vol. IV, pp. 440–442.

[7] Krasnoseltsev, N., considers this commentary to be authentic and he attributes it to John Postnyk (Cf. his *Svyedyeniya o nyekotorykh liturgicheskikh rukopisyakh Vatikanskoy biblioteki* (Kazan: 1885), pp. 306–307). The text of the commentary is given by Krasnoseltsev on pp. 307–311. However we cannot agree with his opinion.

[8] Muretov, S., *Istoricheskiy obzor chinopos. proskomidii do Ustava patr. Filofeva*, (Moskva: 1895), pp. 157–158.

[9] Migne, PG, 89, 825–850.

[10] Migne, PG, 99, 1687–1690.

value and significance of the external forms of worship as was manifested in liturgical forms, and, consequently, thought these to be superstitious. The reaction of the Catholic faithful to these iconoclastic ideas manifested itself in the veneration of icons which were the symbols or representations of their prototypes. The iconoclastic war only strengthened and augmented their love for icons and sacred rites; and incited them to perfect the symbolism connected with liturgical rites and objects.

The first liturgical commentary of this period that merits our attention is the *Mystical Theory*, ascribed to St. Herman, Patriarch of Constantinople (d. 740 A.D.).[11] This commentary has been handed down to us in a number of manuscripts.[12] The first text of the *Mystical Theory* was adulterated by later additions and interpolations. Many authors endeavored to reconstruct and establish the authorship and origin of this primitive text. We make mention here of the research and investigations of Pitra,[13] Krasnoseltsev,[14] Brightman [15] and Borgia,[16] men who achieved some positive results. The question of the authorship of the *Mystical Theory* still remains unclarified. Most manuscripts of the *Mystical Theory* ascribe its authorship to St. Herman, who lived during the time of the iconoclastic persecutions and who, for opposing Emperor Leo III (717–741), had to abandon his patriarchate in Constantinople. Other manuscripts, however, attribute authorship to such various Fathers of the Church as St. Basil, St. Cyril of Jerusalem, St. Cyril of Alexandria (d. 444 A.D.), St. John Chrysostom, St. Athanasius of Alexandria and even St. James the Apostle.[17] Leo Allatius attributes the *Mystical Theory* to Patriarch Herman II (d. 1240 A.D.).[18] However, we must accept the fact that the work was written before the ninth century and that its author was, if not St. Herman, then one of his contemporaries. The time of origin can be deduced from the fact that the *Mystical Theory* was translated into Latin in the ninth century by Anastasius the Librarian, a contemporary of Photius. In the dedication of his work to the Emperor Charles the Bald, Anastasius mentions that the Greeks ascribe the original to St. Herman.[19] The original text of the *Mystical Theory* acquired in later centuries many additions and interpolations. The text quoted in Migne's [20] edition can only have come from the thirteenth century. Hence, in the course of our work we will refer to this commentary as the Pseudo-Herman commentary.

---

11 Migne, PG, 98, 383–454.

12 Expositionis liturgicae de sacris graecis obeundis textus sincerus S.P.N. Germani Patriarchae Constantinopoleos (Nova Patrum Bibliotheca, Vol. X. pars 2, pp. 4–8 Romae: 1905).

13 J. Pitra, *Iuris eccl. Graecorum historia et monumenta* (Paris: 1868), Vol. II, p. 287.

14 Krasnoseltsev, *Svyedyeniya*, pp. 321.

15 F. E. Brightman, *The Historia mystagogica and other greek commentaries on the Byzantine liturgy*, "*Journal of theol. Stud.*", IX. (1908) , p. 255.

16 N. Borgia, *Il commentario liturgico di s. Germano Patriarca Constantinopolitano e la versione latina di Anastasio Bibliotecario* (Grottaferrata: 1912), pp. 1–9.

17 Migne, PG, 98, 11–14 (Notitia de S. Germano).

18 *Ibid.*

19 S. Petrides, *Traites liturgiques de saint Maxime et de saint Germain, traduits par Anastase le Bibliothecaire*, "*Revue de l'Orient Chretien*," X (1905), pp. 287–309.

20 Migne, PG, 98, 383–454.

The *Mystical Theory* is also noted for its symbolism. Unlike the symbolic interpretation of Pseudo-Dionysius and St. Maximos, the Pseudo-Herman commentary was the first to consider the Divine Liturgy as symbolizing the chronological events of Christ's life on earth, His death and His resurrection. The rites of the Divine Liturgy, then, are a symbolic representation or dramatization of the most prominent events in the history of the Redemption. Even in the less significant rites we find symbolic allusions to the events in the life of our Savior.

This symbolic concept of the Divine Liturgy of Pseudo-Herman is unprecedented—it was unknown to Pseudo-Dionysius and St. Maximos. The very charm of originality is perhaps the reason why the *Mystical Theory* was accepted so enthusiastically by all the later Byzantine interpreters of the Divine Liturgy. It is not our intention here to determine where this mystical-symbolic concept of the Divine Liturgy first originated. We may only say that the new concept became the exclusive theory for interpreting the rites and sense of the Divine Liturgy, not only in the Byzantine, but also in the Latin, Syrian, Armenian, Chaldean and Ethiopian liturgical commentaries.[21] We shall see in the second part of our work how this mystical-symbolic concept was applied to each rite and ceremony of the Divine Liturgy. We shall also present a critique of these symbolic interpretations.

Similar to the *Mystical Theory* are the liturgical commentaries of Pseudo-Sophronius (d. 638 A.D.) and Theodore Andides (d. ab. 1270 A.D.). The commentary ascribed to St. Sophronius probably dates back to the twelfth or the thirteenth century. To our knowledge, only one manuscript of Pseudo-Sophronius has been preserved. Cardinal Mai [22] published it and Migne [23] incorporated it in his Patrology. This commentary is incomplete since it ends with the interpretation of the Great Entrance. As to its authorship, it can scarcely be the work of St. Sophronius, Patriach of Jerusalem, because its descriptions of the ritual ceremonies suggest the twelfth or thirteenth century. Some like to ascribe at least some parts of this liturgical commentary,[24] excluding later interpolations, to St. Sophronius (d. 631 A.D.), but the fact is, that the saint most probably had nothing to do with the work.[25]

In character, arrangement and especially symbolism, the Pseudo-Sophronius commentary is identical to the *Mystical Theory* of Pseudo-Herman. We encounter in both commentaries verbatim quotations which suggest a common source. From this similarity we may infer that the Pseudo-Sophronius belongs to a

---

[21] S. Salaville, *Indication sommaire des principales "Explications de la messe orientale" anciennes et modernes* (Liturgies orientales, II, La Messe, Paris: 1942, 2 Partie, pp. 135–148).

[22] Mai, *Specilegium Romanum*, Vol. IV (Romae: 1840), pp. 31–48.

[23] Migne, PG, 87, 3981–4002.

[24] S. Muretov, *Istorich. obzor chinopos. proskom. do Ust. lit. pat. Finlofeya* (Moskva: 1895), pp. 141–142.

[25] M. Solowij, *De commentario liturgico s. Sophronio attribuito* (Romae: 1948), pp. 5–8, 12–13, (reproduction from the "Analecta OSBM," VII–VIII).

group of liturgical commentaries that appear under the title of the *Mystical Theory,* and is only one of the numerous editions of Pseudo-Herman.[26]

To this same group belongs the commentary of Theodore, Bishop of Andida, entitled *A Brief Commentary on the Symbols and Mysteries of the Divine Liturgy.*[27] Although we know little about the author himself, nevertheless, we do know that his commentary belongs to the thirteenth century in which he lived. Theodore's commentary differs in some respects from the previous two. The difference, however, does not lie in its symbolism for Theodore follows faithfully in the footsteps of Pseudo-Herman and Pseudo-Sophronius. But, the work of Theodore is more unified and perfected. We find the individuality of the author clearly expressed in it. He is aware of the existence of other liturgical commentaries; he refers to them, and he profits from them.[28] His approach to the interpretation of the Divine Liturgy is marked by a clear and distinctive method. In the introduction, he emphasizes that the Divine Liturgy, as a whole, is a portrayal or representation of the great work of Redemption; in its rites, all the events of Christ's life are symbolically typified and dramatized.[29] The work of Theodore, therefore, is the first systematic adaptation of the symbolic method to the Divine Liturgy. It is true that the works of Pseudo-Herman and Pseudo-Sophronius express the same theme, but they lack Theodore's clarity, consistency and systematic application of the symbolic method to the rites of the Divine Liturgy.[30]

The most celebrated liturgical commentaries of the Byzantine-Greek period were those of Nicholas Cabasilas (d. 1363) and Simeon of Thessalonica (d. 1429). Precedence undoubtedly should be accorded the commentary of Cabasilas. Until recently scholars were convinced that Cabasilas was the Bishop of Thessalonica, but later research shows that he not only was not an archbishop but that he was not even a member of the clergy. Cabasilas was a lay theologian and without doubt he is to be considered among the better Byzantine theologians and mystics.[31] His *Interpretation of the Divine Liturgy* [32] is an excellent liturgical treatise which, so far, has surpassed all commentaries on the Divine Liturgy in its depth of thought.[33] It is based primarily on numerous quotations drawn

---

[26] *Ibid.* p. 17.

[27] Migne, PG, 140, 417–468.

[28] Migne, PG, 140, col. 424.

[29] Migne, PG, 140, 417–424.

[30] Krasnoseltsev, *Obyasnenie liturhii, sostavlennoye Teodorom, episkopom Andidskim.* Pamyatknik vizantiyskoy dukhovnoy literaturi XII v, "Pravoslav. Sobes." (1884), I, p. 375.

[31] S. Salaville, *Explication de la divine liturgie (de Cabasilas), Introduction et traduction de S. Salaville* (Paris-Lyon: 1943), p. 14; Bossuet considers N. Cabasilas to be "un des plus solides théologiens de l'Église grecque," Salaville, *Explication* . . . ., p. 14.

[32] Migne, PG, 150, 367–492. S. Salaville translated the liturgical commentary of Cabasilas into the French language: *Explication de la divine liturgie* (Paris-Lyon: 1943).

[33] "L'Expositio Liturgiae de Cabasilas. . . . . est un excellent exposé méthodique te doctrinal des rites et des formules de la messe byzantine. Les meilleurs juges ont toujours fait grand cas.". . . . . (p. 13) , "il y a peu de traites de ce genre ou l'on découvre plus de lumière sur les mystères et plus de science ecclésiastique," . . . . . . (p. 15) . "Elle est constamment imprégnée de substance scripturaire et patristique, le tout lie en doctrine cohérente de Thessalonique, le meilleur des théologiens liturgistes postérieurs, n'a fait que l'utiliser et l'imiter avec bien moins de talent" (Salaville, *Exposition* . . . . . ., p. 16).

from Holy Scripture and the Fathers of the Church. In his symbolic interpretations of the liturgical ceremonies and functions, Cabasilas follows the *Mystical
Theory*, but he clearly distinguishes between the symbolic and practical aspects
of the rites of the Liturgy, thus avoiding hyperbolic symbolism. Thus, although
his commentary is traditionally symbolistic, nevertheless, it rests upon a solid
theological foundation and has good organization which sets it apart from the
chaotic *Mystical Theory*.

Cabasilas was the first to discriminate between the "Greeks" and the
"Latins" in regard to the form of Eucharistic Consecration. He supports the
view that not only the words of Christ: "This is My Body, This is My Blood,"
constitute the consecratory form, but that the words of the prayer invoking the
Holy Spirit (the epiklesis) also are part of this form. This view later was
accepted in Byzantine-Greek and Russian theology.

The commentary of Simeon of Thessalonica does not possess the theological
depth of Nicholas Cabasilas, but it is one of the most esteemed, most widely-
quoted and most frequently used of all commentaries. Simeon was an archbishop
and is revered in the Byzantine Church as a saint. This great ascetic was one of
the opponents of the "Latins." Like Cabasilas, he took a stand against the position of the Western Latin theologians who attributed the power of consecration
to the institutional words of Christ.

Simeon left two liturgical commentaries, one short [34] and one long.[35] They
were both known for the symbolism which was almost entirely borrowed from the
Mystical Theory. Simeon became a great authority for all the later interpreters
because of his conciseness and clearness of thought. In addition, he left interpretations for almost all the liturgical functions, i.e. the sacraments,[36] the dedication
and blessing of churches, and the divine office.[37] He gave a brief exposition of
the Liturgy, in the broad sense of the term. He was the first liturgist in the
Byzantine East. Even the renowned liturgist Goar respected and extolled his
works.[38] This, too, enhanced the popularity of Simeon's work. The Byzantine
Church had in his works the first systematic exposition of all the divine services.

In the same century (the fifteenth) two other well-known Byzantine theologians, Bessarion of Nicaea [39] and Mark Eugenicos, Metropolitan of Ephesus,[40] also

---

[34] *On the Holy Liturgy*, Migne, PG, 155, 253–304.

[35] *On the Holy church....and on the divine service*, Migne, PG, 155, 697–750. Cf. also
Goar for the text of this last commentary: *Euchologion sive Rituale Graecorum* (Parisiis:
1647), pp. 212–232: Beati Metropolitae Thessalonices Domini Symeonis de Templo et in
Missam enarratio.

[36] Migne, PG, 155, 176–696.

[37] *Ibid.*

[38] Goar, *Euchologion*......., p. 211 ("vir, si Romanae Ecclesiae fuisset coniunctus, antiquis
Patribus adnumerandus").

[39] "De sacramento Eucharistiae, ex quibus verbis Christi Corpus conficiatur," Cf. Migne,
PG, 161, 493–526.

[40] "Libellus de consecratione eucharistica: quod non solum a voce dominicorum verborum
sanctificantur divina dona, verum a consequente oratione et benedictione sacerdotis, virtute
Sancti Spritus," Migne, PG, 160, 1079–1090.

wrote on the Liturgy. Their concern was not with a systematic exposition of the Divine Liturgy, but rather with determining the precise moment of consecration. Bessarion defended the Western theory that the consecration of the Holy Species is to be attributed to the words of Christ, i.e. the words of institution, while Mark Eugenicos ascribes the consecratory power both to the words of Christ and to the epiklesis.

The next Greek commentary does not appear until the sixteenth century, after a lapse of 150 years. The author of this work was a priest, John Nathanael, and the title of his commentary was *The Divine Liturgy with the Commentaries of Various Teachers.*[41] This work lacked originality; it was a mere mechanical compilation of the liturgical commentaries of Pseudo-Herman, Theodore Andides, Simeon and especially of Nicholas Cabasilas. It does deserve consideration, however, because it was later accepted as the basis for the liturgical commentary *"Skrizhal"* (1656) which was prepared at the request of the Russian Patriarch Nikon.

From the seventeenth century we have a few Greek liturgical commentators, viz. Gabriel Vlasios,[42] Paissius Ligarides,[43] Meletius Sirigos,[44] Kalinnikos from Arkanania [45] and Nicholas Bulgaris.[46] Of these, only one deserves special consideration—Nicholas Bulgaris. His commentary is original, not in content or its novel symbolism, but in its literary form which is the question-answer form. Because of this it is called *Liturgical Catechism*. It was published many times and toward the close of the seventeenth century, the monk Euthymius translated it into Old Slavonic.

In the seventeenth century, the first edition of the *Euchologion* also appeared; its author was the famous Dominican, James Goar.[47] We mention Goar here because of his great influence on the later liturgical commentaries. Still, the *Euchologion* is not itself a liturgical commentary in the strict sense of the word. It contains the text of the Greek divine services: all three Liturgies, the divine office, ceremonies of the holy sacraments, and other divine services, with a corresponding Latin translation. The author added many valuable historical annotations together with quotations from the various Byzantine commentators on the texts and rites of St. John Chrysostom's Liturgy. These historical-crit-

---

[41] Venice 1574, (second edition, Venice: 1712). The Greek title is: *He theia leiturghia meta eksegezeon diaphoron didaschalon.* Cf. E. Legrande, *Bibliographie Hellenique des XVe et XVIe siecles,* Vol. II (Paris: 1885), pp. 201–204.

[42] Gabriel Vlasios was metropolitan of Navpakta and Arta. He died in 1638. The title of his book is: *Eksegesis tes leiturghias.* see Constantine Satas, *Neohelleniki Filologhia* (1453–1821). (Athens: 1868), p. 304.

[43] P. Ligarides died in 1667. His commentary on the Liturgy is entitled: *"Ermeneia tes teias leiturghias.* (Vid. Satas, *Neohellenici.........,* p. 316).

[44] M. Sirigos died in 1667. His commentary was published in 1876 in Constantinople. (Cfr. M. Jugie, *Theologia Dogmatika Christianorum Orientalium,* Vol. I (Parisiis: 1926), p. 514).

[45] C. Satas, *Neohellin. Filologh...,* p. 356.

[46] *Catechesis iera etoi tes theias kai ieras leiturghias eksegesis* (Venice: 1681).

[47] *Euchologion sive Rituale Graecorum* (Lutetiae Parisiorum: 1647:2–da ed. Venetiis: 1730).

ical observations are of great importance because they laid the foundation for a scientific-historical commentary on the Liturgy of St. John Chrysostom. We find Goar's influence evident in the liturgical commentaries of John Dmitrevsky and Benjamin Krasnopievkov.

From the eighteenth century, we have only one known Greek liturgical commentary, written by Constantine Kaisarios (d. 1784).[48] In the nineteenth century, Greek literature on the Liturgy was able to boast of a few great names. In this century, the first textbooks on liturgics appear, and not only do they furnish us with a commentary on the Divine Liturgy, but also with a systematic exposition of all the divine services. One might mention the liturgical works of Dimitrios Darbares,[49] P. Rompotes,[50] H. Palamas,[51] I. Mezolaras,[52] Mina Khamadopulos,[53] John Martinos[54] and Bartholomew Georgiades.[55]

3. Slavonic Liturgical Commentaries

(Twelfth-Twentieth Centuries)

From the very beginning of Christianity in the territories of ancient Rus, the Liturgy became a subject of special interest and love. Because of the lack of literature on theology, the Liturgy, for many centuries, was the sole source of theological inquiry. Love for and attachment to, external ritualism characterized early Christian piety in Rus. This external ritualism often led to ritual exaggeration and formalism.[56] It was especially characteristic of the people from the northern part of Rus (the Russians) to identify external ritual with dogma and Orthodoxy itself. It was the lack of formal higher learning and education that caused the discrimination between rite and dogma to disappear and to give rise to the seventeenth century schism (Raskol). Behind the mask of loyalty to tradition, there arose a ritual formalism and scrupulous fanaticism for the "letter."[57]

The interest shown in liturgical rites in ancient Rus was great indeed, but the understanding of these rites was not on a high level.[58] The first Slavonic liturgical commentaries are not known to possess any great value. Predominantly translations of Greek originals, they were ambiguous, incomplete and, at times,

---

[48] *Eksegesis tes theias leiturghias* (Vienna: 1795).

[49] *Encheiridion christianikon* (Vienna: 1803).

[50] *Christianike leiturghike* (Athens: 1869).

[51] *Orthodoxos christianike leiturghike* (Constantinople: 1886).

[52] *Encheiridion leiturghikes* (Athens: 1895).

[53] *Ermeneia tes ieras leiturghias* (Athens: 1887).

[54] *Leiturghike kai peri Proeghiasmenes* (Athens: 1900).

[55] *Epitome leiturghikes* (Athens: 1892) .

[56] N. Krasnoseltsev, *Tolkovaya Sluzhba i drughiya sochineniya, otnosyashchiyasya k obyasneniyu bogosluzheniya v drevney Rusi do XVII v.* Bibliograficheskiy obzor. (Pravo-Sobes.: 1878), II, p. 3.

[57] Arsen Richynsky, *Problyemy ukrayinskoyi relihiynoyi svidomosty,* (Volodymyr Volynsky: 1933), p. 98.

[58] N. Krasnoseltsev, *op. cit.,* p. 3.

corrupted by additions and insertions borrowed from unreliable and dubious sources. This condition persisted until the seventeenth century when commentaries worthy of consideration began to appear.

To the ancient liturgical commentaries found in the territories of Rus belongs that of St. Cyril of Jerusalem, which was found in manuscripts of the twelfth century.[59] The liturgical commentary of St. Maximos was also known at least in excerpts.[60] In the thirteenth century, the liturgical commentary of Pseudo-Herman appears in manuscripts, although never under his name. In comparison with the Greek editions, it has very many of its own additions and omissions. In regard to the contents of the Pseudo-Herman commentary, the interpretations of the Divine Liturgy that appear under the name of Gregory the Theologian,[61] and the anonymous *"The Interpretation of the Apostolic Catholic Church,"*[62] we find that they are of the same literary caliber. The apocryphal element is very noticeable in these commentaries. Both are of the fifteenth or sixteenth century.[63]

In the manuscripts of the century we frequently encounter commentaries with the titles *Commentary on the Holy and Apostolic Catholic Church,* or *Interpretations of the Liturgy of St. John Chrysostom* by Sichius, or simply *Sluzhba Tolkovaya* or *The Liturgy Interpreted.* This latter must have been widely-known and highly esteemed because the Stohlavy Council of 1551 refers to it as to an authority.[64] We discover the *Sluzhba Tolkovaya* in the moral-pastoral books (kormchi knighi), trebnyks and various collections. It was the main source from which ancient Rus gleaned its knowledge of the meanings and significance of the rites and ceremonies of the Divine Liturgy. The text of the *Sluzhba Tolkovaya* would sometimes be inserted between the texts of the Sluzhebnyks themselves.[65]

The contents of the *Sluzhba Tolkovaya* are divided into three parts: 1) the explanation of the church edifice; 2) the Proskomide; and 3) the Liturgy itself. The explanation of the church edifice and the Proskomide is almost verbatim that of Pseudo-Herman. The commentary on the Divine Liturgy is based predominantly on the commentary of "Gregory the Theologian." In comparison to the Greek-Byzantine interpretations they are quite original. The *Sluzhba Tolkovaya* is, therefore, a compilation of sundry sources with a considerable admixture of aprocryphal-mystical elements.[66]

We know almost nothing about the author of the *Sluzhba Tolkovaya.* In manuscripts this work is never ascribed to St. Herman, but the name Sichius or

---

[59] Krasnoseltsev, *op. cit.,* p. 4.

[60] Krasnoseltsev, *op. cit.,* pp. 5–6.

[61] *Ibid.,* pp. 10–11.

[62] Ibid., pp. 9–10.

[63] Ibid., pp. 9–10; Especially the influence of the apocryphal "Acts of Pilate."

[64] Krasnoseltsev, *op. cit.,* p. 20.

[65] E.g. in the handwritten Sluzhebnyk of the Moscow Synodal Library, no. 366 of the sixteenth century. (See Gorskiy-Nevostruev, *Opisanie rukopisey Mosk. Synod. Bibl.,* III, otd. ch. I, p. 91.)

[66] Krasnoseltsev, *op. cit.* pp. 30–31.

Isichius does very frequently occur in connection with it.[67] Probably this is a reference to Isichius, a monk and priest of the Church of Jerusalem (d. 450 A.D.) who was an expert in the study of Holy Scripture. He adhered to the allegorical method of interpretation which was employed in the Alexandrian School.[68] There are some resemblances [69] between the interpretations of the *Sluzhba Tolkovaya* and the works of Isichius, a fact which lends some foundation for ascribing the *Sluzhba Tolkovaya* to him. Krasnoseltsev even conjectured that the liturgical commentary of Isichius was the most likely source and basis of the Pseudo-Herman commentary.[70] However, we have no evidence in Patristic literature to substantiate his claim.

The seventeenth century marks the beginning of a new era in the history of Slavonic commentaries. The need of a solid commentary on the Liturgy was especially felt when the Moscow Patriarch Nikon began his renowned liturgical ritual reform.

The first liturgical commentary on the century, however, did not appear in Russia but in the Ukraine, almost 40 years before the publication of Nikon's *Skrizhal.* The author of this work was Taras Zemka, priest-monk of the Kievan-Pecherska Lavra, orator, and censor of the Lavra Monastery editions during the time of Metropolitan Peter Mohyla.[71] This commentary served as the preface to the 1629 Sluzhebnyk of Peter Mohyla. It was short but well elaborated. Zemka does not go into a detailed interpretation of the rites of the Divine Liturgy, but gives a brief dogmatic lesson on the sublimity of the Unbloody Sacrifice. In his Introduction, he explains the various names given to the Divine Liturgy, and then he points out its dignity and at the end makes observations concerning its origin and tradition. He also mentions the *Tradition of the Divine Liturgy,* which St. Proclus was supposed to have written. The liturgical commentaries of Taras Zemka are rich in quotations taken from the Fathers of the Church. One can truly call it a "remarkably written liturgical treatise." [72]

Wider acclaim was accorded the commentary entitled *Skrizhal* or "Tablets" of the Divine Liturgy. This commentary is inseparably linked with the name of Patriarch Nikon and his liturgical-ritual reform. Desiring to issue a commentary devoid of deficiencies, Nikon turned to the Patriarch of Constantinople, Paissius, requesting that a liturgical commentary be sent to him in Moscow. Paissius obliged him and sent him "a very useful book, a holy interpretation of the Divine Liturgy, spiritual tablets "Skrizhal" or a revelation of church mysteries." [73]

---

[67] Ibid., pp. 31–32.

[68] B. Altaner, *Patrologia* (Roma: 1944), p. 227.

[69] Krasnoseltsev, *op. cit.*, p. 32.

[70] Ibid., p. 32.

[71] Taras Zemka died in 1632.

[72] "The foreword of Taras L. Zemka is a very beautiful liturgical treatise based on the works of the Holy Fathers and in general on spirit of those theological-historical works of the scholars of the Percherska Laura printing press," (T. Titov, *Tipografiya Kievo-Pecherskoy Lavri,* Vol. I (Kiev: 1916), p. 180–181).

[73] See "Skrizhal"—the foreword of Patriarch Paissius.

The author of the commentary was a well-known Greek priest, John Nathanael. The first edition of Nathanael's work came out in 1574 in Venice. The Ukrainian monk, Epiphany Slavynetsky (d. 1675), later translated this commentary from Greek into Old Slavonic.

The *Skrizhal* was issued in Moscow in 1656. It is a commentary which contains also some liturgical-dogmatic treatises such as the treatise of Gabriel Severus (1616), Metropolitan of Philadelphia (Asia Minor), on the holy sacraments: some excerpts from the works of Maximos the Greek (d. 1556); and the questions of the Patriarch Nikon to Paissius and the latter's corresponding answers.

The liturgical commentary in Nikon's *Skrizhal* is not an original but an eclectic work, because his Greek original, Nathanael's liturgical commentary, is simply a compilation of the various Byzantine commentators. It is comprised of portions borrowed from the interpretations of Simeon, Pseudo-Herman and especially Nicholas Cabasilas. Up to the nineteenth century, the *Skrizhal* remained the exclusive commentary on the Liturgy in Russia.

Ten years after the appearance of the *Skrizhal* a new commentary was published. Its author was the Ukrainian, Hegumenus Theodosius Safonovich.[74] It first appeared in Kiev in the Ukrainian vernacular of 1667, and again in the following year (1668) in Moscow in an Old-Slavonic translation called *An explanation of the holy church, liturgical instruments, the Divine Liturgy,*[75] *and Vespers, taken from St. Simeon, Archbishop of Thessalonica, and other Church writers (John Chrysostom, John Damascene, Nicholas Cabasilas,*[76] *Ambrose of Milan) and translated from the Greek and Latin into the Ruthenian language.* The book of Safonovich was composed of five chapters: 1) the Holy Church; 2) Priestly Vestments; 3) Commentary on the Proskomide; 4) Commentary on the Liturgy; 5) Commentary on the Lytia—Great Vespers. In the text, numerous references are made to Simeon of Tessalonica, Cabasilas, Dionysius Areopagite and Herman. The author made use of the these sources in such a way that his work can truly be said to be original and independent; and it can also be said that he was not an eclectic. His style of writing is original; he uses the question-and-answer technique or the catechetical method. The "Explanation" by far excels the commentary contained in Nikon's *Skrizhal* from both the theological and literary points of view.[77] Safonovich's commentary is remarkable for its brevity, clarity of thought and expression, a clear division of material, perspicuity and thoroughness.

The work of Safonovich stirred up a lively controversy among Ukrainian and Russian theologians, centered upon one of Safonovich's questions dealing

---

[74] Krasnoseltsev, *op. cit.,* p. 37.

[75] It was then that the Ukrainian term for liturgy—*Sluzhba Bozha*—was first used. This term was unknown in Russia.

[76] Safonovich mistakenly ascribes the authorship of the Liturgical commentary to Nilos Cabasilas (d. 1361), and not to Nicholas Cabasilas (d. 1371) the real author and close relative to Nilos, the Archbishop of Thessalonica.

[77] Krasnoseltsev, *op. cit.,* p. 39.

with the Consecration. He maintained that the Consecration of the Sacred Species takes place at the moment the priest utters the words of Christ and not during the words of the epiklesis. The Theologians supporting this view were Metropolitan Gideon Chetvertynsky, Archimandrite of Kievan-Pecherska Lavra, Barlaam Yasinky, Lazar Baranovich, Archbishop of Chernihiv, Dmytry Tuptalenko, Bishop of Rostov, and other theologians of the Academy of Kiev. Innocent Monastersky [78] and Sylvester Medvedev [79] in their writings also defended Safonovich. Two brothers, Joannikios and Sophronios Lykhudes who arrived in Moscow from Greece to take up their residence there, opposed Safonovich and all those who upheld the view that the Consecration takes place when the priest pronounces the words of Christ.[80] The arguments of the two brothers impressed the Muscovite Patriarch Joachim, who prior to their arrival in Moscow was an advocate of the views espoused by the theologians of Kiev.[81] The controversy lasted for a few years and was finally terminated at the council held in Moscow (1690) by the condemnation of the "Little Russian (Ukraine was called Little Russia) doctrine" as a "Latin" heresy. This condemnation was promulgated by the Patriarch Joachim of Moscow, who later ordered a reply or rebuttal to be prepared to the book of Safonovich.[82] Sylvester Medvedev, the most ardent champion of Safonovich's view on the Consecration of the Holy Gifts, was accused by the state of treason and was sentenced to death. He was executed in 1691.[83]

Two publications (1670, 1674) of Safonovich's work in Univ testify to its popularity. Safonovich's name does not appear in either publication. A little later, after the "Explanation" of Safonovich, Simeon Polotsky, a Byelorussian, wrote *A Word on Proper Deportment in the Church of God and the Proper Manner of Participating in the Divine Liturgy*.[84] This work was added to a collection of sermons written by the same author under the title of *Vecheria Dukhovnaya* or *Spiritual Supper*. The *Word* of Simeon Polotsky is didactic and moral in character and does not consider the rites of the Divine Liturgy.

The eighteenth century gave us only two interpretations of the Divine Liturgy. The first was published by a Catholic (Uniate); the second was written by an Orthodox author. The latter, printed in 1792 in Petersburg under the title

---

[78] *"Knizhitsa o bozhestvennoy liturghii,"* which remained a manuscript at the Imperial Public Library in Petrograd, no. 668.

[79] The polemical works of S. Medvedev: *Knigha, glagolemaya chlyeb zhyvotniy*. This work is very similar to the book of Safonovich; it was written in 1686 in the form of question and answer. However, it remained a manuscript. In 1687 Medvedev wrote: *Knigha o Mannye khlyeba zhivotnaho*, and later: *Tetrad na Ioannikiya i Sofroniya Likhudievikh*.

[80] *Akos ili vrachevanie, protivopolagaemoe yadovitim ugrizeniem zmievim* (1688). See G. Mirkovich for more detailed information on the polemics that was then carried on, *O vremeni presushchestvleniya sv. Darov*. Spor, byvshiy v Moskvye vo vtoroy polovinye XVII-ho vyeka, (Vilna: 1886).

[81] Mirkovich, *op. cit.,* pp. 88–90.

[82] The full title is: *Osten, sostroenniy iz dukhovyeshchaniya svyatikh Otsev nizvergayushchiy, otryevayushchiy i probodayushchiy napirayushchiyasya k nemu*, (Cf. *Pravosl. Sobes.*, 1865, Supplement, pp. 1–207).

[83] Mirkovich, *op. cit.,* p. 217.

[84] Issued in Moscow 1683, (See Supplement, f. 8–15).

The Manner of Performing the Rite of Ordination in the Russian Orthodox Church,[85] was prepared by the Metropolitan of Petersburg, Gabriel Petrov (d. 1801). In 1795, it was reprinted and, in 1799, a Creek translation, prepared by Metropolitan Eugene Bulgaris, was published.[86] This commentary is now a bibliographical rarity and, unfortunately, we did not have the opportunity to examine it.

The Uniate commentary appeared first in Pochaiv in 1768 in a collection of Basilian sermons bearing the title, *An Address to the Faithful or a Word to the Catholic Faithful*,[87] and again in 1779 in a separate book entitled, *The Pouchenia* or *Teaching on the Christian Rites*. *The Teaching (Pouchenia)* merits special attention not only because it is the first liturgical commentary published by the Uniates, but also because of its intrinsic value. Hence, we shall examine it closely.

The Teaching consists of seven chapters. The first chapter deals with rites in general, as: their nature, origin and institution, and the reasons why we should respect them. The second chapter, on the transfer of an individual from the Greek Rite to the Latin Rite, is well-elaborated, based on the documents and constitutions of the Roman Popes. In this chapter we learn that it is not permissible for a person to change from the Greek Rite to the Latin Rite. The third chapter consists of commentaries on the church interior and on church vessels. In the fourth chapter the priestly vestments are discussed and the fifth offers a commentary on Vespers, Matins, and other services of the Divine Office. The sixth chapter is dedicated exclusively to the interpretation of the Liturgy. The seventh chapter deals with the burial services and some other minor ceremonies.

The author of *The Teaching* gathered his information mostly from the Byzantine liturgical commentaries, such as Herman, Pseudo-Dionysius, Simeon of Thessalonica, N. Cabasilas and recent authors whom he often cites, as well as from Arkudius, Goar and Western theologians.[88] He was well-acquainted with the various questions of Canon Law and very frequently refers to the Encyclicals of Benedict XIV, and was also familiar with the Pope's *Euchologion* and the Latin Liturgy. In brief, one must admire the erudition of the author of *The Teaching*. His historical observations on some of the rites are borrowed from Goar's *Euchologion*. *The Teaching* is also remarkable for its conciseness and perspicuity. Besides having knowledge of the Liturgy, we find the author to be well-versed in Church History, Canon Law, and Dogma. In reading *The Teaching*, one can sense a great love for the Rite, a love devoid of superfluous dogmatic speculation on ritual practices. His observations concerning the recited

---

[85] Philaret (Gumilevskiy), *Obzor russkoy dukhovnoy literaturi* (Spb.: 1884), pp. 380–381.

[86] The Greek title is: *Teleturghia iera etoi diatipozis syntomos ton ieroteleston* (Spb.: 1799).

[87] *Narodovyeshchanie . . .* , is a collection of catechetical sermons delivered to the people by the Basilian missionaries in the years 1750–1760.

[88] The author, for example, cites the French dogmatist Antoine, the Italian historian Baronius and others.

Divine Liturgy, the "Zeon" (or teplota), and the licitness of an Eastern Rite priest celebrating the Liturgy in Latin Rite vestments are very interesting.[89]

Unfortunately, the author of this remarkable *Teaching* remains unknown. But we do know for certain that he was a Basilian priest-monk from the Pochaiv Monastery. We may venture to say that the *Teaching* was the first attempt at a scientific-historical commentary on the divine services, for, although the author clings to the traditional symbolic method of interpreting the rites, he does not confine himself exclusively to this method, but tries to give a historical-practical interpretation as well. In making this attempt the author was a good century ahead of his time.

The nineteenth century inaugurates a new period in the history of the liturgical commentaries written in Ukraine which at that time was under Russian rule. This century can truly boast of its great number of liturgical commentaries and of its liturgical textbooks.

First of all, there were the works of the Archbishop of Nizhgorod, Benjamin Rumovsky-Krasnopievkov (d. 1811), who achieved great popularity by his *Novaya (New) Skrizhal,* so called to distinguish it from Nikon's *Skrizhal.* In the years following it enjoyed numerous editions in 1806, 1810, 1816, 1823, 1825, 1843, and 1853. By 1908, the 17th edition of the *Novaya Skrizhal* had appeared. The number of editions clearly indicates the wide popularity of the liturgical commentaries of Benjamin Krasnopievkov.[90]

The *Novaya Skrizhal* is the first complete book of Byzantine-Slavonic liturgics. It consists of four separate books. The first book describes and explains the interior of the church edifice, church vessels, etc. The second book is a commentary on Vespers, Compline, Nocturne, Matins, the Hours and all three Liturgies. The third book deals with the various chirotonies (ordinations) and other services such as the dedication of churches and the blessing of the antimension. In the last book diverse prayers, blessings and ceremonies in the Trebnyk, especially the holy sacraments are explained.

It is evident that the reason for the great popularity of Benjamin Krasnopievkov's commentary lay in the fact that it was the first complete and systematic explanation of all the divine services, and the first book of general and special liturgics. In the *Novaya Skrizhal,* the influence of Simeon of Thessalonica is clearly evident. He was the chief authority on liturgics. The author also derived information from Goar's *Euchologion,* which he himself translated into the Russian language. However, for some reason this translation was not published but remained in manuscript.

Benjamin Krasnopievkov profited little from Goar's historical findings. But on the other hand, he treats very extensively the symbolic interpretations of the individual rites and ceremonies of the Liturgy. However, the encumbered his book with too much diverse, and at times contradictory, symbolism with no criti-

---

[89] Page 36.

[90] The full title of the *Novaya Skrizhal* is: *Novaya Skrizhal ili obyasnennie o Tserkvi, o liturghii i o vsyekh sluzhbakh i utvaryakh tserkovnikh.*

cal distinction.[91] Krasnopievkov seems to have tried in this way to preserve as faithfully as possible all the traditional Byzantine symbolic interpretations.

Scarcely a year had passed after the publication of the *Novaya Skrizhal,* when John Dmitrevsky's (d. 1829) *Historical, Dogmatic, and Mystical Interpretation of the Divine Liturgy* appeared in Moscow in 1804. This commentary also enjoyed great popularity and was reprinted many times. Dmitrevsky's work is truly worthy of consideration for he explains only the Divine Liturgy, and that much more profoundly and thoroughly than the author of the *Novaya Skrizhal.* He uses Goar very frequently and conscientiously acknowledges this in his references. In his work we find frequent historical observations regarding the origin of each separate ritual, particularly in his first chapter where he sketches briefly the development of the Liturgy during the first centuries of Christianity. The work of Dmitrevsky required a great deal of labor and research. and it had a profound influence on later liturgical commentaries.[92] His symbolic interpretations are generally marked by more restraint and discernment that those of Krasnopievkov in his *Novaya Skrizhal.*

Besides the works of Krasnopiekov and Dmitrevsky, other commentaries appeared, which, however, did not meet with as much success as the other two. We may recall the commentaries of G. Mansvyetov [93] and G. Debolsky,[94] which belong to the first half of the nineteenth century. In that same period Andrew Muravyov wrote his *Letters on the Divine Services of the Eastern Catholic Church.* His work certainly deserves consideration, if only for its many editions and translations into other languages. The book first appeared in 1836 in Petersburg, and by 1882 it reached its eleventh edition. In 1838, E. Muralt [95] translated the *Letters . . .* into German. Other translations followed, e.g. the Polish translation of 1841, the French translation of 1850, the Greek translation of 1851, the Serbian of 1854, and the English translation of 1866.

The great success of Moravyov's *Letters . . .* must be attributed to his beautiful literary style. Muravyov was no theologian nor even a member of the clergy; he was a lay official at the Holy Synod. But through his wide travels and his great interest in ecclesiastical-liturgical problems, he acquired extensive knowledge in this field. Not only did he visit the more important Church centers of Russia, but he also journeyed to the Holy Land, Asia Minor, Egypt and

---

91 This is the objection which Philaret Gumilevskiy hurls at the author of *Novaya Skrizhal.* He says, "It is a pity that the interpretation of the holy rites and vessels sometimes is ambiguous in that one and the same object is given two or three meanings entirely without reason." (See *Obzor russkoy dukhovnoy literaturi,* Spb.: 1884, p. 401).

92 Philaret, *op. cit.,* p. 412.

93 *Kratkoe obyasnenie na liturghiyu sobrannoe iz raznikh pisateley,* Spb. 1822, (9-te vidannya (Spb.: 1894).

94 *The solicitude of the Orthodox Church for the salvation of the world expressed in her divine services which embrace the whole life of the Christian from the day he was born to the time he dies (from his birth to his death), or the interpretation of rites, needs, mysteries, and divine services of the Orthodox Church* (Spb.: 1843), 4th edition, 1896.

95 E. Muralt, *Briefe ueber den Gottesdienst der morgenlaendischen Kirche,* (Leipzig: 1838).

even Rome where he frequented divine services in St. Peter's Basilica.[96] In his *Letters* . . . he described his experiences and impressions. All that Muravyov wrote about the divine services bespoke great love and enthusiasm for Church ritualism. His work was popular because of his smooth and sublime style, depth of thought and pertinent observations. He reaps his information from Krasnopievkov and Dmitrevsky. To Muravyov the Liturgy was not an intricate system of symbols, but rather an expression of spirituality. Besides commenting on the Divine Liturgy, Muravyov explains other divine services, especially those of Lent and Easter. The explanations were written in the form of private, confidential letters.

The commentary of Nicholas Gogol (d. 1852) possesses similar qualities. He wrote his *Meditations on the Divine Liturgy* during 1845–1852. Gogol, as we know, was a deeply religious man and his explanation was an expression of his piety. His commentary was brief but it was the work of a master for he wrote in a style worthy of the pen of a great writer. He strove to fathom the prayers and rituals of the Divine Liturgy. Since he regarded the Divine Liturgy as an organic whole, there is in him no affectation nor over-elaborated or forced symbolistic interpretation. It was not until after Gogol's death that his *Meditations on the Divine Liturgy* were published by Panko Kulish in 1857. Later the well-known Russian liturgist, Alex Maltsev, incorporated it in his German translation of the Sluzhebnyk [97] with a parallel German translation. Besides the German, it was also translated into Serbian, French and Dutch.[98] In 1938, a new edition of this commentary appeared once again in a German translation.[99]

During the second half of the nineteenth century, especially toward the end, there was a proliferation of new liturgical commentaries. It is impossible to consider all of them, and indeed not all are deserving of special consideration. Hence, we shall mention only the more significant authors, such as Rozhdestvensky,[100] Sokolov,[101] N. Antonov,[102] Pavlov,[103] Arseniy,[104] Vikhrov [105] and Vladislav-

---

[96] In his descriptions of the services celebrated in St. Peter's Basilica in Rome Muravyov is quite one-sided and tendentious.

[97] A. Maltsev, *Liturgikon (Sluzhebnik). Die Liturgien der orthodox-katholischen Kirche des Morgenlandes* . . . , (Berlin: 1902). Vide p. IX–CVIII: "Betrachtungen ueber die goettliche Liturgie, aus dem Russischen des Gogol".

[98] The Serbian translation was issued in 1909 in Sremski Karlovtsi. The French translation came out in 1938 (*La divine Liturgie meditee*, Amay-sur-Meuse: 1938). The Dutch translation was issued the same year 'Gooddelijke liturgie bemediteerd door Gogol, Amay-sur-Meuse: 1938).

[99] *Betrachtungen ueber die goettliche Liturgie* (Freiburg in Br.: 1938).

[100] Rozhdestvenskiy, *Izyasnenie Liturghii po chinu sv. Ioanna Zlatoustaho* (Spb.: 1860).

[101] D. Sokolov, *Uchenie o bogosluzheniyu pravoslavnoy tserkvi*, (Spb.: 1892, 10-te vidannya). Morozov translated this book of Sokolov's into the German language; *Darstellung des Gottesdienstes der orthodox-katholischen Kirche* von D. Sokolov (Berlin: 1893).

[102] A. Antonov, *Khram Bozhiy i tserkovnyya sluzhbi* (Spb.: 1912).

[103] A. Pavlov, *Nauka ob liturghii pravoslavnoy tserkvi*, (Moskva: 1886) . Written in question and answer form.

[104] Arseniy (Mitrop. Kievskiy) , *Izyasnenie bozhestvennoy liturghii* (Kiev: 1879, 2-te vidannya). This commentary is written somewhat chaotically and unsystematically.

[105] A. Vikhrov, *Obyasnenie Bozhestvennoy liturghii sv. Ioanna Zlatoustaho,* (Novgorod: 1893).

lev.[106] The last commentary, written in the form of liturgical sermons, was considered among the best of those mentioned. The short sermons of V. Nordov [107] on the Liturgy are also good.

Of the many textbooks on liturgics that have been published, we have: Chernaev,[108] Khitrovo,[109] Smolodovich,[110] Petrov,[111] Khorunzhov,[112] Lebedev,[113] Bishop G. Hermogen,[114] Archimandrite Gabriel,[115] Alkhimovich,[116] Belyustin [117] and Nestorovsky.[118] The last can perhaps be classified as one of the best. However, the greatest scholarly work on the Liturgy was written by the Serbian liturgist, Lazar Mirkovich, in three volumes.[119] It was not strcktly his own original work, but a revision of the book originally written by the Rumanian professor of liturgics, Dr. V. Mitrofanovich, amplified by T. Tarnavsky and N. Kotlyarchuk.[120] The liturgics of Mirkovich was based entirely on the principles of modern liturgical science.[121]

Before concluding our survey of the Orthodox commentaries and liturgical textbooks, we must mention several others worthy of our consideration. K. Nikolsky and S. Bulgakov are important authors because in their works they concentrated mainly on the practical aspect of the rites of the divine service.

---

[106] V. Vladislavlev, *Obyasnenie bogosluzheniya svyatoy, pravoslavnoy tserkvi. Voskzesnaya, Vsenoshchnaya, i bozhestvennaya liturghiya,* (2 chasti) (Tver: 1862; 2-he vidannya Tver: 1876).

[107] V. Nordov, *Besyedi na bozhestvennuyu liturghiyu* (Moskva: 1842).

[108] Al. Chernaev, *Podrobnoe, sistematicheskoe ukazanie sostava Liturgiki, nauka o bogosluzheniyu pravoslavnoy tserkvi* (Kharkov: 1859).

[109] H. G. Khitrovo, *Uchenie pravoslavnoy tserkvi o bogosluzhenii ili Liturghika* (Tambov: 1869).

[110] D. Smolodovich, *Liturghika ili nauka o bogosluzhenii pravoslavnoy vostochnoy katolicheskoy Tserkvi* (Kiev: 1861, 2-he vidannya).

[117] I. Belyustin, *O tserkovnom bogosluzhenii v 2 chastyakh* (Spb.: 1897).

[112] T. Khorunzhov, *Pravoslavnaya khristiyanskaya Liturghika* (Spb.: 1877).

[113] P. Lebedev, *Nauka o bogosluzhenii pravoslavnoy tserkvi* (Moskva: 1881). Other editions Moskva: 1904 and 1913).

[114] EP. (bishop) Hermogen, *Liturghika ili uchenie o bogosluzhenii pravoslavnoy tserkvi* (Spb.: 1884).

[115] Arkhimandrite Gavryil, *Rukovodstvo po Liturghikye, ili nauka o pravoslavnom bogosluzhenii* (Tver: 1886).

[116] I. Alkhimovich, *Liturghika* (Spb.: 1891).

[117] I. Belyustin, *O tserkovnom bogosluzhenii v 2 chastyakh* (Spb.: 1897).

[118] E. Nestorovskiy, *Liturghika ili nauka o Bogosluzhenii Pravoslavnoy Tserkvi,* (Kursk: 1895, Vol. I), (Kursk: 1900, Vol. II), (2-he vidannya: Moskva: 1905–1909).

[119] L. Mirkovich, *Pravoslavna Liturghika* (Sremski Karlovtsi: 1918) (Vol. I), 1920 (Vol. II), 1926 (Vol. III).

[120] Cf. Mitrofanovichi-Tarnavschi-Kotlyarchuk, *Liturgica Bisericei ortodoxe cursui universitare* (de Dr. Vasile Mitrofanovichi, prelucrate, completetate si editate de Prof. Dr. T. Tarnavshchi si acum din non editate si completate de Nectarie Nicolae Cotlarciuk) ; new edition (Cernauti: 1929).

[121] Besides Lazar Mirkovich there are other Serbian authors who dealt with the source of Liturgics and the interpretation of the Divine Liturgy: I. Vitkovich, *Sokrovishche khristiyanskoe, liturghiysko pouchenie* (Budim: 1818) ; N. Vukichevich, *Izyasnene svete liturghie* (Panchevo: 1879); A. Zhivanovich, *Nauka o bogosluzhenyu sv. pravoslavne tserkve ili pravoslavna liturghika* (Sremski Karlovtsi: 1900), 2-he vidannya, Zagreb: 1908); N. Zhikovich, *Liturghika ili nauka o bogosluzhenu sv. pravoslavne tserkve* (Zagreb: 1885).

However, they were not concerned with an interpretation of the Divine Liturgy, or at most only indirectly so. The *Guide for Studying the Order of Celebration in the Orthodox Church* by K. Nikolsky [122] is an excellent practical textbook for studying the rites and ceremonies of the Divine Liturgy and other divine services. *A Handbook for Ministers of the Liturgies* by S. Bulgakov [123] is also practical.

Another liturgical commentary, that of Bishop Bessarion (Basil Nechayev, d. 1905), deserves special mention. In our opinion, it is the best ever produced by Russian Orthodox authors. In many points it differs from the other Russian liturgical commentaries. The most significant characteristic of Bessarion's commentary is that he focused his entire attention on the text of the Divine Liturgy. Scarcely any commentator on the Divine Liturgy before Bessarion had given special attention to the text; [124] they were interested only in symbolic interpretations. At times, they gave exclusive attention to the external rites and ceremonies. Bessarion, on the contrary, strove to probe the sense of the liturgical prayers. He explained them beautifully and disclosed their original meaning which were composed of quotations from Holy Scripture, e.g. the Psalms.[125] He also have an explanation of the private prayers of the priest, which also had not been taken into consideration by the Byzantine commentators and their Russian followers. Bessarion objected to the use of the symbolic method in explaining the Divine Liturgy, and thus avoided the symbolic techniques of interpretation, for according to him such techniques were not based on the liturgical texts and had no intrinsic connection with them.[126] This is the distinctive characteristic of Bessarion's commentary.

The most recent Orthodox commentary on the Divine Liturgy, published after World War II, is that of the Archimandrite Cyprian, a Professor of Theology in the Orthodox Theological Institute in Paris. His work, which appeared in Paris in 1947 under the title *Evkharistya* or *Eucharist*,[127] is based upon the most current theological-liturgical research. The commentary itself is prefaced with a historical introduction containing a history of Christian worship in the first centuries and an analysis of the most important liturgical anaphoras and liturgical types. Although in interpreting the prayers and rituals of the Divine Liturgy, Archimandrite Cyprian at times applies the old and obsolete symbolic method, he does also offer observations of a historical-critical nature. Cyprian's

---

[122] The first edition of *"the Guide"* appeared in Spb., 1862, (in 1907 the 7th edition appeared.)

[123] Kharkiv: 1892).

[124] The full title of Bessarion's commentary is: *Tolkovanie na bozhestvennuyu liturghiyu po chinu sv. Ioanna Zlatoustaho i sv. Vasiliya Velikaho*, (Moskva: 1884, 3-tye vid.; 1895 4-te vid.).

[125] See e.g., the beautiful commentary on the antiphons (*Tolkovanie....*, pp. 50–118). We quote the 1895 edition.

[126] Cfr. the preface to the *Tolkovaniya na bozhest. Iiturghiyu* of Bessarion (pp. V–VI).

[127] Arkhim Kipriyan, *Evkharistiya. (Iz chteniy v pravoslavnom bogoslovskom Institutye v Parizhye) (Parizh: 1947).

work is in parts unsystematic, seemingly without definite plan or division, but this lack of order does not minimize its scientific value.

Thus far we have discussed Orthodox liturgical commentaries, predominantly by Russian authors in the nineteenth and twentieth centuries. Let us now take a quick glance at the commentaries of the Uniate-Catholics.

Apart from the *Teachings* mentioned earlier, first published in Pochaiv in 1774, Ukrainian liturgical literature was, in general, very scarce in the nineteenth century. Little was written about the Divine Liturgy and that little was superficial and cursory. Not until the second half of the nineteenth century was the Liturgy given more consideration.

In the year 1815, the Bishop of Kholm, F. Tsikhanovsky (1810–1828), published *The Order of Celebration of the Divine Services for the Eparchy of Kholm* in the Polish language,[128] which is simply a set of rubrics for the celebration of the Liturgy. That same year (1815) J. Bazylovych, a Basilian Provincial of the Monastery at Mukachevo, wrote *The Interpretation of the Divine Liturgy, the True Unbloody Sacrifice of the New Testament*. Unfortunately, the commentary was not printed but remained in manuscript preserved as No. 2667[129] in the Mukachevo Monastery. The manuscript contains the Ruthenian and Latin texts in parallel columns. The two texts, though identical, are to be considered original.[130] The manuscript, which is 780 pages in length, consists of three parts. In the first part, the author explains the general notion of sacrifice, the sacrifice of the Old Testament and finally the institution of the New Testament Sacrifice. Then briefly, he reviews the history of the Divine Liturgy stressing especially the Liturgy of the *Apostolic Constitutions*. In the second part, the author analyzes the Liturgies of the East and of the West. Of the Western Liturgies, he analyzes the Roman, Ambrosian, Gallic and Spanish, and of the Eastern Liturgies he treats the Liturgy of St. James, St. Mark, the Ethiopian, the Maronite, and the Coptic Liturgies. Finally, the author furnishes information on all three Byzantine Liturgies. The third part presents a detailed explanation of the Liturgy of St. John Chrysostom. In the last chapter, Bazylovych gives a short history of the Eastern Rite and its spread through Slavic lands. From this concise description we may infer that his liturgical commentary is original. It is unfortunate that it was never printed.[131]

In the middle of the nineteenth century, the commentary of Michael Malynovsky appeared in Galicia.[132] Although he writes in Old Slavonic, the author

---

[128] *Porzadek nabozenstwa i cerkiewnego na dycezye Chelmska przepisany* (Warszawa: 1815). (Vid. K. Estreicher, *Bibliografia polska XIX stulecia*, Vol. X., [Krakow: 1885], pp. 51–52).

[129] N. Rusznak, *Epiklizis* (Pryashev: 1926) , p. 88.

[130] The latin text is: "*Explicatio Sacrae Liturgiae Novae legis veri incruenti Sacrificii….*" auctore R. Patre Joannicio Basilovits OSBM, 1815.

[131] We follow the description of the commentary of Bazylovych given by Rusznak (*op. cit.*, pp. 88–89).

[132] M. Malynovsky, *Izyasnenie na bozhestvennuyu liturghiyu* (Lvov: 1845).

frequently inserts lengthy quotations taken from the various German theological and homiletic works. Malynovsky's work is very obscure; it lacks all division of parts or chapters, and as a result is very difficult to read. In content and character, it lacks originality. He quotes Dmitrevsky almost verbatim, and yet, nowhere mentions his name. It is surprising that Malynovsky, in borrowing so great a part of his work from Dmitrevsky fails to borrow his clear division. In a word: the work of Malynovsky is a new, but corrupt, edition of the liturgical commentary of Dmitrevsky.[133]

The commentary of Alexander Dukhnovych, also written in Old Slavonic and published in 1851 in Budyn (present-day Budapest), is more original and clear. The author used the catechetical method in explaining the Divine Liturgy; hence, his work is called: *Liturghichesky Katekism*, i.e., *Liturgical Catechism*.[134] The book is divided into two parts, each having eight chapters. In the first part, the author discussed the interior of the church, the altar and the other parts of the sanctuary and church. He then explained the church vessels, priestly vestments, etc. Finally, he comments on the Proskomide and the Divine Liturgy itself. In the second part, the author briefly explained the church services (Vespers, Orthros). He also included a few words about fast, the Sacrament of Baptism, the blessing of water and other blessings contained in the Trebnyk.

Dukhnovych's view regarding the precise moment of Consecration is very interesting, for he, although a Catholic, contended that it consists in the epiklesis and not in the recitation of the words of Christ.[135] He was perhaps influenced by Orthodox interpretations and notably by the author of the *Novaya Skrizhal*. In fact, the title itself states that the liturgical catechism follows the *Novaya Skrizhal*. With regard to its intrinsic merits, it by far surpasses Malynovsky. In the second edition of the *Liturgical Catechism,* however, which was published in 1854 in Lviv,[136] a chapter where Dukhnovych defended the epiklesis was omitted. This omission was made at the request of the Austrian Nuncio, who was informed by responsible Church authorities of the erroneous view of Dukhnovych regarding the Consecration of the Holy Gifts.[137]

In the year 1858, a commentary written by an anonymous author appeared in Budapest.[138] Another anonymous commentary was published two years later

---

[133] The same lack of perspicacity can be seen, for example, in his German work: *Die Kirchen und Staat-Satzungen des gr. kathol. Ritus der Ruthenen in Galizien*, (Lemberg: 1864). It was written chaotically, without plan or system.

[134] *Liturghichesskiy katekhism ili izyasnenie sv. liturghii i nyekotorikh tserkovnikh obryadov po novoy skrizhali* (Budin: 1851).

[135] *Op. cit.*, pp. 105–111.

[136] J. Levitskiy, *Galitsko-russkaya bibliografiya XIX stolyetiya*, (1801–1886), Vol. I (Lvov: 1888), p. 64.

[137] Spiridion Lytvynovich, later metropolitan of Galicia, and Dr. Shashkevich drew the attention of the Nuncio to this view of Dukhnovych; Cfr. J. Levitskiy, *Galitsko-russkaya bibliografiya*, I, p. 64.

[138] *Izyasnenie na sv. Liturghiyu pravoslavnoy katolicheskoy vostochnoy tserkvi*," Budin 1858, (Levitskiy, *Gal. russk. bibliogr.* I., p. 106).

in Lviv.[139] In 1861, the textbook of Marcel Popel on liturgics was also published in Lviv.[140] This same author re-edited his book in 1862 [141] and 1863.[142] The work appeared during the period of the strong ritual polemics previously waged by Naumovych, and is filled with attacks against the "Latin Rite" practices in the Galician Church.[143]

In the second half of the nineteenth century, two authors, I. Halka [144] and A. Dobriansky,[145] wrote short commentaries on the Divine Liturgy. Both wrote for the people and, therefore, used a style that was simple and popular. The commentaries of Dobriansky, which are in the form of short liturgical instructions (*sermons*) are especially noteworthy for their clarity of expression and content.

From this period we have two textbooks on liturgics, one by E. Fencik [146] and the other by the well-known and learned historian, Bishop Julian Pelesh.[147] Fencik's work, written in the Pod-Carpathian vernacular with a mixture of Old Slavonic, was published in Budapest in 1878. It is composed of two parts: the first part treats of the church and its interior, church vessels, priestly vestments, liturgical books, Vespers, Matins and the Divine Liturgy. In the second part the book explains the sacraments, Church blessings, the blessing of water on the holy day of the Epiphany, fasts and feast days. Its form recalls the *Liturgical Catechism* of Dukhnovych. The questions and answers are brief and clear. Some of the historical annotations below the text are borrowed from Dmitrevsky. Fencik frequently alludes to the *Novaya Skrizhal* and the commentary of Dmitrevsky. He also cites Muravyov's *Letters* and Popel's liturgics. The liturgics of Fencik are noteworthy for its clearness of expression.

The work of Bishop Pelesh is the first truly scholarly texbook on liturgics written for Uniate Catholics. It constitutes the second part (over six hundred pages in length) of the author's voluminous *Pastoral Theology* issued in Vienna in 1877. It is unfortunate that this section was not issued as a separate book because it tends to be lost among the other volumes. The author's intention was

---

[139] *Liturghiya ili viyasnenie liturghii kostela greko-katolitskaho,* (Lvov: 1860, Tipografiya Stauropighii), p. 80). Levitskiy, *op. cit.,* I, p. 119).

[140] M. Popel, *Liturghika ili nauka o bogosluzhenyu tserkvi grekokatolicheskoy* (Lvov: 1861). (Levitskiy, *Galitsko-russkaya bibliografiya,* Vol. II, Lvov: 1895, p. 6).

[141] M. Popel, *Liturghika tserkvi greko-katolicheskoy, Uchebnaya knigha dlya shkol serednikh v derzhavye Avstriyskoy* (Lvov: 1862), p. XI–286, (Levitskiy, *Gal. russ. bibl.,* II, p. 19).

[142] M. Popel *Liturghika ili nauka . . . ,* (Lvov: 1863), p. XXVI–584–XII tablits; (Levitskiy, *op. cit.,* II, p. 32).

[143] See O. Botsyan, *Prelat Izydor Dolnytsky";* (*Bohosloviya,* Vol. II, (1942), kn. 1–4, pp. 133–134) : "The spirit of Popel's liturgics criticized on every point the practice of our church. No other textbook either for learning nor for practical use was available." (Unfortunately we could not locate a copy of Popel's liturgics and as a result we do not possess personal and exact knowledge of its contents or spirit.).

[144] I. Halka, *Dukh vecherni, utreni i liturghii gr. kat. tserkvi* (Lvov: 1861).

[145] A. Dobrianskiy, *Obyasnenie sluzhbi Bozhoy dlya selskikh zhiteley* (Peremisl: 1880).

[146] *Liturghika, ili obyasnenie bogosluzheniya svyatoy, vostochnoy, pravoslavno-katolicheskoy tserkvy* (Budapes(h)t: 1878).

[147] J. Pelesh, *Liturghika,* ("Pastirskoye Bogoslovie," Chapt 2, pp. 265–877) (Viden [Vienna] 1877) The second edition came out in Vienna 1885.

to provide a complete practical text on theology for his clergy, and he gathered all the information necessary for such a project. Much of the information, unfortunately is irrelevant and without direct bearing on the subject matter of his work, which as a result is somewhat cluttered with extensive treatises on Dogma, Moral Theology and Canon Law. It is full of decrees, regulations, dispatches and letters of the Metropolitan Consistory, Austrian State officials, etc. This is without doubt the methodological-scientific drawback of Pelesh's *Liturghika*, which today, in many respects, renders the work obsolete. Nevertheless, in Ukrainian theological literature it is still regarded as the first scientifically elaborated book on liturgics.

Pelesh patterned his work after the German authors, F. Schmid[148] and J. Fluck.[149] He divides his treatment into two parts: 1) General Liturgics and 2) Special Liturgics. In his General Liturgics he explains and supplies general concepts and information about the divine services—their elements and form. He presents information about the various elements of Christian worship, holydays (e.g. liturgical year), holy places (church, sanctuary), and holy things (vestments, icons, crosses, bells, in general, objects pertaining to religious worship). The second part treats of various church services, the Divine Liturgy, Divine Office, services held throughout the liturgical year, the sacraments, various dedications and blessings. He diligently uses all available references on the Liturgy. The commentary on the Divine Liturgy, which is our main interest here, is very well-elaborated. Though it retains the traditional symbolism which refers all the rites and ceremonies to events in the life of Christ, there are several historical observations and instructions of a practical-rubrical nature.[150]

Another author worth mentioning is I. Dolnytsky who dedicated himself untiringly to scientific research on the Divine Liturgy. He is known mainly for his remarkable *Typik*.[151] A member of the liturgical-ritual pre-synodal commission which prepared for the Synod of Lviv (1891) a complete Order of Celebration or Typikon for the Divine Liturgy, Dolnytsky possessed extensive knowledge of the Liturgy. He was the first of all learned Catholic-Uniate liturgists to consider the Greek liturgical handwritten and printed Liturgikons, and also the first to apply the comparative method in his research. It pained Dolnytsky to see ritual diversity and the disputes it generated in the Ukrainian Uniate Church during his time. He refrained from taking sides in these polemics because he was convinced that the ritual question should be solved by applying the scientific-comparative method and not by futile disputes. Hence, he gave his complete attention to scientific investigation of the Liturgy and its historical development.[152] In 1885, Dolnytsky published a small booklet entitled, *Sacred*

---

[148] Franz X. Schmid, *Liturgik der christlich-katholischen Religion* (Passau: 1832) 3 Baende; —*Grundriss der christlich-katholischen Liturgik* (Passau: 1836).

[149] J. Fluck, *Katholische Liturgik* (Regensburg: 1853–1855) 2 Theile.

[150] See the Part II of this book.

[151] I. Dolnytsky, *Tipik tserkve rusko-katolicheskiya*, (Lvov: 1899).

[152] Bishop Joseph Botsyan, *op. cit.*, pp. 118–195. Here bishop Botsyan, a disciple of I. Dolnytsky, gives a good survey of the liturgical-scientific activities of Rev. Isidore Dolnytsky.

Rites of the Greek-Ruthenian Church. This booklet was lithographed and reprinted many times.[153] Later it formed the basis for his well-known *Typik.* Dolnytsky did not interpret the Divine Liturgy, but gave more of his attention to the ceremonies of the Liturgy. Toward the end of the World War I, he prepared *An Order of Celebration for All the Liturgies of Our Rite* but this book, unfortunately, was never printed.[154]

At the beginning of the twentieth century, only a few authors supply us with literature on the Liturgy. These authors were priests not from Galicia, but from Pod-Carpathia who, in general, devoted more time to the understanding and popularizing of the Liturgy than did the Galician clergy. We mention here Alexander Mykyta, Simeon Szabo, George Mikulash, Paul Bihun and Nicholas Rusznak.

Besides a textbook on liturgics in the Hungarian language,[155] Alexander Mytyka also prepared *A Manual on the Church Typikon.*[156] Like Dolnytsky, he devoted his attention exclusively to the ceremonial-ritual aspect of the Divine Litury. His comments on the Divine Liturgy are only cursory and incidental.

The work of Szabo was written in Latin and was called *Expositio ss. liturgiae s. Joannis Chrysostomi historica, dogmatica et moralis,* (Ungvarini, 1902).[157] It is patterned especially after the liturgical commentary of John Dmitrevsky, whom Szabo quotes frequently and like whom he also gives historical references. His book rests on a solid theological basis; however, his explanation is too incoherent. The author availed himself of Western authors, especially of Goar, Renaudot [158] and others.

The *Interpretation of the Liturgy* of George Mikulash, also written in Latin, is smaller and not as erudite as that of Szabo. Mikulash tended more to the theological aspects of the Divine Liturgy and rarely uses any historical references.

The *Interpretation of the Divine Liturgy* of Paul Bihun, printed in Hungarian in 1906 at Uzhorod,[160] is a popular, brief commentary written in the form of nineteen liturgical sermons. This work was based on a commentary of an anonymous author which was published in Budapest in 1858, and on the commentaries of M. Malynovsky and the *Typik* of Alexander Mykyta.

---

[153] Unfortunately all these issues were lithographed. The students of the Lviv Seminary published them for their own private use. We availed ourselves of the edition prepared in 1891 by Spiridion Karkhut: *O svyashchennikh Obryadakh grek-russ. tserkvi,* third corrected edition (Lvov: 1891).

[154] This book even had the approbation of Metropolitan Ordinary in Lviv, 8.11. 1919.

[155] *Liturgika* (Ungvar: 1891).

[156] *Rukovodstvo v Tserkovniy Tipikon* (Ungvar: 1911).

[157] S. Szabo. *Expositio ss. liturgiae s. Joannis Chrysostomi historica, dogmatica et moralis* (Ungvarini: 1902).

[158] E. Renaudot, *Liturgiarum orientalium collectio,* I–II (Paris: 1716).

[159] G. Mikulash, *Liturgiae sancti Joannis Chrysostomi interpretatio.* (Dissertatio inauguralis) (Magno-Varadini: 1903).

[160] Pal Bihun, *Szent Liturgianak ertelmezese* (Ungvar: 1906).

Thus far, the best Carpathian liturgical commentary is the *Liturgies of the Eastern Church* written in 1915 by Nicholas Rusznak.[161] In a Hungarian translation, Rusznak published the texts of the three Liturgies of the Byzantine Rite together with historical-explanatory notes. The text is prefaced by an extensive historical-theological introduction in which the author explained the general notion of the Divine Liturgy as a sacrifice of the New Testament and its relation to the sacrifice on the cross and to the feast of the Jewish Passover. Further on, Rusznak treated the dogmatic aspects of the Divine Liturgy, its essential elements, its worth, effects and significance. After briefly reviewing the more important Western and Eastern Liturgies, the author explained the significance of the Divine Liturgy from the symbolical point of view. The book is rich in references to various authors not only of the West but also to Russian authors, e.g. Petrovsky, Makarius and others. Rusznak's work is distinguished for its truly scientific character.[162]

Of the Galician authors of the Liturgy, there are Levynsky, Luzhnytsky, and Myshkovsky. A. Levynsky wrote *A Sermon on the Divine Liturgy*, in 1906, in which he briefly presented in popular style the most important theological teachings on the Divine Liturgy, the significance and meaning of its component parts, its external rites, and on how one should participate in it.[163]

The book of L. Luzhnytsky is a textbook on Greek-Catholic liturgics for high-school students.[164] In it the Divine Liturgy, as well as all the other divine services, is discussed briefly and clearly. In accord with the character and purpose of his book, Luzhnytsky does not give a detailed exposition of the history of the rites of the Divine Liturgy, but is satisfied with presenting only a general description of these rites with their symbolic content.

The commentary of T. Myshkovsky, which was written in Russian,[165] deserves special attention. Myshkovsky was one of the ritual purists. Prior to World War I, he had already written a polemical brochure, *Our Rite and Its Latinization*,[166] in which he severely attacked the Latin Rite practices in the Ukrainian Uniate Church. Although the author was, without doubt, partially justified in what he wrote, nevertheless, his belligerent and antagonistic tone won little sympathy.[167] The same polemical tone can be detected in places in his

---

[161] Miklos Rusznak, *A Keleti Egyhaz Misei. A mise dogmatikus, toertenelmi es szoevegkritikai eloeadasa Aranyszaju szent Janos, nagy szent Vazul es Dia logosz szent Gergely misevei* (Budapest: 1915).

[162] Dr. Rusznak is also the author of the theological work on the Epiklesis: *"Epiklisis,"* napisal Nikolay Rusznak, (Pryashev: 1926).

[163] A. Levynsky, *Nauka o Sluzhbi Bozhi* (Lviv: 1906), p. 43.

[164] L. Luzhnytsky, *Liturghika greko-katolitskoyi tserkvy. Uchebnyk dlya molodizhy serednykh shkil* (Lviv: 1922).

[165] T. Myshkovskiy, *Izlozhenie Tsaregradskoy Liturghii sv. Vasiliya V. i sv. Ioanna Zlatousta po yeya drevnemu smislu i dukhu* (Lvov: 1926).

[166] Lvov: 1913.

[167] Rev. Mark Halushchynsky, CSBM carried on polemics with the author on ritual themes. Cf. his article: *Orhanism nashoho obryadu,* "Nyva," 1914, ch. 12, pp. 329–343.

Exposition of the Constantinopolitan Liturgy of St. Basil the Great and St. John Chrysostom according to its old sense and spirit, of 1926. Nevertheless, the commentary itself does merit praise for its especially fine explanation of the prayers of the Divine Liturgy. It examined the private prayers of the priest in the two Byzantine Liturgies—St. Basil and St. John Chrysostom—and showed their common prayer-content. Thus, the author contributed to a better understanding of the spirit and content of the liturgical prayers, which had been very much disregarded or at best superficially treated, by former interpreters of the Divine Liturgy. This quality of Myshkovsky's commentary reminds us of that of Bessarion. Myshkovsky was well acquainted with the ritual-ceremonial aspect of the Liturgy, and on this point he furnished us with valuable observations which, however are unfortunately of a polemical nature. Unfortunately also, the author was very parsimonious in his use of historical data. He exhibited an almost total lack of knowledge of and familiarity with everything previously written on the history of the Divine Liturgy by Western authors and even by Russian liturgical scholars. Hence, his inferences and conclusions are not always accurate and are incapable of withstanding historical criticism. The critics are also quite justified in accusing the author of fallacious theological views regarding the nature of Christ's presence under the Eucharistic Species.[168] Aside from these deficiencies in his commentary, T. Myshkovsky offered new and positive information which made for a better comprehension of the sense and spirit of the Byzantine Liturgies.

We shall conclude our critical survey of the various Catholic-Uniate commentaries on the Divine Liturgy with the last liturgical commentary written by D. Nyarady, Bishop of Kryzhevtsi, in 1932,[169] a very good popular interpretation. It is notable for its consistent application of the traditional concept of the Divine Liturgy, which is the mystical-symbolic chronology of the life of Christ and all the events relating to our redemption. Hence, Bishop Nyarady's commentary is more a narrative of the events in the life of Christ than a commentary on the rites of the Divine Liturgy. The author, going through the prayers and rites of the Divine Liturgy, goes through the whole life of Christ from which he derives practical applications for everyday living. The Divine Liturgy to the author is, therefore, only a framework within which all the events of the Gospel take place. The commentary of D. Nyarady was written with great love for the Liturgy and for its ritual, and in a lucid, easily understood style. As a popular commentary it is exemplary, but the method of interpretation, which is the method of exaggerated symbolism, can scarcely be accepted today as correct and scientifically justified.

---

[168] For the evaluations of the book by T. Mishkovskiy see Rev. Paul Theodorovich "Analecta OSBM," V. (1927), kn. 1–4, pp. 251–253 and the Studite monk Rev. Leo Zhilet, *"Bohoslo-viya."* Both critics express their doubt about some of the theological views of T. Mishkovskiy which he had voiced in the foreword of his liturgical commentary.

[169] Dionisiy Nyarady, *Sluzhba Bozha abo Liturghiya* (Dyakovo: 1932).

4. The Scientific-Critical Interpretation of the Divine Liturgy

As a conclusion to this chapter on the various liturgical commentaries, we shall discuss briefly the progress of the science of liturgics and the scientific-critical interpretations of the Divine Liturgy.

In considering the commentaries of the Patristic Age, and particularly those of the Byzantine Era, we noted that they were all based on the mystical-symbolic interpretation of the rites and prayers of the Divine Liturgy. This method was common among Slavic commentators, who aimed in their commentaries to introduce those interested to the symbolism which, in their view, is hidden in the sacred rites. These interpreters did not even think of applying the historical method of interpretation; at no time did they think to determine the origin of any particular rite or prayer, or the original sense of this or that ritual practice or ceremony. They were concerned rather to discover every kind of symbol, analogy and allusion that could possibly be fitted within the framework of the symbolistic concept of the Divine Liturgy. Beginning with the commentaries of Pseudo-Herman and Theodore Andides, almost all the liturgical literature was preoccupied with this aspect. The method, more often than not, led to an artificial and far-fetched or forced interpretation of the liturgical rites and prayers and to a ready-made symbolic scheme. Even the least insignificant ceremony had to have a symbolic allusion to some event in the life of our Saviour, or to an event relating to the history of man's redemption. So far did this tendency go that the same rite was whimsically interpreted in two or more different ways according to the author's inventive ingenuity. We might add that the symbolic interpretation became commonplace not only in the Byzantine-Slavonic world but also in the Western and Eastern Churches that were not Orthodox. Not only did Pseudo-Herman, Theodore, Simeon of Thessalonica and Benjamin Krasnopievkov interpret the Liturgy symbolically, but symbolic interpretations were in vogue even in the West. Amalarius and other Western liturgists [170] indulged in symbolism. In the Catholic East, many interpreters likewise fell victim to the exaggerated use of symbols, such as the Syrians, Moses Bar Kepha,[171] Jacob Bar Salibi,[172] Jacob Bar Shakako,[173] and the Chaldean Abraham Bar Liphen,[174] the Armenian Chozroes the Great,[175] and Nerses of Lampron,[176] and the Coptic

---

[170] M. Righetti, *Manuale di storia liturgica*, Vol. I., *Introduzione generale* (Milano-Geneva: 1945) , pp. 55–60.

[171] R. H. Connoly and W. Corrington, *Two Commentaries on the jacobite Liturgy, by Georg, bishop of the Arab Tribes, and Moses Bar Kepha*......., (London: 1913).

[172] D. J. Bar Salibi, *Exposition liturgiae* ("*Corpus Scriptorum Christianorum*"), Scrpt. Syri, series 2, Vol. 92) (Parisiis et Romae: 1915).

[173] J. Bar Shakako, *Espositio officiorum et orationum* (Vid. Th. J. Lamy, *Dissertatio de Syrorum fide, et disciplina in re eucharistica*, Louvain: 1859).

[174] A. Bar Liphen, *Interpretatio officiorum*, (in *Corpus Scrip. Christ. orientalium* [Chabot-Hyvernat]) , Scriptores Syri, Ser. 2., Vol. 92, (Parisiis et Romae: 1915) .

[175] Chosroes, *Explicatio precum missae* (P. Vetter, *Commentarius de orationibus Missae*), (Freiburg in Br.: 1880).

[176] Nerses Lampronensis, *Explicatio liturgiae Armenae* (E. Dulaurier, *Recueil des Histories des Croisades. Historiens Armeniens*, Vol. I.), (Paris: 1869), pp. 569–578.

Shams-al-Riasah-Barakat ibn Kabar.[177] In short, the symbolistic interpretation of the Liturgy was for many centuries the only correct and traditionally sanctioned method.

But with the progress of liturgical studies came a complete renaissance in interpretation. Scientific investigations into the history and evolution of the Liturgy itself actually began in the second half of the nineteenth century. Although previously some attempts had been made at historical-scientific research on the Liturgy, as in Goar, Lebrun,[178] and other liturgists of the eighteenth centrury, the real renaissance came in the second half of the nineteenth century. This century tends to be called the *"saeculum historicum,"* i.e., the historical age for, like other branches of science, liturgics also had recourse to history and to investigation of primary sources.[179] Not only in the West did the scholars begin examining ancient manuscripts and focusing their attention on the history and evolution of the Liturgy, but also in the East, the Byzantine Liturgy especially had its own untiring researchers among whom were the Russian scholars, Krasnoseltsev, Muretov, Petrovsky, Golubtsov, Orlov, Karabinov and especially A. Dmitrievsky. Through their works, these scholars aroused interest in the Liturgy. In the light of ancient liturgical monuments, the symbolic method of interpreting the Divine Liturgy began to lose its popularity and to make room for a new method—the historical-genetic method. The mystical-symbolical theory, which had been considered throughout the centuries to be the only correct and established theory, could not satisfy the minds that began to seek a historical-genetic analysis of the rites and prayers of Christian church services.

The development of the science of liturgics was, therefore, responsible for introducing a new method of interpreting the Divine Liturgy—a method which produced wonderful results. Twentieth-century commentators on the Roman Liturgy have long ago abandoned the symbolic-mystical interpretations and have interpreted the rites and prayers of the Divine Liturgy in terms of their historical development and their intrinsic meaning.[180] The interpretation of the Byzantine Liturgy in terms of the historical-genetic method is still in an infant stage of development. To many interpreters, the symbolism of the old Byzantine commentators still retains its charm and, consequently, they enjoy using this method without realizing that it has no solid foundation.

The historical-genetic method, however, is now being applied in some new works as in the commentary of Bessarion which is free of the traditional symbol-

---

177 *Lampas tenebrarum et expositio mysterii,* (Vid. Villecourt-Tisserant-Wiet, *Livre de la lampe des ténèbres et de l'éxposition* [*lumineuse*] *du service* [*de l'Eglise*], *Patrologia Orientalis* [Graffin-Nau], Vol. 20, pp. 575–734, Paris: 1929). Cf. L. Villecourt, *Les observances liturgiques et la discipline du jeune dans l'Église copte,* "Museon," 36 (1923), pp. 249–292; 37 (1924), pp. 201–280.

178 P. Lebrun, *Explication litterale, historique, et dogmatique des prieres et des ceremonies de la messe* (Paris: 1716–1726), 4 Vol.

179 P. Oppenheim, *Introductio historica in litteras liturgicas,* 2-da ed., p. 56 ss (Torino: 1945).

180 P. Parsch, *Messerklaerung* (Klosterneuburg b. Wien: 1937); A. Jungmann, *Missarum solemnia.* Eine genetische Erklaerung der roemishchen Messe, (2 Baende) (Wien: 1948); J. Brinktrine, *Die heilige Messe in ihrem Werden und Wesen* (1931).

ism, and in the liturgical commentary of T. Myshkovsky. Among Western writers on the Byzantine Liturgy, who strove to explain it from the historical-genetic
aspect, the following are deserving of mention: P. De Meester, F. Moreau, S.
Salaville, M. Hanssens and A Raes.[181]

In our commentary we will employ the historical-critical method in
interpreting the rites and texts of the Divine Liturgy. We will avoid the symbolic interpretative methods of the past because today they are considered obsolete, subjective and inconsistent. The mystagogues of the past centuries were primarily interested in the subjective-ascetic aspect of interpretation; hence, they
endowed every rite with a mystical meaning, in order to impress the reader and
incite him to mediate upon the events of the redemption. Such interpretations
undoubtedly were edifying and increased devotion, but at the same time, they
caused the historico-practical aspect of the rites of the Divine Liturgy to be
neglected.[182]

A greater part of the liturgical rites derived their origin from practical
needs and the influence of the synagogue and even the hellenistic-oriental mysteries. Only later did the mystagogues attach a mystical-symbolical sense to the
rites.[183] Hence, the liturgical researchers should, above all, strive to ascertain the
historical origin and development of a given rite in order to determine its original purpose, and then proceed to the interpretation of its sense.

The historical method has been wholly vindicated and currently established;
hence there is no need to defend its principles here. The historical-genetic
method of interpreting the Divine Liturgy has yet to complete the great task
which the symbolic interpretations of the past century failed to accomplish, i.e.
to discover the proper and original sense of the rites of the Liturgy, to explain
these rites in relation to their intrinsic connection with the Eucharistic Sacrifice,
to indicate the source of ritual practices, to explain its historical background,
and thus, to widen our knowledge of the Divine Liturgy. Every interpretation of
the Divine Liturgy not based on history or on critical analysis is likely to be
exposed to subjectivism.[184] If history is to be called *"magistra vitae"*—the
"teacher of life"—then the liturgical commentaries, if they are to be fruitful and
practical, must rest upon solid historical data.

---

[181] PL. De Meester, *"Les origines et les developpements"* pp. 245–357;— (Liturgies)
grecques, *DACL*, VI, cols. 1591–1662; F. Moreau, *Les liturgies eucharistiques.* Notes sur leur origine et leur developpement (Bruxelles: 1924) ; S. Salaville, *Liturgies orientales, Notion gene-
rales, elements principaux* (Paris: 1932) , II, La Messe, (2 parties) (Paris: 1942) ; M. I. Hanssens,
Institutiones liturgicae de ritibus orientalibus, De Missa rituum orientalium, Vols. II–III,
(Romae: 1930–1932); A. Raes, *Introductio in liturgiam orientalem* (Romae: 1947).

[182] J. Botsyan, *Liturhia na skhodi;* "Nyva," IV (1907), p. 345.

[183] *Ibid.,* pp. 172–173, 345.

[184] "A theory on the church services not based on historical data is faulty in itself and
damaging in its effects, here we have arbitrariness running rampant and causing the mind and
heart to be obscured. We find one and the same rite and one and the same object used in the
performance of a rite being interpreted in five or six different ways, one way by Simeon of
Thessalonica, another by Cabasilas, and still others by other commentators. Hence the reason
for a historical inquiry into the divine services." (Philaret Gumilevskiy, *Istoricheskiy obzor
pyesnopyevtsev,* Spb.: 1902, (3 izd.) p. 5).

SELECT BIBLIOGRAPHY

Brightman, F. E. *The Historia mystagogica and other greek commentaries on the byzanitne liturgy*, "Journal of Theological Studies," Vol. IX. (1908), pp. 248–267, 387–397.

Borgia, N. *Il commentario liturgico di S. Germano Patriarca Constantinopolitano e la versione latina di Anastasio Bibliotecario.* Grottaferrata: 1912.

Zhivkovich, I. *Kratki pregled knizhevnosti nauke o bogosluzhenu,* (Otlomak iz liturghike): Bogoslovski Glasnik, VI (1904), 5, pp. 345–353; 6, pp. 429–442.

Krasnoseltsev, N. *"Tolkovaya Sluzhba" i drughiya sochineniya otnosyashchiyasya k obyasneniyu bogosluzheniya v drevnei Rusi do XVIII v.* (Pravoslav. Sobes.: 1878 II., pp. 3–43).

Krasnoseltsev, N. *O drevnikh liturghicheskikh tolkovaniyakh.* Odessa: 1894.

Krasnoseltsev, N. *Drevniya tolkovaniya liturghii kak istochnik yeya istorii* (See the Prilozhenie II. of the work by the same author: *"Svyedyenniya o nyekotorykh liturghicheskikh rukopisakh vatikanskoy biblioteki,"* Kazan: 1885, p. 305. . . .).

Muretov, N. *Grecheskiy podlinnik Nikonovskoy Skrizhali.* (Bibliograf. Zapiski, n. 7). Moskva: 1892.

Oppenheim, P. *Introductio historica in litteras liturgicas.* Torino: 1945 (2-da).

Petrides, S., *Traites liturgiques de S. Maxime e de S. Germain traduis par Anastase le Bibliothecaire,* "Revue de l'Orient Chretien," X. (1905), pp. 287–309.

Salaville, S. *Indication sommaire des principales "Explications de la Messe orientale" anciennes et modernes,* (II.) Appendix in "Liturgies Orientales," La Messe, II. Paris: 1942 pp. 135–148).

Solowij, M. *De commentario liturgico s. Sophronio attribuito.* Romae: 1949.

PART TWO

A COMMENTARY ON THE PRAYERS
AND RITES OF THE DIVINE LITURGY

INTRODUCTION

Having reviewed the historical background of the Divine Liturgy, we now come to the systematic interpretation of its prayers and rites.

This interpretation or commentary of the Divine Liturgy is divided into three principal parts: I. the Proskomide, II. the Liturgy of the Catechumens (or the Liturgy of the Word), and III. the Liturgy of the Faithful (or the Liturgy of Sacrifice). This division, which is ancient and traditional, is based upon the structure of the Divine Liturgy itself. All three principal parts have their own constituent elements, origin and distinct causes and factors underlying their development.

The first part of the Divine Liturgy is the Proskomide, the purpose of which is to prepare for the Divine Liturgy. It includes the preparation of the priest and of the sacrificial gifts: bread and wine.

The second part, the Liturgy of the Catechumens or of the Word, begins with the doxology or invocation of the Holy Trinity, "Blessed be the Kingdom etc.," and terminates with the dismissal of the catechumens: "Catechumens, depart, etc." Because of its content and character, the Liturgy of the Catechumens is frequently called the homiletic-didactic service or the service of the word. Its origin dates back to the time of the Apostles and it is an adaptation of the Jewish synagogue services.

The last part of the Divine Liturgy is called the Liturgy of the Faithful or Liturgy of Sacrifice. It is the most important part of the entire Divine Liturgy, since in this part the eucharistic sacrifice is consummated. It begins with prayers for the faithful and the Great Entrance and concludes with the dismissal of the faithful. Not only is the Liturgy of the Faithful the most significant part of the Divine Liturgy, but it is also the oldest, since its origin and essential elements can be traced to Christ Himself who celebrated the first Divine Liturgy at the last Supper.

To acquire a better understanding of these three main divisions of the Divine Liturgy, we shall, in our commentary, offer a few preliminary remarks about the origin, nature and character of each part, as well as about their role in relation to the Divine Liturgy as a whole.

Section 1, THE PROSKOMIDE

Chapter I

PRELIMINARY REMARKS

The Proskomide is the first of the three components of the Divine Liturgy. It is the introduction to and the preparation for the two other parts of the Divine Liturgy: the Liturgy of the Catechumens [1] and the Liturgy of the Faithful.[2] In this lie the role and the significance of the Proskomide.

To many, the Proskomide is almost unknown and strange. A great number of the faithful who are otherwise fairly well informed about the structure and course of the Divine Liturgy are erroneously convinced that the Proskomide was an unimportant addition to the Divine Liturgy or mere private rite of the priest. Perhaps the reason for such want of familiarity with the Proskomide, is that it is performed in private, without the participation of the people. The priest celebrates it alone behind the closed Royal Doors, at a side table called the Table of Prothesis or Table of Preparation.

Although the Proskomide appears non-essential, it plays an important role in the Liturgy. Moreover, its origin and historical development furnish the researcher with a key to the comprehension of the many rites and to the structure of the Divine Liturgy. For this reason we shall, in the introduction to the rites and texts of the Proskomide, present some general facts about the name, origin, historical development, role, place and minister of this rite.

---

[1] Although the first part of the Liturgy is sometimes referred to as the "liturgy of the cate-chumens," we shall designate it as the "liturgy of the word," because this is actually the more proper term and the one which Vatican Council II has adopted, thus making it official. (See Vatican Council II, Constitution on the Sacred Liturgy, art. 56, Collegeville, Minn.: The Liturgical Press; 1964)

[2] While the terms "liturgy of the faithful," "liturgy of sacrifice," and "eucharistic liturgy" are used indiscriminately, the latter two terms are to be preferred because they best express the nature of the second part of the Divine Liturgy and because Vatican Council II has adopted them. (See Vatican Council II, Constitution on the Sacred Liturgy, art. 56, Collegeville, Minn.: The Liturgical Press; 1964)

1 The Name—Proskomide

Etymologically, the name *Proskomide* comes from the Greek word *proskomidzo*" which means, "I offer," "I bring," "I sacrifice." The Proskomide is a rite of offering up gifts. This offering applies to the eucharistic gifts or elements, bread and wine. In other words, the Proskomide is the offering of bread and wine, which later in the course of the Divine Liturgy is changed into the Body and Blood of Jesus Christ by virtue of the words of Consecration pronounced by the priest.

The Proskomide goes by another name also, one very often met with in the old texts of the Divine Liturgy, i.e. "Prothesis." In the Slavonic Sluzhebnyks the word *prothesis* is translated as *predlozhenie* and in English, "oblation or proposition." The term "prothesis" has survived to our day, signifying, however, not the whole Proskomide, but only its last part, namely, the prayer, which terminates the rite. This prayer is called "the prayer of prothesis," and the place where the rite of Proskomide is performed is called the Table of Prothesis.

In the Liturgies of other Rites, both Eastern and Western, we find other terms designating the preparation of the eucharistic gifts, but all have the same meaning. In the Latin Rite, the Proskomide is called the *Offertorium* or "Offertory."

2. Origin of the Proskomide

The origin of the Proskomide can be traced back to the Apostolic Age. Since it was a preparation of the eucharistic gifts, it was part of the original Liturgy. However, in the original Liturgy it had a slightly different form and character. The Proskomide, as we have it today, originated and evolved from the old Christian ceremony of community gift-offering.

From the earliest liturgical documents we learn that the faithful, gathering to celebrate the Divine Liturgy, brought bread and wine and offered them to the Lord. Part of these offerings were intended for liturgical purposes, i.e. for the eucharistic gifts; the remainder were set aside for the love banquet, the so-called agape. In their generosity and love for sacrifice, the faithful were accustomed to bringing more than was needed for the Divine Liturgy and the love banquet. Besides bread and wine, they also brought oil, honey, fruit, wool, wax, silver, gold and other valuable articles.[3]

---

[3] We find in the Old Testament shewbread some elements of our Proskomide. In describing the various offerings the Jewish people made to God, Father Roland De Vaux, in his *Ancient Israel its Life and Institutions,* says: "Rather similar to the offerings just described is the shewbread, called in Hebrew *lehem happanim* ('the bread of the face' (of God), or 'the bread of the Presence') or *lehem hamma'areketh* (the 'shewbread')."

According to Lv 24:5–, twelve cakes of pure wheaten flour were laid out in two lines on a table which stood in front of the Holy of Holies; they were renewed every sabbath day. They were a pledge of the Covenant between the twelve tribes and Yahweh. These cakes, or loaves, were eaten at the end of the week by the priests, but they were not placed on the altar; incense, however, was placed alongside each line of loaves as an *azkarah*, and was burnt (on the altar of perfumes) when the loaves were changed. The fact that incense was placed there justifies us in regarding the loaves as something like a sacrificial offering, and Ezechiel himself likens the table on which they were put to an altar (Ez 41:21–22).(De Vaux, *Ancient Israel, its Life and Institutions,* New York, 1961, p. 422).

The faithful presented these gifts to the deacons, who placed them in the sanctuary on a table of preparation. The minister or celebrant (the bishop or the priest) then recited a prayer over the gifts, in which he implored the Lord to accept the offering from those who brought them and those who blessed them. During the ceremony of community offering, the names of those who brought the gifts to be offered and those for whom they were offered, were read.

In the course of time, the custom of community offering, from which the rite of Proskomide originated and developed, underwent a change in character and form. First, the love banquet was separated from the Liturgy proper because it became an occasion for sundry abuses and excesses. Later, all other offerings except bread and wine were eliminated. For instance, the third and fourth Rules of the Apostles forbade bishops and priests to accept and to bring to the altar such gifts as honey, milk, fruit, animals, or spirits instead of wine.

The new circumstances under which the Christians in the first centuries were forced to live also contributed to the modification of the form and character of the Proskomide. During the severe persecutions, the Church was not legally recognized as a religious institution. The faithful themselves had to support the Church, the clergy and in general the poorer Christians. The ancient Christian custom of community gift offering, besides providing gifts for purely liturgical purposes, had also provided gifts for charitable purposes. Thus, the gifts which were presented in the rite of gift-offering, served the needs of the Church as well. A portion was given for the support of the priest, and a portion was set aside for the destitute, widows, orphans and the sick. After securing religious freedom (313 A.D.), the economic status of the Church and its clergy improved considerably. Churches were now able to secure their own possessions, and the clergy were eventually supported by the income of the Church. Sources of support were the benefices of the faithful and the state; this meant that the clergy no longer had to depend for support on the liturgical gift-offering as they had during the persecutions. As a result of this economic growth, the custom of community gift-offerings slowly disappeared. Gift-offering was no longer a necessity nor an obligation.

3. Development of the Proskomide

It is difficult to determine exactly when the ancient Christian custom of community gift-offering ceased to be practiced. It probably happened about the fifth and sixth centuries. It must have occurred slowly and gradually, for we learn from certain documents that, even after the custom had ceased to be a general practice, it was still retained by the Emperor's family and by the more prominent and affluent people. The Emperors enjoyed the special privilege of entering the sanctuary and presenting their gifts there. With the gradual disappearance of the community gift-offering, the rites of the original Proskomide lost much of their solemnity and pristine meaning. The Proskomide ceased to be a community rite in which all the faithful took an active part, and became exclusively the private function of the priest and the deacon.

After losing its original meaning, the rite of Proskomide was transferred from its original place in the Liturgy, i.e., from the beginning of the Liturgy of the Faithful, to the beginning of the Liturgy of the Catechumens. That the original place of the Proskomide was at one time at the beginning of the Liturgy of the Faithful can be substantiated by certain testimonies and allusions found in liturgical documents. One of the oldest documents in which we find many liturgical prescriptions, the so-called "Testament of Our Lord Jesus Christ," contains, among other things, a prescription that forbids any acceptance of gifts from the catechumens: "It is not allowed to accept bread from a catechumen, even though he has a believing son or wife for whom he would like to offer gifts; his gifts shall not be accepted until he is baptized." From this restriction we may deduce that the gift-offering among the ancient Christians was part of the Liturgy of the Faithful, since the catechumens were not allowed to take part in it. The rite of gift-offering was the initial rite of the Liturgy of the Faithful (the Liturgy of the Sacrifice). After the rite of gift-offering followed the Anaphora or Eucharistic Canon.

The transposition of the Proskomide to the beginning of the Liturgy of the Catechumens most likely occurred at the time when the catechumenate ceased to be a practice, i.e., about the sixth and seventh centuries. When the catechumenate ceased to exist as a distinct class, there was no longer a need to continue the practice of community gift-offering in the Liturgy of the Faithful. In any event, the Proskomide is the initial rite of the Liturgy in the oldest manuscript of the Divine Liturgy of the Byzantine Rite—the Barberini Codex of the eighth-ninth centuries.

4. Role and Purpose of the Proskomide

When the Proskomide ceased to be a rite of community gift-offering and when it was moved from its original place in the Liturgy of the Faithful and became the initial rite of the Liturgy of the Catechumens, it also lost its original character, its original role and purpose.

As we have mentioned, the original rite of the Proskomide was not only a preparation of the eucharistic matter (bread and wine), but it was also a public act of Christian charity. This community gift-offering was an exterior manifestation of the love the Christians had for their Church, their clergy and for all those who were under the protection of the Church. The rite of gift-offering was considered a natural obligation of all the faithful. It was even customary to sacrifice the offerings for those unable to come to church, the persecuted, members of the family, relatives, the deceased, etc. In this ancient community gift-offering the whole Church was symbolically represented. The whole community participated in the offering of gifts which were symbols of their love for the Church community and an external sign of their gratitude for God's gifts—the Holy Eucharist, which the faithful received during the Unbloody Sacrifice of the Liturgy.

It is clear, then, why the original character of the rite of Proskomide had to change. Now it is no longer a public act but strictly a private one—a liturgical act of the priest. It is not an overt act of charity or an outward sign of Christian love, but exclusively a preparation of the sacrificial or eucharistic matter necessary for the Consecration. The role of the Proskomide is now that of a purely liturgical rite, in which the faithful as a whole do not actively participate.

5. Place and Minister of the Proskomide

The Proskomide, as we know it today, takes place at the side altar called the Table of Prothesis, which is located to the left of the main altar (the north side of the sanctuary).

In its new place (i.e., at the beginning of the Liturgy) the Proskomide becomes a secondary rite, in the sense that no external solemnity accompanies it. One of the priests assisting or concelebrating at the Divine Liturgy performs the rite which is short and simple. The Proskomide in St. John Chrysostom's Liturgy (eighth-ninth centuries), as recorded in the Barberini Codex includes a prayer of prothesis or oblation with a prescription stating that this prayer be recited "in the sacristy when the priest places the prosphora or altar-breads upon the diskos." In the oldest commentaries on the Divine Liturgy of the Byzantine Rite we discover that the rites of the Proskomide were not fully developed. According to their descriptions, the Proskomide consisted of the rites of preparing the sacrificial bread, the pouring of wine and water into the poterion or chalice and the prayer of Prothesis. The earliest manuscripts of the Byzantine Liturgy do not mention other ritual additions which we have today in the modern Proskomide.

6. Rites and Texts of the Proskomide

Not until after the ninth century do the liturgical documents reveal a development in the rites and texts of the Proskomide. In the tenth and eleventh-century manuscripts of the Byzantine Liturgy, various new formulas and texts begin to appear in company with the rite of preparing the bread. Thus, for instance, the rite of cutting the bread is given a symbolic meaning, because the accompanying text alludes to the death of the Lamb, Jesus Christ, on Golgotha.

In the liturgical documents of the eleventh century, we find various short prayers taken from the psalms that distinctly suggest a symbolic meaning. In the Proskomide commemorations and, later, the prayers accompanying the covering or veiling of the diskos and chalice are mentioned. In the eleventh and twelfth centuries, we find the practice of using the asteriskos to protect the bread on the diskos against contact with foreign objects, and this too was soon given a symbolic meaning. We shall discuss this symbolism when we speak in general about the symbolism of the other rites of the Proskomide.

A further phase of development is the arrangement of the particles on the diskos. In the twelfth century the rites of cutting particles from the prosphora and offering them in honor of the Blessed Virgin Mary and the saints enriched the Proskomide. Later other particles were added to commemorate the living and the dead. The commemoration of the saints, at first, was general; only the various classes or groups of saints were mentioned, e.g., the apostles, martyrs, etc. But later the catalogue of saints increased and the names of particular saints from the different classes began to appear, and with this increasing number of saints, the number of prosphorae increased from one to three, then to five, and sometimes to seven.

Although in the thirteenth and fourteenth centuries the rites and texts of the Proskomide reached their highest point of development, the rite still suffered from a lack of uniformity. Philotheus, the Patriarch of Constantinople (1354-1376), wishing to do away with this chaotic diversity in the performance of the Proskomide, prepared the *Diataxis*, in which he accurately described and specified such rites as the manner of cutting out the portion representing the Amnos or Lamb and particles from the prosphorae. He stabilized the texts regarding the commemoration of saints and other prayer formulas, and in general brought order and system into the rites and texts of the Proskomide.

The *Diataxis* of Philotheus was accepted not only on Byzantine soil, but also in the Slav territories. It was the Kievan Metropolitan Cyprian (1406) who introduced it in the Ukraine. But even the *Diataxis* failed to remove all the differences, however insignificant and non-essential they were. When the printed Sluzhebnyks began to appear in the fifteenth-sixteenth centuries, the rites and texts of the Proskomide received their final form; only in non-essential points did they differ from the present day texts and rites.

7. Symbolism of the Proskomide

We shall discuss the symbolism of each of the separate rites of the Proskomide when we describe and explain them in detail.

We have stated that the Proskomide evolved from the ancient Christian practice of community gift-offering, and hence in its original form it had its practical purpose and its own symbolism. The practical purpose consisted of the priest selecting those gifts that were needed for the celebration of the Liturgy and the setting aside of the remainder for his own support and for other charitable purposes. The symbolism of the original Proskomide was expressed in the gift-offering, which was a sign and symbol of Christian love and solidarity. The gifts offered by the faithful were the symbol of their sincere love of sacrifice and an external sign of their active faith and membership in the Church.

From this it can be seen that only true members of the Church, i.e. the faithful, and not the catechumens, could have participated in the Proskomide. When the original Proskomide changed in purpose, its symbolism changed also. In ancient manuscripts dealing with the Proskomide of the eighth-ninth centuries, we do not find a symbolic text or allusion except for the prayer of oblation in which the sacrificial bread on the diskos represents "the heavenly bread, food for the world," Jesus Christ. From this first symbolic interpretation of the bread there later sprang other symbolism that enriched the rites of Proskomide. Liturgical commentators, sometimes, on the basis of the texts of the rite and sometimes on their own subjective interpretations, tried to attach a symbolic meaning to even the most insignificant and most practical rites.

According to the medieval interpretation of the Byzantine Divine Liturgy, the Proskomide, as a whole, symbolizes Christ's sacrifice on Golgotha. In this interpretation, the Lamb which is cut from the prosphora represents the Lamb of God, Jesus Christ. The rite of cutting out the Lamb symbolizes Christ's humanity—the fact that he was mankind's representative, to be offered as a sacrifice for the sins of His brothers according to the flesh. He allows Himself to be "cut out," i.e. to be chosen from among "the prosphora," which symbolize mankind, to be sacrificed to the last drop of blood and water which flowed from His pierced side. Hence, the liturgical lance used in the rite of the Proskomide recalls the spear or lance with which the Roman centurion opened the side of Jesus Christ, and the wine and water symbolize the blood and water that flowed from that sacred wound. The small particles of bread placed about the Lamb are the Mystical Body of Christ, His Church, His faithful, whom he redeemed with His Blood. The Table of Prothesis represents Golgotha where Christ died, as well as the sepulcher in which His body was laid. The priestly vestments are intended to recall the events of Christ's passion, and the *aër* or larger veil which covers the diskos and the chalice is a symbol of the linens in which His Body was wrapped. The incense with its fragrance symbolizes the myrrh and precious oils with which the Body of Christ was anointed before being laid in the tomb.

We can see how the early commentators attempted to give a symbolic meaning to every rite performed during the Proskomide. To them the Proskomide was a mystical symbolization and dramatization of the sacrifice of Jesus Christ on the cross. But there were those who were not satisfied with these particular interpretations and sought to attribute other symbolic meanings to the rites and texts of the Proskomide. According to the latter group the Proskomide as a whole was a mystical representation of the Birth of Christ and His hidden life.

These men felt that each separate rite and text of the Proskomide recalled some one of the various events of Christ's childhood. The prosphora from which the priest cuts the Lamb is the symbol of the Blessed Virgin Mary, who gave birth to Jesus Christ. The lance signifies the operation or action of the Holy Spirit at the Conception and Nativity of our Lord. The deacon represents the angel Gabriel, who announced the birth of Christ to the Blessed Virgin Mary. The diskos is the manger or crib where Mary placed the child Jesus. The asteriskos or star symbolizes the star of Bethlehem which shone above the stable where Christ was born. The veils are symbols of the swaddling clothes in which Jesus was wrapped; the incense represents the gifts of the three wise men from the East. The act of covering the holy gifts, symbolizes the hidden life of Jesus Christ in Nazareth.

We shall give a more extensive and comprehensive critical evaluation of the interpretation of each separate rite and text in connection with our detailed commentary on the Proskomide. Here we have presented only a general outline of the early symbolic interpretation. What connection, if any, each symbolic interpretation had with the general plan and purpose of the Proskomide we shall determine in our commentary on the rite.

8. The Division and Plan of the Proskomide

In its present form the Proskomide has a two fold purpose: 1) properly to prepare and predispose the priest for the Proskomide as well as for the Divine Liturgy as a whole, and 2) more important to prepare the eucharistic gifts (bread and wine). Although these two purposes are distinct, the distinction is difficult to perceive. Generally speaking, this division into the twofold purpose, like all the other divisions in the Divine Liturgy, is conventional and arbitrary, and is the work of commentators and liturgists.

In our commentary on the rites and texts of the Proskomide, we shall, for the sake of clarity, divide the rite into: 1) the preparation of the priest, and 2) the preparation of the eucharistic gifts. The preparation of the priest includes the introductory and preparatory prayers of the priest and the deacon before the iconostasis, his entrance into the sanctuary and the rites of vesting and washing of hands. The second preparation involves the actual rites proper to the Proskomide, such as the cutting out of the Lamb and the particles, the commemorations, and all that is associated or connected with the preparation of the eucharistic gifts.

In our commentary, we shall adhere to the historical-scientific method in interpreting the rites and texts of the Proskomide. We shall investigate their origin, historical developments and original meanings. Our interpretations will thus have an historical basis.

SELECT BIBLIOGRAPHY

Muretov, S., *Istoricheskiy obzor chinoposlyedovaniya proskomidii*, ("Chtenie v Obshchestvye lyu-bopitateley dukhovnaho prosvyeshcheniya," dekabr, 1893, p. 627 ff.); *Istoricheskiy obzor chinoposlyedovaniya proskomidii do "Ustava liturghii" Konstantinopolskaho patriarkha Filofeya*, Moskva, 1895;-*K materialam dlya istorii chinoposlyedovaniya liturghii*, Sergiev-Posad, 1895.

Petrovskiy, A., *Drevniy akt prinosheniya veshchestva dlya tainstva evhkaristii i poslyedovanie proskomidii*, ("Khrist. Cht.," (1904), pp. 402–432).

Engdahl, R., *Die Proskomidie der Liturgien des Chrysostomus und des Basilius waehrend des Mittelalters*, Berlin, 1908.

Mandala, M., *La protesi della liturgia nel rito bizantino-greco*, Grottaferrata, 1935.

Petrides, S., *La preparation des oblats dans le rit grec*, ("Echos d'Orient," III, pp. 65–78).

De Meester, P., OSB, *Les origines et les developpements du texte grec de la liturgie de S. J. Chrysostom*, ("Chrysostomika," Roma, 1908, pp. 245–357).

De Vaux, R., *Ancient Israel, its Life and Institutions*, New York, 1961.

Chapter II

THE PREPARATION OF THE PRIEST

The dignity of the Divine Liturgy requires that the priest approach the altar properly prepared. The Old Testament priests were obliged to undergo various ritual purifications before carrying out their priestly functions, and before offering their sacrifices. God Himself exacted of the levites and priests purity and holiness because they were His servants: "Be holy because Your Lord is holy." (Lev. 11:44; 20:7)

If the priests of the Old Testament had to fulfill their offices with a proper attitude and disposition, then what can be said of the priests of the New Testament, who offer the Eucharistic Sacrifice of the Body and Blood of Jesus Christ? They too should predispose and prepare themselves properly before celebrating the Divine Liturgy, and the nature of the first part of the Proskomide requires such preparation on the part of the priest. This preparation is remote and proximate: the remote preparation involves the preparation of the priest's body and soul, his spiritual and corporal preparation, while the proximate preparation embraces the prayers before the iconostasis, his petitions before his entrance into the sanctuary, and the prayers he recites while vesting and washing his hands.

1. The Spiritual Disposition of the Priest

The priest's first act in preparing himself for the Divine Liturgy is to predispose himself properly. St. Paul admonishes all Christians to attend the Divine Liturgy with a disposition proper to its sublime nature.

> But let a man prove himself: and so let him eat of that bread and drink of that chalice. For he that eateth and drinketh unworthily eateth and drinketh judgment to himself, not discerning the body of the Lord. (1 Cor 11:28–29).

The Apostle's warning pertains especially to the priest, who not only receives the holy gifts during the Divine Liturgy, but also performs the act of Consecration by virtue of the grace conferred upon him by Jesus Christ.

This spiritual disposition or internal preparation of the priest consists chiefly in his being in the state of sanctifying grace, i.e. being free from mortal sin—a prerequisite so natural and self-evident that it is not even mentioned in any of the texts of the Proskomide. However, at the very beginning of the rite there is a prescription reminding the priest of one very important requirement for celebrating the Divine Liturgy worthily—that he approach the altar with a heart free from all animosity and hate:

The priest, before celebrating the Divine Liturgy, should first of all be reconciled with all, and should have no animosity in his heart, and his soul, and in so far as it is possible, should be free from all evil thoughts.

This prescription found both in the opening rite and in the Divine Liturgy as a whole is a re-echoing of Christ's words:

If therefore thou offer thy gift at the altar, and there thou remember that thy brother hath anything against thee, leave there thy offering and go first to be reconciled to thy brother; and then coming thou shalt offer thy gift. (Mt 5:23–25)

Although these words are addressed to all Christians, they refer especially to the priest who, in the name of all Christians, offers the Unbloody Sacrifice. The Divine Liturgy in essence is a sacrifice of reconciliation between God and mankind. Hence, the one who offers this sacrifice of reconciliation should himself be reconciled with his neighbor and should not harbor any malice toward him. Only in this way can the priest be a reflection of Christ the "High Priest," his prototype.

The heart of the priest must be free not only from animosity and aversion, but also from all evil thoughts, because the Divine Liturgy is the holiest of all priestly functions. He must approach the altar with a clean heart, for the priest, in the eyes of the Church, is the image of the "innocent Lamb," Jesus Christ.

2. Corporal Disposition of the Priest

Before celebrating the Divine Liturgy, not only must the priest's heart and soul be predisposed, but also his body, i.e. he must abstain from food and drink. We read of this abstinence in the rite of Proskomide:

The priest should, before celebrating the Divine Liturgy, abstain from food and remain temperate to the time he begins his priestly functions.

This is called the eucharistic abstinence or eucharistic fast.

The law and custom of the eucharistic fast developed gradually in the Church. After Our Lord's ascension the first Christians gathered together for the Unbloody Sacrifice in commemoration of the Last Supper, and also attended the love supper or agape. However, even during the time of the Apostles various abuses arose. We know that St. Paul severely rebuked the faithful of Corinth because they congregated, not to eat the Lord's supper, but to partake of the food they had brought for themselves, so that some went hungry while others drank to excess. (1 Cor 11:28–23)

To eliminate these abuses, the custom of celebrating the Divine Liturgy in the morning rather than in the evening, and apart from the community fraternal repast or love meal (apage), was soon introduced. It was from this time that the Christians began to set aside Sunday to commemorate Christ's resurrection.

To celebrate the glorious resurrection of Christ, which occurred in the early morning on Sunday, the Christians began to hold the Divine Liturgy on Sunday morning. Probably it was from this time that the Christians began fasting before receiving the Holy Eucharist. We have evident references to the fact that the custom of the eucharistic fast began around the end of the second century and the beginning of the third (e.g. the testimonies of the Church writers Tertullian and St. Hippolytus). By the time of St. Augustine the eucharistic fast was already a general custom and law in all the Christian churches, and we may, therefore, reasonably conclude that it was practiced throughout the fourth century.

The principal motive for introducing eucharistic abstinence for the priest as well as for the faithful was the great respect for the Holy Eucharist. The restriction of not eating or drinking anything before receiving the Holy Eucharist was based on the assumption that the Eucharist should be the first food taken by the Christians before all other wordly food. From it the Christian should draw new strength and life. And because the liturgical day began in the evening, the eucharistic abstinence also began in the evening. That the priest should "abstain from supper" is mentioned in the rubrics found in the rite of Proskomide.

Another motive for introducing the eucharistic fast was the practice of self-denial. As a token of gratitude for the Unbloody Sacrifice, the Church exacted from her faithful and priests the denial of their corporal needs or pleasures. The eucharistic fast presented an opportunity for Christians to demonstrate their spirit of sacrifice. The ancient church prescriptions demanded that the minister and the recipient of the sacraments observe a fast before receiving Baptism, Penance and especially before receiving any of the degrees of Holy Orders.

Throughout the centuries the prescriptions for the eucharistic fast were very stringent. It is only recently that the Church has relaxed the old prescriptions of the fast for the faithful and the priest. These new regulations went into effect in 1953–56 as a result of the Apostolic Constitutions of Pius XII.

3. The Prayers of the Priest Before the Iconostasis

The spiritual and bodily disposition of the priest was a remote preparation for the celebration of the Divine Liturgy. Besides this, the rite of the Proskomide prescribes a proximate or immediate preparation in the form of a whole series of introductory or preparatory prayers for the priest and deacon before entering the sanctuary.

These introductory prayers, which include the so-called penitential troparia and three prayers before the iconostasis, were added to the rite of Proskomide rather late. The liturgical manuscripts before the eleventh century do not contain any such introductory prayers. This fact, of course, does not mean that priests did not recite any preparatory prayers before celebrating the Divine Liturgy; it is simply that these prayers were not yet definitely formulated and fixed but were left to the choice of the individual.

The eleventh-century manuscripts of the Divine Liturgy do contain at the beginning of the Proskomide the prayer: "Lord, stretch forth Thy hand . . .," from which we may conclude that this is the most significant and the oldest of all the prayers the priest recites before entering the sanctuary. In the liturgical documents of the thirteenth century, the priest is instructed to bow three times upon entering the church. Not until the fifteenth and sixteenth centuries do the preparatory prayers as we know them today begin to appear in the Sluzhebnyks. This is especially true of the prayers said while kissing the icons of the Savior and Blessed Virgin Mary; in fact, the preparatory prayers before the iconostasis represent a later extension of the rite of Proskomide.

The rite of Proskomide prescribes that priest and deacon "standing before the Royal Doors" make three metanias in the direction of the East, i.e., facing the altar which, according to the ancient custom, was erected facing the East. The prayers open with the invocation: "Blessed be our God always, now and ever, and unto ages of ages," which is followed by the "Customary Beginning" which consists of the following prayers: "O heavenly King . . .," "Holy God, Holy Mighty One . . .," "Glory be to the Father . . .," "O most Holy Trinity . . .," and the "Our Father."

Since all church services begin with these prayers, which incidentally, do not require any special interpretation, they are called the "Customary Beginning" (i.e. the common, usual, ordinary beginning). The "customary Beginning" has also been integrated into the daily prayers of the faithful of the Byzantine-Slavonic Rite.

After the "Customary Beginning" the priest recites three penitential *troparia* which are most appropriate in preparing him for a worthy celebration of the Divine Liturgy. They remind the priest that, although he has been endowed with the dignity and the grace of the priesthood of Christ, before God he is still a sinner and is in need of God's mercy. Therefore, when he approaches the sanctuary before the Royal Doors he says:

> Have mercy on us, O Lord, have mercy on us: for having no excuse for our sins, as guilty servants we offer this prayer to Thee: have mercy on us.

> O Lord, have mercy on us, for we have hoped in Thee. Be not exceedingly angry at us nor remember our transgressions; but even today look down upon us mercifully, and deliver us from our enemies: for Thou art our God and we are Thy people, the work of Thy Hands, and we invoke Thy name.

> O Blessed Mother of God, open to us the doors of mercy, that we who hope in thee may not perish, but that we may be delivered through thee from all miseries: for thou art the salvation of Christian people.

After reciting these three penitential *troparia,* the priest then goes up to the icon of the Savior and, kissing it, prays:

> Thy most pure image we revere, O Gracious One, entreating forgiveness for our offenses, Christ, O God. For of Thine own will Thou wast graciously pleased to ascend the cross in the flesh, that Thou mightest deliver from

bondage of the enemy those whom Thou hast made. Therefore we gratefully cry to Thee: Thou didst fill all with joy, O our Savior, in coming to save the world.

The priest then goes and stands before the icon of the Blessed Virgin Mary and, kissing it, prays:

Thou who are the fount of mercy, O Mother of God, vouchsafe compassion unto us. Look down upon the people who have sinned. Manifest thy power as ever; for hoping in thee we cry unto thee: Hail! as did once Gabriel, chieftain of the incorporeal.

The prayers before the iconostasis end with the prayer: "Lord, stretch forth Thy hand," which we have previously mentioned as being the most significant and oldest of all the preparatory prayers in the Proskomide. The priest recites this prayer with bowed head before the Royal Doors. He implores God to bless him before he celebrates the Liturgy:

Lord, stretch forth Thy hand from Thy holy dwelling place on high, and strengthen me for Thy appointed service; that I may stand without blame before Thy awesome altar, and may offer the unbloody sacrifice. For Thine is the power unto ages of ages. Amen.

The contents of these prayers before the iconostasis include the sentiments that should dominate the soul of the priest before he approaches the altar to celebrate the Divine Liturgy. His first sentiment should be one of atonement for his sins and the sins of the people. Hence, the priest, who is the representative of sinners, expresses sorrow before God for his own sins and the sins of the people and begs forgiveness. The other sentiment which the preparatory prayers should evoke within the priest, is profound confidence in God's mercy. Representing the congregation, the priest dares to approach the altar, filled with hope in Gods mercy. And although sinners cannot by themselves achieve "justification," God is nevertheless their God and sinners are His people, the work of His hand. Confidence in God's mercy further increases because sinners have another "source of mercy," the Blessed Virgin Mary, who can open "the doors of mercy" and save them from eternal damnation.

The external expression of atonement and hope in God's mercy is found in the three metanias which the priest makes before the iconostasis and in his kissing of the icons of the Blessed Virgin Mary and our Savior. This is all a beautiful symbol of expiation, conversion and reconciliation with Him before entering the sanctuary. Only after this sincere public confession before God, the Blessed Virgin Mary, and the heavenly court which the iconostasis symbolizes, does the priest dare ask God to place His "hand" upon him, to give him the strength and grace to celebrate this Unbloody Sacrifice" without judgment or condemnation."

As we can see, the preparatory prayers of the priest before his entering the sanctuary are beautifully designed to predispose and prepare him for a worthy celebration of the Divine Liturgy.

4. Entrance of the Priest into the Sanctuary

After the priest has expressed his sorrow before God, his hope in His mercy, and has asked God's blessing for a worthy celebration of the Liturgy, he enters the sanctuary praying:

> I will enter into Thy house; I will bow in Thy holy temple in Thy fear. Guide me, O Lord, with Thy righteousness; because of my enemies make straight my path before Thee. For there is no truth in their mouth; their heart is vain; their throat is an open sepulchre; with their tongues have they dealt deceitfully. Judge them, O God. Let them fall from their devices. According to the multitude of their iniquities cast Thou them out, for they have provoked Thee exceedingly, O Lord. And let all be joyful who trust in Thee; they shall rejoice forever, and Thou shalt dwell in them; and those who love Thy name shall glory in Thee. For Thou, O Lord, wilt bless the just, as with the shield of benevolence hast Thou crowned us.

These words, taken from Psalm 5, recall the scene when the priests of the Old Testament entered the sanctuary of the Temple of Jerusalem. Only once a year were the Old Testament arch-priests allowed to cross the threshold of the temple and enter the Holy of Holies to incense the tabernacle of the covenant. Otherwise, it was forbidden under severe penalty.

The New Testament sanctuary is, without comparison, holier than the Old Testament Holy of Holies. There God dwelt in the form of a cloud; here the God-Man Jesus Christ dwells in the Holy Eucharist, really and truly present under the appearances of bread and wine. The Holy Eucharist is a greater treasure than those memorials which were concealed in the tabernacle of the covenant—the miraculous manna, the tablets of the law and the rod of Aaron which blossomed miraculously. Hence, the priest, on entering the sanctuary, invokes Our Lord to "show him the way" to God.

Once he arrives in the sanctuary and stands before the altar, the priest again makes three bows or metanias and, approaching the altar, kisses the gospel book on the altar, the altar itself and the altar cross. The three bows and the kissing of the gospel book have been in the rite of Proskomide since the thirteenth century but the kissing of the altar and altar cross were not added until later. It was not until the fifteenth and sixteenth centuries that we find the rite of entering the sanctuary as practiced today.

The three kisses following the entrance into the sacristy have their own symbolic meaning. It is Christ who is being kissed three times, for the gospel book, altar and altar cross all symbolize Him. The gospel book symbolizes Christ the Divine teacher; the altar represents Christ the victim or sacrifice, and High Priest; and the altar cross represents our redemption and the victory of Christ over sin and death. The priest who kisses these three symbols represents Christ's Church which St. Paul calls the bride whom Christ redeemed with His Blood (Ephes 5:23–28). Thus Christ's Church (the bride) in this manner gives her heavenly Bridegroom a kiss of reconciliation and love.

Medieval liturgical commentators were fond of elaborating on the meaning of the altar, and have left us a great variety of symbolic interpretations. For example, according to Simeon of Thessalonica (1429), the altar symbolized Christ's tomb, the sanctuary His sepulcher. The altar was also the symbol of the table at which Christ instituted the sacrament of the Holy Eucharist, and the table at which He will sit to judge the world. Again the division of the church into the nave (for the faithful) and the sanctuary symbolized the divine and human natures in Christ; the sanctuary referring to God, the divine nature, and the nave to human nature. Finally the division of the church into sanctuary and church proper (or nave) recalls and represents human nature which is composed of body and soul.[1]

However, not all these symbolic interpretations correspond to the real meaning of the rite and texts of the Divine Liturgy. We mention them only because they are still used in current commentaries on the Divine Liturgy.

5. The Vesting of the Priest

After the priest kisses the altar, altar cross and gospel book, he dons the priestly vestments. But before the vesting, the rite of the Proskomide prescribes that he makes three bows "toward the East." With each bow he recites the prayer of the publican: "Lord have mercy on me a sinner." Then follows the rite of vesting. The priests dons the *stikharion, epitrakhelion, zone, epimanikia* and *phelonion*. When the deacon concelebrates with the priest, he asks the priest for his blessing before vesting: "Bless, master, the *stikharion* with the *orarion*." And the priest responds: "Blessed be our God always, now and ever, and unto ages of ages."

As he dons each vestment, the priest recites a short prayer which clearly reveals the vestment's symbolism. The vesting prayers were incorporated into the rite of the Proskimide at about the same time as the introductory prayers before the iconostasis. The use of priestly vestments for the celebration of the Divine Liturgy is an older custom. Some liturgists affirm that the Apostles themselves prescribed the practice. However, current research shows that in the first two centuries of Christianity, the garb used in the celebration of the Divine Liturgy and other divine services was simply the daily attire worn by the people in those times. Not until the third and fourth centuries do we find special vestments being used for different services.

As to their form, the priestly vestments originated from the ancient Roman garb. For example, the *stikharion* is reminiscent of the ancient Roman tunic, and the *phelonion,* the Roman cloak used for traveling. The vestments used by the Old Testament priests, Roman Emperors, dignitaries and even the pagan priests all had their influence upon vestments of the bishop and priest. The deacon's *orarion,* for instance, owes its origin to an item worn by the pagan priests for the celebration of their mysteries.

In the early ages, the Church had no detailed regulations regarding the form and color of the priestly vestments. As a result, great freedom and diversity prevailed. Even the accompanying prayers and symbolic interpretations of the priestly vestments were not readily accepted nor were they the same everywhere. In the present-day rite of the Proskomide, as we have seen, the rites of vesting is accompanied by corresponding prayers composed of Psalms. These short prayers themselves carry a symbol and endow each vestment with a meaning.

While putting on the *stikharion,* the priest says the words taken from the prophet Isaias:

> My soul shall be exalted in the Lord, for He hath clothed me with the robe of salvation and He hath arrayed me in the garment of joy; as on a bridegroom He hath put a crown on my head and as a bride He hath adorned me with jewels. (Is 41:10)

Taking the *epitrakhelion,* the priest repeats the words of the Psalmist:

> Blessed be God, who poureth out upon His priests His grace, as ointment upon the head, which runneth down upon the beard, the beard of Aaron, which runneth down to the hem of his garment. (Ps 132:2)

Girding himself with the *zone,* he utters the words:

> Blessed be God, who girdeth me with strength, and hath made my way sinless, and hath made my feet like unto the deer, and hath set me upon high places. (Ps 17:33–34)

Putting an *epimanikion* or cuff on the right hand, he prays:

> Thy right hand, O Lord, is glorified in strength. Thy right hand, O Lord, hath annihilated the enemy, and through the multitude of Thy glory Thou hast crushed the adversaries. (Ex 15:16)

While putting the other *epimanikion* on the left hand, the priest repeats with the Psalmist:

> Thy hands have made me and formed me. Give me understanding, and I will learn Thy commandments. (Ps 118:73)

Finally, before donning the *phelonion,* he blesses and kisses it saying:

> Thy priests, O Lord, shall be clothed with righteousness, and Thy saints shall rejoice with joy always, now and ever, and unto ages of ages. Amen. (Ps 131:9)

These prayers recited while he is vesting remind the priest of his great dignity and authority. The priestly vestments distinguish the priest from the people. They symbolize his office as priest of Christ, and emphasize the dignity of his priesthood. They are a visible sign of invisible grace which the priest has received through the sacrament of the priesthood. The person vested in the priestly garments no longer represents an ordinary man, but a sacred person, the servant and priest of Jesus Christ, by whose power and grace he celebrates the Unbloody Sacrifice of the Divine Liturgy.

Although the short vesting prayers were chosen at random, they are, nevertheless, beautiful symbols of the dignity of the priest of Christ. They remind him that he is the "bridegroom" and the "bride" of Christ and hence is set apart from all the other faithful in that he is dressed in the "attire of salvation" and carries on his head the "crown" of God's chosen one. Our Lord, bestowing on him the grace of the priesthood, poured upon his head the fragrant "myrrh," girded him with his "power" and placed him "above" so that, strengthened by the "right hand" of the Most High and garbed in "truth;" he could offer the Sacrifice worthily.

In many of the medieval and current commentaries on the Divine Liturgy, the priestly garments are made to symbolize Christ's passion. The *stikharion* refers to Christ's garments which were covered with blood in the flagellation; the *epimanikia* or cuffs and *zone* recall the cords with which He was bound; the *phelonion* represents the purple robe which was put on Him in derision. Such Byzantine commentators as Herman, Theodore of Andida and Simeon of Thessalonica attribute to every diaconal, sacerdotal and pontifical garment various, and at times antithetic, symbolic meanings; they try to discover in each vestment at least a remote allusion to the life and passion of Christ.[1]

As we remarked earlier regarding the symbolism of the altar, not all these symbolic interpretations have any basis in the liturgical texts. The prayers said while vesting in no way suggest Christ's passion, but they do stress the power and dignity of the priest.

6. The Washing of the Hands

The final act of preparation is the washing of the hands. As the priest performs this rite, he utters the words taken from the Psalm:

> I will wash my hands among the innocent, and will compass Thy altar, O Lord, that I may hear the voice of Thy praise, and tell of all Thy wondrous works. Lord, I have loved the beauty of Thy house and the place where Thy glory dwelleth. Destroy not my soul with the wicked, nor my life with the men of blood, in whose hands are iniquities; their right hand is full of gifts. But I have walked in my innocence; deliver me, O Lord, and have mercy on me. My foot hath been set in righteousness; in the churches I will among the innocent, and will compass Thy altar, O Lord . . .[2]

The ceremony of washing the hands before the divine functions has its origin in the oldest and most widely known rites, not only in Christian worship but also in the Old Testament and even pagan cults. The ancient Greeks washed their hands before offering sacrifices to their gods. In the Old Testament, it was prescribed that the priest not only wash his hands but that he bathe his whole body. At God's command Moses designed a special basin to be used in washing the feet and hands of those who took part in the ceremonies and sacrifices. (Ex 40:30–32; 3:18–21) The liturgical practice of washing the hands is

---

[1] Simeon of Thessalonica, *On the Divine Liturgy;* Migne, PG, 155, 291–294.

mentioned in the earliest liturgical documents of the first centuries. *The Apostolic Constitutions* and the *Mystagogical Catechism* of St. Cyril of Jerusalem give an account of the rite before the Eucharistic Sacrifice. The washing of hands once followed the community offering; the priest and the deacon, after taking the gifts from the people, cleansed their hands. When, therefore, the rite of gift-offering was moved to the beginning of the Liturgy, so also was the washing of the hands, and it was not until the thirteenth and fourteenth centuries that the ceremony appeared in the manuscripts of the Divine Liturgy. However, this fact does not mean that the washing of the hands became a part of the Proskomide at so late a date. Some Eastern Rites, as well as the Latin Rite, retained the rite in its original place, before the Eucharistic Canon. In the Byzantine Divine Liturgy, we have it at the beginning of the Divine Liturgy.

There is no doubt that the rite of washing hands before the celebration of the Divine Liturgy has, besides its practical purpose, a profound symbolism. Not only did necessity require the washing of hands before the gift-offering, but also the desire to approach the altar with a clean heart. The *Apostolic Constitutions* and St. Cyril in his *Mystagogical Catechism* explain this rite symbolically. St. Cyril says of it:

> You have observed the deacon giving water to the priest and to others who stand with him at the altar that they might wash their hands. However, he does not give the water to purify the body, because no one enters the church dirty and unwashed. The water symbolizes the necessity of purifying one's soul from sin and iniquity, for hands are symbols of our deeds, and by washing them, we wish to represent the purity of our deeds. This same thought is conveyed by the royal Prophet David: "I will wash my hands among the innocent, and will compass They altar, O Lord . ..[2]

Other ancient documents and sources give evidence that the people as well as the priests washed their hands before the divine services. In the time of St. John Chrysostom, water basins were placed at the entrance of the church so that the faithful could cleanse their hands as a sign of their desire to serve and pray to God with purity of heart. The Jews preserve, to this very day, the custom of washing their hands before every function, and especially before every prayer, because to them the washing of hands was a symbol of purity of intention and a preparation before performing a good deed.

The words of the Psalm which the priest recites during the ceremony emphasize the profound meaning of the rite of washing hands before the Divine Liturgy. The priest expresses his desire to be among the "innocent." He wishes to have no part with the "ungodly" and with those whose consciences are burdened with iniquity. On the contrary, the priest desires to wash his hands with the "innocent" and "approach the altar of God" with a soul free of sin.

---

[2] Migne, PG, 33, 1110 ff.

The rite of washing the hands is also a beautiful termination to priest's preparation for the Proskomide and the Divine Liturgy. When we reflect upon the previous rites of this preparation—the introductory prayers before the iconostasis, the kissing of the icons, the altar, gospel book and altar cross and finally the donning of the priestly vestments—we find among them an intrinsic harmony. The washing of the hands complements and perfects all the preceding rites. The priest, who in the preparatory prayers expressed sorrow for his sins and confidence in God's mercy and, in kissing the holy objects, his reconciliation with God, becomes a new man entirely once he vests. No longer is he just an ordinary man, but the chosen one of God, "the bridegroom" of Christ, who is to offer the sacrifice of reconciliation for sinful mankind. For this reason he washes his hands as a sign of his desire to be pure, and with an unstained conscience he "blesses" God and "proclaims his wondrous works."

SELECT BIBLIOGRAPHY

Golubstov, A. P., *Istoricheskoe obyasnenie obrayadov liturghii,* ("Bogoslovskiy vyestnik," 1915, II, pp. 565–601).

Dolotskiy, V. J., *O svyashchennikh odezhdakh,* ("Khrist. Cht.," 1848, I., p. 325 ff.).

Nikolskiy, K., *O svyashchennikh odezhdakh tserkovnosluzhiteley,* ("Khrist. Cht.," 1889, I, pp. 378–394).

Wawryk, M., OSBM, *Prypysy evkharystinoho postu,* ("Slovo Dobroho Pastyrya," VII, nos. 3–4, March-April 1956), New York, 1956.

Browe, P., *Die Nuechternheit vor der Messe und Kommunion im Mittelalter,* ("Ephemerides Liturgicae," 1931).

Frochisse, I. M., *A propos des origines du jeune eucharistique,* ("Revue d'histoire Eccl.," 1932).

Braun, J., *Der chistliche Altar in seiner geschichtlichen Entwicklung,* Muenchen 1924 (2 Baende) ; *Das christliche Altargeraet,* Muenchen: 1932; *Die liturgische Gewandung in Occident und Orient,* Freiburg in Br. 1907; *I paramenti sacri.* Loro uso, storia e simbolismo, Torino, 1914.

Bernardakis, P., *Les ornements liturgiques chez les Grecs,* ("Echos d'Orient," 1902, V., no. 3 pp. 128–139).

Schuemmer, J., *Die altchristliche Fastenpraxis,* Muenster, 1933.

Roulin, *Vetements liturgiques,* Paris, 1930.

Bock, *Geschichte der liturgischen Gewaender des Mittelalters,* Bonn, 1857–1871 (3 Baende).

Chapter III

THE PREPARATION OF THE EUCHARISTIC GIFTS

The preparation of the priest is only an introduction to the most important rite of the Proskomide: the preparation of the bread and wine and the prayer of Prothesis or the prayer of Oblation.

In the present-day Proskomide we have, besides these two basic rites, still others which, in the course of centuries, became part of the Proskomide, completing it and forming one liturgical whole.

We shall closely study and analyze each rite connected with the preparation of the eucharistic gifts, and thus acquire a better and deeper understanding of the Proskomide as a whole.

1. The Offering of the Eucharistic Lamb

After washing his hands, the priest with the deacon makes three metanias before the Prothesis, reciting at the same time the publican's prayer: "Lord have mercy on me a sinner." This is the fourth time this triple *metania* occurs in the rite of Proskomide. Just as before the iconostasis, the triple metania here expresses repentance and hope in God's mercy. The priest, remembering that it was humility that saved the publican, also humbles himself before God. After the triple metania, the priest says the *troparion,* taken from the services of Good Friday.

> Thou has redeemed us from the curse of the law by Thy precious Blood, nailed to the cross and pierced with a lance. Thou hast bestowed immortality to men. Our Savior, Glory be to Thee.

The words of the *troparion* serve as an immediate introduction to the rite of the cutting of the eucharistic Lamb, which represents Christ dying on the cross for the salvation of mankind. The priest begins the preparation of the eucharistic gifts by cutting out the Lamb from the prosphora or altar-bread and then offering the Lamb to God.

This rite begins with the words intoned by the priest: "Blessed be our God always now and always and forevermore. Amen." Then he takes the prosphora in his left hand, and the lance in his right and makes the sign of the cross over the seal of the prosphora saying three times:

In remembrance of our Lord God and Savior Jesus Christ.

121

The seal imprinted on top of the prosphora consists of a cross and the Greek letters "IC-XC-NI-KA," signifying "Jesus Christ Conquers." The priest cuts into all four sides of this seal. While making an incision on the right side of the seal he repeats the words of the Prophet Isaias:

> He was led as a sheep to the slaughter; (Is 53:7–8)

cutting into the left side he continues with the words of the same prophet,

> And as a spotless lamb is silent before his shearers, so He did not open His mouth.

The priest again cuts the seal, this time the lower and upper part. Cutting the upper part of the seal, he recites the prayer:

> In His humiliation His judgment was taken away.

Cutting the seal at the bottom of the lower part, he prays:

> Who shall indeed describe His generation? *(Ibid.)*

Then cutting into the seal on all four sides and lifting out the cube of bread bearing the inscription, "Jesus Christ Conquers," the priest says:

> For His life shall be taken away from the earth. *(Ibid.)*

After uttering these words, he places on the diskos the seal which has been cut out of the prosphora. This portion of the prosphora is called the Lamb, for it symbolizes Christ, of whom the Baptist spoke as "the lamb of God who takes away the sins of the world." (Jn 1:29) The words of the prophet recited by the priest as he cuts the eucharistic Lamb from the prosphora allude to the Lamb of God. Isaias, the most celebrated of the Old Testament prophets, depicted in his prophecies the Messiah who was to suffer and die voluntarily. Christ is represented as the innocent Lamb who, without murmuring, freely offers himself as a sacrifice, although no one can "describe His generation" since He is the Son of God.

To show more dramatically the manner in which the Lamb of God was slain, the rite of the Proskomide directs the priest to pierce the eucharistic Lamb with the lance. Hence placing it on the diskos the priest incises a cross in it, saying:

> The Lamb of God who takes away the sins of the world is sacrificed for the life and salvation of the world.

Once he has said these words, the priest turns the Lamb over so that the seal of the prosphora faces upward. Then he pierces it with the lance repeating the words of the gospel:

> One of the soldiers pierced His side with a lance and immediately there came forth blood and water. And he bore witness and his testimony is true. (Jn 19:34–35)

Not until the tenth century was the offering of the Lamb on the diskos practiced as it is in our present-day rite of Proskomide. Originally the priest placed the whole bread on the diskos and poured wine and a little water into the chalice without any accompanying prayers. This manner of offering the bread was recorded in the manuscripts of the eighth and ninth centuries. In the liturgical documents of the ninth and tenth centuries, we find the liturgical lance being used. Afterward the rite developed of cutting the Lamb from the prosphora with accompanying appropriate prayers from Isaias, giving the rite a symbolic meaning. To the words of the prophet were also added the words of St. John the Evangelist, which compare the piercing of the Lamb to the piercing of Christ's side by the centurion.

There are very few rites in the Divine Liturgy with such beautiful, natural and profound symbolism, as the rite of offering the eucharistic Lamb. The rite of excision (cutting the Lamb) and of piercing the Lamb during the Proskomide, with the attendant prayers, are a dramatic representation of Christ's death on the cross, of the unbloody repetition, renewal and continuation of the Bloody Sacrifice of the God-Man on Golgotha. The Lamb of the Proskomide is the symbol of the Lamb of God, Jesus Christ, who gave up His life for the sins of the world. Although the actual moment in which Christ offers Himself in the Divine Liturgy as an unbloody sacrifice is not during the Proskomide but at the moment of consecration, nevertheless, the sacrifice of the Lamb of God is represented symbolically at the Proskomide in the rites of cutting out and of piercing the Lamb.

2. The Offering of Wine and Water

The offering of the bread in the form of the Lamb is inseparably connected with the offering of wine and water. The rite of the Proskomide prescribes that the deacon pour wine and a little water into the chalice after the priest has said:

> One of the soldiers pierced His side with a lance, and immediately there came forth blood and water. And He who saw it bore witness and his testimony is true.

When the priest celebrates the Liturgy alone without the deacon, he pours the wine and water himself.

The custom of mixing wine with water was borrowed from the Old Testament. The Jews are known to have drunk wine diluted with a little water; never clear wine. Jesus Christ, in instituting the Divine Liturgy at the Last Supper used wine mingled with a little water, and the Apostles and their successors retained this custom. Hence, the practice of pouring wine mingled with water into the chalice.

The Holy Fathers and the Church writers added a symbolical interpretation to this mixing of water with the wine, according to which the wine and water symbolize the blood and water that flowed from the side of Jesus when it was pierced by the spear of the Roman centurion. This symbolism is confirmed by the words of the Evangelist which the priest says before pouring the wine and water into the chalice:

> One of the soldiers pierced His side with a lance, and immediately there came forth blood and water. . . .

There was another interpretation also which explained the wine and water as symbols of the two natures in Christ—the wine, His Divine Nature, and the water of His human nature. This interpretation was used by the Byzantine pole-mists as an argument against the Armenians who used wine alone with no admixture of water in their Liturgy. In the Armenian custom Byzantine writers detected the heresy that Christ was not true man, and therefore condemned the Armenians for this strange liturgical practice which did not conform to Christian tradition.

Wine, water and bread could also be regarded as symbols of human life because bread and water serve as basic food for man's sustenance and are, therefore, natural symbols; and wine "which gladdens the heart of man" (Ps 103:15) from time immemorial has been considered a symbol of courage, joy and contentment. Besides this, wine symbolized blood, which, circulating throughout the whole body, brings life to all its parts and members as well as to the cells of the various organisms. The shedding of blood meant the deterioration and destruction of human and animal life. From this originated the restriction of eating raw meat, i.e. meat in which there was blood, for blood was regarded as a principle or source of life. If bread, water and wine by their very natures symbolize human life in all its positive implications, then the offering of bread, wine and water in the Liturgy is a fitting symbol of the offering of human life to God, the Lord and Giver of this life. From the very beginning the main purpose of sacrifice has been to acknowledge God as Master and Lord over life and death. The external sign of this acknowledgment was the burning and total destruction of the sacrificial offering which represented human life and took the place of man. The sacrificing of animals, fruits or other objects useful to man replaced human sacrifices in the sense that through them man deprived himself of these goods in order to manifest his dependence upon the deity. Hence, all sacrifices are symbols of human life and its dependence upon the source of this life—God.

The eucharistic offerings, offered to the Lord in the Divine Liturgy, are also symbols expressive of human life. By sacrificing bread, wine and water to God, we render to God both our body and our blood, i.e., our entire life as witness of our acknowledgement that all things come from and depend upon God. These offerings take the place of man's life. For this reason Jesus Christ in His divine wisdom chose bread, wine and water as the elements of the New Testament sacrifice and wished to make them the eucharistic species of His Body and Blood. The offerings of bread and of wine mingled with water, which so aptly symbolize human life, were chosen by Jesus Christ to represent His own sacrifices. Christ gave Himself up as a sacrifice by dying on the cross; in the Divine Liturgy, the unbloody continuation and repetition of the Bloody Sacrifice of Christ, the same Christ, by virtue of the eucharistic Consecration, changes the bread into His Body and the wine into His Blood.

We can see, then, that the eucharistic gifts, which the priest offers during the Proskomide, unite the offerings of man with the sacrifice of Jesus Christ, making both offerings one. On the one hand, the bread and wine sacrificed symbolize human life and, on the other hand, these same offerings represent the Lamb of God, Jesus Christ, who gave up His Body and shed His Blood on the cross for mankind. The rites of cutting the Lamb from the prosphora, the piercing of this Lamb and finally the pouring of wine and water impress upon these human offerings the mark of our dependence upon Jesus Christ. The Eucharistic offerings of man become holy gifts, designated to become the Body and Blood of Christ at the moment of Consecration. Hence, in the rite of Proskomide they are for the first time called "holy" ("holy bread," "holy or sacred chalice," "holy oblation") and in the texts and rubrics of the Divine Liturgy of the eucharistic Consecration, we encounter the terms or expressions "holy things," "holy diskos," "holy chalice," "divine gifts," "holy or sacred gifts," and "oblation of worthy gifts."

3. The Commemorations of the Proskomide

We have already mentioned that in the ancient records of the Divine Liturgy the Proskomide was composed of the rites of the offering of bread and wine and the prayer of prothesis. (Prothesis, proposition, oblation, preparation; Proskomide and offertory or offering are synonyms.) Not until the beginning of the tenth century does the primitive rite of the Proskomide become enriched with new ceremonies, first with the complicated rite of cutting the Lamb from the prosphora, then later with other rites, such as the cutting and offering of the particles of bread in honor of the Blessed Virgin Mary, the saints and the living and the dead. This latter rite is called the Proskomide rite of commemoration, We say "Proskomide" commemoration in order to distinguish it from the eucharistic commemorations which follow the consecration of the holy gifts.

The triple commemoration made its way into the Proskomide and developed in the eleventh and twelfth centuries. The scholars Muretov and Petrovskij affirm that the commemorations of the saints, the dead and the living in the Proskomide were taken from the triple commemoration which followed the Consecration in the Liturgy of the Faithful. Originally the Proskomide commemorations of saints and of the living and the dead were left to the discretion of the priest; hence, in the manuscripts of the Proskomide of the twelfth and fourteenth centuries, we observe a long list of names, notably of saints. These numerous additions in the commemorations and the extremely complicated system of cutting particles in memory of the saints, the living and the dead were remedied by Patriarch Philotheus (1354–1376) in his *Diataxis*." He revised the method of commemorations, fixed their order and the number of *prosphorae* and selected prayers suitable to the rite of cutting particles.

In the present Proskomide, the priest commemorates the Blessed Virgin Mary first, then the saints, the living, the dead, and finally concludes with a remembrance of himself. As he commemorates the names, the priest cuts from the phosphora one particle at a time and arranges each particle on the diskos in the prescribed order next to the eucharistic Lamb.

The commemoration of the saints opens with the commemoration of the Blessed Virgin Mary. The priest cuts from a separate prosphora a particle and prays:

> In honor and in memory of our most blessed Lady, the Mother of God and ever-virgin Mary through whose prayers, O Lord, accept this sacrifice upon Thy own altar in heaven.

Placing the particle to the right of the eucharistic Lamb, he adds:

> At Thy right hand stood the Queen dressed in golden vesture adorned with many colors. (Ps 44:10)

Then the priest cuts out a particle in honor of the different classes of saints and, placing them on the diskos he mentions their titles. The next commemoration is that of the angels:

> In honor and memory of the honored, incorporeal powers of heaven,

to be followed by the prophets, apostles, fathers and bishops of the Church, martyrs, miracle-workers, the religious, the parents of the Blessed Virgin Mary and finally the saint of the day.

The particle in honor of the Blessed Virgin Mary is smaller than that of the eucharistic Lamb but larger than those in honor of the saints. The particles of the saints are arranged on the left side of the eucharistic Lamb; that of the Blessed Virgin Mary, as we have noted, on the right. In this way the dignity of the Blessed Virgin Mary among the saints is emphasized. On account of her dignity, her role in the redemption and her great sanctity, she occupies the first place after Jesus Christ. For this reason the words of the Psalmist, recited during the Proskomide, refer to the Blessed Virgin Mary as a "Queen," who stands "at the right" of Jesus Christ, the King of the universe.

From each category of saints only certain ones of the most outstanding are mentioned, as for example, of the prophets, St. John the Baptist, of the apostles, Sts. Peter and Paul, of the fathers and holy men, St. Basil, St. Gregory the Theologian, St. John Chrysostom, St. Nicholas, Sts. Cyril and Methodius and St. Josaphat. The commemoration of the saints concludes with the words:

> And all the saints through whose prayers protect us, O God.

In the commemoration of the living, which follows that of the saints, the priest first mentions the Church, the hierarchy, the Pope of Rome, the archbishop and metropolitan, bishops of the diocese by name and all the bishops, priests, deacons, superiors of monasteries and all those who concelebrate or assist at the Divine Liturgy. This commemoration of the ecclesiastical hierarchy ends with the commemoration of all our brothers whom Thou hast called into Thy communion, through Thy tenderness of heart, all-gracious Lord.

This is a general commemoration of all the religious whom God has called to His service.

The priest then commemorates in a special way those for whom he personally wishes to pray. The particles of the living are placed below or at the bottom of the Lamb.

Finally, we have the commemoration of the dead, among whom the founders of the monastery and church are given first mention. The priest can also, if he so desires, commemorate a deceased bishop from whom he received the sacrament of Holy Orders, and his departed parents, relatives, friends, benefactors, etc. Finally, in the end he commemorates

all our fathers and brothers of the true faith who have fallen asleep in the hope of resurrection, eternal life and communion with Thee, O Lord, Lover of men.

The triple commemoration concludes with the commemoration of the priest himself:

Lord, according to Thy great mercy, remember my own unworthiness, and forgive me all my sins, both voluntary and involuntary.

The commemorations of the Proskomide, though developed at a comparatively later date—eleventh to fourteenth centuries—must be regarded as a remnant of the old ancient Christian community gift-offering. As we mentioned earlier, in the first centuries of Christianity there prevailed the custom of community gift-offering in which the faithful offered gifts not only for themselves but also for those who were not present in church, for those who had requested that gifts be offered up in their name as well as for the deceased. When the Divine Liturgy was celebrated at the tomb of a martyr or saint, the faithful also offered gifts in his honor. Hence, the commemoration of saints, and the commemoration of the living and the dead in the rite of the Proskomide are obviously a vestige of this ancient practice, with the difference that the priest alone, instead of the people, now makes these community offerings. The particles of bread which he cuts and places on the diskos symbolize the faithful who participate in the Divine Liturgy and partake of the fruit of Christ's unbloody Sacrifice.

The commemoration of the saints, the living and the dead express the Christian dogma concerning the Communion of Saints. The Church of Christ is His Mystical Body, a holy community, composed of the saints in heaven (Church Triumphant), the faithful on earth (Church Militant) and the souls in Purgatory (Church Suffering). All the members of Christ's Mystical Body, including the Blessed Virgin Mary, owe their redemption and sanctification to the Lamb of God.

Hence the particles, which the priest cuts out in honor of the saints and in memory of the deceased are placed next to the eucharistic Lamb, who is the head and lifegiving principle of His Mystical Body, the Communion of Saints.

4. The Use of the Prosphora or Altar-Bread in the Rite of Proskomide

In cutting the eucharistic Lamb and the smaller particles for the triple commemoration, the rite of Proskomide prescribes the use of the prosphorae. They are small breads set aside especially for the eucharistic offering, hence the name *prosphora* which comes from the Greek word *prosphero*—I bring forth,—I present,—I offer, and *prosphoron*—that which is offered.

The earliest liturgical manuscript makes no mention of the prosphorae. All that they record is that the priest places "bread" on the diskos. The number of prosphorae was not immediately established. When, at the beginning of the eleventh century, the practice of the triple commemoration and the rite of cutting small particles were introduced into the rite of Proskomide, the number of prosphorae increased. In some liturgical manuscripts three, four and five prosphorae were mentioned, while in others as many as six or seven. Not until the fourteenth century, when the *Diataxis* of Patriarch Philotheus appeared, did the custom of using five prosphorae finally become established. However, not all Churches use all five; some use one or three; the old Russian ritualists retained the custom of using five.

From the first prosphora, the priest cuts the eucharistic Lamb, from the second a particle in honor of the Blessed Virgin Mary, from the third, particles in memory of the saints, from the fourth, particles in commemoration of the dead, and from the last, particles in remembrance of the living. In the cutting of the Lamb from the prosphora Byzantine liturgical commentators saw a symbol representing Jesus Christ as being born of the Blessed Virgin Mary, from whom Jesus Christ, the Lamb of God, assumed human flesh.

This interpretation is a little too artificial and farfetched, and it is completely out of keeping with the prayers that accompany the rite of excision. These prayers do not allude to Christ's being born of the Blessed Virgin Mary, but to the voluntary sacrifice of the Lamb of God, His passion and death. According to the opinion of the Byzantine liturgist, Nicholas Cabasilas, the prosphora from which the priest cuts the Lamb represents mankind, i.e., "the human race." Christ, "the first born of every creature," willed to take upon Himself a human body in order to sacrifice it in atonement for the sins of mankind. The rite of cutting the Lamb from the prosphora was supposed to symbolize the willingness of the Lamb of God to sacrifice Himself.[1]

If the first prosphora symbolizes Jesus Christ, the Lamb of God, then the second prosphora from which a particle is cut in memory of our Blessed Virgin Mary symbolizes her role in the sacrifice of the Lamb. The same can be said of the prosphora from which particles in honor of the saints are cut: it symbolizes the Church Triumphant which owes its heavenly glory to the sacrifice of the Lamb of God. The fourth prosphora is the symbol of the Church Militant, the fifth, of the Church Suffering, for from the fourth and fifth prosphorae, particles are cut in memory of the living and the dead.

---

[1] N. Cabasilas, *A Commentary on the Divine Liturgy;* Migne, PG, 150, 379–380.

From this we may see the profound symbolism the rite of cutting the Lamb and particles conveys. As we have mentioned, the particles on the diskos symbolize the Mystical Body of Christ with Christ the eucharistic Lamb as its head and center. Around Christ is gathered His whole Church, which He redeemed with the price of His Blood. Here we recall the vision of St. John which spontaneously suggests itself:

> After this I saw a great multitude, which no man could number, of all nations, and tribes, and peoples, and tongues, standing before the throne, and in sight of the Lamb, clothed with white robes, and palms in their hands: And they cried with a loud voice, saying: Salvation to our God, who sitteth upon the throne, and to the Lamb. (Apoc 7:9, 10)

5. The Rite of Veiling or Covering the Holy Gifts

When the priest concludes the rite of cutting the particles from the prosphorae in honor of the saints and in memory of the living and the dead, he covers the holy gifts. The rite of covering is accompanied by the incensing of the star and the veils; we shall explain these two acts separately.

First of all, after the priest has finished cutting the Lamb and particles from the prosphorae and placing them on the diskos, he places over them the asteriskos or star. The purpose of the star is to protect the Lamb and the particles from contact with the veil with which the priest covers them. But before placing the star over the holy gifts, the priest first holds it over the thurible to be incensed, and as he places it on the diskos, he repeats the words of the Gospel:

And the star stood over the place where the child was. (Mt 2:9)

The priest covers the diskos and the asteriskos with the veil after he has incensed it and recites the words of the Psalmist:

> The Lord hath reigned, He is clothed with beauty. The Lord is clothed with strength and hath girded Himself. For He hath made the earth firm, which shall not be moved. Thy throne is prepared from of old: Thou art from everlasting. The floods have lifted up, O Lord; the floods have lifted up their voices; the floods have lifted up their waves, with the noise of many waters. Wonderful are the surges of the sea: wonderful is the Lord on high. Thy testimonies are become exceedingly credible. Holiness becometh Thy house, O Lord, unto length of days. (Ps 92:1–7)

Finally, the priest covers both the diskos and the chalice with a larger third veil called the *"aer"* or firmament. While performing the rite of the last veiling or covering the priests says the *troparion*:

> Shelter us with the shadow of Thy wings, and drive away from us every foe and adversary. Make our life peaceful, O Lord, have mercy on us, and on Thy world, and save our souls, as a Good One and Lover of men.

The present-day rite of veiling the holy gifts was prescribed by Philotheus, in his *Diataxis*. This rite is of much later origin. We come across the use of the asteriskos in the rite of the Proskomide in the fourteenth century, although it was known to exist in some places toward the end of the eleventh.

The star and the veils serve to protect the holy gifts from dirt, dust, flies, insects and other foreign matter. However, as in other rites, so also in this rite of veiling interpreters of the Liturgy searched for a symbolic meaning. Medieval Byzantine commentators explained the star as a symbol of the Star of Bethlehem which stood over the new-born Christ. Under the influence of this symbolic interpretation, the attendant prayer was added to the rite of Proskomide:

And the star came and stood over the place where the child was. (Mt 2:9)

Under the same influence the veils came to represent the swaddling clothes in which the Blessed Virgin Mary wrapped the Child Jesus after His birth. To some commentators they symbolize the linens in which the Body of the dead Christ was wrapped. Still others use both symbols antithetically—as representing both the birth and the burial of our Lord. Most probably, though, the asteriskos and veils have a purely practical purpose; therefore it would be pointless to seek out their symbolic meaning. As for the prayers accompanying the veiling, it must be said that they were arbitrarily chosen and bear no real relation to the liturgical rite. They originated at a time when it was the fashion to use verses and passages from Holy Scripture, adapting them to the various rites regardless of whether or not they had any bearing on the rites.

6. The Rite of Incensing the Holy Gifts

The incensing of the holy gifts is connected with the rite of veiling, for the priest incenses the star and three veils before he places them over the holy gifts. When he has finished covering the holy gifts, he takes the thurible with burning incense and incenses them while reciting the prayer of Prothesis.

Although we first meet with the incensing of the holy gifts in the liturgical manuscripts of the eleventh century, the custom of incensing during the rite of the Proskomide and the Divine Liturgy is of ancient date. In the first centuries of Christianity, the Church did not use the censer in the divine services. Some of the Fathers objected to the use of incense and there were even explicit restrictions issued against it. The reason for this attitude was that the censer was regarded as a symbol of pagan worship during the period of the persecutions and a sign of apostasy. When the Christians were forced to renounce Jesus Christ, they had to offer incense as a sacrifice to the gods as a sign of their renunciation. However, when the Church was granted religious freedom in the later centuries, and Christianity eventually prevailed over paganism, her attitude toward the use of incense changed. No longer was incensing a symbol of pagan sacrifices but like the Old Testament sacrifices and ceremonies, it became a part of the New Testament Christian worship.

Incense and rite of incensation in Christian worship has the same meaning and symbolism as it had in the pagan and Old Testament cults. From remotest antiquity the burning of fragrant seeds or incense on hot coals was regarded as a natural sign of adoration and veneration of the deity. It symbolized the subjection and resignation of man's will to that of the deity, his readiness to offer any sacrifice to the deity, and the desire to be as pleasing to Him as the odor of the incense which rises from the man-made altar to the heavenly throne of God. In short, incense is the symbol of adoration, especially of our desire to please God, to obtain answers to our prayers and to secure additional graces from Him.

This incense has this same meaning when in the rite of Proskomide, the priest incenses the holy gifts. It is a symbol of our desire to have God receive and accept our sacrifices, to have Him remember us and to have Him shower His heavenly graces upon those who offer the sacrifices. We shall see later that the prayer of Prothesis, which is accompanied by the incensing of the priest, expresses that which the incensing symbolizes. In the rite of Proskomide it is called the "prayer of incensation":

> Unto Thee, O Christ our God, do we offer incense for an odor of spiritual fragrance: which do Thou accept upon Thy most heavenly altar, and send us in return the grace of Thy most Holy Spirit.

It is evident from these words that incense is a symbol of the spirit of sacrifice. Through the rite of incensing, the priest, on behalf of all the people, asks God to accept the holy gifts along with the prayers of the people and to bestow upon them His graces. The Psalmist prayed in like manner, comparing his prayers to incense:

> Let my prayer be directed as incense in Thy sight; the lifting up of my hands, as evening sacrifice. (Ps 140:2)

St. John also describes in one of his visions how:

> . . . when he had opened the book, the four living creatures and the four and twenty ancients fell down before the Lamb, having every one of them harps, and golden vials full of odors, which are the prayers of saints. (Apoc 5:8)

In the interpretations of the medieval commentators on the Byzantine Liturgy, the incensing of the holy gifts referred to the gifts of gold, myrrh and frankincense which the Wise Men brought from the Orient and presented to the Child Jesus. The commentary assigned to St. Herman gives us another symbolic interpretation of the rite of incensing that is very original: the thurible symbolizes the human nature of Christ, the hot coals His divinity, the smoke the fragrant breath of the Holy Spirit. The rite of incensing itself signifies the sweetly-scented balsam and ointment with which the Body of Christ was anointed, as well as the gifts of the Wise Men, and finally the good deeds of the Christian.[2] We can perceive in these ideas the creative, and fertile imaginations of the old liturgical commentators, who, unfortunately, encumbered their works with such superfluous and irrelevant symbolic interpretations having little or no intrinsic relation to the ritual actions and liturgical texts.

---

[2] Migne, PG, 98, 400.

7. The Prayer of Prothesis

The offering of the eucharistic Lamb and the prayer of Prothesis are the most significant and the oldest parts of the Proskomide. The prayer of Prothesis is regarded as the essence of the whole rite, for by it the priest offers up to God the holy gifts and begs that they be accepted by Him.

The introduction to the prayer of Prothesis is the invocation:

Blessed be our God Who thus is well pleased,

and the invitation to pray:

For the offered precious gifts, let us pray to the Lord.

Then the priest recites the prayer itself:

O God, our God, who didst send the heavenly bread, the nourishment of the whole world, our Lord and God Jesus Christ, our Savior and Redeemer and Benefactor, blessing and sanctifying us: Thyself bless this oblation, and accept it on Thy most heavenly altar. Remember as a Good One and Lover of men those who have offered and those for whom they have offered; and preserve us blameless in the sacerdotal ministry of Thy divine mysteries. For hallowed and glorified be Thy most honorable and majestic name of the Father and the Son and the Holy Spirit now and forever and unto ages of ages. Amen.

The words of the prayer of Prothesis are convincing proof that the prayer originated at the time when community gift-offering was practiced in the Church. In it, those who "brought" the gifts of oblation as well as those "for whom these gifts were brought and offered" were mentioned. The prayer of Prothesis is, therefore, a prayer which the priest recited after the community offering and the reading of the diptychs or list of donors or benefactors. It was preserved in the rite of Proskomide even after the community offering had fallen into disuse and the rite of Proskomide had been moved to the beginning of the Mass as a private liturgical function of the priest.

The contents of the prayer of Prothesis claim special attention, for in it Christ is called the "heavenly bread" and "the food for the world," "Savior, Redeemer and Benefactor" of man, for He blesses and sanctifies him. The object of the prayer is to entreat God "to accept and bless" the holy gifts. The words: "most heavenly altar" are an allusion to heaven where God dwells and to the altar which St. John describes in his "Apocalypse":

And I saw: and behold in the midst of the throne and of the four living creatures, and in the midst of the ancients, a Lamb standing as it were slain, having seven horns and seven eyes: which are the seven Spirits of God, sent forth into all the earth. Saying with a loud voice: The Lamb that was slain is worthy to receive power, and divinity, and wisdom, and strength, and honor, and glory, and benediction. And every creature which is in heaven, and on the earth, and under the earth, and such as are in the sea, and all that are in them, I heard all saying: To Him that sitteth on the throne, and to the Lamb, benediction, and honor, and glory, and power, for ever and ever. (Apoc 5:6; 12:13)

The rite of incensing the holy gifts and the prayer of Prothesis are the formal act of gift-offering. In the prayer the priest turns to the Heavenly Father, who deigned to give the world the "heavenly bread" in the person of Jesus Christ, asking Him to bless and accept these gifts. And because the holy gifts symbolize Jesus Christ the Lamb of God, along with His Mystical Body, the priest asks at the end of the prayer of Prothesis that he "without judgment" be made worthy to perform the priestly functions of the Divine Liturgy. Hence, the priest desires not only that God accept the holy gifts which are pleasing to Him, since they represent Christ and mankind redeemed by Him, but also that his personal participation in the Divine Liturgy be pleasing to God.

8. The Conclusion of the Proskomide

In the ancient rite, the prayer of Prothesis concluded the rites and prayers of the Proskomide. In the present-day rite, the prayer of Prothesis is followed by a "dismissal" and then a *troparion*: "In the grave . . .," which concludes the Proskomide and at the same time effects a transition to the Liturgy of the Catechumens. The "dismissal" is said by the priest, and the *troparion*, "in the grave bodily," by the deacon as he begins to incense the altar and the sanctuary.

The "dismissal" was introduced into the Proskomide probably to make it evident that the Proskomide is a separate liturgical function. In fact, each liturgical rite and service has its own conclusion or "dismissal." The aim of the dismissal is to express gratitude, to render praise to Christ our God and to wish all the participants abundant grace and salvation through the intercession of the Blessed Virgin Mary and the saints.

Besides the general dismissal, the rite of Proskomide includes still another *troparion,* taken from the services of Holy Saturday. This *troparion* is apparently a later insertion of the fourteenth century. The *Diataxis* of Philotheus already mentioned it, but not all the handwritten or printed Sluzhebnyks or Liturgikons had it in the rite of Proskomide. The *troparion* was added, probably under the influence of the symbolic interpretations of the Proskomide and the altar. In medieval commentaries on the Divine Liturgy, the altar represented the grave where Christ was laid, and the placing of the holy gifts on the altar was symbolic of the placing of Christ in the sepulcher.

The words of the *troparion* clearly allude to the burial of Christ:

> In the grave bodily, in limbo with the soul as God, in paradise with the thief, and on the throne Thou wast, O Christ, with the Father and the Holy Spirit filling all things, O Uncircumscribed.

The *troparion* has profound dogmatic meaning savoring of a paradox, for it speaks of the inscrutable mystery of the ubiquity of Christ and the inseparability of the hypostic union of the divine and the human natures in Christ. Yet despite the profundity of its meaning, it does not seem to have any special connection with the prayer of Oblation or with the other prayers and rites of the Proskomide. The author of this *troparion* is supposed to have been St. John Damascene.

SELECT BIBLIOGRAPHY

Dmitrevskiy, J., *Istoricheskoe, dogmaticheskoe i tainstvennoe izyasnenie na liturghiyu,* Moskva, 1804.

Bessarion, bishop., *Tolkovanie na bozhestvennu liturghiyu po chinu sv. I. Zlatoustaho i sv. Vasiliya V.,* Moskva, 1895.

Muretov, S., *O pominovenii bezplotnikh sil na proskomidii,* Moskva, 1897.

———— *K svidyetelstvam o chislye prosfor na proskomidii v grecheskoy tserkve,* Moskva, 1896.

Palmov, N., *O prosforakh na proskomidii,* Kiev, 1902; S. Ch., *Istoricheskoe proiskhozhdenie i znamenie izyatiya chastits iz prosfor,* ("Vyera i Razum," 1906, no. 6, pp. 345–353) .

———— *O chislye prosfor na proskomidii po drevlepismennim Solovetskim Sluzhebnikam,* ("Pravo. Sobes.," 1856, pp. 148–169).

Mandala, M., *La Protesi della liturgia nel rito bizantino-greco,* Grottaferrata, 1935.

Borgia, Nilo, *Le Liturgie Orientali e la Liturgia Bizantina,* ("Il Bolletino della Badia di Grottaferrata," no. 4, Dicembre, 1933).

Petrides, S., *Asterisque,* ("Dict. d'Arch. Chret. et de la Liturgie," I, 2. partie, pp. 3002–3003).

Atchley, G. G., *A history of use of Incense,* London, 1909.

Fehrenback, E., *Encens,* ("Dict. d'Arch. chr. et de la Lit.," V, 1 partie, pp. 1–21), Paris, 1922.

Leclerque, N., *Encensoir,* ("Dict. d'Arch. chr. et de la Lit.," V., 1 partie, pp. 22–33), Paris, 1922.

Section 2, *THE LITURGY OF THE CATECHUMENS*
(Liturgy of the Word)

Chapter I

PRELIMINARY REMARKS

The Liturgy of the Catechumens constitutes the second part of the Divine Liturgy. It follows immediately the rite of Proskomide and includes the rites and prayers from the invocation of the Triune God to the end of the ektene of the catechumens before the Great Entrance.

Today, the Liturgy of the Catechumens is so closely united with the Liturgy of the Faithful that one can hardly perceive their distinct characters, origins and roles although in the first centuries of Christianity this distinction was noticeable.

In order to promote a better understanding of the rites, prayers, structure and spirit of the Liturgy of the Catechumens, we offer some preliminary remarks about its name, origin, historical, evolution, characteristic traits, role and symbolism.

1. The Name—Liturgy of the Catechumens

The second part of the Divine Liturgy was known for many centuries as the Liturgy of the "Catechumens" because during this part of the primitive Divine Liturgy not only Christians i.e., those who were baptized, were allowed to be present but also those who were not yet baptized, but were preparing themselves for the reception of Baptism. These formed a separate class of people called the "catechumens," a name derived from the Greek word *catechein* which means to teach aloud, to instruct. The verb is literally translated into the Old Slavonic as *ohlashaty* which means to inform or notify someone orally, by voice, and the noun *catechumen* is translated as *ohlasheny*.

The catechumens were not regarded as members of the Christian community and were excluded from participating in the rites of the Unbloody Sacrifice and Holy Communion. On the other hand, they were permitted to participate in that part of the Divine Liturgy in which the reading of the Scriptures took place, and so this part of the Divine Liturgy was referred to as the "Liturgy of the Catechumens."

Contemporary liturgists, however, call the Liturgy of the Catechumens, the Liturgy of the Word, or the homiletic-didactic part of the Liturgy. The latter name corresponds best to the essence and character of the Liturgy of the Catechumens, for in this Liturgy, it is the word of God, i.e., the reading of the Sacred Scriptures that is inculcated and not sacrifice, as in the Liturgy of the Faithful.

2. Origin of the Liturgy of the Catechumens

The structure and constituent parts of the Liturgy of the Catechumens do not directly owe their origins to Jesus Christ. Although it originated in Apostolic times, its internal structure was largely due to the influence of the Jewish synagogue. The Apostles and their successors used the services of the synagogue as a model, giving them a Christian character, meaning and form.

The Jews had two services—one involving bloody and unbloody sacrifices offered in the temple of Jerusalem and the other the service conducted every Saturday in the synagogue. This latter consisted of community prayers interwoven with the chanting of Psalms, the reading and explanation of the Scriptures and a community prayer which concluded the services. The synagogue service was characterized by prayer and instruction and had nothing to do with sacrifices or sacrificial offerings.

The Gospels are evidence that Jesus and the Apostles attended the Saturday synagogue services. St. Luke gives us an account of one such occasion, when Christ stood in the midst of those present and read and explained a passage from the Scriptures (Lk 4:16–21). The Apostles followed the example of Christ, for even after His Ascension they frequented the Saturday synagogue services. Only for the "breaking of bread," i.e., the offering of the eucharistic sacrifice, did they meet with the other Christians in private homes. The Saturday synagogue services proved very useful to the Apostles who themselves were Jews, for listening to the Scriptures being read and explained, they had the opportunity to confirm the fulfillment of the Old Testament prophecies concerning Jesus Christ and to explain the true sense and meaning of the Scriptures to the new Christian converts. This prayer-instruction service was adopted from the Jewish synagogue by the primitive Church and very rapidly assumed a Christian character and meaning, for, besides the reading of the Old Testament, the reading of the New Testament (i.e. the Gospels, Acts of the Apostles, the Letters of St. Paul and other Apostles) eventually became a practice.

3. Historical Development of the Liturgy of the Catechumens

As early as the first century there came about a complete separation of the first Christians from the synagogue, because the Christians became convinced that their hopes of converting the Jews to the Christian faith were futile. Indeed a great gulf arose between the two groups. The Christians were ostracized and so there was no room for them in the synagogue. They came to be regarded as traitors to the faith of their ancestors and to the laws of the Old Testament, and were excommunicated from the Saturday services. Besides, the pagans were being converted in large numbers and they had no knowledge of Jewish religious services which to them were strange and foreign. For several reasons, then, the Christians abandoned the synagogue and began to conduct their services separately.

The christianization of the synagogue (sabbath) services can clearly be seen from the fact that the Christians began conducting their services on Sunday and not on Saturday, as before. They also gathered on other days for community prayer and the reading of the Scriptures. In this latter, preference was given to the books of the New Testament, although the Jewish custom of singing Psalms and reading selections from the Old Testament, especially those that referred to Jesus Christ, the Messiah, was still retained.

A further step toward christianization of the synagogue services was taken when the Christians began to hold these prayer-instruction services in conjunction with the "breaking of bread," i.e., the Eucharistic Sacrifice. This became an established practice in the post-Apostolic period. From the description of the ancient Christian Liturgy given by St. Justin, the Martyr, we can conclude that the homiletic-didactic service served, at that time, as an introduction to Eucharistic Sacrifice and that together they formed one whole. The Divine Liturgy, according to Justin's description, began with the reading of both the New and the Old Testaments, followed by a sermon in which the one presiding over the congregation explained the Scriptures and exhorted his listeners to observe the commandments. The faithful then recited common prayers and greeted one another with the kiss of peace. After this the deacons brought bread, wine and water for the Eucharistic Sacrifice which, after being consecrated, was distributed to the faithful in Holy Communion.

In later centuries the Liturgy of the Word, i.e. the homiletic-didactic service, merged with the Liturgy of the Faithful, and although to the Christians the service was one in practice, theoretically they were two entirely distinct services, for while the catechumens were permitted to assist at the Liturgy of the Word, only baptized believers took part in the Liturgy of the Faithful. Even after these two Liturgies were united, the custom of celebrating them separately still prevailed. For example, Silvia Etherea, a pious pilgrim (end of the fourth century) who journeyed to the Holy Land, relates in her diary titled *Pilgrimage* that in Jerusalem, after celebrating the Liturgy of the Catechumens in one church, the bishop, with the faithful, would immediately proceed to another and there celebrate the Liturgy of the Faithful. The same pilgrim writes that the Liturgy of the Catechumens was omitted on Wednesdays and Fridays of Lent and that only the Liturgy of the Faithful was celebrated on those days. It is clear, then, that at that time there existed a distinction beween the two services.

4. Character of the Liturgy of the Catechumens

The Liturgy of the Catechumens differs from that of the Faithful not only by reason of its origin and unique historical development, but also by its internal character. The structure and scheme of the Liturgy of the Catechumens suggests its origin in the homiletic-didactic service of the synagogue. Actually the basic characteristic of the Liturgy of the Catechumens is that it is the Liturgy of the Word, while the Liturgy of the Faithful is the Liturgy of Sacrifice.

Therefore, in the rites and texts of the Liturgy of the Catechumens we find nothing directly relating to the Eucharistic Sacrifice, and if there are allusions to it, they are interpolations and additions of a later date. In this there is an essential difference between the Liturgy of the Catechumens and that of the first part of the Divine Liturgy, the Proskomide, which is a preparation of the priest for the Eucharistic Sacrifice and a preparation of the eucharistic elements. The rites, prayers, structure and symbolism of the Proskomide reveal its relation to the Eucharistic Sacrifice. Although the Proskomide is separated from the Liturgy of Sacrifice by the Liturgy of the Catechumens, nevertheless, in content, purpose, and character, it is related to the Liturgy of Sacrifice. We have already mentioned this in the commentary on the Proskomide where it was pointed out that the original and true position of the Proskomide was not at the very beginning of the Liturgy, but at the beginning of the Liturgy of the Faithful or the Liturgy of Sacrifice.

The Liturgy of the Catechumens is not so directly related to the Liturgy of the Faithful as is the Proskomide. The contents of the Liturgy of the Catechumens consists of prayers and songs of a general nature, and even readings and explanations of Holy Scripture. The prayers, chants, and the reading and explanation of Holy Scripture in today's Liturgy help to predispose and prepare the priest and faithful for the Eucharistic Sacrifice and Holy Communion. Nonetheless, each component part of the Liturgy of the Catechumens has its own purpose and character even though it bears no relation to the Liturgy of Sacrifice. The object of the prayers and chants in the Liturgy of the Catechumens is to glorify God, to thank Him for all His blessings and to make known our many needs. The reading and explanation of the Holy Scripture also has its purpose, namely, to enlighten Christians with the word of God and to give them direction in life.

The distinctive character of the ancient Liturgy of the Catechumens lies also in the fact that it was substituted at times by other services, as for example, Vespers, the rite of Baptism, the Consecration of a bishop and the ordination of a priest or a deacon. Various liturgical documents testify that in place of the Liturgy of the Catechumens, the sacrament of Baptism was sometimes administered to be followed immediately by the Liturgy of the Sacrifice, during which the newly baptised person or persons received Holy Communion. Even today we may detect a vestige of this ancient practice of celebrating the Divine Liturgy with Vespers, before the holy days of Christmas and Epiphany, and on Holy Thursday and Holy Saturday. In such celebrations, Vespers almost completely replaces the Liturgy of the Catechumens. Indeed the very structure of Vespers is quite similar to that of the Liturgy of the Catchumens. especially Solemn Vespers, which includes besides the prayers, songs and Psalms, the reading of the Holy Scripture.

Another distinct characteristic of the Liturgy of the Catechumens is that it was sometimes regarded as part of the divine office, i.e. the everyday services, which the monks conducted in their churches. Thus, for example, in the larger monasteries of Palestine, the monks of various nationalities—Greeks, Syrians, Armenians—after celebrating in their respective churches the Liturgy of the Word, along with the other services, would all convene in one particular (e.g., Greek) church and there celebrate in common the Liturgy of Sacrifice.

The practice of celebrating the Liturgy of the Catechumens only on Sundays and feastdays, and on ordinary days the Liturgy of the Faithful was alone retained by the Nestorians until the eighteenth century and serves as a proof that the Liturgy of the Word had no direct or intrinsic connection with the Liturgy of Sacrifice. Although it formed one liturgical unit with the Liturgy of the Faithful, nevertheless, it remained distinct from it.

5. Role of the Liturgy of the Catechumens in the Divine Liturgy

As we mentioned in the preceding section, the purpose of the Liturgy of the Catechumens is to glorify God through song, common prayer for the various needs of the faithful, and through learning and adopting the Christian way of life by means of reading and explaining the word of God. Hence, its role consists in a general worship of God and not in particular expressions of this divine worship, as for example, in the offering of sacrifice.

Another characteristic of the Liturgy of the Catechumens is that the people take a greater part in it than in the Liturgy of the Faithful. In it the people along with the deacon, engage in common prayer. The deacon sings the *ektene* of petition, and the people prayerfully respond. Even in the chantings of the antiphons, *troparia* and hymns, the faithful participate actively. While the priest gives the intonations and recites the silent prayers, the people and the deacon accompany him by singing their supplications. The role of the priest in the Liturgy of the Catechumens does become greater when he celebrates without the deacon, for then he recites all that which, according to the Order of Celebration, the deacon should recite. However, the actual role of the priest begins with the Liturgy of the Faithful when he offers the unbloody Sacrifice of the New Testament. The priest, by virtue of his office, is primarily one who offers sacrifice to God in the name of the people. The other functions which he performs in his various capacities as teacher, pastor, preacher and superior are actually secondary to his first and essential function of one who offers sacrifices.

Precisely because the Liturgy of the Catechumens is of its nature and character the Liturgy of the Word and not of Sacrifice, it permits a greater community participation. Theoretically at least, the Liturgy of the Catechumens could be celebrated with or without a minimum participation of the priest. So it was in the first centuries when the priest celebrated the Liturgy of Sacrifice, while the Liturgy of the Word was celebrated without his participation.

However, we do not wish to be understood as saying that the Liturgy of the Word had no relation whatever to the Eucharistic Sacrifice, for in the present-day Divine Liturgy we do not discern the sharp distinction between the Liturgy of the Faithful and the Liturgy of the Catechumens that was made in the first centuries. Today, at least, the division appears to be a purely scientific one. Nevertheless, in interpreting the prayers and rites of the Divine Liturgy, attention must be drawn to the origin, historical development and character of each constituent part in order to understand their roles, aims and significance in relation to the Divine Liturgy as a whole.

6. Symbolism of the Liturgy of the Catechumens

In the various interpretations of the rites and texts of the Proskomide we saw the great role of symbolism which the texts and rites themselves suggest and which the commentators sought to develop. Now, before beginning our interpretation of the rites and texts of the Liturgy of the Catechumens, we may well inquire whether this part also possesses its own symbolism.

In the Liturgy of the Catechumens there are undoubtedly many rites and texts capable of symbolic interpretation. We shall discuss this later when we examine each of its rites and texts.

Nicholas Cabasilas, one of the proficient Byzantine commentators of the Divine Liturgy, in the very introduction to his commentary, stresses that the Divine Liturgy in its entirety represents Christ and His work of salvation. The Eucharistic consecration represents His death, resurrection and ascension; all the rites preceding the Eucharistic consecration represent the events that occurred prior to Christ's passion.[1] In another place, he says that the Divine Liturgy is "the history" of what Christ did for our salvation.[2] This is not exclusively the opinion of Cabasilas, for before him there were commentators who viewed the Divine Liturgy as a liturgical chronology of the life and death of Jesus Christ.

Thus, for example, Theodore Andides, a mid thirteenth century commentator, in the introduction to his liturgical commentary, tries to prove that the Divine Liturgy is a representation of the life of Jesus Christ. A great number of priests, says Theodore, know that the Divine Liturgy typifies the death and resurrection of Christ, but few realize that the Liturgy is also a mystical portrayal or representation of His whole life—His conception, birth, hidden life, baptism in the Jordan, three years public life as a teacher, His passion and death. According to Theodore Andides, all the rites of the Divine Liturgy are symbols of Christ's great work of redemption.[3]

---

[1] N. Cabasilas, *A Commentary on the Divine Liturgy*, Migne, PG, 150, 369–371.

[2] *Ibid.* 404.

[3] Theodore Andides, bishop, *A Brief commentary on the symbols and mysteries of the Divine Liturgy*, Migne, PG, 140, 417–421.

According to this concept, the Proskomide represents Christ's birth and His hidden life in Nazareth. The Liturgy of the Catechumens symbolizes His epiphany or public appearance and His preaching of good tidings—the Gospel, and all the events in His life before His triumphal entrance into the city of Jerusalem and His passion. The Liturgy of the Faithful is the dramatic and symbolic representation of all those events from His triumphant entry into Jerusalem to His passion, death, resurrection, ascension and pentecost.

Now, the Divine Liturgy is, without doubt, a memorial to Jesus Christ and His great work of salvation. Christ, Himself, in instituting the Liturgy at the Last Supper, ordered the Apostles to celebrate it in His memory. (Lk 22:20) The Divine Liturgy is a living memorial of the sacrifice of Jesus Christ, for in every Divine Liturgy that very sacrifice is renewed, repeated and continued in a mysterious and unbloody manner. Nevertheless, there is no rational basis for regarding the Divine Liturgy as a chronology of events and mysteries connected with the life of Our Savior. Such an interpretation has very little foundation in the structure, contents and historical development of the rites and prayers of the Divine Liturgy. Hence, a symbolic interpretation of every one of these rites and texts as representing and recalling the various events in the life of Jesus Christ cannot withstand criticism.

In our interpretation of the Liturgy of the Catechumens, as in our interpretation of the Proskomide, we shall acknowledge only such symbolic interpretations as have a rational basis in the liturgical rites and texts. Those which are not intrinsically related to the texts and rites we shall regard as merely subjective views or interesting theories of the various liturgical commentators.

Chapter II

THE BEGINNING OF THE LITURGY
OF THE CATECHUMENS

In its present form the Liturgy of the Catechumens has a well developed beginning which embraces the rite of incensing, introductory prayers and a short dialogue between priest and deacon, and culminates in a solemn doxology or invocation honoring the Blessed Trinity. Let us analyze each part of this prelude or introduction.

1. The Rite of the First Incensing

The initial rite in the Liturgy of the Catechumens is the incensing of the table of Prothesis, altar, sanctuary, iconostasis and the faithful. This incensation begins immediately after the concluding prayer of the *Proskomide,* called the prayer of dismissal, thus, marking the transition to the Liturgy of the Catechumens.

This incensing is performed by the deacon, or by the priest in the event he is celebrating without the assistance of the deacon. During the incensing of the altar, the Order of Celebration prescribes the recitation of the *troparion:* "In the grave bodily. . . ." The words of the *troparion* suggest a symbolic allusion to the altar, and that is probably why it was introduced into the Divine Liturgy. Immediately following this *troparion,* the celebrant, while incensing, recites the penitential Psalm (Ps 50) :

Have mercy on me, O God, according to the greatness of Thy mercy. . . .

It also prescribes in detail the order of incensing.

The rite of incensing at the beginning of the Divine Liturgy is not peculiar to the Byzantine-Slav Rite alone, for other rites also begin in the same manner. Moreover, it is prescribed for other divine services besides the Divine Liturgy. These facts indicate that it must be of ancient origin and undoubtedly possesses some special significance of its own.

There is one reference to the rite of incensing at the beginning of the Divine Liturgy in a commentary assigned to Dionysius the Areopagite,[1] from which we may conclude that the ceremony was already known at that time. In the liturgical commentaries of later centuries, symbolic interpretations of this rite appear. Beginning with the thirteenth century, we find rubrics which pre-

---

[1] Migne, PG, 3, 425.

scribe, for the first incensing, the recitation of the penitential Psalm 50 or Psalm 25. We also find in the ancient rubrics a direction to recite the following prayer: "Unto Thee, O Christ our God, do we offer incense. . . ."

As was pointed out in our discussion of the Proskomide, incense is a symbol of divine worship, of the spirit of sacrifice and prayer. The rite of incensing is an externalization of man's desire to have God accept his prayers and sacrifices. Such is the general meaning and symbolism of the rite of incensing not only in the Proskomide, but also in the other functions of the Divine Liturgy. The first incensing here in the Liturgy of the Catechumens also has its own additional and separate role and significance.

The first incensing must be regarded as a salutatory rite, an act of greeting those present at the Divine Liturgy. The Order of Celebration directs that not only the altar, the sanctuary, and the icons be incensed but also the faithful present in the church. The incensing of the icons and of the faithful is an expression of reverence and a sign of respect. In the East there existed the custom of washing the feet of guests and of incensing them with precious frankincense, a custom that was prevalent among the Jews, who washed the feet of their guests and anointed them with precious ointments. We have evidence of this in the touching scene in the Gospel where Mary Magdalene washed the feet of Jesus and anointed them with precious oils. (Jn 12:3–9; Lk 7:35–48)

The significance and symbolism of the first incensation, however, does not end here, for it indicates also purification and sanctification. The various peoples of the East had a deep-rooted conviction that demons roamed the places of divine worship, and so it was thought necessary to purge these places of demonic presence at the beginning of divine worship. The outward expression of this purgation was the rite of incensing,[2] which was supposed, according to this ancient belief, to have the power of purifying and sanctifying. Despite the naivete which this primitive concept reveals, nonetheless, this conviction was responsible for the introduction of the rite of incensing at the beginning of the Divine Liturgy and other religious ceremonies. The purgative character of the first incensing in the Liturgy of the Catechumens is suggested by the 50th Psalm which accompanies this rite "Have mercy on me O God . . . " and which gives expression to the repentance felt by the soul that desires to be cleansed of its sins and to "become white as snow." The words of the Psalm remind both priest and people that the evil spirits or demons which actually hover even over holy places are their sins. Sin defiles the soul, the living temple of God, and the means of purifying the soul are sincere repentance, prayer and good deeds. These truths, therefore, are expressed in a symbolic manner by the first incensing.

The character of sanctification is also joined with the purifying role of the rite of first incensing. In the Old Testament a white cloud rose above the Holy of Holies as a visible sign of God's presence in the temple of Jerusalem. In Christian churches the presence of God is made manifest in a special and more

---

[2] J. Dmitrevskiy, *Ist. Dogm. i tainstvennoe izyasnenie na liturghiyu*, Moskva, 1804, p. 47.

mysterious manner, of which the rite of incensing is only a theophanical symbol. The liturgical commentary ascribed to Dionysius the Areopagite [3] already mentioned also alludes to the symbolic sanctifying character of the first rite of incensing. Simeon of Thessalonica (fourteenth century) in his commentary, explains the sanctifying character of the rite of first incensing in the following manner: the fragrant odor of incense signifies the fullness of spiritual grace and blessings. The source of these spiritual graces and blessings is Jesus Christ, who is represented in a mysterious manner by the holy gifts. According to Simeon, the reason why the rite of incensing begins with the holy gifts on the Prothesis, is that sanctification comes from Jesus Christ whom these gifts symbolize. This sanctification is bestowed upon priest and people alike, for from Christ the grace of the Holy Spirit flows upon all.[4]

It is interesting to note that a similar symbolic implication of the rite of the first incensing is found in other Liturgies such as the Maronite, Coptic, Ethiopian and Syrian. In them we discover short prayers accompanying the rite of the first incensing in which God is asked to forgive the sins of those who participate in the Divine Liturgy and to make them holy.

2. Introductory Prayers of the Liturgy of the Catechumens

Following the first incensation, the priest, with the deacon, stands before the altar where both bow three times and recite the preparatory prayers. These prayers were once left to the free choice of the priest, but in the later manuscripts of the Divine Liturgy, they are determined by certain rubrics.[5] To the present-day form of the Liturgy of the Catechumens belong the following preparatory prayers: "O heavenly King . . . ", "Glory to God in the highest . . . ", and "O Lord, Thou wilt open my lips. . .".

In the first prayer the priest prays with the deacon to the Holy Spirit asking His assistance. The prayer "O heavenly King" is one of the most widely used, and certainly, one of the most beautiful liturgical prayers in the Byzantine-Slavonic Rite. The petitions in this prayer are concise and clear. We implore the Holy Spirit "who is everywhere present and fillest all things" to come and "dwell within us, and to cleanse us from every stain, and to save our souls" for He is the "Treasury of good things and Giver of life. . . ." The prayer "O heavenly King" is, to a certain extent, a continuation of the thought expressed in the rite of incensing and the 50th Psalm. This means that the prayer is also indicative of purification and sanctification of the soul.

The ensuing brief prayer "Glory be to God in the highest . . . " recalls the song the angels sang over the place where Christ was born. It was most likely inserted into the Liturgy of the Catechumens at the time when interpreters of the Divine Liturgy began to attach symbolic meanings such as the Nativity, to

---

[3] Migne, PG, 3, 425.

[4] *Ibid.*, 155, 288–289.

[5] De Meester, *Les origines* . . . . . , p. 313.

the Proskomide, and the Liturgy of the Catechumens. This assumption is confirmed by older documents on the Divine Liturgy which do not contain the prayer. Before the fourteenth century, we do not find the "Glory be to God in the highest . . . ", although we do find "O heavenly King," and "O Lord, Thou wilt open my lips. . . ." The content of this prayer clearly reveals the main purpose of the Divine Liturgy as a sacrifice of the New Testament which glorifies God and brings His peace to men through forgiveness of sins.

The final prayer in the introduction to the Liturgy of the Catechumens is a sincere and earnest supplication to the Lord to "open the lips" of the priest that they may "declare the praise of God." The words are again taken from Psalm 50. Its contents are related to the rite of the first incensing, to the main petition of Psalm 50 and to the prayer: "O heavenly King"; it is also a petition imploring spiritual purification and sanctification of the soul.

After this final introductory prayer, the priest kisses the gospel book, and the deacon the altar. This twofold kiss is an allusion to Jesus Christ whom the Gospels and altar symbolize. The kissing of the gospel book and the altar signifies that Christ is the author of the priesthood and the source of that divine power which the priest has received from the High Priest Christ to celebrate the Unbloody Sacrifice of the New Testament. Just as the lips of the Prophet Isaias were purified by the coals taken from the altar of God, thus making him a prophet and the ambassador of the Lord (Is 6:7), so too, the kissing of Christ, symbolized by the Holy Gospel and altar, is a symbolic purification and anointing of the priest, which makes him worthy to offer the Divine Liturgy.

It is quite evident, then, that the rite of first incensing and the introductory prayers at the beginning of the Divine Liturgy form an organic and symbolic whole. The ruling thought in the ceremony is the desire to approach the altar and celebrate the Divine Liturgy—the Unbloody Sacrifice—with a clean and holy heart for the glory of God and the reconciliation of mankind.

3. Dialogue Between the Deacon and the Priest

When the Divine Liturgy is celebrated with the participation of a deacon (which the Order of Celebration always anticipates) a short dialogue takes place between the deacon and the priest, after which follow the introductory prayers and the kissing of the gospel book and altar. A similar dialogue takes place later, immediately after the transference of the holy gifts from the table of Prothesis to the altar (The Great Entrance).

The dialogue between priest and deacon at the beginning of the Liturgy of the Catechumens first appeared in the liturgical documents of the twelfth century. Here it varies in form, but yet always retains the same character, i.e., the same petition of the deacon that the priest bless and pray for him before commencing the services. In the Byzantine Order of Celebration, the deacon performs the duty of an assistant to the priest in the Divine Liturgy. He is the mediator between the priest and the people. Interpreters of the Divine Liturgy call the deacon an "angel" or messenger of the priest. Just as the angels are the "spiritual assistants" of God in the work of salvation, so also are deacons "the angels" of the priest, who assist him in performing the service of the Divine Liturgy.

The role of the deacon in the Divine Liturgy is revealed in the introductory dialogue where he reminds the priest that "the time has come to sacrifice unto the Lord," and therefore asks the priest to "bless," "pray for" and "remember" him. The priest, answering the deacon, first of all glorifies God's name:

Blessed be our God always, now and ever, and unto ages of ages.

and then wishes the deacon, "May the Lord direct thy steps." The dialogue ends with the deacon saying, "Amen" and bowing, he leaves and goes in front of the iconostasis and immediately begins the Divine Liturgy.

The words: "It is time to sacrifice unto the Lord; bless, Master," taken from Psalm 118 (v. 126) signify that the Divine Liturgy is that service of God which renders Him the greatest glory. The word "bless" has a twofold meaning; it is a translation of the Greek word *eulogein* which etymologically means to glorify someone, to praise, to wish good things to another; the second meaning is to confer upon another a blessing before some undertaking. In the first meaning, the words "Bless, Master" are an appeal to the priest to give glory to God through the celebration of the Divine Liturgy. In the second meaning, they are a request that the priest bless the deacon for the service of the Divine Liturgy.

The dialogue emphasizes the high office of the priesthood. The priest is the representative of Jesus Christ, the High Priest—Master. For this reason the deacon calls the priest "Master," although the title traditionally pertains to the bishop. The bishop, as well as the priest represents Christ at the Divine Liturgy whom the Liturgy acknowledges as the "one who offers and is offered, receives, and is received."

4. The Doxology or the Glorification of the Holy Trinity

The Liturgy begins with a doxology or a solemn invocation in honor of the Blessed Trinity:

Blessed be the Kingdom of the Father and of the Son and of the Holy Spirit, now and ever, and unto ages of ages.

The priest was called upon by the deacon to give glory—that is, the deacon asked the priest's blessing, with the words "Bless, Master." While intoning these words of the doxology, the priest takes the book of gospels in his two hands and makes the sign of the cross with it over the altar.

The Divine Liturgy has many other invocations or doxologies similar to the first invocation honoring the Blessed Trinity most of which conclude the ektenies and the silent prayers of the priest. This invocation in honor of the Triune God is of ancient Christian origin. Its frequent usage in the Divine Liturgy recalls the times when the various heretics denied the existence of the Blessed Trinity, or refused to worship the Second and Third Persons of the Trinity (or denied that honor was due them).

The invocation of the Holy Trinity at the very beginning of the Divine Liturgy serves to emphasize that, although the Divine Liturgy is an unbloody renewal and perpetuation of the sacrifice on the cross of Jesus Christ, the Second Person of the Divine Trinity, it does not cease to be a glorification of all the Persons of the Divine Trinity. Here at the beginning of the Divine Liturgy the doxology is a beautiful introduction to the supplication. One of the best of the Byzantine liturgical commentators, Nicholas Cabasilas, remarks that it is proper that the Divine Liturgy begin with a prayer of glorification or doxology and that only after this adoration should prayers of petition be offered to God. This doxology at the beginning of the Liturgy is also an expression of our gratitude to God. One who petitions thinks first of himself; but he who expresses gratitude to God and praises Him seeks first the glory of God. The very order of things demands that we begin the Divine Liturgy with a prayer of praise and not of petition. He who approaches God should first contemplate the grandeur, majesty and glory of God, for only then will the sentiment of awe arise in his soul and culminate in the glorification of God. One must contemplate God's goodness and mercy in order to awaken in his soul sentiments of gratitude. Only after such manifestation of praise and thanksgiving will we find it proper to present our needs to God. The beginning of our prayer should always be characterized by unselfishness and should always bear the character of praise.[6]

Certain commentators who see in the Divine Liturgy a symbolic chronology of Christ's life on earth, associate the first invocation in honor of the Holy Trinity with the sermon of John the Baptist in which he exhorts all the Jews to repent, saying;

Do penance for the kingdom of heaven is at hand. (Mt 3:1–3)

The priest, in beginning the Divine Liturgy with the doxology, symbolizes St. John the Baptist, but only until the Little Entrance with the gospel book which, in its turn, symbolizes the first Epiphany or public appearance when our Lord delivered the sermon on the Kingdom of Heaven.[7] Such symbolic explanation of the first portion of the Liturgy of the Catechumens, although original, does not harmonize with the texts or with the structure of the Divine Liturgy as a whole.

To the doxology the faithful respond with the word "Amen," a formula frequently employed in the Liturgies of the various rites. The word, which is of Hebrew derivation, means "so be it." Among the Jews this word was frequently used, especially in their solemnities, to express consent or agreement. (Deut 27:15–26. Jesus Christ too used to repeatedly on many occasions, "Amen, Amen, I say unto you. . . ." With these words He wished to accentuate the gravity as well as the veracity of His words.

In the Liturgy the word "Amen" is a grave and solemn response of the people to the doxological invocation of the priest. By it the faithful declare

---

[6] N. Cabasilas, *A commentary on the Divine Liturgy;* Migne, PG, 150, 392.

[7] Migne, PG, 98, 401. (The Liturgical Commentary of Pseudo-Herman); 87, 3992 (The Liturgical Commentary of Pseudo-Sophronius); 140, 432 (The Liturgical Commentary of Theodore Andides).

their willingness to praise God, to glorify His goodness and mercy, to render Him honor and service. St. Augustine beautifully remarks: "to say 'Amen' means to endorse something." [8] By this word those present at the Divine Liturgy endorse and subscribe to all the priest says when glorifying the Triune God; they all join him in a hymn of praise of adoration.

---

[8] F. Cabrol, *Amen*, DACL, I, 1554–72; I. Cecchelli, *L'Amen nella Scriptura e nella liturgia*, Roma, 1942.

Chapter III

THE GREAT EKTENE OR EKTENE OF PEACE

The Divine Liturgy begins with the invocation "Blessed be the Kingdom" which also marks the beginning of the Great Ektene or the Litany of Peace. This ektene contains a series of short supplications, each possessing its own characteristic content. Ordinarily, it is the function of the deacon to sing the ektene, but if there is no deacon, the priest himself does so.

Since the ektene appears very frequently in the Divine Liturgy, it is worthwhile to study its structure, origin, history and usage. In the Divine Liturgy we meet with various types of ektenes: 1) The Great Ektene, or Ektene of Peace; 2) The Little Ektene; 3) The Triple Ektene or the Insistent Ektene and 4) The Ektene of Supplication or Petition. Besides these main types there is a special ektene, as for example, that for the deceased. Ektenes or litanies are also used in other services such as orthros or matins, vespers, moleben, parastas, the rites of the sacraments, etc.

1. Origin and History of the Ektene

Primarily, the ektene is a liturgical community prayer which is distinct from the other prayers by virtue of its form and individual characteristics. The name *ektene* is derived from the Greek word *ekteinein* which means to continue or to prolong. Therefore it is a continued, prolong, insistent prayer. The characteristic trait and the distinctive form of the ektene consist in the fact that it is not a long protracted prayer like the private prayers of the priest, but a series of short petitions with the same ending and the same prayerful response of the faithful. By its very nature the ektene is "an antiphonal prayer," i.e., a prayer recited alternately. Therefore, its form and structure makes it suitable for community, congregational prayer, for which reason it is interspersed throughout the Divine Liturgy. The ektene as a congregational prayer in the complete sense of the word is the most acceptable form of prayer, not only in the Divine Liturgy, but also in the other divine services and rites. The other Eastern Liturgies—Armenian, Coptic, Chaldean, Ethiopian, Syrian—also have this form of prayer. It is found as well in the Western, or Latin services, especially in the form of the litany.

The manner of praying in the ektene form testifies to its ancient origin. Since we do not encounter this form of prayer in the Jewish Old Testament services, some liturgists such as A. Baumstark,[1] trace its origin to the pagans. As

---

[1] A. Baumstark, *Vom geschichtlichem Werden der Liturgie*, 22–23.

a matter of fact certain pagan mystery-religions (e.g., the mystery of Isis) did know a form of prayer analogous to our ektene, and this might be regarded as one of the proofs of pagan, or to be more accurate, of hellenistic influence on parts of our Divine Liturgy, as we have earlier mentioned.[2]

In the writings of Clement of Rome (1st century) we can discern traces of our ektene. In his Epistle to the Corinthians, St. Clement gives a whole series of petitions for a wide variey of needs. These may have been excerpted from the eucharistic prayer, for the series does not have the present day form of the ektene. Furthermore, we have some allusions to the ektene form of prayer in the works of St. Justin and St. Hippolytus. Conclusive evidence of the use of the ektene in the services of the fourth century can also be found in the works of St. Basil the Great, St. John Chrysostom and in Etheria's *Pilgrimage*.[3] The latter describes the services which she personally witnessed in Jerusalem and mentions the ektene which the deacon recited and to which the faithful responded with the prayer: "Lord have mercy."

The first texts or formulae of the ektene appeared in the *Apostolic Constitutions*[4] and in another liturgical document of about the same time, *The Testament of Our Lord, Jesus Christ*.[5] Most akin to the form and content of our ektene of peace is the ektene called "Megale Synapte," a large collection of prayers found in one of the oldest Christian Liturgies, that of St. James.[6] The Great Ektene also bears this title in several manuscripts of the Byzantine Liturgy. In the Slavonic manuscripts it usually comes under the heading of "The Ektene of Peace" because it begins with the petition for peace.

The ektenes, therefore, are among the oldest parts of the Divine Liturgy, although we cannot affirm that the ektene as we know it today originated in the fourth or fifth century. Like other liturgical rites and prayers, it too has undergone some changes throughout the centuries. Not until much later, in the eleventh century, do we find the Ektene of Peace appearing in the liturgical documents. This can be explained by the fact that the oldest manuscripts of our Divine Liturgy predating the eleventh century contained only the prayers and functions of the priest, and not those of the deacon. The ektenes, since they were the deacon's prayers, were found in the *Diakonikon*. It was in the twelfth century that the prayers and functions of the deacon became incorporated into the text of Liturgy. Comparing the ektenes of ancient liturgical documents with

---

[2] Cf. above, Part I.

[3] For the testimony of St. Basil, see Migne, PG, 32, 612; for that of St. John Chrysostom, Migne, PG, 60, 266 and other places. For the *Pilgrimage* of Etheria, see Duchesne, *Origines du culte chret.*, 1925, p. 514; Krasnoseltsev, *Bogosluzhenie Yerusalimskoy tserkvi v k. IV*, v., "Pravo. Sobes.," 1888, III, 350–384.

[4] *Apostolic Constitutions*, VIII, see Funk, *Didascalia et Constitutiones Apostolorum*, Paderborn, 1905, I., 478–494.

[5] The *Testamentum Domini nostri Jesu Christi* probably dates back to the fifth century. Cf. the article of A. Petrovsky, *Liturghiya po novootkrytomu pamyatkniku "Testamentum Domini nostri Jesu Christi"* (Khrist. Cht., 217 (1904) , pp. 473–482) .

[6] Skabalanovich calls he ektene in the Liturgy of St. James the "first edition" of our Ektene of Peace. (Cf. his research work: *"Ektenii"* in "Trudy K. D. A.," 1911, III. 1–32).

the text and content of the present Ektene of Peace, we perceive only slight and insignificant differences.

2. Content and Signification of the Ektene of Peace

The Great Ektene as we have just said, is a series of short petitions, twelve in number, for various needs. We may well examine and analyze each petition since each contains much instruction and serves as a good example of community prayer which is truly catholic in nature.

1. *The first prayer* is a petition for *"peace"*:

"In peace, let us pray, to the Lord".

This prayer is not exactly a petition; but rather an invitation to begin our prayer in "peace." Nicholas Cabasilas says aptly of this first petition, that it admonishes and reminds us of how we should pray and what our prayers should be like. To pray in "peace" means to pray with a pure and innocent heart, for only he whose soul is free of sin and inordinate attachment to the world prays in "peace." Without this internal peace and serenity it is impossible to pray, for God is not a God of dissipation and vexation, but a "God of peace" (I Cor 14:13). Rightly then does Holy Scripture tell us that "there is no peace for the wicked" (Is 48:21; 57:21). During prayer our souls and our hearts should be peaceful and serene; they should not be disturbed and confused by worldly care and the movements of the passions. "Whoever prays without internal peace," says Cabasilas, "does not pray well and his prayers are of no avail." [7]

2. *The second petition* is similar to the first in that it also is a petition of peace:

For peace from on high, and for the salvation of our souls, let us pray to the Lord.

"Peace from on high" and "the salvation of our souls" are one and the same thing. Christ came into the world to bring "the peace of God, which surpasses all understanding." (Phil. 4:7) "The peace of God" is actually the result of that reconciliation with God which has been achieved through Christ's death on the cross. He brought us "salvation," for He reconciled us with God. Thus at the beginning of the ektene we implore God that we may always enjoy this heavenly peace, never forfeit it but increase it in our hearts.

3. In *the third petition* the theme is again "peace":

For the peace of the whole world, for the welfare of all the holy churches of God, and for the union of all, let us pray to the Lord.

This petition has two parts and although in each part there are different words: "welfare of the church"[8] and "union of all," nevertheless, in essence, these words are synonymous with "peace."

---

[7] Migne, PG, 150, 392.

[8] The Slavonic text has the word: "blahostoyaniye." This word is a literal translation of the Greek *eustateia* which means: prosperity, well-being, security or a flourishing state.

First of all, we ask God for peace in the world. We must not here understand peace in the ordinary sense of the word, negatively, as the absence of
wars. Of this the Liturgy treats in another petition, the ninth. Rather it must be
understood in the sense the Holy Scriptures, the Holy Fathers, and the Liturgy
itself understand it—as heavenly peace, the peace of God, the symbol of the
Messianic graces which Christ, the "King of Peace" bestowed upon the world.
Here we ask that the kingdom of peace reign in the world, that everyone
become a partaker of the salvation and reconciliation with God which we have
achieved through Jesus Christ. This is the original and true meaning of the
word "peace" so oft-repeated in our Divine Liturgy.[9]

So that this peace of Christ will reign successfully throughout the whole
world, we continue to pray for "the welfare of the holy churches of God." Here
we must understand internal peace, i.e., peace within and among the individual
churches, as well as concord and unity among the members who make up
Christ's Universal Church. Only this internal harmony within the Mystical Body
of Christ is the sure guarantee that the Church will fulfill the mission which
Christ entrusted to her, namely, the spread of God's Kingdom throughout the
world and the bestowal upon all peoples of the peace of Christ. We will fully
understand the petition for harmony within and for the growth of the Church
if we recall the turbulent times of internal dissension, schisms, dogmatic altercations, and heresies so prevalent in the fourth and fifth centuries and which still
shake the Church to its very foundation.

For this reason the Liturgy further begs for "the unity of all." This petition
is reminiscent of the prayer Christ prayed before His passion "that all may be
one," (Jn 17:21) that all form one Body. The Liturgy reminds us that all
good Christians should pray for the unity of Christ's Kingdom—His Church.

The peace for which we ask, whether in our souls, among the churches, or
throughout the world, is so important that the Church in the Liturgy places it
above all other needs. This petition is none other than the petition for *the realization of God's Kingdom on earth* which Christ mentions in the Our Father:
"Thy kingdom come"—hence its significance in the Divine Liturgy.

4. *"For this holy temple,* and for those who enter therein with faith, piety,
and fear of God, let us pray to the Lord."

After praying for the world, all the churches and all peoples in general,
our petitions become more specific; however, the peace of Christ is still the main
theme. We pray that those assembled in church be blessed with this peace. By
the word "church" we do not mean exclusively an edifice but the "church" taken
in its original sense as designating the faithful present in the church who "with
faith and devotion" come to church to render honor and glory to God.

---

[9] For the meaning of peace see the beautiful articles written by P. M. Tarchnishvili S.J.C.,
Die idee des christlichen Friedens in der byzantinischen Liturgie, (Das Wort in der Zeit, 6,
(1937), pp. 219–226); *Die byzantinische Liturgie als Verwirlkichung der Einheit und Gemein-
schaft im Dogma, (Das oestliche Christentum,* Heft 9), Wuerzburg; 1939, pp. 49–56.

5 and 6. The two succeeding petitions are for *the Church hierarchy,* for the "teaching Church."

> For our holy universal Supreme Pontiff N . . ., Pope of Rome, let us pray to the Lord.
> For our most reverend Archbishop and Metropolitan N . . ., for our God-loving Bishop N . . ., for the venerable priesthood, diaconate in Christ, for all the clergy and people, let us pray to the Lord.

This is natural because the Church's hierarchy, beginning with its supreme pastor, the head of the Universal Church, and ending with the church assistants, is entrusted with a truly responsible mission—that of spreading Christ's Kingdom on earth, each according to his capacity or office. Like the hierarchy, so too the priests, and, in general, all the "clergy" have, besides attaining their own salvation, the obligation to help save the souls of others.

A prayer for the "people" is also joined to the prayer for the hierarchy or Church authorities. This petition embraces the whole Church of Christ which is composed of not only the pastors, "the teaching Church," but also of the community of Christians—the "listening Church", or "the people of God".

7. Following the prayer for the Church, its officials and members, we have a *prayer for civil authorities*:

> For our God-protected Emperor, (or King) N . . . (or) our sovereign authorities and for all armed forces, let us pray to the Lord.

In the various editions of the Sluzhebnyk, this petition is found in different forms, owing to the fact that in the course of centuries the form of government in countries and nations that once belonged to the Byzantine-Greek Rite has undergone various changes. Hence we encounter petitions for emperors, czars, kings, princes, lords, hetmen and the like. In the most recent edition of the Sluzhebnyk [10] this petition has a more universal application ("for our sovereign authorities") than it had in the older editions, and can be applied to all types of government. Such a form of petition is very convenient, especially in our turbulent and uncertain age, when forms of government change almost every decade. In any event, this comprehensive and general petition for civil rulers corresponds closely to the earlier prayer for rulers which was not a very long enumeration of the names of the emperors, their wives, sons, daughters and in general, the whole royal family, as we so frequently encounter in the Russian-Orthodox Sluzhebnyks before World War I. [11] In its comprehensive form this

---

[10] That is, the Roman edition of 1940. The words "o prederzhashchykh vlastekh" are a literal if not a servile translation of the Greek words *hyperechuse eksuzia,* which means "higher authority:, higher authorized power." These words are taken from St. Paul's Letter to the Romans, Chapter 13.

[11] In the Russian-Orthodox Sluzhebnyks besides prayers for the reigning Czar there are also petitions for the Czarina, the successor to the throne, the prominent princes and other members of the royal family, although they had nothing to do with governing the state. Such an elaboration of the ektene petitions must be considered a deviation from the spirit and purpose of

prayer for civil authorities and rulers places the Liturgy above and beyond the fleeting circumstances of time and politics and adds to its dignity.

The prayer for civil rulers is in no sense "servile," nor is it solely a relic of "Byzantinism." It was a practice of the primitive Church and we find it in one form or another in all liturgies. Its antiquity is evidenced by the fact that it is found in the commemorations of the Anaphora following the Consecration. St. Paul himself instructed the first Christians to pray for their rulers:

> I desire therefore, first of all, that supplications, prayers, intercessions, and thanksgivings be made for all men: For kings, and for all that are in high stations: that we may lead a quiet and a peaceable life in all piety and chastity. For this is good and acceptable in the sight of God our Savior, Who will have all men to be saved, and to come to the knowledge of the truth. (1 Tim, 2:1,4)

In these beautiful words St. Paul gives us the key to the proper understanding of the liturgical prayer for rulers: it is not an expression of servility toward a particular ruler, nor an expression of loyalty to, or servile acknowledgement of any single form of government, nor an endorsement of its political leanings, attitudes, actions, or ideology, but conversely, it is a prayer for the *salvation of those endowed with authority*, that they too may "be saved and come to the knowledge of the truth." The prayer reminds us that it is the duty of every good Christian to be concerned not only with his own salvation, but with the salvation of others as well, especially of those who have been raised to higher offices and who can easily become oblivious of the first and foremost purpose of life, the salvation of one's soul.

Understood in this way, it extends to governments that are usurped, forcefully imposed, as happens often in our times, and even to those of atheistic ideology. The Liturgy is entirely indifferent to the type of civil authority, its form, origin, and politics. It urges us to pray for every civil authority, so that under its direction the faithful can "live a peaceable life," that the wordly powers with their shortcomings, ideologies and laws may not impede Christians in their en-

---

the Liturgy and the liturgical prayer for civil authority. The Divine Liturgy prays for *civil authority and its legal representatives,* which are, however, not to be regarded as the members of the royal family. A further departure from the spirit of the liturgical prayer are the seemingly superfluous and pompous titles and epithets attached to the name of the Czar, of which the Russian-Orthodox Sluzhebnyks are so guilty. Such pompous epithets are: "our most devout, most autocratic, great ruler", the "Emperor."

Comparing these flamboyant and pretentious titles with those contained in the petition for the Church hierarchy, we find the epithets of the latter to be simple and unassuming.

In our opinion, the petition for "our devoutly believing people" which often replaced the petition for the Emperor does not entirely correspond to the nature of the petition for civil authority, *for the people as such are not the civil authority; the Liturgy wishes here to remember active authority.* The petition for the people, however, could have its place in the Liturgy and could exist as a separate petition. Special petitions for various needs could be inserted into the Great Ektene. However, the petition for the people cannot supplant the petition for civil authority.

deavor to attain salvation. St. Paul, in his first letter to Timothy, instructed all to pray for those who held high posts in the state at that time, even though they were pagans opposed to everything that Christianity stood for. Therefore, this intercession for civil authorities has, and will always have, its place; and even more so when the authorities do not recognize the Church, God, man's God-given inalienable rights or when they actually persecute the Church.

The prayer for "all armed forces" should also be taken in this same all-embracing sense. We do not pray for "the armed forces" in general as the mainstay of the state, but for the individual soldiers who make up those forces, that they may attain eternal salvation in military life which is so filled with dangers to soul and body, and that they may not forget their final destiny.

The prayer for civil authorities then, taken in its original meaning, is nothing other than a prayer for the Kingdom of Christ, for the peace of God and for the salvation of souls. In it we ask God to remove all the civil obstacles that might hinder the diffusion of His Kingdom. Thus understood, this petition is instrinsically related to the first petition for the "peace of God" on earth.[12]

8. In *the eighth petition* we pray to God

> For this city (or for this village or for this holy monastic community), for every city and country, and for the faithful who dwell therein, let us pray to the Lord.

The Liturgy does not forget our cities, villages and towns which are so dear to us. Since we are citizens of a given country, we are naturally bound to remember our native land in our prayers. Not only must we remember our native land in general, but we must also remember the province, city or village [13] in which we happen to live, for it is God's will that we live there and there work out our final destiny. The words: "and for all the faithful who dwell therein" reveals the ancient origin of this petition. Christians living among the pagans and associating with them daily could have easily succumbed to the pagan mode of life and compromised their salvation. Hence, the Christians remembered their brothers in faith and prayed for them so that they might live "in faith" and by their faith surmount all the dangers of their environment.

9. *The ninth petition:*

> For good weather, for abundance of the fruits of the earth, and for peaceful times, let us pray to the Lord,

is cogent proof that we can and should pray not for spiritual blessings only, but also for temporal goods for ourselves as well as for others. The Liturgy recognizes the fact that we live on earth and that our life depends to a great extent on the fruits of the earth. Hence, we are urged to pray for "good weather," i.e., favorable weather on which depends the productiveness of the land and consequently our material well-being. This petition asks also for "the abundance of

---

[12] Some pertinent observations on the sense and meaning of the prayer for civil authority can be found in T. Mishkovskiy's *Izlozhenie tsaregradskoy liturghii,* Lviv, 1926, pp. 46–49.

[13] In the Greek text we have the word *Khora* which means village, hamlet, suburbs.

the fruits of the earth" because, while an accumulation of wealth and a surplus of material goods can certainly prove detrimental and cause a person to neglect his soul, by the same token, a lack of these necessary goods can destroy faith and hope in God. This petition also expresses unwavering faith in God's providence. In praying for the fruits of the land, fertility of the soil and a plentiful harvest, we express implicitly our faith that God is the Supreme Lord of the world. Although the phenomena of nature have their causes in the immutable laws of nature, nevertheless, the Lord of these laws is no other than God Himself. He has endowed nature with her laws; He is her creator and legislator and, being free, He can do whatever He pleases with the nature of things. In His providence He has wrought miracles whenever the good of His creatures warranted them and whenever they did not go contrary to His plan.

In our prayer of petition we also pray for "peaceful times." "Peace" here is to be assumed in its ordinary sense as freedom from war, its disasters and consequences. This petition has never lost its timeliness; perhaps it is more timely now than it ever was in ancient times.

10. The Liturgy does not forget to pray for those *"traveling by air, sea and land, the sick, the suffering, the imprisoned, and for their salvation."* For a better understanding of this petition, we must go back to the times when this ektene originated. Long ago traveling by sea and by land was not so convenient and pleasurable and safe as it is today—it was hazardous. In those days travelers were exposed to many dangers, not to mention the various natural inconveniences and difficulties of the journey itself. We must admire the material solicitude the Church shows for the welfare of her children in introducing the prayer for travelers into the Liturgy. The Liturgy goes still farther, for it remembers those of whom we are often least mindful, namely, the destitute, ailing, weak (mentally and physically), bedridden, unfortunate prisoners who have been deprived of all human rights and whom a callous victor has exploited shamelessly. In *The Apostolic Constitutions* we find in the text of one ektene, a petition also for those "condemned to heavy labor," i.e., those who were sentenced by pagan masters to hard labor in the mines for professing their Christian faith. This indicates how dear to the Church her children are, especially those stricken by misfortune and suffering. She prays for "their salvation," for she knows that the heavy blows of fate can easily break a man and cause him to despair and thus compromise his salvation. From this we can see that the Liturgy looks upon all the needs of man from the viewpoint of his eternal salvation.

11. *"That we may be delivered from all affliction, wrath and need, let us pray to the Lord."*

In *the eleventh petition* we ask God to "deliver us from affliction, wrath and need." The words "affliction, wrath and need" are taken from the book of the prophet Sophonius (1:15) who predicted to the people the wrath of God which was to fall upon them in punishment for their sins of infidelity and idolatry. In this petition the Church reminds us that by our sins we have made ourselves unworthy that God should hear our prayers, and that we deserve to be smitten with God's wrath, affliction and need. Hence, we beg God in His infinite mercy to deliver us from all misfortunes, misery, suffering and destitution, and we entreat Him not to punish us by His just wrath, but to be a merciful Father toward us.

12. *In the next petition* we solicit God for His graces:

Help, save, have mercy and protect us, O God, by Thy grace.

In the preceding petition we asked God to deliver us from misfortune and distress; now we ask Him for His graces. The former petition was negative; the second implies supplications for positive goods, especially for the greatest of all goods man is capable of possessing here on earth, the grace of God, without which it is impossible for man to save his soul and to attain his ultimate goal. Without the God's grace man cannot perform any salutary acts. We ask God for this grace for ourselves, so that it may "help, save, bestow mercy and protect us" in our life. In a very real sense this petition contains implicitly all the other solicitations of the Great Ektene and, therefore, is the most important of them all. Without the grace and mercy of God we cannot accomplish "peace," "the salvation of our souls," nor can we be "free of wrath, affliction and need."

13. The petition for God's grace marks the conclusion of the *ektene*. It is the last link in the chain of supplications. However, before concluding the ektene, the Liturgy draws our attention to *the commemoration* of "our most holy, most pure, most blessed and glorious Lady, the Mother of God and ever-virgin Mary, with all the saints," so that through their intercession we may present our prayers and *"commend* ourselves, each other, and all of our life to Christ, God." Conscious of our numerous grave sins and our weakness we turn to those who stand before the throne of God and ask them to intercede for us. First of all we turn to our dear heavenly Mother, the Mother of God and Queen of Heaven, for through her divine grace flows upon mankind. The Mother of God and the saints are our heavenly ambassadors before God and, therefore, it is altogether fitting to commemorate them and to solicit their aid.

Not only does this petition emphasize the powerful intercession of our Blessed Mother and the saints, but it also reveals a boundless confidence in our Lord Jesus Christ, our Mediator between heaven and earth. As a token of this confidence we offer Him *"ourselves, each other and all of our life"* to do with as He wills. Perhaps there is no better prayer than one in which we place our full trust in God; commit ourselves to Christ, place at His feet all our needs, all our worldly cares, troubles, all our sufferings, in fact our whole life. To place all our trust in, and resign ourselves to, His holy will and providence is the most perfect and most efficacious prayer. This filial trust in God is the last refrain of our prayer, the last chord of the Great Ektene, the prayerful hymn to God's mercy. As a sign of the faithful's desire to live with this trust in God, the whole Church answers: *"To Thee, O Lord."* To You, Lord, we offer our petitions, at Your feet we place our supplications, to You we commend ourselves without reservation, to You we give back our life and all that You have given us, in You we place all our trust and know that You will not fail us in our hopes!

3. "Lord, have Mercy"

To each petition of the ektene the faithful exclaim: *"Lord, have mercy."* This ejaculatory prayer reflecting the fervor of the faithful is terse but very meaningful. It is one of the prayers most frequently used not only in the Divine Liturgy, but also in other divine services.

This short prayer was found among the pagans (Virgil, Epictetus). It also appears very frequently in the Old Testament especially in the Psalms. It became one of the most cherished prayers in Christian services. According to Baumstark [14] this prayer made its way into Christian services from the pagan cult, of the Sun god. We find it in liturgical documents of the fourth century, as well as in the *Apostolic Constitutions* and the *Pilgrimage* of Sylvia Etheria. This prayer was quickly adopted by the Liturgies of both the East and West.

"Lord, have mercy" sums up the entire Great Ektene. In this short supplication we appeal to God's mercy, upon which depends the fulfillment of our prayers and supplications. This prayer expresses the exclusive dependence of the answers to our prayers upon God's mercy and grace, and not upon our own merits and prayers. "Lord, have mercy" is the cry of a soul that is aware of its sinfulness and unworthiness. A more beautiful prayer invoking the mercy of God cannot be found. It is a prayer in which the soul expresses its longing for God, His grace and mercy. The "Lord, have mercy" re-echoes the importunate plea of the blind men of Jericho whom Christ cured because of their faith, or the petition of the lepers who called after Him: "Lord, have mercy." This prayer is an expression of the unshakable faith and confidence of the Canaanite woman, and echoes the sorrowful signs of the penitent soul so frequently heard in the Psalms of David. Briefly, the prayer, "Lord, have mercy" is one of the most beautiful, most profound, most meaningful prayers of our Divine Liturgy. [15]

4. The Prayer of the Great Ektene

The chain of petitions of the Great Ektene is climaxed with the doxology or invocation glorifying the Blessed Trinity:

> For to Thee is due all glory, honor and adoration, to the Father, and to the Son, and to the Holy Ghost, now and ever, and unto ages of ages.

This invocation is actually the conclusion of the short private prayer of the priest and the final ekphonesis glorifying God. By "ekphonesis" is meant the audible singing of the final phrase of a silent prayer, i.e., a doxology.

---

[14] See A. Baumstark, *op. cit.*, p. 27.

[15] E. Bishop, *Kyrie eleison, A liturgical consultation,* (Liturgica-historica 1918) ; F. Cabrol, *Kyrie eleison,* (DACL, VIII, col. 308–916), Paris, 1928.

The silent prayers of the priest constitute the greater part of the Divine Liturgy. Moreover, they are to be considered the most important function of the priest in the Divine Liturgy. The priest does not say the most important prayers aloud, but privately and silently. This is true especially of the Anaphora which he recites mostly in silence and rarely aloud. At one time, in the primitive Church, the priest recited everything aloud, including the Anaphora. But because the prayers of the original Liturgies were usually long and because the people took only a passive part, they were abbreviated and assigned to the priest to be said in silence, while the people sang or chanted some hymn or recited the petitions of an ektene with the deacon. Thus it became customary for the priest to recite the majority of the liturgical prayers silently and only during the most important parts of the Liturgy would he conclude his prayer in an audible voice. We are not going to offer a detailed analysis of this gradual transition from the audible to the inaudible prayers in our Liturgy or conclude whether as a result of the transition the Liturgy gained or lost.[16] It is a fact, though, that these silent, inaudible prayers, ordinarily profound, are as a rule unkown to the people. The faithful know very little or nothing at all about them, and this certainly is not conducive to a better understanding and appreciation of the Divine Liturgy, its profound content and beautiful prayers. This is precisely one of the reasons why we will devote special attention to the private or secret prayers of the priest and will strive to unveil and explain their contents. Without this knowledge it is impossible to acquire a thorough understanding of the Liturgy, for actually, it is the priestly prayers that form the foundation and skeleton of the whole Liturgy.

To understand the first silent prayer recited by the priest at the conclusion of the Great Ektene, we must direct our attention to the style and character of silent prayer in the Liturgy. The private prayers of the priest have a typical style and composition, which clearly distinguishes them from the other liturgical prayers, as for example, the ektene supplications. Almost every private prayer that the priest says is composed of three elements: a short introduction (an opening), the prayer itself and the conclusion. In the first part there is usually a short reflection in which the priest recalls God's perfections or attributes, His majesty, goodness, etc. Then, in the prayer itself he places before God the needs

---

[16] The problem regarding silent prayers in the Liturgy is treated by B. J. Sove, *Evkharistiya drevney tserkvi i sovremennaya praktika*, "Zhivoe Predanie," Paris, 1937, and A. Golubtsov, *O prichinakh i vremeni zamyeny glasnaho chteniya liturgiynykh molitv taynymi*, (Bog. Vyestnik, 1905, sentyabr, pp. 68–77).

Shortly before World War I there arose among the Russian-Orthodox liturgists and the clergy a movement which sought to revive the ancient Christian practice of having the priest recite his private prayers aloud. Many representatives of the higher clergy even approved of this reform. The main reason advanced for the change was the desire to render the liturgy more "popular" and living and to have the people take the greatest possible active part in it. However, the War and adverse conditions in the Russian-Orthodox Church did not permit the realization of this desire. A more extensive treatment of this project of liturgical reform can be found in the collection: *"Otzyvi eparkhialnykh arkhiereyev po voprosu o tserkovnoy reformye,"* Sb., 1906.

and petitions of the congregation. Finally, the prayer concludes with the *ekpho-nesis* addressed to the Holy Trinity (Trinitarian doxology) which the priest recites or sings aloud. In Old Slavonic it is called the *Vozhlas.*

A classical example of this type of prayer is the prayer toward the end of the Great Ektene which we have already mentioned. While the deacon and the people are reciting their ektene petitions, the priest stands at the altar and as a mediator between God and His flock commends the prayers of His flock to God:

> Lord our God, Whose might is beyond utterance, and glory is incomprehen-sible, Whose mercy is measureless, and love of man is ineffable: Thyself, O Master, look down with Thy mercy upon us, and upon this holy house, and grant to us, and to those who pray with us, the riches of Thy mercy, and of Thy compassion. (*Ekphonesis*) For to Thee is due all glory, honor and ado-ration, to the Father, and to the Son, and to the Holy Ghost, now and ever, and unto ages of ages.

This beautiful prayer begins with a meditation on God's omnipotence, mercy and love for man. Meditating on these divine attributes, the priest is moved to continue the prayer proper. Since God's mercy is "measureless and His love of man ineffable," the priest, appealing to this mercy, implores God to look down upon His people, gathered in prayer, and to fulfill their petitions and sup-plications. He does not mention the particular needs of his flock. The silent prayer of the priest is, therefore, a recapitulation of the whole ektene; in it, like rays of light in a prism, each particular petition of the Great Ektene converges.

Now we shall consider another aspect of the private prayer—its form. Such expressions as "ineffable, inaccessible, immeasurable, indefinable and unspeaka-ble" indicate that the composer of this prayer was one who was well acquainted with Hellenism, for in it the hellenistic style and mentality are quite evident.[17]

The Great Ektene concludes with the doxology addressed to the Blessed Trinity. Here we have the quintessence of a liturgical prayer—every prayer begins and ends with the Trinitarian doxology or invocation honoring the Blessed Trinity. The Great Ektene began with glorification and ends with glorification. The glorification of God is the closing point of the liturgical prayer, and gives it a supernatural and holy character which renders it distinct from the private individual prayers of Christians.

---

[17] We have spoken earlier of the influence of Hellenism, its style, *modus cogitandi*, philoso-phy, etc., upon the formation of our Liturgy. Justly do liturgists draw attention to the influ-ence of the Hellenistic style and lexicon upon the Divine Liturgy and other Eastern Liturgies. This influence is evident in the numerous epithets describing the name of God, especially the adjectives involving the "alpha privative" which are so well illustrated in the Great Ektene "e.g. *an- eikastos*—inexpressible; *a- kaliptos*—un attainable (in-accessible) ; *a- metretos*—immea-surable; *a- fatos*—ineffable). Other extensive works on Hellenistic influence on the Divine Lit-urgy are given by the following authors: E. Norden, *Agnostos Theos, Untersuchungen zur For-mengeschichte religioeser Rede*, Leipzig, 1913; F. J. Doelger, *Sol salutis, Gebet und Gesang im christlichen Altertum*, Muenster in W., 1920; P. Wendland, *Die hellenistisch-roemische Kultur in ihren Beziehungen zu Judentum und Christentum*, Tuebingen, 1907; A. Loisy, *Les mysteres paiens et le Mystere chretien*, Paris, 1919 (written in the spirit of modernism); A. Baumstark, *Vom geschichtlichen Werden der Liturgie*, Fr. im Br., 1923, pp. 21–29.

5. Characteristic Traits of the Great Ektene

Looking at the form and content of the Great Ektene, one can easily recognize certain traits which distinguish the liturgical prayer from private prayer. When we compare the contents of the ektene petitions with our own personal prayer, we immediately discern striking contrasts.

Catholicity or universality is the first characteristic of the liturgical prayer of the ektene; indeed, in many Greek manuscripts, the Great Ektene is called the "Katolike Synapte" or "Catholic prayer," for this prayer embraces in its petitions the most diverse, and most universal needs. In it we pray for all people. We pray for such very significant needs as God's peace in the world, the salvation of the world, the unity, growth and spread of God's kingdom on earth, the welfare of the Church, for the local Church and its faithful; for the pope, bishops and clergy; for civil authorities; for the welfare of city and state; for material prosperity; for the various needs of the faithful; for deliverance from evil, and for God's protection. What individual person remembers to pray for the great needs of God's kingdom on earth as the Liturgy prays? How limited are the petitions of our prayers! They tend usually to be egocentric, self-centered, for we only know our needs. As a rule we begin our prayer with our own "I." Not often do we pray for others and their needs and when we do so, it is usually for someone who is related to us in one way or another, e.g., parents, family, friends, etc. Does anyone of us ever embrace in our prayer the salvation of the world, the dispersion of God's kingdom throughout the world, the unity of all people in the peace of God?

The prayer of the Liturgy teaches us to be mindful not only of our personal needs but also of the needs of the whole Church and of the whole world; it makes us aware of the obligation to pray for all people, to forget no one and to include as many people and needs as possible in our prayer. The Liturgy not only remembers Church and civil authorities, but also remembers and prays for the neglected whom no one thinks or cares about, for whom no one prays—the poor, the destitute, the sick, the disabled, prisoners, and the afflicted. The Church includes everyone in her prayer, for the Church is Mother to all and she wishes to bring salvation to all. She commends all to the mercy of God. When we compare liturgical prayer with its catholic and altruistic character with our daily prayers, it becomes apparent how deficient the latter are and how selfish we are.

The Liturgical prayer is catholic, i.e., universal in content and spirit, because it is *the official prayer of the Universal Church.* Why is it the official prayer of the Church? We realize why when we consider that the Liturgy is offered in the name of the whole Church and for the whole Church. Many of the petitions it contains are lacking in the private prayers of the faithful. The Liturgy remembers those needs which we are not accustomed to pray for or for which we feel no need to pray. In these mementoes lie the great significance of liturgical prayer, and its utility for all members of Christ's Church. The Liturgy is the prayer of the whole Church for the whole Church. Hence the priest, in celebrating the Liturgy, does so not in his capacity as a private person, but as a representative and delegate of the entire Church. That is the reason why the priest's prayers are usually in the plural rather than in the singular person. The priest acts as a spokesman, not for his congregation alone but for all the people of God, the whole Church. He serves as God's ambassador for mankind.

Besides this catholic-universal spirit, *liturgical prayer has another characteristic,* namely, it reveals a hierarchy of needs. Here we refer to the order of requests in the petitions of the Great Ektene. The Liturgy begins with man's most important spiritual need—the peace of God, eternal salvation, the needs of the Church; it then considers the various states of life, the hierarchy, clergy, civil and national authorities, nations, city; finally, it considers man's material needs—the harvest, general welfare, etc. The Church, then knows not only the spiritual needs of her children but also their material needs and prays for both; but she also observes the proper hierarchical order and she sees all these things from the viewpoint of the "peace of God" and man's salvation. We should most certainly pray for our material and earthly needs and for the success of our daily negotiations or undertakings, but our first and foremost prayer must be for our own salvation and the salvation of the world.

These few reflections on the Great Ektene should convince us that our private prayers, good, praiseworthy and necessary as they are, do not compare in content and significance with the liturgical prayer of the Church. If we wish our private prayer to have more value before God, then we must strive to model it on the liturgical prayer. Liturgical prayer, with its catholic and altruistic character, should be the basis for our private prayers, for only then will the latter possess the priestly character of liturgical prayer and not savor of selfishness, egoism and individualism.

SELECT BIBLIOGRAPHY

Petrovskiy, A., *Ekteniya,* ("Pravo. Bog. Ents.," Vol. 5, pp. 376–378).

Skaballanovich, N.J., *Ekteniya,* (Tr. K.D.A. 1911, III, 9, pp. 1–39; and 1912, II, 6, pp. 181–202) .

Soloviyev, J., *Velikaya ekteniya, opit istolkovaniya yeya smisla i znacheniya kak molitvi tserkovno-bogosluzhebnoy.* Moskva, 1911.

Philaret, Bishop of Moscow, *Znachenie tserkovnoy molitvi o soyedenenii tserkvey,* (Prib. k tvor. sv. Otsev, 1860, XIX).

Palmov, N., *K izyasneniyu tretyaho prosheniya velikoy ektenii,* ("Rukovod. dlya selskikh pastirey," 1910, nos. 36–38).

Z., *O kakovom soyedenii vsyekh molimsya mi v 3-m proshenii velikoy ektenii,* Rukovod. d. selsk, past.," 1910.

Doelger, F. J., *Sol salutis,* Muenster in W., 1920.

Schuster, I., *La preghiera litanica,* (Delle origini e dello sviluppo del canto liturgico), "Rassegna gregoriana," XII, (1913), pp. 47–54.

Cabrol, F., *Litanies,* (DACL, IX, col. 1540–1571).

Thibaut, J. B., *Le Pseudo-Denys l'Areopagite et la "priere catholique" de l'Eglise primitive,* (l'Echos d'Orient, XX (1921), pp. 283–294).

De Puniet, P., *La grande supplication pour tous,* (La vie et les arts liturgiques), 1922.

Connoly, R. H., *Liturgical prayers of intercession,* (Journal of th. studies, 1920, XXI, pp. 219–223).

Pio Alfonso, *Oratio fidelium, Origine e sviluppo eucologico della prece dei fedeli,* Finalphia, 1928.

Chapter IV

THE ANTIPHONS

The antiphons follow the Great Ektene. While the purpose of the Great Ektene was to present all our petitions to God and to implore His grace and mercy, the aim of the antiphons is to give God homage by singing Psalms. In the former we have the element of supplication while in the latter we may perceive the element of praise.

The antiphons consist of the psalmody or the singing of Psalms.

1. The Origin and History of the Antiphons

Antiphons derive from the Jewish synagogue services, whence they found their way into the Christian services. The oldest documents witnessing to the use of Psalms in Christian services are St. Paul's epistles to the Ephesians and Colossians. In the Epistle to the Colossians he encourages the Christians to "teach, and admonish one another by *Psalms, hymns and spiritual songs,* singing in your hearts to God by His grace." (Col 3:16; cf. Ephes 5:19) Psalmody was integrated not only into the Divine Liturgy but also into other divine services, and was adopted by all the Liturgies.

There are three types of Psalm singing. The first type, called "declamatory," consists in having one lector sing the Psalms while the others listen attentively. The second type is called "symphonic," and consists in everyone singing or reading the Psalms in unison. In the third type, the "alternate" singing of Psalms, the congregation is divided into two choirs, one of which sings one versicle of the Psalm and the other the following versicle and so forth; or one choir sings one versicle or passage of the Psalm and the other choir responds in the same refrain. This last type is called "antiphonal singing or chanting" for the two choirs sing alternately.[1]

The antiphonal manner of singing Psalms, hymns or songs is very old. It was already known to the Hebrews, as witness the well known song of Moses and his sister Miriam which the Hebrews sang after they had crossed the Red Sea. It was sung antiphonally or alternately. This antiphonal manner of singing was also known in Greek drama and tragedy, where it was used to heighten

---

[1] The word *anti-phonein* is a Greek word which means to sing alternately, to sing in response. The Psalms were called antiphons from this manner of singing, i.e., antiphonal singing. Briefly then, by antiphons we understand those Psalms which are sung or recited at the Divine Liturgy.

suspense. Greek drama also inspired the introduction and development of antiphonal singing in Christian services. In any event, we find this type of singing in the services of the various Jewish sects and in the pagan services. For example, Philo, the renowned Jewish philosopher (first century) after Christ, mentions antiphonal singing among the Therapeuts, a Jewish sect. The *Younger Plinius* (second century) mentions this antiphonal chanting in Christian services in his famous letter to Emperor Trajan. However, we cannot be sure whether the antiphons were sung in all Christian churches.

According to the Church historian Socrates (fifth century), it was St. Ignatius of Antioch who introduced the antiphons into the Divine Liturgy. He was supposed to have had a vision of heaven in which he saw the angels praising God with antiphonal singing, and in order to imitate this manner of singing, he ordered it to be introduced into the divine services.[2] Another Byzantine historian, Theodoret,[3] ascribes the introduction of antiphonal singing into the Liturgy to two monks: Diodorus and Flavianus (middle of the fourth century). But N. Khoniates, an eleventh-century Byzantine historian, attempted to reconcile the contradictory statements of Socrates and Theodoret by ascribing to St. Ignatius the incorporation of the antiphons into the Liturgy of the Antiochian Church (in the Syrian language), and to Diodorus and Flavianus the translation of these antiphons from the Syrian language into Greek as well as their introduction into the Byzantine Church.[4]

The testimony of the Byzantine historians is, however, somewhat disputable. The introduction of the antiphons into the Liturgy, at least in Asia Minor, can be assigned to St. Basil the Great. This we know from a letter which he wrote to the clergy of Neo-Caesarea, in which he justifies himself for introducing the singing of Psalms by two choirs in the ecclesiastical province of Cappodocia.[5] As an argument he appeals to the custom of the antiphonal singing of the Psalms which was practiced in the other Christian churches, as for example, in Syria, Palestine, and Egypt. St. John Chrysostom introduced the practice in Constantinople to protect the faithful from the Arians, who, by means of this type of singing were attracting the Catholic faithful. A record of the existence of antiphons and their use is found in the *Pilgrimage* of Etheria where we come across the word "antiphon" twenty-nine times.[6] According to the testimony of St. Augustine, St. Ambrose introduced the antiphons as sung in the Greek Rite into the Liturgy of the Western Church" so that the faithful would not be bored.[7]

However, we should not conclude from these witnesses that the present-day antiphons are from the fourth and fifth centuries or that they were used in the Liturgy of that time. In the documents prior to the eighth century there is no

---

[2] Migne, PG, 67, 692 (Church history by Socrates). H. Leclerque regards this story as a "legend," Antienne, DACL, I, 2284.

[3] *Ibid.*, 82, 1060–1061. (Church History, bk. 2, chapter 19).

[4] *Ibid.*, 139, 1390.

[5] *Ibid.*, 32, 763.

[6] *Ibid.*, 67, 769–770; L. Duchesne, *Les origines du culte chretien,* Paris, 1925, pp. 513–514.

[7] Migne, PL, 32, 769–770, ("The Confessions of St. Augustine," bk. 9, chapters 6–7).

mention of the antiphons that we have; in those dating from the third to the eighth centuries, we do not encounter any antiphons at all at the beginning of the Liturgy, which began with the Little Entrance. The first information we discover bearing on the present day antiphons at the beginning of the Liturgy comes from Pseudo-Herman and Amalarius.[8] The antiphons were, at that time, a variable part of the Liturgy. As late as the ninth century and even the tenth, these Psalms were still not an integral part of the Liturgy, for we have documents testifying that they were omitted, for example, on days when the Great Vespers was being sung.[9] In all probability the antiphons were not part of the original Liturgy but were taken over from another service.[10]

Not until the end of the first millenium do antiphons in the present form begin to appear. The triple antiphon is mentioned in the liturgical commentaries of Pseudo-Herman, Pseudo-Sophronius, Theodore Andides, Nicholas Cabasilas and Simeon of Thessalonica. These men were familiar with the present-day texts of the daily antiphons which each attempted to explain.[11] One must remember that originally antiphons were entire Psalms, and that the singing of entire Psalms existed in some places up to the ninth century.[12] But, this custom must have disappeared later, for the aforementioned liturgical commentators explain only the first versicles of the Psalm. Simeon and Cabasilas explain the antiphons as we have them today, i.e. consisting not of complete Psalms but of the first three passages.

Of even later date are the so-called "typika" or "typological antiphons" and the "makarismoi" or "beatitudes" which certain Churches of the Byzantine Rite recite, especially on Sundays and Holy Days [13] instead of our daily antiphons. We are not going to discuss their history or their incorporation into the Liturgy. We shall instead explain the antiphons together with their ektenes and the christological hymn; *Monogenes,* and at the close of our commentary we shall say a few words about the role and significance of the antiphons in the Divine Liturgy.

---

[8] Amalarius reports that he heard the Psalm "Come let us adore" sung in the Church of St. Sophia at the beginning of the Divine Liturgy. (Migne, P.L., 105, 1243–1316: *"De ordine antiphonarii."*

[9] Cf. Krasnoseltsev, *Tipik tserkvi Sv. Sofii v Konstantinopolye,* (Lyetopis istoriko-filologicheskaho Obshchestva, I, Odessa, 1892, p. 202).

[10] According to De Meester all those prayers preceding the little Entrance (the Great Ektene and the antiphons) are "later additions," which probably date back to the eighth century. The singing of the antiphons, according to De Meester, was inserted in the Liturgy under the influence of the psalmody sung during the divine office, especially at vespers. See his work, p. 317.

[11] Migne, PG, 98, 401–405; 150, 400–412; 87, 3994; 140, 432–33; 155, 292, 717–719, 632–636.

[12] Cf. Moreau, F., *Les liturgies eucharistiques,* p. 114 (Footnote).

[13] For the "Typical" and "Beatitudes" antiphons see Mishkovskiy, *Izlozheniya tsaregrad liturghii,* pp. 40–41. Select Literature on the subject: Petrovskiy, A., *Antifon,* "Pravo. Bogo. Enst.," I. (1900), 318–820; Pantelakes, E., *Antifon,* Triskeutike Khr. Enk.," I, Athens, 1936, cols. 1211–1217; Amalarius, *De ordine antiphonarii,* Migne, PL. 105, 1243–1316; Leclercq, H., DACL, I, (1907), cols. 2282–2319; Petit, L., DACL, I., cols. 2461–2488; Baudot, *L'Antiphonaire,* Paris, 1912; Wagner, P., *Origine et developpement du chant liturg,* Tournai, 1904.

2. Explanation of the Antiphons

The antiphons belong to the variable parts of the Divine Liturgy, that is they change according to the Holydays or Feast Days. There are three types of antiphons: 1) the daily or weekday, 2) Sunday, 3) the holyday or feast day antiphons. The festal antiphons are sung only on major holydays in the liturgical year as on the Christological feasts of the Epiphany and Nativity of our Lord, etc. They are usually selected from those Psalms that have some immediate relation to the given holyday or to the theme corresponding to the mysteries of the feast day. In our commentary we will not explain all the antiphons which appear in our Divine Liturgy throughout the whole liturgical year, but will limit ourselves to those more frequently used, namely, the Sunday and weekday antiphons.[14]

A. The First Antiphon.

As we have mentioned, originally the antiphons were entire Psalms, and not only selected versicles as they are today. To understand the antiphons properly it is essential that we know the theme of the Psalm from which the antiphonal versicles are drawn. Only then can we avoid a fictitious and exaggerated interpretation of the liturgical texts. In our commentary we shall adhere to the literal or real interpretation of each Psalm—an interpretation based on an internal analysis of the texts themselves.

a) *The first weekday antiphon* is taken from the first, second and fifteenth verses of Psalm 91.

> It is good to give praise to the Lord: and to sing to Thy name, O Most High.
> By the prayers of the Mother of God, O Savior, save us.
> To proclaim Thy mercy in the morning, and Thy truth every night.
> By the prayers of the Mother of God, O Savior, save us.
> For the Lord our God is righteous, and there is no iniquity in Him.
> By the prayers of the Mother of God, O Savior, save us.
> Glory be to the Father, and to the Son, and to the Holy Spirit, and now and ever, and unto ages of ages. Amen.
> By the prayers of the Mother of God, O Savior, save us.

The predominant thought of the 91st Psalm is that the Lord is deserving of our constant worship. Atheists who do not want to know God and do not accord Him due honor will be punished by Him, but the just who praise Him and render Him homage will be exalted like the "cedars of Lebanon" (12th verse). Hence, the Psalmist calls everyone to honor and glorify God, for it is "meet, good, and just." We should glorify Him in the "morning" and "night," i.e.,

---

[14] A beautiful commentary on the weekday, Sunday and Feast-Day antiphons, as well as the "Typika" and "the antiphons composed of the beatitudes" is given by Nechaev (Bishop Bessarion), in his commentary. *Tolkovanie na Bozhestvennu Liturghiyu po chinu sv. I. Zlatousaho*, Spb., 1895 (4 izdan.), pp. 50–116.

every moment, every minute, and in every circumstance. The motivation for honoring and glorifying God is His mercy, His justice, and all His perfections. For in God there is no "falsehood" and He is "just."

The motif of this first Psalm is, therefore, as we have seen, the adoration of God. He is our Lord, Creator and God. Our life's purpose is to serve Him. To Him we must sing all our lives, "morning and night." Our life should be a "hymn to God."

b) Similar to this theme is that of *the first Sunday antiphon* composed of the first, second and third verses of Psalm 65 which exhort us to praise God for His providence as it was manifested in the liberation of the Chosen People from Egyptian captivity.

> Shout with joy to God, all the earth: sing ye a psalm to His name: give glory to His praise.
> By the prayers of the Mother of God, O Savior, save us.
> Say to God: how terrible are Thy works, in the multitude of Thy strength Thy enemies shall lie to Thee.
> By the prayers of the Mother of God, O Savior, save us.
> Let all the earth adore Thee and sing to Thee: let it sing a psalm to Thy name, O Most High.
> By the prayers of the Mother of God, O Savior, save us.
> Glory be to the Father, and to the Son, and to the Holy Spirit, and now and ever, and unto ages of ages. Amen.
> By the prayers of the Mother of God, O Savior, save us.

In this prayer the Psalmist calls upon all nations and the whole universe to praise God for the "mighty works" in which His omnipotence is displayed. Here the Psalmist alludes to the miraculous works wrought by God through Moses, which finally impelled the Egyptians to grant the Hebrews their freedom. Thus, the Psalmist says that even the "enemies" themselves dared not resist God's will and, in order to "appease" Him, set His people free.

The Church applies this Psalm to Christ's resurrection and sings it every Sunday, since Sunday is dedicated to the memory of His resurrection. The exodus of the Chosen People from Egypt is a prefiguring of Christ's resurrection and of His victory and that of His new Chosen People over the powers of darkness. Thus the first Sunday antiphon is a hymn of jubilation and victory of the souls redeemed by the death and resurrection of Jesus Christ. In this antiphon, we sing praise to the providence of God and His omnipotence exhibited in His Son's resurrection and at the same time in our own resurrection.

The weekday antiphon and the Sunday antiphon both have the same antiphonal refrain: "By the prayers of the Mother of God, O Savior, save us." This refrain accentuates the role of the Blessed Virgin Mary as the Mediatrix between her Son Jesus Christ and the faithful.

B. The Second Antiphon.

a) *The second weekday antiphon* is composed of three versicles from the 92nd Psalm; the first, second and fifth. This Paslm praises God as the Almighty

King of the Universe and Mighty Defender of the Chosen People:

> The Lord hath reigned, He is clothed with strength and hath girded Himself.
> By the prayers of Thy saints, O Savior, save us.
> For He hath established the universe, which shall not be moved.
> By the prayers of Thy saints, O Savior, save us.
> Thy testimonies become exceedingly credible.
> Holiness becometh Thy house, O Lord, unto length of days.
> By the prayers of Thy saints, O Savior, save us.

We saw the words of this Psalm in the Proskomide during the rite of covering the Lamb. The expression "He is clothed with strength" is one of the metaphors expressing God's dominion over all creatures. The Psalm, "The Lord hath reigned" describes God as the powerful Creator of the Universe clad in the full brightness of His grandeur and holding in the palm of His hand the universe which He "hath established and which shall not be moved"; He is a strong and powerful Lord, who "is clothed with strength." Power and grandeur are His royal apparel. Without His willing, nothing transpires in the world. He holds all things in His hands, He is faithful and true to His covenant promises. He is immutable as are His laws of the universe. Hence, honor and homage are His due. We should praise Him fervently and constantly in His churches ("houses") ("all the days"). The "house" of God perhaps alludes to the temple of Jerusalem where God was worshiped by the Jews. The Psalmist probably wished to remind the Jews to adore the one true God in His temple and not strange or false gods.

The dominant theme of this Psalm, and of the second antiphon, is rendering God, King and Lord of the universe, due honor and homage, especially because He is powerful and true to His promises.

b) *The second Sunday antiphon,* like the second weekday antiphon, extols God's might and power, and particularly His mercy toward man. He is remarkable for His wonderful sincerity and truthfulness. This antiphon is composed of the first, second and the third versicles of the 66th Psalm.

> O God, be generous to us, and bless us: cause the light of Thy countenance to shine upon us: and have mercy on us.
> O Son of God, risen from the dead, save us, who sing to Thee: alleluia.
> That we know Thy way upon earth: Thy salvation in all nations.
> O Son of God, risen from the dead, save us, who sing to Thee: alleluia.
> Let the people confess to Thee, O God: let all the people give praise to Thee.
> O Son of God, risen from the dead, save us, who sing to Thee: alleluia.

The motif of this Psalm is the abundant harvest with which the Chosen People were blessed by God, for the seventh versicle mentions that "the earth yielded its fruits." The Psalmist gives thanks to God for showing His mercy so generously, for "causing the light of His countenance to shine upon us." Not only does he express his gratitude for earthly blessings such as the fruitful harvest, but also for all His blessings and help. Here the Psalmist desires all people to be thankful to God always for all the blessings bestowed upon them, that they all understand "God's ways" and His mercy to all peoples, and thus "acknowledge" and "profess" the Lord God. The resurrection of Christ is the bountiful harvest on which depends our eternal life. Christ's resurrection is the guarantee or insurance of our resurrection and eternal life, for without it, as St. Paul says, "our faith would be vain." (Cor 15:14)

The second Sunday antiphon contains certain allusions to the resurrection of Christ, and instead of the weekday refrain "By the prayers of Thy saints, O Lord, save us," the refrain: "O Son of God, risen from the dead, save us" is sung in honor of Our Savior's victorious resurrection.

C. The Third Antiphon.

The third antiphon is the same for both Sundays and weekdays. Comprised of the first three versicles of the 94th Psalm, its subject is again one of triumph and praise:

Come let us praise the Lord with joy; let us joyfully sing to God our Savior.

(On Sunday): O Son of God, risen from the dead, save us, who sing to Thee: alleluia.

(On weekdays): O Son of God, wonderful in the saints, save us, who sing to Thee: alleluia.
Let us come before His presence with thanksgiving; and make a joyful noise to Him with psalms.
O Son of God . . .
For the Lord is a great God, and a great King over all the earth.
O Son of God . . .

In the refrain the weekday antiphon honors the Son of God, Who is "wonderful in the saints" while the Sunday antiphon honors His resurrection.

The third antiphon is an act of homage. The 94th Psalm, from which it is taken, invites us to manifest our reverence and submission to Him. The Psalmist encourages his people to be faithful to God who is more powerful than all gods and idols. He created all things; in His hands are the heavens, waters and firmaments, and all men are people of "His fold and sheep of His hand." (7th versicle) God is the shepherd of all peoples; hence, all must listen to His voice and not to the voice of strange shepherds. The Psalmist warns the people to remain faithful to God always and never again to abandon Him as they had done so frequently in the past.

To understand better the true sense of the antiphon, we may recall the Little Entrance when the priest carries the gospel book in procession around the altar while this antiphon is being sung: "Come let us praise the Lord with joy: let us joyfully sing to God, Our Savior." This prayer has a direct reference to Christ, who is symbolized by the gospel book. This antiphon exhorts us to render homage to Christ and to manifest our loyalty to Him who is our "God and King". The Gospels are our New Testament Tablets. We must preserve and cherish them; we must disregard other strange tablets, false philosophies and false prophets and avoid following the footsteps of the idolatrous.

3. Meaning and Role of the Antiphons

From our analysis of the contents of the antiphons we may conclude that, although composed of different Psalms, they share a common theme, a common motif—the extolling of God's perfections: His power, grandeur, beauty, might, goodness, mercy and province. We observe that in every antiphon the Psalmist repeats the same idea—praise the Lord, render Him due honor, bow down to Him, be faithful to Him, for He is our Lord, King and Ruler! All our antiphons are an expression of divine worship.

We may ask whether, besides this original and literal meaning, one can attribute a metaphorical or symbolic meaning to the antiphons? Can a symbolic role be ascribed to them in the rite of the Divine Liturgy?

The Byzantine commentators on our Divine Liturgy without exception strive to place them within the framework of symbolism. They seem to be looking constantly for a symbolic theme, even though it can be had only by forcing and stretching a text beyond its proper limits. They treat our antiphons in the same manner.

According the Pseudo-Herman, we sing the antiphons during the Liturgy because they represent the prophecies concerning Christ's advent into the world.[15] With His coming the prophecies were fulfilled. This same dominant idea is found in Theodore Andides.[16] He refers the antiphons to Christ, Who came into the world to fulfill the Law and Prophets and to announce the glad tidings of the New Testament.

Nicholas Cabasilas [17] discusses the antiphons still more extensively. In his opinion, psalmody plays a twofold role in the Divine Liturgy: first, to prepare and predispose us for sacrifice, and second to portray and symbolize certain episodes in the life and works of Jesus Christ. According to Cabasilas, then, the antiphons, like the beginning of the Divine Liturgy, symbolize the Nativity of Jesus Christ and His hidden life before His epiphany or public manifestation. This interpretation, however, is subjective and arbitrary. According to Simeon of Thessalonica also, the antiphons have a symbolic meaning—the versicles of the Old Testament Psalms contain the prophecies about Christ's incarnation, while the refrains ("By the prayers . . . Save us, O Son of God") represent the fulfillment of these prophecies.[18]

Other commentators of the modern school adhered to the same interpretation that the antiphons allude to the advent of Christ, His Nativity, or to His

---

15 Migne, PG, 98, 401.
16 *Ibid.*, 140, 432.
17 *Ibid.*, 150, 405–412.
18 *Ibid.*, 155, 717.

hidden life.[19]

Unfortunately, all these interpretations are subjective. We are firmly convinced that the texts of the antiphons themselves do not suggest the slightest prophetical allusion to the coming of Christ, His incarnation or hidden life. Even the Sunday, weekday, or holy day antiphons contain no prophetical reference to His birth or hidden life with the exception of those composed of the messianic Psalms sung on the Feast of our Lord's Nativity.

To refer the antiphons to events in Christ's life or to Christ Himself presents another difficulty, namely, that the Old Testament Psalms, with the exception of a few messianic Psalms, deal with the Old Testament concepts of God, His essence and existence. To interpret the Psalms according to our own ideas and not according to those objectively presented by the texts themselves would be to go counter to all sound exegesis. It is true that the central theme of the antiphons is Jesus Christ, for the refrains of the second and third antiphons testify to this. However, the theme does not allude exclusively to the person of Jesus Christ nor to any particular mystery of His life. The purpose of the antiphons is not to memorialize the mysteries of Christ's life, but rather to give God due honor and worship. We have seen that the fundamental thought of all the antiphons is to exhort all creatures to praise God; all are imbued with the idea of rendering worship. They are songs eulogizing the might, grandeur and mercy which are revealed in the works of God. They are intended to generate in our souls sentiments of gratitude, fidelity and sincere dedication to the Lord. They should enkindle within our souls a love for God and a strong resolution to serve Him the rest of our lives. In other words the antiphons incite us to offer our entire lives wholly and without reservation to God and to render them pleasing to Him.

4. The Small Ektenes and the Secret Prayers of the Priest

The antiphons are interwoven with the small *ektenes*. Between the first and second antiphons, and between the second and the third, we have a small or short *Ektene*. The second antiphon is followed by the hymn *Monogenes* or "Only-begotten Son".

The Small Ektene is so called to distinguish it from the Great Ektene or Ektene of Peace. It is an abridgement of the Great Ektene and does not contain its own petitions. Every small ektene is composed of the first and last petitions of the Great Ektene, i.e., petitions for peace—"Again and again in peace let us pray to the Lord"—and the petition for God's grace—"Help, save, have mercy, and protect us, O God, by Thy grace." The Small Ektene is, therefore, a reiteration of the most important petitions of the Great Ektene and the last part com-

[19] "The antiphons drawn from the Psalms typify or portray the advent of the Son of God into the world," N. Gogol, *Razmishleniya o Bozhestvennoy liturghii*, p. XXV, see *"Sluzhebnik"* of A. Maltsev, Berlin, 1902; According to Pelesh the antiphons express and typify "the expectation of the Saviour by the nations," see *Pasterskoe Bogosloviye*, p. 482.

memorating the Blessed Virgin Mary and the saints and the commending of ourselves, our neighbor and our entire lives to Christ our God. Finally, every small
ektene has its own private prayer which closes with an invocation honoring the
Blessed Trinity.

In the preceding chapter we explained the petitions repeated in the smaller
ektenes; therefore we will treat here only silent prayers of the priest. These
secret prayers come under the heading of "prayers of antiphons." In many of
the Greek and Slavonic Sluzhebnyks, they are placed after the invocation rather
than before it as they should rightfully be. In the handwritten texts of our Liturgy, we find it stated that the priest, when celebrating without a deacon, recites
the antiphonal prayer while the antiphons are being sung. Under the influence
of this transposition and the growing lack of deacons, we find the "prayers of
antiphons" appearing in certain printed Sluzhebnyks after the Small Ektene.
Therefore, this transposition could have also crept in, for as we have mentioned
earlier, only the services of the priest were found in the oldest liturgical
manuscripts, while the ektenes were found in a service book prepared exclusively
for the deacon. When in the course of time the deacon's services began appearing with the secret prayers of the priest, the latter were then moved to another
place. The words: "antiphonal prayers" were understood by many to mean that
they were to be recited during the antiphons, and not before the antiphons, i.e.,
before the invocations preceding the antiphons.

Reverting to the theme of the private prayers which the priest recites at the
end of every small ektene, we must direct our attention to an existing similarity
between them and the secret prayer of the Great Ektene. The contents of these
three prayers are so similar that *they may be considered variations of one and
the same prayer.* The common characteristic of all three is that they do not contain the particular or detailed petitions of the Great Ektene, but adhere to a
general form which includes all its petitions. Here the priestly character is
clearly shown. The priest is the representative or mediator between God and the
community. The priest does not pray as the people do who present various petitions; rather he combines the supplications of the people to form one general
prayer which he in turn offers to God.

The prayer of the first small ektene is in essence and form a continuation of
the private prayer of the Great Ektene. The priest prays:

> O Lord our God, save Thy people, and bless Thy inheritance (Ps 27:9).
> Sanctify those who love the beauty of Thy House (Ps 25:8): glorify them
> by Thy divine might in recompense; and forsake not us who put our trust
> in Thee (Ps 26:0).

In his first *secret prayer of "Antiphon"* the priest asks God to look with
mercy upon him and those who pray with him. In the second prayer he continues
the petition of the first, commending his flock to God and asking Him to save and
sanctify His faithful, His Chosen People, participants of His future Kingdom,
and to reward those who "love the beauty in His house." This refers not merely
to the external beauty of His house or church, but to the zealous fulfillment of

our religious obligations. It is for these zealous Christians that the priest prays, so that God may reward them with His grace.[20] The prayer closes with an appeal to God's might and power, that He never abandon those who hope in Him:

> (*Ekphonesis*) For Thine is the might and Thine is the Kingdom and power, and glory, of the Father, and of the Son, and of the Holy Spirit, and now and ever, and unto ages of ages.

This same prayer is repeated at the closing of the Divine Liturgy and is the beginning of the so-called "prayer behind the ambo." We could call the prayer of the first small ektene *a prayer for the Church and her preservation in the fullness of God's grace and life*. It is composed almost entirely of quotations from Holy Scripture—a characteristic, not of this prayer only, but of almost all the other prayers in our Liturgy.

The prayer of the second small ektene is obviously related to the preceding two prayers but it omits the usual beginning, the invocation of God's name, and begins with a petition:

> Thou who hast granted us these common and united prayers, who didst promise to grant the petitions of two or three gathered together in Thy name (Mt 18:19), do Thou now fulfill the petitions of Thy servants for their good; giving us also the knowledge of Thy truth in the present age, and granting everlasting life hereafter (*Ekphonesis*). For Thou are a good God and Lover of men and we render glory to Thee, to the Father, and to the Son, and to the Holy Spirit, now and ever and unto ages of ages. Amen.

This prayer, like the previous two, is a prayer for "the Church," which gathers for "common and united prayer." The priest recalls Christ's promise that whenever two or three gather to pray in His name, He will hear them. This consoling thought gives the priest confidence to ask God to hear the prayers of those present in the church. The prayer of the priest centers around two main petitions, namely, that God grant him and the faithful knowledge of the truth and the grace to contemplate Him in heaven face to face in the beatific vision. The prayer, like the others, closes with an appeal to God's mercy and His love for man, the sole source of His abundant grace. The doxology again brings it to an end.

We do not know the author of these prayers; however, we do recognize in their form and content *an air of antiquity*. Most likely they are compositions of the period of St. Basil and St. John Chrysostom.

5. The Hymn MONOGENES or "Only Begotten Son"

After the second antiphon the hymn *Monogenes* or "Only begotten Son" is sung. This hymn would seem at first glance to be an interpolation of a date

---

[20] In the Greek text the word is *antidoksazon* which means to express gratitude by means of praise, to praise someone, to reward someone.

later than that of the three antiphons because its theme does not coincide with theirs. We still do not know why or when this hymn was added to the antiphon. Some are of the opinion that it was inserted into the Divine Liturgy earlier than the antiphons themselves; [21] however, we have no reliable testimony to substantiate this.[22]

We do know, however, more about the origin and the author of this hymn. According to the testimony given by the Byzantine historian, Theophanes,[23] the author of this dogmatic hymn is generally considered to be the Emperor Justinian (527–565), one of the most renowned rulers of the Eastern-Roman Empire, who ordered that it be sung in the Divine Liturgy. Some scholars such as J. Puyade, and others, ascribe the hymn to the Monophysite Patriarch of Antioch, Severus, because the Syrian (Jacobite) Liturgy contains a very similar hymn ascribed to him.[24] Others again, like Grumel, assert that the *Monogenes* more likely owes its origin to Justinian, or that it was at least inspired by him, because in his writings and expressions we encounter the same thoughts, the same terminology and phraseology found in the hymn. At any rate, it must have originated in the time of Justinian because its character savors of a dogmatic-apologetic nature. It was written in refutation of two Christological heresies which prevailed at the time, namely, Nestorianism which denied unity of person to Christ and Monophysitism which denied the two natures in Him. Theophanes' testimony, then, can be taken as confirming the origin of the hymn *Monogenes* between the years 535–536.

Pseudo-Herman, in his liturgical commentary, affirms that the *Monogenes* was the composition of Joseph of Arimathea and Nicodemus who sang it while carrying the body of Christ to the tomb, for they believed that Christ was not only man but also God.[25] This testimony of Pseudo-Herman is considered bold, for one certainly has to be daring to ascribe this composition with its well developed terminology and dogmatic concept of the person of Jesus Christ to Joseph of Arimathea and Nicodemus. Needless to say, no great importance should be attached to this bit of testimony.[26]

As we have just mentioned, the *Monogenes* is a dogmatic-apologetic hymn, directed against the Nestorians and the Monophysites. It contains profound truths concerning Christ's nature, incarnation, death and resurrection. Although it is short, it is very expressive and thematic—a resumé of all the dogmas regarding Jesus Christ.

The whole of the dogmatic treatise on Christology is epitomized in this hymn. Let us examine closely its contents:

---

[21] De Meester, *Les origines...*, p. 321.
[22] We first meet with the *Monogenes* in the codices of the ninth and tenth centuries.
[23] Migne, PG, 108, 477.
[24] *Le tropaire "Ho Monogenes"*, "Revue de l'Orient. Chret.," 1912, XVII, pp. 253–267.
[25] Migne, PG, 98, 404.
[26] *Pseudo-Herman* himself, when ascribing the *Monogenes* to Joseph of Arimathea and Nicodemus, adds that others consider Emperor Justinian to be its author. Hence Pseudo-Herman himself does not take his bold conjecture too seriously (*ibid*).

O Only-begotten Son and Word of God, Thou who are immortal, and who for the sake of our salvation didst deign to become incarnate of the holy Mother of God, and ever-virgin Mary; who without change didst become man and wast crucified, O Christ God, who didst trample death by death, who art one of the Holy Trinity, and art glorified with the Father and the Holy Spirit, save us.

First of all, Christ is the "Only-begotten Son of God," for He is the Second Person of the Trinity, equal in nature to the Father, He is the true Son of God, not adopted like those who have been redeemed by Him. Christ is God's natural and true Son, and not a son by grace and adoption as we are. He is also the "Word of God" (Jn 1:14), the image and reflection of the Father (Hebr 1:3) and, therefore, whoever sees Christ and believes in Him, sees and believes in the Father also. (Jn 14:9) This Christ, equal to the Father, wished to become man for our salvation and to assume human flesh of the Blessed Virgin Mary. Taking upon Himself our human nature, He did not lose or change His divine nature, and therefore, we sing in the hymn that Christ "without change did become man" (in Greek—*atreptos*—"without changing"). The work of the incarnation and redemption was accomplished by Christ's death and resurrection. He "trampled death by death," for He is not an ordinary man, but "one of the Divine Trinity," to whom is also due the honor and glory which is given to the Father and Holy Spirit.

Some commentators refer the *Monogenes* to Christ's nativity,[27] an allusion that is unfounded and irrelevant. This symbolic application lacks rational foundation, not only because the rites of the Divine Liturgy are not a chronology of the life of Christ, but primarily because the theme of the hymn cannot be referred exclusively to His nativity. As we have just seen, the "Only Begotten Son" is ostensibly a dogmatic hymn about Christ and recalls, besides His incarnation, His death and resurrection. The fact that the hymn is placed in the first part of the Divine Liturgy has no bearing on this point, for it could well have been inserted in another part and still have retained its original meaning and theme. To refer the *Monogenes* exclusively to the nativity of Christ would be to disregard its true content and meaning.

---

[27] Theodore, Andides, Migne, PG, 140, 433; J. Pelesh, *Past. Bog.* p. 482; Archiman. Kypriyan, *Eucharistia*, Paris, 1947, p. 168 passim. LITERATURE: J. Puyade, OSB, *o.c.*; V. Grumel, *L'auteur et la date de composition du tropaire Ho Monogenes*, "Echos d'Or.," 22, (1923) Oct.–Dec., pp. 398–418.

Chapter V

THE LITTLE ENTRANCE

The Little Entrance takes place while the third antiphon is being sung. It is called "little" to distinguish it from the Great Entrance in the Liturgy of the Faithful. The Little Entrance is the entrance with the gospel book while the Great Entrance is the entrance with the holy gifts. Except for the reading of the Gospels, this is the most solemn moment in the Liturgy of the Catechumens. Its external solemnity implies that we are dealing here with some important rite of the Divine Liturgy.

The Little Entrance is a solemn procession around the altar with the gospel book. While the choir is singing the third antiphon, the Royal Doors are opened and the priest and deacon execute three metanias before the altar, after which the priest takes the gospel book from the altar and gives it to the deacon. Then the priest, following the deacon who is preceded by acolytes or candlebearers, proceeds around the altar, out of the sanctuary through the deacon doors and stands before the Royal Doors where he silently recites the entrance prayer. After the recitation of the prayer and the singing of the third antiphon, the priest makes the sign of the cross with his hand, blesses the sanctuary and kisses the gospel book, whereupon the deacon raises the book aloft and exclaims: "Wisdom, stand upright." In response to these words the choir sings the entrance song and the *troparion*. The priest then enters the sanctuary accompanied by the deacon who replaces the book on the altar as the priest silently recites the prayer of *Trisagion*. After this prayer and the *troparion*, the priest recites (or sings) the invocation:

> For Thou art holy, O our God, and we render glory to Thee, to the Father, and to the Son, and to the Holy Spirit, now and ever.

Then follows the *Trisagion* hymn: "Holy God, Holy Mighty One, Holy Immortal One, have mercy on us."

We shall examine the Little Entrance with its prayer and hymn of the *Trisagion,* for these two rites once constituted one liturgical whole. The prayer and hymn in honor of the Holy Trinity form the continuation and complement of the Entrance.

1. Origin and History of the Little Entrance

The Little Entrance is one of those rites which have lost their original significance. Hence, it would be difficult to understand it without first investigating its historical background. *The Little Entrance is a remnant of the bishop's entry*

176

into the sanctuary and only in the course of centuries was it transformed into the present-day entrance, i.e. the entrance with the gospel book.

Unfortunately, we are unable to find an adequate explanation of the Little Entrance in any of the liturgical commentators, for the main reason that it had lost its original significance. The Little Entrance is usually described *as a solemn procession around the altar with the gospel book.* The rite is obvious; it explains itself, for in reality the gospel book is carried from the sanctuary into the church and is given to the people to kiss; then it is raised aloft ("Wisdom, stand upright") and carried back to the sanctuary to be placed again on the altar. As we can see, the entire external rite of the Little Entrance centers around the gospel book. It is worth noting that at one time the book did not rest on the main altar from the beginning of the Divine Liturgy, but remained on the side altar close to the sacristy. Just prior to making the Little Entrance, the deacon, with the whole procession, went to the sacristy, took the book and carried it to the altar.[1] The Little Entrance, judging from externals, was to have been a solemn rite whereby the gospel book was carried out of the sanctuary and presented to the people. According to some liturgical commentators, the Little Entrance is a symbolic representation of Christ, the Teacher, who under the mystical image of the gospel book comes into the church to teach His faithful the truths of Gospel.[2]

Such an explanation of the Little Entrance is hardly satisfying, for it ignores its pristine origin. Originally it was not *an entrance or a procession with the gospel book,* for no allusion to this effect is to be found in the ancient liturgical documents. Mention of this Little Entrance was made much later.[3] We must conclude, then, that originally the Little Entrance was something other than it is today. In the oldest liturgical documents available, the Little Entrance is described *as the natural act of the bishop or priest entering the sanctuary to begin the Liturgy.* In the liturgical documents dating before the eighth century, *the Divine Liturgy begins with the Little Entrance,* that is, with the bishop or the priest entering the sanctuary. The Liturgy begins, according to the *Apostolic Constitutions,* the *Pilgrimage* of Etheria and the descriptions which St. John Chrysostom left us in his homilies, with the Little Entrance. All liturgical documents up to the eighth century betray no knowledge of antiphons, ektenes, or the Proskomide at the beginning of the Liturgy. Before the eighth century,[4] the Liturgy began as the priest entered the sanctuary and the people chanted a song, psalm or hymm.[5] The priest turned to the assembly of the faithful with a saluta-

---

[1] J. Dmitrevskiy, *Istor. Dogm. i tainstv. tolkovanie na liturghiyu,* Moskva, 1804, pp. 29–30; 133–134.

[2] We shall discuss the symbolic interpretation of the Little Entrance in a later chapter.

[3] The first testimony or witness to the Little Entrance is the liturgical commentary of *Pseudo-Herman,* hence around the eighth and ninth centuries.

[4] De Meester, *op. cit.,* pp. 315–318, 30–84. Cf. also the above interpretation of the Proskomide.

[5] *Ibid.,* p. 316. In liturgical documents the Entrance Hymn is called *"izodikon"* or *"eisodikon,"* meaning "entry" or "entrance."

tion of peace ("Peace be to all"), then proceeded to the throne or chair behind the altar and began the reading of the Holy Scriptures (Epistle and Gospel) which in turn was followed by a homily or sermon, the prayers for the catechumens and finally the dismissal of the catechumens. Then followed the sacrificial offering.

Most likely it was in the eighth century that a great change took place in the first part of the Liturgy.[6] The preparation of the bread and wine or the Proskomide was moved to the beginning of the Divine Liturgy and about that same time the antiphons and Great and Little Ektenes make their appearance. As a result of these changes, the Little Entrance lost its original meaning and character. No longer is it the beginning of the Liturgy but gradually becomes the entrance with the gospel book, with which it originally had no connection. For the Little Entrance is not so much an "entrance with the gospel book" as an "exit." Of the old entrance, only the name stayed with us, but its meaning and character changed beyond recognition.

That the Little Entrance is an entrance of the priest and not an entrance with the gospel book is clearly shown by the solemn Liturgy with the bishop participating. Here the original meaning and character of the Little Entrance is still preserved. The bishop begins the Divine Liturgy with the Little Entrance. Although he is present during the Great Ektene and the antiphons, he is not present in the sanctuary but outside it. He takes his appointed place in the church where he sits on a chair called the "throne" or "cathedra" and has no active part in the ceremonies until the end of the antiphons when he leaves his throne and, with the assisting priests and other concelebrants, solemnly enters the sanctuary, incenses it, walks round the altar, proceeds through the deacon's door and goes back to the altar through the Royal Door and, standing before it, begins to take active part in the Divine Liturgy. *The Little Entrance, therefore, here assumes its original meaning as the entrance of the priest into the sanctuary and the actual beginning of the Liturgy.*

To prove that the Little Entrance originally was the entrance of the priest into the sanctuary, we add that it can be found with this meaning in one form or another in both Eastern and Western Liturgies. These Liturgies also have an entrance prayer which is ordinarily the first liturgical prayer in which the priest asks God to grant him the grace of beginning the Liturgy worthily. Besides the purely structural, or external reason mentioned above for the change in the Little Entrance, i.e. the transfer of the Proskomide to the beginning of the Liturgy and the addition of the antiphons and ektenes, symbolism probably played a great role in changing its original character. Long ago the bishop and not the priest was the minister of the Divine Liturgy. At one time every city and every large community had its own bishop who was considered *Christ's representative,* endowed with the fullness of priestly authority to lead and teach the faithful.

---

[6] This change had to come about slowly, for usually all liturgical changes do not happen abruptly but gradually.

This concept of the bishop has been transmitted to us by St. Ignatius of Antioch (+ 117). The bishop was a figure of Christ and was acknowledged as such by the community in the rite of the Little Entrance. True, the priest also is a representative and priest of Christ; however, in the first centuries he did not possess full authority. With the spread of Christianity the number of bishops diminished, and not all church communities were able to have their own. The role of the bishop in the Divine Liturgy was, consequently, assumed by the priest. Since the entrance of the priest did not have the same significance as that of the bishop, i.e., the entrance of Christ—the High Priest in the person of the bishop —it became customary to look upon the gospel book as representing Christ. The bishop now no longer represents or symbolizes Christ in His entrance into the sanctuary. The gospel book is now accorded the deference once accorded the bishop. Today, under the symbolism of the gospel book, the people greet and pay homage to Christ Himself. Thus the character and original significance of the Little Entrance changed: it is now the entrance of the gospels which symbolizes Christ and not the bishop's entrance.[7]

In the light of these facts, we can now proceed with the explanation of the Little Entrance. Some elements of its original significance are retained not only in the Pontifical Divine Liturgy, but also in the Liturgy celebrated by the priest. This is confirmed by *the entrance prayer* which the priest recites during the Little Entrance.

2. Prayer of the Little Entrance

The prayer of the Little Entrance is ascribed to St. Basil the Great.[8] Although we have no positive proof of his authorship, its ancient origin is apparent. From an internal analysis we can affirm with certitude that it originated when the Little Entrance was still the bishop's entrance into the sanctuary and the beginning of the Divine Liturgy.

The prayer of the Little Entrance begins with a brief reflection, goes on to petition and ends with a doxology. The prayer is as follows:

O Master, our Lord God, who hast established in heaven the orders and armies of angels and archangels for the ministry of Thy glory: grant that with our entrance may enter the holy angels who with us serve and together glorify Thy goodness.
For to Thee is due all glory, honor, and adoration to the Father, and to the Son, and to the Holy Spirit, now and ever, and unto ages of ages. Amen.

This prayer confirms what we have already said about the primitive character and meaning of the Little Entrance. The content *of the prayer alludes to the entrance of the minister, and not the entrance with the gospel book.* There is in

---

[7] De Meester, *op. cit.,* p. 322.

[8] At least this is what Dmitrevskiy asserts p. 134. LITERATURE: Petrovskiy, A., *Vkhod v altar velikiy i malyj,* (Pravo. Bog. Ent., III, (1902), pp. 1064–1075); Leclercq, H. *Introit* (DACL, VII (1926) cols. 1212–1220.)

it no slightest allusion to the entrance with the Gospel, so that while the external rite of the Little Entrance centers on the gospel book the attendant prayer refers to the entrance of the priest. Here we have an excellent example of the evolution of the Divine Liturgy in which rite and prayer are at variance with each other and do not share a common theme. Such examples are numerous in the Divine Liturgy, especially in those rites which came into being in later centuries. The absence of harmony between the rite and its concomitant prayer proves that liturgical evolution, especially evolution of the ritual aspect of the Divine Liturgy, did not always go hand in hand with the theme and was not always consequential and relevant.

In the prayer, the entrance of the priest into the sanctuary is called the "entrance of the saints." What precisely does the expression, "entrance of the saints" mean? How are we to interpret the words "Blessed is the entrance of Thy saints, always, now and ever, and unto ages of ages," which the priest says immediately before entering the sanctuary, while imparting a blessing to this holy place? Some interpret the "entrance of the saints" as entrance into a holy place, i.e. the sanctuary.[9] This explanation, however, is wide of the point. "The entrance of the saints" is the entrance of the priest and his concelebrants, of those who are saintly and holy by virtue of the indelible character of the priesthood. Finally the term "saint" in ancient expression had a broader connotation than it has today. If we recall, St. Paul calls all Christians [10] "saints" who were baptized in the name of Christ. Taken in this sense, the word "saint" means every believing Christian, chosen by God and made an heir of His kingdom. The word "saint" can be applied *a fortiori* to priests, not only because they are God's chosen ones, but because, by virtue of vocation they are dutybound to lead all people to holiness. Hence the word "saint" in the liturgical connotation rightly refers to those who enter into the sanctuary. Taken in this sense, the word retains its ancient meaning and there is no reason why it should be altered.

Another explanation deserving special attention is that the Little Entrance of the priest is compared to the "entrance of the angels." The prayer alludes to the angels and archangels, who praise God unceasingly. God created them to render Him continuous "sacrifice of praise." The priest, about to enter the sanctuary to begin the Liturgy, recalls that eternal, perpetual service the angels and archangels render to God. Aware of his unworthiness, the priest begs God to make his entrance into the sanctuary resemble an entrance of the angels themselves, so that they, along with him, may offer service to Him.

---

[9] For example, Nechayev, (Bishop Bessarion) : The Deacon asks the priest to bless the holy entrance, "for the place where the entrance begins and ends is holy, i.e. the sanctuary, for it is the place of God's presence. Hence the priest prays and blesses the Little Entrance saying: "Blessed be the entrance of Your saints (i.e. the entrance into Your sanctuary). See his *Tolkovanie na Bozh. liturghiyu,* pp. 123–124. J. Dmitrevskiy also strives to explain the words "Vkhod Svyatikh Tvoikh" in similar manner in his *"Istor., dog., i tainstv. tolkov. na Bozh. lit.,* p. 135.

[10] Cf. the titles of St. Paul's Epistles to the Corinthians, Ephesians, Phillipians and others.

In short, the priest prays that his entrance be like that of angels, that his service will be an imitation and reflection of the service the angels render before the throne of God. This imitation and reflection of the heavenly service was the favorite theme not only of our Liturgy, but of ancient patristic tradition. It dominates the mystical works of Pseudo-Dionysius (fifth centrury) and is one of the salient features of his theological-mystical thought. Pseudo-Dionysius divides the whole created world into two "hierarchies of being," the celestial and the terrestrial. To the celestial hierarchy belong the choir of angels and to the terrestrial hierarchy, man. Both hierarchies have their own subdivisions. The terrestrial hierarchy is but the reflection and imitation of the heavenly one; hence, the service of people should also be a reflection of the service of angels.[11]

It is not our intention to give a detailed analysis of this original theological concept of the two mystical hierarchical services which so pervade our Liturgy. We should only be further convinved that the concept of Pseudo-Dionysius had an influence on the formation of our Liturgy, its prayers and rites.[12] Therefore, the liturgical text of the Little Entrance reminds the priest that he is a reflection of the angels whose service his service should resemble. His entrance into the sanctuary should be the "entrance of the angels."

3. Symbolism of the Little Entrance

What significance, then, does the Little Entrance have in our Divine Liturgy?

This question was answered only partially when we treated of its original significance and its evolution through the centuries. We have pointed out that in the primitive Liturgy the Little Entrance was actually the beginning of the Liturgy and the entrance of the minister or celebrant into the sanctuary. Later, the meaning changed to that of the entrance with the gospel book which symbolizes Jesus Christ who mysteriously comes to teach us the truths of His doctrine.

Many commentators, however, are not satisfied with this particular symbolic explanation. They add other meanings. According to *St. Maximos,* the bishop's entrance into the sanctuary symbolizes the advent of Christ into the world.[13] For Pseudo-Sophronius, the priest carrying the gospel book in the Little Entrance typifies Christ carrying His Cross. When the deacon carries it, then he symbolizes Simon the Cyrenian who helped Christ with His burden. When the bishop alone celebrates the Liturgy, his entrance symbolizes the Epiphany—the manifestation of Christ and the Holy Trinity at the River Jordan. The priest who precedes

---

[11] Cf. the works of Pseudo-Dionysius: *"The Celestial Hierarchy,"* Migne, P.G., 3. 119–370, and the *"Ecclesiastical Hierarchy,"* ibid., cols. 369–584.

[12] The influence of *Pseudo-Dionysius'* views is evident in the "Great Entrance" (the "Cherubic Hymn") and in certain places of the Anaphora. We shall discuss this influence later in our commentary on the Great Entrance and the Anaphora.

[13] Cf. Migne, PG, 91, 688.

the bishop in the prosession and at the entrance to the sanctuary gives precedence to the bishop, symbolizes St. John the Baptist, who announced at the River
Jordan that "He (Christ) must increase, but I must decrease." (Jn 3:30) Thus
the priest gives precedence to the bishop that the bishop may perform the services of the Divine Liturgy. When during the Little Entrance procession the
people sing together with the clergy, "Come, let us adore and fall down before
Christ," the clergy symbolize Christ's first Apostles who cried out in joy: "We
have found the Messias, which is, being interpreted, the Christ," (Jn 1:41) and
who came, saw and remained with Christ that day.[14]

Pseudo-Herman provides us with a similar symbol.[15] For him the Little
Entrance represents Christ's coming into the world. It also symbolizes His
epiphany, and the priest going before the bishop, giving him precedence, symbolizes St. John the Baptist.

Theodore of Andida [16] explains the Little Entrance in like manner, repeating almost verbatim Pseudo-Sophronius. *Nicholas Cabasilas* [17] compares the rite
with the manifestation of Christ at the Jordan River. For him the Little
Entrance also symbolizes the end or sealing of the Old Testament and the beginning of the New, for after the Little Entrance there are no allusions to the Old
Testament in the prayers (as in the antiphons), but instead the *troparia* and
hymns with New Testament themes are sung and the Gospel is read.

Simeon of Thessalonica sees in the Little Entrance the symbol of Christ's
ascension into heaven.[18] The bishop, entering the sanctuary, is Christ Himself,
who after His resurrection, ascended into heaven. The assistants (concelebrants)
of the priest portray the twelve Apostles, and the deacons, the angels who were
present at the ascension of Christ. Thus the Royal Doors, which were hitherto
closed, are opened for Christ to enter. The sanctuary symbolized heaven, the
church the world. After his entrance, the bishop incenses the altar and the sanctuary, signifying the descent of the Holy Spirit upon the Apostles after Christ's
glorious ascension.

We cite these symbolisms of the Little Entrance only to give an example of
the symbolic method of interpreting the Byzantine Divine Liturgy.

All that these commentators needed for the fabrication of a symbol was
some very remote or superficial analogy which had no real reference or connection with a given rite or prayer. The symbolic interpretations mentioned managed to account for all of Christ's entrances or comings—His coming into the
world and to the River Jordan, His going to Golgotha, and even His ascension
into heaven are all remembered and applied to the Little Entrance. Not one
commentator, however, considered the original significance of the rite. With so
many subjective ideas applied, it is no wonder that the real meaning and sym-

---

14 *Ibid.*, 87, 3993–3996.
15 *Ibid.*, 98, 405–408.
16 *Ibid.*, 140, 436.
17 *Ibid.*, 150, 412.
18 *Ibid.*, 155, 720–721.

bolism of the Little Entrance was lost; there was no real connection between rite and text and their symbols. Although we must admire the vivid and fertile imaginations and the incontestable inventiveness and ingenuity that went into these symbolic fabrications, they still contribute little to the proper understanding of the Little Entrance—in fact, they obscure it. Unfortunately, this symbolic method of explaining the Divine Liturgy is still rampant in many of the commentaries on the Byzantine Liturgy and is still carried to extremes.[19]

4. Prayer of the TRISAGION or Thrice-Holy Hymn

The third antiphon accompanies the Little Entrance. After the deacon's information, "Wisdom, stand upright," the choir sings the entrance verse, "Come, let us adore and fall down before Christ. O Son of God, risen from the dead, save us, who sing to Thee. Alleluia." This verse is actually a continuation and conclusion of the third antiphon; for it is taken from the same Psalm of which the third antiphon is composed.[20]

The *troparion* and *kontakion* [21] which correspond and change according to the feastday and the day, are then sung while the priest enters the sanctuary and, standing before the altar recites a silent prayer called the "prayer of the *Trisagion*" which is recited before the hymn of the *Trisagion*.

This prayer of the *Trisagion* was not a part of the early Liturgy (i.e. up to the fourth century inclusive) but probably became a part of it at the time when

---

[19] For example, according to Pelesh: "The Little Entrance signifies Christ's public manifestation at the River Jordan. The deacon or the sexton, who carries a lighted candle, represents St. John the Baptist, who preceded Christ as the star precedes the rising sun; the priest dressed in sacred vestments symbolizes Jesus Christ clothed in human flesh . . . the raising aloft of the Gospels by the deacon or the priest portrays the epiphany or manifestation of Christ, to whom the Heavenly Father gave witness that he was His Beloved Son; therefore, the faithful bowing sing: 'Come let us adore.....' " (See *Past. Bogoslovie*, p. 483). We are confronted with a similar interpretation in Mishkovskiy: "The Little Entrance symbolizes Christ preaching and as the angels ministered to Christ in the desert (Mat. 4:11), so in the prayer of the Entrance, the priest asks the angels to accompany him during the Entrance into the sanctuary and offer along with him the service of angels." (See *Izlozh. tsaregrad, liturghii*, pp. 68–69) M. Malinovskiy also refers the Little Entrance to the manifestation of Christ at the River Jordan. (See *Izyasnenie na Bozhestvennuyu liturghiyu*, Lvov, 1845, p. 83)

[20] "Come let us adore....." is the sixth versicle of Psalm 94. Only the phrase "before Christ" is an addition to the text of the Psalm, and therefore, evidently bears a relation to Christ symbolized in the Gospel book.

[21] The *Troparia* and *Kontakia* are *short eulogistic hymns*, composed in honor of the saints, the Blessed Virgin Mary, and Jesus Christ or some feast day or holy day. Their contents indicate the mystery of a given holyday; they eulogize or extol the life, merits and virtues of the saints, or the mysteries and events in the life of Jesus Christ and the Blessed Virgin Mary. We shall not discuss the derivation of the *troparia* or *kontakia*, their etymological or real definitions, nor shall we discuss their authors for this belongs to the domain of general liturgics. We shall present only certain literature pertaining to them: J. Molitor, *Byzantinische Troparia und Kondakia in syromelchitischen Ueberlieferung*, (Oriens Christ., 1930, 1–36, 179–199; 1930, 191–201) ; E. Bouvy, *Poetes, et melodes*, Nimes, 1886; L. Gautier, *Les tropes*, Paris, 1886; Pitra, *L'hymnographie dans l'Eglise grecque*, Rom, 1837; S. Petrides, *Notes d'hymnographie byzantine*, (Byzant. Zeitschrift, XIII (1904), 422–428); P. Mass, *Fruehbyzantinische Kirchepoesie*.

the hymn of the *Trisagion* was introduced, around the middle of the fifth century.[22] Our assumption is confirmed by the obvious relationship existing between the hymn of the *Trisagion* and its antecedent prayer which serves simply as a preparation or introduction to the hymn. Not until the eighth century, however, do we find it in the oldest Byzantine liturgical codex.[23]

In content this prayer is similar to the prayer of the Little Entrance, for in it are the same allusions to the angels and their heavenly service before the throne of God. Actually it is a continuation of the prayer of the Little Entrance, a development of its basic theme. Hence, the prayer of the *Trisagion* is the link between the Little Entrance and the hymn of the *Trisagion*.

Most of the words and expressions in this prayer are quotations from Holy Scripture and are noted for their great eloquence. The first portion of the prayer is especially long, i.e. the introductory reflection:

> O holy God, who restest in the holy places (Is 57:15), who art praised by the thrice-holy hymn of the seraphim (Is 6:2) and art glorified by the cherubim, and art adored by all the heavenly powers.

These words clearly reveal a connection between this prayer and the prayer of the Little Entrance, in the theme of the celestial service of the angels.

After recalling this theme, the priest considers the creation of the visible world:

> Who didst bring all things out of nothingness into being (Wisd 1:14), didst make man to Thine own image and likeness (Gen 1:26) and didst adorn him with Thy every gift: Thou givest wisdom and understanding to him that asks (2 Par 1:10) and scornest not the sinner, but ordainest repentance unto salvation; Thou hast deigned to us Thy sinful and unworthy servants to stand also at this moment before the glory of Thy holy altar and to offer adoration and glorification due Thee; . . .

Recalling that the aim of all creatures is the glory of God, the priest further continues to ask God not to despise his acts of praise but to give him the grace of glorifying Him:

> Do Thou, O Master, receive also out of the mouth of us sinners the thrice-holy hymn and visit us in Thy goodness. Forgive us every transgression, voluntary and involuntary, sanctify our souls and bodies, and grant that we may worship Thee in holiness all the days of our life, by the prayers of the holy Mother of God and all the saints of the ages who have pleased Thee, (*Ekphonesis*) —For Thou art holy, O our God, and we render glory to Thee, to the Father, and to the Son, and to the Holy Spirit, now and ever, unto ages of ages. Amen.

Examining this prayer more closely, we immediately recall the first prayer of the priest at the altar, in which he reminds himself that God permitted him to

---

[22] Even T. Mishkovskiy shows an inclination toward the theory that the prayer of the *Trisagion* is older in origin than the hymn of the *Trisagion* and that the prayer was the occasion for the hymn (Cf. Izlozhen. tsaregrad. lit., p. 43, below the text).

[23] That is, in the *Barberini Codex* which liturgists assign to the eighth century.

"stand also before the glory of Thy holy altar" to celebrate the Divine Liturgy. As a matter of fact, when there were no ektenes or antiphons at the beginning of the Liturgy, this was the first prayer the priest said after his entrance into the sanctuary. This explains its significance.

There is a great resemblance also between the prayer of the *Trisagion* and the prayer of the priest before "Holy, Holy, Holy . . . " in the Anaphora, as well as the prayerful hymn *Cherubikon*. In all three there are references to angels, their heavenly service, the creation and redemption of mankind, as well as to man's service as an imitation and reflection of the service of the angels in heaven. This is especially true of the *Hagiology*, "Holy, Holy, Holy . . ." which, as we shall see, is a true sister to the prayer of the *Trisagion*. The principal purpose of both is to awaken in the priest pious sentiments, to arouse him to zeal in God's service and to make him realize that his is not ordinary service but one which reflects that of the angels in heaven.

5. The Hymn of the Trisagion

The prayer of the *Trisagion* is only a preparation and an introduction to the hymn of the *Trisagion*: *"Holy God, Holy Mighty One, Holy Immortal One, have mercy on us."* This hymn plays an important role not only in the Divine Liturgy, but in other divine services as well. The *Trisagion* is one of the most frequently used of all hymns. It even became part of the *"Customary Beginning,"* i.e. of the introductory prayers of the Church services and the daily prayers of the people. Let us briefly examine its origin, history and significance.

a. History of the Hymm of the Trisagion

We have more testimonies regarding the origin of the hymn of the *Trisagion* than we have concerning the other liturgical hymns. However, because of their apocryphal nature, not all merit equal credence. Liturgists to this day are unable to ascertain who the author of the *Trisagion* hymn was, where the hymn originated, what occasioned its composition, or its original meaning and external form.

The first mention of the hymn occurs in the acts of the Ecumenical Council of Chalcedon (451).[24] Its author, however, is not mentioned. The Byzantine Church historians *Theophanes,*[25] *Cedrenus,*[26] *Nicephorus Callistus,*[27] and others [28] give us a legendary account which ascribes the origin of the hymn to a miracle. The substance of the account is as follows: In the time of St. Proclus,

---

[24] Mansi, 6, 936.

[25] Migne, PG, 108, 244–248.

[26] *Ibid.*, 121, 652.

[27] *Ibid.*, 146, 1217.

[28] We also find this legend of the miraculous origin of the hymn of the *Trisagion* in other Byzantine historical-theological sources, as for instance in the Letter of Acacius, Archbishop of Constantinople, to Peter Fullo, Mansi, 7, 1121–1124, St. John Damascene tells the same story (Migne, P.G., 94, 1021; or 95, 37).

Patriarch of Constantinople (434–446), the city was visited with an earthquake. The populace, in great terror, abandoned the city. Outside the city they implored God's mercy. While they were praying, a small boy fell into an ecstasy and an unearthly power seized him and lifted him up above the people. In his ecstasy, he turned to Proclus and the multitude, saying that he saw and heard angels singing before the throne of God the hymn of the *Trisagion*: "Holy God, Holy Mighty One, Holy Immortal One, have mercy on us." At once people and clergy started to sing this hymn, the earthquake ceased immediately and St. Proclus ordered the hymn to be introduced into the Liturgy. Queen Pulcheria and Emperor Theodosius ordered the hymn to sung throughout the Eastern-Roman Empire.[29] Syrian sources attribute the hymn to Joseph of Arimathea and Nicodemus, who are said to have sung the *Trisagion* along with the angels at the burial of Christ.[30]

Perhaps more important than the origin of the hymn of the *Trisagion* is its authorship. To whom should this hymn be ascribed? This question has piqued the minds of theologians and, as a result has engendered long disputes.

The cause for these disputes was the addition of the words still used in some of the Eastern monophysite churches, "*You, Who offered Yourself to be crucified for us.*" These words in the hymn of the Monophysite *Trisagion*, which allude to Jesus Christ alone and not to the Holy Trinity, are sung as follows: "Holy God, Holy Mighty One, Holy Immortal One, Who offered Yourself to be crucified for us, have mercy on us."

The Byzantine theologians protested this addition and considered it heretical since the *Trisagion* refers to the Holy Trinity. The addition provoked disputations and polemics between the two camps for many years. While the Catholics rejected and condemned it, the heretics introduced it into the Liturgy. The Byzantine Church never adopted this addition. When the Emperor Anastasius (491–518), who sympathized with the Monophysites, also wished to introduce it in the capital city of Constantinople, an insurrection arose which led the Emperor to abandon his intention. Two centuries later the Council of Trullo (692) condemned the addition as heresy and strictly forbade its incorporation into the *Trisagion hymn*.[31]

We do not know exactly who the author of the interpolation was. Byzantine sources generally ascribe it to the monophysite Patriarch of Antioch, Peter Fullo (+480).[32] However, it is difficult to determine the degree of veracity contained in these testimonies.[33] The question of the origin and history of the *Trisagion* is still open to discussion.

---

[29] Migne, PG, 108, 248.

[30] *Moyses bar Kepha, Explanatio mysteriorum oblationis:* ed. R. H. Connoly et W. Codrington, (Two commentaries on the Jacobite Liturgy, London, 1913, p. 26 ss.)

[31] Mansi, II, col. 977.

[32] *Ibid.,* 7, 1121, in the "Epistle of Acacius to Fullo."

[33] Very good is the work of M. Hanssens who treats of the history and origin and the disputes relating to the hymn of the *Trisagion* most extensively: *Institutiones liturgicae de ritibus orientalibus,* III, 108–156, Romae, 1932.

b. Meaning of the Hymn

Although liturgical researchers still cannot determine the original form of this hymn, with or without the addition discussed above, nevertheless, we may give the hymn a Christological or Trinitarian connotation. Should we take the hymn in its monophysite meaning, then, it becomes clear that it cannot be applied to the Trinity as a whole since only Christ "offered Himself up to be crucified for us." Hence, the contemporary monophysite refers it to Jesus Christ.

The Byzantine *Trisagion,* on the other hand, does not have this addition. Hence, it can be applied to the Holy Trinity. In fact, from the very beginning, the hymn had a Trinitarian and not a Christological connotation. This is the meaning St. John Damascene gives it in a treatise especially devoted to it.[34]

The Liturgy itself gives the *Trisagion* the same Trinitarian meaning. An internal analysis of the prayer has revealed this, for there we find a reference to the Holy Trinity. In the *Trisagion* prayer, the Liturgy makes mention of the Three Divine Persons. A beautiful commentary on the hymn is found in one of the verses sung during the vesper services of the Pentecost, where we sing:

> Holy God, who created all things through the Son and Holy Spirit; Holy Mighty One, through whom we know the Father, and the Holy Spirit came into the world; Holy Immortal One, the Spirit of joy, who comes from the Father and rests in the Son, Holy Trinity, Glory be to You

St. Damascene and other theologians and commentators on the Byzantine Liturgy strive to explain why, in the hymn, we call the Father, God, the Son, Mighty, and the Holy Spirit, Immortal. We call the Father God because He is the "source and the eternal principle" of the Son and the Holy Spirit. We call the Father God because from Him proceed the Son and the Holy Spirit. We call the Son "Mighty" because it was Christ who delivered mankind from the bondage of the devil.[35] We call the Holy Spirit "Immortal" because He is our source of grace and everlasting life. The words of the *Trisagion* are not to be taken in the exclusive sense but as referring to all Three Persons. This means, that the epithets used to describe each Divine Person, do not refer only to one Person to the exclusion of the others, for each Person shares in the same Divine Nature, and so each is equally and substantially Holy, Mighty, and Immortal. In other words, all three epithets in the hymn can be attributed to each Divine Person— to the Father, to the Son and to the Holy Spirit. Perhaps this is the reason why we sing the hymn three times. In this way we refer the "thrice-Holy" to all the Divine Persons together, and to each One individually.

---

34 Migne, PG, 95, 21–62.

35 Cf. the commentary of Pseudo-Herman, Migne, PG, 98, 408–409. LITERATURE: St. J. Damascene, Migne, PG, 95, 21–62; Furlani, G., *Il trattato di Yeso'yabh d'Arzonsul sul Trisagion,* "Riv. delli studi orientali," 7 (1916–1918), pp. 691–693; Engberding, H., OSB., *Zum formgeschichtlichen Vertaendnis des Hagios Ho Teos....,* "Jhb, f. Liturgiewissenschaft", 10 (1930); Hanssens, J. M., *Inst. Liturgicae de ritibus orientalibus,* III, 108–156 (R. 1932); Brou L, OSB., *Le Trisagion de la messe mozarabe,* "Ephemerides liturgicae, LXI, 1947, fasc. IV, pp. 309–334.

Chapter VI

THE READING OF HOLY SCRIPTURES

The most important part and at the same time the culmination point of the Liturgy of the Catechumens is *the reading of the Scriptures* (the Gospel and the Epistle). It is the heart and soul of the homiletic-didactic service. All other parts of the Liturgy of the Catechumens—the ektenes, antiphons, the hymns, *Monogenes,* the *Trisagion, troparia* and *kontakia*—are either a remote preparation or the framework for the reading of the Scriptures. Therefore, the reading of the Scriptures is basically the most essential part of the Liturgy of the Catechumens.

The reading of the Bible is also *the oldest integral part of the Liturgy of the Catechumens.* The pristine Liturgy contained no antiphons or hymns as the *Trisagion* and the *Monogenes,* but it did have the reading of the Scriptures. The ancient Liturgy began with the entrance of the bishop, which was immediately followed by readings from the Old and New Testaments. The Little Entrance and the reading of the Bible are the oldest and most important parts of the Liturgy of the Catechumens. All other liturgies possess these elements in one form or other.

The immediate preparation for the reading of the Scriptures begins when the priest or minister goes to the *"throne."* From the "throne" (cathedra or chair) which is located behind the altar, the minister greets the congregation with the salutation *"Peace to all."* This greeting is followed by the singing of the prokimenon, the Epistle and the Gospel. The *"Alleluia"* is sung after the reading of the Epistle and is followed by the reading of the Gospel. Great solemnity accompanies the reading of the Sacred Scriptures, especially the Gospels. Just as in the ektenes, we have the element of supplication, and in the antiphons and hymns, the element of praise, so in the reading of the Bible we have a third element, namely, that of indoctrination or instruction.

1. History and Development of the Reading
of Holy Scripture during the Liturgy

Before explaining each separate rite connected with the reading of the Holy Scripture, let us study its origin, history and development.

As to its origin, as we mentioned in the first part of our book, there is no doubt that the Church borrowed the custom from the Jewish synagogue. In all the services of the synagogue, the reading of the Scriptures played the most important role. Biblical reading also plays an important role in Christian services.

There are extant a score of ancient Christian references to the reading of Holy Scripture. These references are of great value to us because, with them, we are able to follow the development of biblical reading, beginning with the second century of the Christian era. St. Justin, the Martyr, mentions the reading of the Scriptures in his *Apology:* "On the day of the sun (that is Sunday), those living in the cities and in the villages gather together and there read the *Epistles of the Apostles and the Prophets* as long as time permits. After the reading, the one presiding over the assembly preaches to those present and exhorts them to observe all that has been read." [1]

Tertullian, another witness, also mentions the reading of the Scriptures: "Gathering together, we read the Holy Scriptures in order to derive a lesson for future or present application. With the Holy Word we confirm ourselves in faith, nourish our hope, and strengthen our confidence." [2] Other witnesses are: Origen,[3] St. Cyril of Jerusalem,[4] St. Basil the Great,[5] the *Apostolic Constitutions,*[6] the *Pilgrimage* of Etheria,[7] the works of St. John Chrysostom,[8] and other writers and Fathers of the Church. Not only do we learn from these sources that there were biblical readings, but we also learn of the *manner of reading,* the selection of the readings and the amount of reading.

In the pristine liturgy there was no one, definite manner of reading the Scriptures. What was to be read and the length of the reading depended upon the choice and discretion of the bishop conducting the services. The bishop selected passages from the Holy Scriptures that corresponded to the circumstances of time and the need of the faithful, as well as to certain occasions and holidays. At times in choosing a chapter from Holy Scripture, especially from the Old Testament, the order which the Jews observed in their scriptural readings was imitated. Thus, in the first centuries there was no one standard system employed in reading the Holy Scripture.

In the third century, we discover attempts being made at standardizing the order of the readings.[9] In the fourth and fifth centuries a definite system begins to develop. St. John Chrysostom, in one of his homilies, advises his hearers to read at home beforehand a chapter from the Scriptures to be read at the forthcoming services.[10] From this we may conclude that the choice and order of biblical readings no longer depended exclusively on the will or choice of the minister conducting the eucharistic service, but that there was already a certain established system. It was probably in the fourth and fifth centuries that the first

---

[1] Apology, chapter 67, Otto, *Corpus Apologetarum,* I, p. 184.

[2] Migne, PL, I, 468–469.

[3] Migne, PG, 13, 1819.

[4] *Ibid.,* 33, 340, 344, 456, 589.

[5] *Ibid.,* 31, 425, 1437.

[6] *Apostolic Constitutions,* Chapter II and VII; cf. Funk, *op. cit.,* I, pp. 161–163, 476.

[7] Duchesne, *Les origines du culte chretien,* Paris, 1925, pp. 515, 518, 520, 524.

[8] Migne, PG 63, 75–76.

[9] Cf. V. Dolotskiy, *O chtenii sv. Pisma pri bogosluzheniyu,* "Khrist. Cht.", 1846, II, p. 150.

[10] Migne, PG, 59, 77; also 48, 991–992.

"lectionaries" appeared, i.e. books which contained passages and chapters arranged in order. Unfortunately, not one of these books has been preserved, and consequently our knowledge about the order of biblical readings is fragmentary. We do know, however, that during Passion week the Gospel accounts of the passion of our Lord were read; during the Easter season, the accounts of the resurrection; and during the Pentecost season, the Acts of the Apostles were read.[11]

Of course, the order of biblical readings was not the same in all Churches and Rites. Almost every Church had its own custom and reasons for selecting their own scriptural readings. Therefore, the diversity we see in the system of biblical reading in the present-day Liturgies should not surprise us.

Our system of biblical reading is based on the *principle of continuous reading (lectio-continua)*, i.e., the reading of the entire New Testament in the course of one ecclesiastical year. Although we do not know exactly when this practice of continuous reading became prevalent, it could not have been earlier than the fifth or sixth century. We will not examine in detail, the question of how the order of biblical reading, *"the pericope system,"* which we have at the present, originated, developed and became fixed. Tradition has it that it was St Sophronius of Jerusalem (seventh century) who arranged the order of scriptural reading, and that he finally fixed the order of biblical pericopes. The final phase of arranging and stabilizing the order of pericopes came in the period of St. John Damascene (eighth century) and St. Theodore Studite (ninth century). The *Studite Typikon* is associated with the Monastery of Studium in Constantinople where Theodore was superior. This *Typikon* not only gives us the order of reading of the biblical pericopes, but also contains liturgical prescriptions or rubrics and rules for the monastic life.

In our Liturgy the reading of the Epistle and Gospel on week days is based upon the principle of continued reading. On the feast days of our Lord, the Blessed Virgin Mary and special saints, however, readings are selected appropriate to the theme of feast days. This practice is quite ancient. We find it in all Liturgies, Eastern and Western alike. The custom of continued reading is practiced during most of the Church year. This practice also remains in the Armenian Church.

The number of biblical readings varies with each Rite. The system of selecting two readings (Epistle and the Gospel) was retained in the Eastern and the Latin Rite. Other Rites have more readings. For example, the Armenian Church has three (Old Testament, Epistle and Gospel); the Egyptian (Coptic) Church has four, all from the New Testament (St. Paul, other Epistles, Acts of the Apostles and the Gospel); the Chaldean Church (Nestorian) also has four (two from the Old Testament and two from the New); the Syrian Church has six readings (three from the Old and three from the New Testament).

---

[11] Cf. Dolotskiy, *op cit.*, p. 152.

Our Liturgy has no readings from the Old Testament, although this was not so originally. In the liturgical documents from the second to the fifth centuries, Old Testament readings are assigned to be read before the New Testament readings of St. Paul, the other Epistles and the Gospel. However, by the ninth century reading of the Old Testament disappeared from the Byzantine Liturgy [12] and was retained only in other church services (e.g., Vespers, during Lent, and in the Liturgy of the Presanctified Gifts). Other Liturgies, as the Armenian, Chaldean and Syrian, as we have just seen, have kept the original practice to this day and still read selections from the Old Testament.

The principle of continuous reading which we have considered applies to both Gospel and Epistle. To give the faithful and the priest an opportunity to become better acquainted with the New Testament, the New Testament is divided into pericopes. This is not the same as the division into chapters and passages because each has its distinct purpose and, consequently its distinct character. The division into pericopes is liturgical, and thus each pericope constitutes a whole or a certain event in the life of Christ, His miracles, etc. The purpose of these pericopes is to give an excerpt from the four Gospels and from St. Paul and the other Apostles for each day. The reading of all these pericopes is called a "cycle" which begins with Easter. The cycle of the Epistles begins with the Acts of the Apostles, and the cycle of the Gospels begins with St. John. Each is divided into 67 pericopes and is read throughout the season of the Pentecost (beginning with Easter to the Descent of the Holy Spirit). Then comes the Gospel of St. Matthew which is divided into 116 pericopes and begins with Pentecost and extends to the eleventh Sunday after Pentecost. From the eleventh to the seventeenth Sunday after Pentecost, the Gospels of St. Mark (divided into 71 pericopes) are read, and from the seventeenth Sunday after Pentecost to the twenty-ninth Sunday, the Gospels of St. Luke (divided into 114 pericopes) are read. On the last Sundays after Pentecost and on the Sundays before Lent (the Sunday of the Publican and Pharisee, Prodigal Son, Meat-fare, Cheese-fare), the second part of the pericopes of St. Mark are read.

The readings of the Apostles begin with the Acts of the Apostles; when they are finished, the Epistles of St. Paul and the other Epistles are read. There are in all 335 pericopes in the Epistles. In this way, in the course of the church year, the entire New Testament (with the exception of the Apocalypse) is read.

In ancient times there existed separate editions of the Epistles and the Gospels together with their respective divisions of pericopes. They were called *Aprakos* from the Greek word which literally means "a day on which no work was done," hence, Sunday. [13]

---

12 Hanssens, *Institutiones liturgicae....* II, p. 162.
13 Cf. Dolotskiy, op. cit.

2. Procession to the "Throne"

The procession to the "throne" marks the beginning of the biblical readings. From the documents of the pristine liturgy, we learn that the minister, after entering the sanctuary, left the altar and proceeded to the throne located behind the altar. Our present day procession to the "throne" is a survival of this ancient liturgical rite.

The Church historian Eusebius of Caesarea [14] tells us about this throne, or bishop's cathedra. He tells that St. James, the first bishop of Jerusalem, had a chair elevated on a platform behind the altar. Tertullian also mentions a cathedra (chair) behind the altar in Alexandria, from which "the letters of the Apostles are read." [15] The *Apostolic Constitutions* also make mention of the throne.

As he proceeds to the throne, the minister says a silent prayer, taken from the 117th Psalm (v. 26): "Blessed is He that cometh in the name of the Lord." When he reaches the throne, the deacon asks him to bless it: "Bless, Master, the seat on high." Then the priest says silently:

Blessed art Thou on the throne of the glory of Thy Kingdom, who sittest upon the Cherubim, always, now and ever, and unto ages of ages.

In some manuscripts we have another prayer of different context.[16]

Byzantine liturgical commentators, as might be expected, interpret this procession symbolically. As is clear from their interpretations, they did not know its real origin, and therefore, they interpreted freely and allowed subjective conjecture to dominate their interpretations. Pseudo-Sophronius sees this procession as Christ's transfiguration. After the *Trisagion*, according to him, the bishop, attended by the deacons and priest, proceeds to the throne; the deacons represent the angels, the priests, the Apostles who accompanied Jesus to Mt. Tabor. The procession also symbolizes Christ's departure into heaven and the conversion of the Jewish nation, which began after Christ's baptism. Christ, sitting on the throne, signifies that, although possessing human nature, He was elevated above all things and sits at the right hand of the Father.[17]

Pseudo-Herman offers a similar interpretation. The procession to the throne and the sitting upon it symbolizes Christ's elevation into the heavens and the glorification of His human nature, which God the Father accepted as a pleasing sacrifice for the human race. Thus He says to Christ: "Sit at my right." [18] Theodore Andides [19] and Simeon of Thessalonica [20] give the same interpretation.

---

[14] Migne, PG 20, 681.

[15] Migne, PL., 2, 49.

[16] "Lord Master, God of the heavenly powers, save your people and reconcile them by the strength of your Holy Spirit and by the image of the holy cross of Your Only-begotten Son, with whom You are blessed for ever and ever. Amen." This prayer is found in the oldest document of our Liturgy—The Barberini Codex. (Eighth century)

[17] Migne, PG, 87, 3996.

[18] *Ibid.*, 98, 409.

[19] *Ibid.*, 140, 437.

[20] *Ibid.*, 155, 721.

These symbolic interpretations are irrelevant and inadequate because they overlook the original meaning of the procession to, and the sitting upon the throne. As we mentioned, the present procession to the throne is simply a survival of the ancient custom of the bishop's procession to the throne.

The reason why the bishop proceeded to the throne was that the reading of the Scriptures immediately followed, and according to ancient Christian custom, bishop, priests and faithful were seated during the readings.[21] We also recall that in the early Church the reading of the Scripture lasted longer than it does today, for selections from the Old Testament as well as the New Testament were read and were followed by a homily delivered by the bishop or the presiding minister. Thus the procession to the throne and the sitting had a practical purpose. Symbolic interpretation of this rite came later. Perhaps it was under the influence of this symbolic interpretation of all rites and prayers that the prayer accompanying the procession to the throne was introduced into the Liturgy. In it the "throne of the kingdom" upon which Christ sits surrounded by the Cherubim was mentioned. The earliest codices of our Divine Liturgy, as we have already mentioned, do not contain this prayer, hence, we can consider it a later interpolation, introduced into the Liturgy under the symbolic-interpretative influence.

The "throne," in our opinion, originated with the synagogue. It was customary among the Jews for the one who taught Holy Scripture and explained it to remained seated. To be seated on the cathedra, according to the Jews implied authority to judge and to teach. The Gospels themselves relate that Christ entered the synagogue and began to explain the Scriptures:

> And he came to Nazareth, where he was brought up: and he went into the synagogue, according to his custom, on the sabbath day; and he rose up to read. And the book of Isaias the prophet was delivered unto him. And as he unfolded the book, the found the place where it was written: 'The Spirit of the Lord is upon me, wherefore he hath anointed me to preach the gospel to the poor. . . .' And when he had folded the book, he restored it to the minister, and sat down. And the eyes of all in the synagogue were fixed on him. And he began to say to them: This day is fulfilled this scripture in your ears. (Lk 4:16–21)

Therefore, sitting on the throne symbolized the power to teach with authority. Christ spoke to the people about the Scribes and Pharisees:

> The scribes and the Pharisees have sitten on the chair of Moses. All things therefore whatsoever they shall say to you, observe and do: but according to their works do ye not; for they say, and do not (Mt 23:2–3).

By the words "the chair of Moses," Christ understood the power to make and enforce laws and the power to teach, which God gave to Moses, whose unworthy successors were the Scribes and Pharisees.

The idea of the cathedra symbolizing authority to teach was adapted from the synagogue by the Christian Church. Here one must look for the true sense

---

[21] Dolotskiy, *op. cit.*, Khr. Cht., 1846, 2, pp. 159–160.

and origin of our "cathedra." *The throne is a symbol of the teaching power of the minister.* For this reason the priest sits upon it while the Scriptures are being read, i.e. during the reading of the Epistle and Gospel.[22] Hence there is no need to refer the procession to the throne to Christ's transfiguration and his ascension, and the sitting upon the throne to His "sitting on the right hand of the Father." [23]

3. The Greeting of Peace

"Attention, Peace to All. Wisdom, Attention."

Besides the procession to the cathedra, there is another rite preparatory to the reading of the Scriptures and that is the *"greeting of peace"* which is a series of short acclamations of the priest or deacon. Its purpose is to bring the attention of the faithful to the reading of the Gospel. Such acclamations are: *"Attention," "Wisdom," "Stand Upright," "Peace to You,"* and *"Peace to All."* We encountered this acclamation at the Little Entrance when the deacon, lifting the Gospel, proclaims: *"Wisdom, stand upright."* The closer we approach the reading of the Scriptures, the more intensified and insistent these acclamations become. As soon as the priest reaches the throne his first words are to draw the attention of the congregation to the reading of the Scripture: *"Attention, Peace to All, Wisdom, Attention."* And when the choir finishes singing the *prokimenon,* again he exhorts: *"Wisdom!"* When the lector reads the title of the Epistle, he once more exclaims: *"Attention."* These same exhortatory acclamations also precede the reading of the Gospel.

It will be useful to consider the true significance of these words since their frequent repetition naturally tends to dull their force and rob them of their original sense. What is their real meaning? They have a long tradition. St. John Chrysostom mentions them frequently in his sermons. They were used very often

---

[22] When we say during the reading "of the Scriptures," we mean during the reading of both Epistle and Gospel, for in the primitive Church the minister and the people sat not only during the reading of the Old Testament and Acts of the Apostles, but also during the reading of the Gospel. This can be inferred from the testimony of St. Justin Martyr and other sources. In the fourth century, it was customary to listen to the Gospel standing, in order to show respect to Christ who speaks through the Gospel. The historian Sozomen, however, relates that in his time in Alexandria (fifth century) the pristine custom of listening to the Gospel sitting down was still retained (see Dolotskiy, V., Khrist. Chten., 1846, 2, p. 160).

[23] The custom of referring the cathedra to Christ probably dates back to the time when the Divine Liturgy was celebrated not only by the bishop but by the priest also. We have said that the bishop was the figure or personification of Christ Himself. When the priest took the place of the bishop in celebrating the Divine Liturgy, then the Gospel and the throne of the bishop became the symbols of Christ. The cathedra as a symbol of Christ was also introduced into Christian iconography. We mention here some well known ancient pictorial representations of Christ's throne called "ETOIMASIA." ETOIMASIA is one of the most popular motifs in the art of Mozaic: It is a picture of Christ's throne, representing or symbolizing Christ the Ruler (Pantocrator) and His forthcoming PAROUSIA (Last Judgment), or His second coming on earth.

in Christian services; with them the deacon carried out his function of directing the attention of the faithful to the more solemn moments of the Divine Liturgy. Since a great number of people took part in the services, it was necessary from time to time, for the sake of maintaining order, to rouse the faithful from their distractions and exhort them to recollect their thoughts, to observe silence and to maintain a pious attitude. No wonder these acclamations become more frequent the closer we approach the scriptural readings. They have a real purpose and significance.

The acclamation *"Attention"* indicates the necessity of attention during the scriptural readings. Christ exacted this same attentiveness when He spoke to His listeners: "He that hath ears to hear, let him hear." (Mt. 11:15 and elsewhere). This means, "Whoever listens to my words, let him listen with attentiveness, reflection and understanding."

"Wisdom"—this acclamation draws attention of the people to the profound doctrine of the Bible, to the wisdom of God contained in the Scriptures and written down under the inspiration of the Holy Spirit. Its author is no other than the all-wise and inscrutable God Himself.

The acclamation, *"Upright,"* *"Stand upright,"* directs one's attention to the proper disposition of the body. Long ago the faithful sat during the reading of the Scriptures. Gradually, however, the custom of standing at least for the reading of the Gospel was introduced. The exhortation to "stand up", then, must be taken in its literal sense. This and other similar acclamations in our divine services, are analogous to the military command, "Attention." During the reading of the Scripture we should predispose ourselves not only bodily but also spiritually. Our bodily disposition is actually only an outward expression of the internal disposition of recollection which is essential during the reading of the Gospel, if the seed of God's word is to take root in the soil of the soul. In His parable of the Sower, Christ compared those who listen inattentively to His word to the seed that fell on hard ground and was eaten up by the birds (Lk 8:5–7). That is what happens to those who do not listen to the reading of the Scriptures with proper attention; the word cannot take root in the soul, for a distracted, wandering mind filled with worldly cares does not allow the seed of God's word to bear fruit a hundredfold. The Liturgy warns us against the danger of such useless and fruitless listening.

The salutation of the priest, *"Peace to all,"* has a similar meaning. Here the priest expresses his desire that the congregation listen to the word of God in "peace," that God with His heavenly peace be present in the hearts of man during the reading of His word.

The intonation of peace ("Peace to all," etc.) occurs frequently during the Divine Liturgy and other services—it is, in our Liturgy, *a common formula of liturgical greeting.* The Liturgy adopted this *greeting* from our Lord Himself who addressed His disciples after the resurrection with the words: "Peace to you." (Jn 20:19) The Apostles and first Christians, in imitation of the Master, began using the words as a salutation. "Peace be to all" expresses a sincere wish for good things for others. We have already spoken of the meaning of tne word "peace" as used in Holy Scripture as well as in the Liturgy.[24] With this greeting of peace the priest not only salutes the congregation, but *also draws their attention to a new part of the service which is about to begin*. Every important part of the Liturgy begins with a salutation of peace, hence, it is not only a blessing bestowed upon the faithful but also an introduction to an important part in the Liturgy.

To these greetings of peace, the people answer: *"And to your spirit,"* or *"And with your spirit."* These expressions are Hebraisms. "And to your spirit" means "To you"—"To your person"; and "With your spirit" means "With you" or "With your person." The faithful express the desire that this peace which the priest wishes them be also with him and never abandon him.

To the Byzantine commentators the greeting of peace symbolizes Christ's farewell to His disciples before His ascension into heaven.[25] Pseudo-Sophronius sees in the greeting which precedes the reading of the Epistle, a symbol of the fulfillment of all the prophecies concerning Christ and the beginning of the New Testament.[26]

4. The Reading of the Epistle

The reading of the Epistle is preceded by the singing of the *prokimenon,* a short versicle taken from a Psalm. It is sung not only before the reading of the Epistle in the Liturgy, but also before the readings in Vespers, Hours and other divine services. *Prokimenon* is a Greek word which means "that which is placed before;" so it is a verse or song that comes before, or precedes, the reading of the Scriptures.

The *prokimenon,* like the antiphons, *troparia* and *kontakia,* belongs to the fluid or variable parts of the Divine Liturgy. These are the daily *prokimena* which correspond to the theme the particular day on which the Liturgy is celebrated. For example, the angels are mentioned in Monday's *prokimenon* because Monday is the day dedicated to the angels. ("Who makest Thy angels spirits, and Thy ministers a burning fire" (Ps 103:4). Wednesday's *prokimenon* is dedicated to our Blessed Lady; thus we have the hymn of praise: "My soul doth magnify the Lord, and my spirit hath rejoiced in God, my Savior." (Lk 1:46–47). Besides the daily *prokimena,* we have Sunday, holyday and feastday *prokimena* which correspond to the mystery of the particular day.

The *prokimenon* is probably a remnant of the ancient rite of reading selections from the Old Testment which was once present in the Liturgy. Now however, it serves as a preparation for the Epistle. At one time the *prokimenon* was composed either of a whole, or at least the greater part of a Psalm. Today it is

---

24 See the commentary on the Great Ektene.
25 Migne, PG 98, 409.
26 *Ibid.,* 87, 3997.

composed of a single verse, repeated once. Certain Liturgies (e.g., the Chaldean) still retain the custom of reading entire Psalms before each reading of the Scripture.[27]

The purpose of the *prokimenon,* as we have said, is to prepare the listeners for the reading of the Epistle. Some give it a symbolic meaning, e.g., Pseudo-Herman, for whom it represents the prophecies relating to Christ.[28] This interpretation is without foundation. As a matter of fact we have in the Liturgy very few *prokimena* that can be applied directly to Christ. For example, how can we apply to Jesus Christ the daily *prokimena* or those relating to the saints and the Blessed Virgin Mary?

The reading of the Epistle follows the chanting of the *prokimenon.* Since we have already discussed the history of scriptural reading, we need say no more here. There is no Liturgy in existence that does not have the reading of the Epistle for the reason that the Epistle is one of the oldest parts of the Liturgy of the Catechumens. Of all the Epistles, those of St. Paul are most frequently used, although the Epistles of the other Apostles—Peter, James, John and Jude as well as the Acts—are also read. The Apocalypse is omitted, probably because of its abstruse contents which over the centuries have given rise to various unorthodox interpretations, such as chiliasm.

The Epistle readings, like the Gospel pericopes, are arranged according to the principle of continuous reading. Therefore, the theme of the Gospel rarely coincides with that of the Epistles as it does in the Roman Liturgy where the Epistles are selected as a rule to suit the theme of the Gospel in some degree at least.

Byzantine commentators see the reading of the Epistle as signifying the calling of the Apostles and their mission to preach the Gospel throughout the world. Such is the interpretation of Theodore Andides.[29] If the procession to the throne symbolizes Christ's ascension, then evidently the reading of the Epistle symbolizes the mission of the Apostles. To the question why we read the Epistle before the Gospel, N. Cabasilas answers that it is because Christ first sent the Apostles to preach, and then afterwards preached Himself. "And after these things the Lord appointed also other seventy-two, and he sent them two and two before his face into every city and place whither He Himself was to come." (Lk 10:1)[30] Simeon of Thessalonica gives the same explanation.[31]

---

[27] That the practice of singing entire Psalms between the readings existed in the Liturgy also is proven by the rubric in the Sluzhebnyk after the greeting of peace before the reading of the Epistle—"And the choir sings the prokimenon, a Psalm of David." This custom is ancient, for it is derived from the synagogue service in which a Psalm was sung between the two readings. It was later retained by the Christian Liturgy. Entire Psalms were sung as early as the fifth century.

[28] Migne, PG, 98, 409.

[29] *Ibid.,* 140, 437.

[30] *Ibid.,* 150, 416–417.

[31] *Ibid.,* 155, 724.

At one time the Scriptures were read facing the people. This custom has been retained only for the Gospel, although in certain districts of Greece it is still practiced for the Epistle as well.[32] This ancient manner of reading the Epistle certainly is in accord with the spirit of the Liturgy for, reading the Epistle facing the people, gives the word "Brethren" more meaning and sense, than reading it facing the altar.

5. Alleluia

Just as the *prokimenon* is an introduction to the reading of the Epistles, so the hymn *"Alleluia"* introduces the reading of the Gospel. This is the oldest and most widely used hymn in all Liturgies. The word itself indicates its ancient derivation. *Alleluia* is a Hebrew word *(Hallelu-Ya)* which means "Praise the Lord," or "Praise God." It was used in the Old Testament (Job 13:18). There are many Psalms, especially the Psalms of praise that have the *Alleluia* at the beginning or at the end— (e.g., Ps. 103–104, 111–117). We also encounter the *Alleluia* in the New Testament. In the Apocalypse of St. John, it is a paean or hymn of praise and victory sung by the saints in heaven: "After these things I heard, as it were, the voice of many people in heaven, saying: Alleluia. Salvation and glory, and power is to our God." (Apoc 19:1)

The chanting of the *Alleluia* was quickly adopted in the Liturgy. St. Basil,[33] the Synod of Laodicea [34] and other liturgical documents mention it. In ancient times the chanting of the *Alleluia* was wide-spread and highly revered. It was not sung only during the Liturgy, but on other occasions—by sailors during a storm, by harvesters in the fields, and by soldiers marching on their way to war. It was also sung at funerals.[35]

The *Alleluia* holds a very special place in the Liturgy. As can be determined by the disputes concerning its use, this hymn was considered very significant. For example, one of the accusations of Cerularius against Rome was that the "Latins" do not sing the *Alleluia* during Lent. Cerularius quoted this as one of the "Latin errors".

Another dispute arose in Muscovy (Russia) at the beginning of the fifteenth century in the city of Pskov, about the number of times the *Alleluia* was to be sung—whether two or three times. Metropolitan Photius decreed that it be sung three times (1419). Thirty years later, however, the argument was reopened. The cause of the disagreement was that some referred the *Alleluia* to the Triune God and therefore sang it three times, while others referred it to Jesus Christ and therefore sang it twice. This *dispute* was one of the factors that brought about a schism (raskol) in the Russian Orthodox Church. The ritual conserva-

---

[32] Cyprian Archim., *Eucharistiya*, Paris, 1947, p. 180.
[33] Migne, PG, 29, 304.
[34] Mansi, II, 567, A.
[35] See the article of Cabrol, quoted in the literature relating to this chapter.

tists retained the practice of singing it twice. The Stohlavy Synod (1551) decreed that the *Alleluia* should be sung twice in the Muscovite (Russian) Church, but the Synod of 1667 decreed that it be sung three times. These two historical *disputes* bear witness, on one hand, to human limitation, religious fanaticism, pharisaical formalism, religious hyprocrisy, and on the other, to the significance that was, at one time, attached to the hymn *Alleluia.*

The *Alleluia,* like the *prokimenon,* was at one time sung after each line of the entire Psalm. Gradually, only two verses corresponding to the theme of a given holyday or feastday were sung. The *Alleluia,* as a solemn hymn of praise and joy, occupies a very suitable place in the Liturgy, i.e., before the reading of the Gospel. This is the "joyous news" of Christ's doctrine and grace, and the book is the symbol of Christ who speaks to us in the Gospel. Hence, the chanting of the *Alleluia* before the reading of the Gospel is not only an expression of spiritual joy but the greeting of the glorified risen Christ, who comes to us in His word, under the symbol of His Gospel.

Pseudo-Herman refers the *Alleluia* to the Trinity in a manner characteristic of all the old liturgical commentators. According to him, *Al* means God the Father, *El* means God the Son, *luia* means the Holy Spirit. When we, as he claims, analyze the word in Hebrew, then Alleluia means: *Al* = Came, *El* = God, and *Luia* = Praise Him. On the basis of this "etymological" analysis, then, Pseudo-Herman decides that the Alleluia refers to the Holy Trinity.[36] Here we have a classical example of the mania for seeking out every kind of mystical and symbolic meaning in the prayers and rites of the Divine Liturgy.[37]

6. The Reading of the Gospel

The apex of the Liturgy of the Catechumens is reached in the *reading of the Gospel.* There is no need to prove here that this is the most important part of the homiletic-didactic or instruction service. What the reading of the Torah, i.e. the Law of Moses, was in the synagogue services, the reading of the Gospel is in the Divine Liturgy. "For the law was given by Moses; grace and truth came by Jesus Christ." (Jn 1:17) The reading of the Gospel announces this truth and grace in every Divine Liturgy; it heralds the "joyous good tidings" of our Lord and Teacher, Jesus Christ. It is consequently appropriate that the reading of the Gospel constitute the most solemn action in the Liturgy of the Catechumens, an

---

[36] Migne, PG, 98, 412.

[37] The interpretation of Pseudo-Herman betrays a complete lack of knowledge of the Hebrew language on the part of the author. Small wonder, then, that his "philological" excursion is also strained as are most of his symbolic conjectures. A similar ignorance of the Hebrew tongue is found in the other Byzantine commentators of the symbolistic school. Simeon of Thessalonica explains the Alleluia in the spirit of Pseudo-Herman (Migne, PG, 155, 724). E. Malov justly remarks about these commentaries: "It is understood that on such explanations one should not base one's commentary. These explanations only serve to prove that it is unreasonable to undertake an explanation of something one knows nothing about . . ." (See his article in the list of the above literature).

action surrounded by impressive rites and ceremonies. Only the Little Entrance enjoys a similar framework of external solemnity, but then this rite too is associated with the reading of the Gospel.

We have mentioned that the *Alleluia* is an immediate preparation for the reading of the Gospel. There are besides two other preparatory rites—the rite of incensing, a silent prayer, *"Illumine our hearts"* and the blessing the priest bestows upon the deacon before reading the Gospel.

The rite of incensing, which takes place while the *Alleluia* is being sung, is an ancient rite. Both Pseudo-Herman and Pseudo-Sophronius mention and interpret it symbolically. The *Pilgrimage* of Etheria [38] also speaks of the incensing before the Gospel is read. Pseudo-Sophronius [39] sees in the rite a symbol of grace arfd charism which the Apostles received from Christ to preach the good tidings, to cure the sick, exorcise demongs, etc. But Pseudo-Herman gives us the most original interpretation. According to him the thurible represents the human nature of Christ, the fire His Divinity, and the pleasant odor, the Holy Spirit. He has still another interpretation in which the thurible is the blessed womb of the Blessed Virgin Mary which bore the divinity.[40] Theodore Andides interprets the incensing as a symbol of the grace given to the Apostles to heal the sick.[41]

These subjective and arbitrary interpretations of the rite of incensing are in no sense satisfying. We have already discussed the meaning of incensing,[42] pointing out that it is an expression of reverence shown to the object or person being incensed. Therefore, the rite of incensing before the Gospel is, primarily, an expression of reverence for the Gospel, the symbol of Christ. True, we are not incensing the book itself, but what the book represents, namely, the Gospel or the Incarnate Word. Like the *Alleluia,* the rite of incensing is the greeting of Christ and an act of homage to Him. It has meaning too for the people present in church, inciting them to listen to the word of Christ. Symbolically, it is a prayer petitioning God to predispose out hearts and our souls to receive His Word. The Apostle Paul expresses his gratitude that God through him, i.e. through his preaching, "always maketh us to triumph in Christ Jesus, and manifesteth the odor of His knowledge by us in every place." (2 Cor 2:14) Here St. Paul compares the preaching of the Holy Gospel to a pleasant odor which diffuses itself and fills the air. According to some liturgical commentators, the incensing before the reading of the Gospel signifies the blessings of the preaching of the Gospel throughout the world, especially in the hearts of the faithful.[43]

---

[38] Duchesne, *Origines du culte chretien,* (Paris, 1925), p. 515.

[39] Migne, PG, 87, 3997.

[40] *Ibid.,* 98, 412.

[41] *Ibid.,* 140, 440–441.

[42] Cf. our interpretation of the rite of incensation at the Proskomide and the beginning of the Divine Liturgy.

[43] Cf. *Tolk. na Bozhestv. Lit.* of Bessarion, pp. 158–159, and the commentary of Malynovsky, pp. 95–96. The priest performs the rite of incensing before the Holy Gospel "to show reverence toward the Gospel about to be read as well as to signify mystically that, through the preaching of the Gospel, the grace of the Holy Spirit flowed upon the four corners of the earth and filled the hearts of man with the pleasant odor of Christ's doctrine" (2 Cor 2:4) .

In certain Eastern Rites as, for example, the Armenian Rite, there exists a custom of incensing the reader of the Gospel throughout the reading. This incensing refers to none other than Christ Himself who, through the deacon or priest, teaches us the truths of His Gospel.

The prayer before the reading of the Gospel: "Illumine our hearts . . . " was introduced into the Liturgy in a later century, for we do not come across it in the ancient liturgical manuscripts. It is a sincere petition to Christ for the grace of understanding the Gospel and of translating its principles into actions:

> Illumine our hearts, O Master, Lover of men, with the spotless light of Thy divine knowledge, and open the eyes of our mind to the understanding of Thy gospel preaching. Instill in us also the fear of Thy blessed commandments, that trampling upon all carnal desires, we may enter upon a spiritual life, thinking and doing all that is well-pleasing unto Thee. For Thou art the enlightenment of our souls and bodies, Christ O God, and we render glory to Thee, together with Thine eternal Father, and Thy most holy and good and life-giving Spirit, now and ever, and unto ages of ages. Amen.

In this prayer, which is one of the most beautiful prayers of the Byzantine Liturgy, the significance of the Gospel in our life is expressed. We must accept its message as the basis of our philosophy of life and our morals, "thinking and doing" all things according to its principles. However, our "carnal desires" are a great impediment to making the Gospel principles our guiding light. These desires are the briars which choke the seed of God's word in our souls and prevent it from taking root and producing fruit. Therefore, we ask God to instill in us "fear of the blessed commandments," for fear of the Lord is the beginning of wisdom. The fear of God gives us more strength to subdue our passions and to "enter upon a spiritual life." By ourselves we are weak and incapable of leading a spiritual life. Not until we are enlightened by the grace of God will the seed of His word take root in our souls. Hence, the priest prays God to open "the eyes of our mind," to bestow His grace of enlightenment upon our souls. The grace of God is the Divine Sun, without which there can be no life, development or progress in the spiritual life.

After this silent prayer, the Gospel is read. When the Liturgy is celebrated with the deacon, then *he asks the priest to bless him* before he reads the Gospel. The priest sings:

> May God, by the prayers of the holy, glorious, all-laudable Apostle and Evangelist N . . ., grant thee to evangelize the word with great power in the fulfillment of the gospel of His beloved Son, our Lord Jesus Christ.

Then he solemnly announces the reading of Gospel with the usual exhortative acclamations: *"Wisdom, let us stand upright to listen to the Holy Gospel. Peace be to all."* Just before the reading, we again hear the acclamation, alerting the people to pay attention, *"Let us attend."* More solemnity is added to the rite by the fact that the people listen to the Gospel standing and the acolytes stand holding lighted candles. Thus, great respect is shown to Christ whom the Gospel symbolizes, for as Pseudo-Sophronius remarks, "The Gospel is a symbol of Christ, the Son of God, who appeared to us not in figure but really and truly, and that which we read are His words, God's truth, God's doctrine."[44]

At the beginning and the end of reading the Gospel, the people exclaim, *"Glory be to Thee, O Lord, glory be to Thee."* St. John Chrysostom, among other things, mentions this prayer, "When the priest begins to read the Gospel, we stand and say, *'Glory be to Thee. O Lord.'* "[45]

It was also an old custom to hold lighted candles during the reading of the Gospels to symbolize the Gospel as the light of our lives. Regarding the lighted candles, St. Jerome remarks, "In all the Eastern churches, before the reading of the Gospels candles are lit, even during the day when the sun is shining. They are lit not to dispel the darkness, but as a sign of solemnity and joy."[46] The reason for all the solemnity attending the reading of the Gospel is that Christ here appears among us and speaks to us as He once did in person to the Jews and to His Apostles. In the reading of the Gospel God's word and doctrine is re-echoed.

In ancient times the bishop or president of the assembly delivered a homily or sermon after the Gospel. This was a constituent part of the Liturgy of the Catechumens, and the custom of having a sermon has survived to our own day. In some places, however, it is delivered not after the Gospel but after the prayer behind the Ambo.[47] Yet it must be said that the proper place for the sermon is immediately after the Gospel, of which it is the continuation and explanation.

---

[44] Migne, PG, 87, 4000.

[45] *Ibid.,* 62, 484.

[46] Migne, PL, 23, 346 (Contra Vigilantium).

[47] The custom of preaching after the prayer behind the Ambo is still prevalent in the Russian-Orthodox Church. In the Ukraine as well as in the Greek Church the sermon is usually delivered after the Gospel. Perhaps the reason for moving the sermon to the end of the Liturgy, was that the faithful after having heard the sermon after the Gospel, left the church thus omitting the most important part of the Divine Liturgy—the eucharistic-sacrificial part. Even St. John Chrysostom complained in his homilies that many Christians came to church only to hear the grandiloquence of the preacher and after having heard, left. (cf. Migne, PG, 48, 725).

SELECT BIBLIOGRAPHY

Nikolskiy, K. T., *Obozryenie bogosluzhebnykh knigh po otnosheniyu ikh k tserkovnomu ustavu,* Spb., 1856.

Dolotskiy, V., *O chtenii sv. pisaniya pri bogosluzheniyu,* (Khrist. Cht., 1846, 2, pp. 145–160).

Ranke, E., *Das kirchliche Perikopensystem,* Berlin, 1847.

Schu, *Die biblischen Lesungen,* Treves, 1861.

Beissel, S. *Entstehung der Perikopen des roemischen Messbuches,* Freiburg. in Br., 1906.

Fortescue, A., *Lessons in the liturgy* (The Cath. Enc. 1910, Vol. IX, pp. 193–199).

Godu, G., *Evangiles,* (DACL, V, (1922), cols. 852–923)m

Godu, G., *Epitres,* (DACL, V. (1922), cols. 245–344).

Mosler, *Lesungen,* (Kraus-Realencyclop., 1888, Vol. II, pp. 292–295).

Herwegen, I., *Die Heilige Schrift in der Liturgie der Kirche,* 1931.

Rahfls, A., *Die alttestamentlichen Lektionen der griechischen Kirche,* 1915.

Glaue, P., *Die Vorlesung der hl. Schrift im Gottesdienst,* 1907.

Baumstark, Anton, *Die sonntaeglichen Evangelienlesungen im vorbyzantinischen Jerusalem,* (Byzant. Zeitschrift XXX, (1930), pp. 350–359).

Smirnov, P., *Alliluya, tserkovnaya pyesn,* (Pravo. Bog. Ents., I., 1900, pp. 542–548).

Golubinskiy, E., *O pyesni alliluya,* (Bog. Vyestnik, 1892. May, pp. 197–223).

Malov, E. *Ob alliluya. Vrazumlenie staroobryadtsam,* (Prav. Sob., 1891, III, noyabr, pp. 187–208; dekabr, pp. 251–266).

Nilskiy, J. *K istorii sporov ob alliluya,* (Khrist. Cht., 1884, I, pp. 690–729).

Klyuchevskiy, V. *Pskovskie spory,* "Pravo. Obozryenie," 1872, Vol. II, pp. 283–307, 466–491, 709–741 (spory pro Alliluya).

Cabrol, F., *Alleluia. Acclamation liturgique,* (DACL, I., cols. 1229–1246).

Wagner, P. *Alleluia (Chant),* (DACL, I., cols. 1226–1229).

Leonardi Cecconi De Montalto, *Dissertazione sopra Alleluia,* Velletri, 1769.

O'Mahony, *Alleluia's story,* (Dublin Review, Vol. 120 (1897), p. 345–350).

Salvadori, *L'Alleluia,* Roma, 1899.

Chapter VII

THE CONCLUSION OF THE
LITURGY OF THE CATECHUMENS

The homiletic-didactic (instructive) portion of the Liturgy climaxes with the reading of the Gospel and a homily. After this, the prayer for the catechumens is said and at this point, in the ancient Liturgy, the catechumens withdrew from the church. It now remains to analyze and explain this last part of the Liturgy of the Catechumens and its ending. This conclusion is reminiscent of the beginning of the Liturgy which opened with the Great Ektene or the litany of peace. The Liturgy of the Catechumens also concludes with an ektene. After the Word of God is read, the whole assembly—priest, deacon and faithful—return to the ektene form of prayer. In the order of ektenes we have three—an ektene of supplication, one for the deceased and one for the catechumens.

1. The Ektene of Supplication

In the Greek Liturgikons this ektene is appropriately called the *"ektene ikesia,"* i.e., ektene of supplication or entreaty. The Old-Slavonic name "Suhuba" ("double") is not an adequate name for this ektene, because the ektene is not a "double" but a "triple" ektene; i.e., to most of its petitions the people respond with three "Lord have Mercy's" and not two.

Regarding the origin of the ektene which is sometimes called the triple ektene of supplication, besides the general data given in the explanation of the Great Ektene, we can add that it is very similar to one of the ektenes in the Liturgy of St. James. This ektene appears first in the liturgical manuscripts of the twelfth century, and by the fifteenth century, we encounter its present-day form.

As to its structure and form, *the triple ektene* differs from the others, in that it is not so much an ektene of petitions for various needs as for various persons and their positions in the Church. The Great Ektene is a supplication for both the various needs and stations of life; the ektene of supplication is a petition only for various persons, notably for the Church hierarchy.

The first three petitions of the triple ektene are an invitation to prayer. Like the other ektenes, the triple ektene begins with the invocation:

> Let us say with our whole soul and whole mind let us say. "Lord, have mercy." "O Lord almighty, God of our fathers, we pray Thee, hear us and have mercy." "Lord, have mercy." "Have mercy on us, O God, according to Thy great mercy; we pray Thee, hear us and have mercy." "Lord, have mercy." "Lord, have mercy." "Lord, have mercy."

After such persistent appeal to the goodness and mercy of God, we propound our petitions to Him:

> Again we pray for our holy universal Supreme Pontiff N . . ., Pope of Rome, and for our most reverend Archbishop and Metropolitan N . . ., and for our God-loving Bishop N . . ., and for those who labor and serve in this holy church or monastery, and for our spiritual fathers, and for all our brethren in Christ. "Lord, have mercy" (3 times).
> Again we pray (for our God-protected Emperor (or King) N . . ., for his health and salvation (or)) for our sovereign authorities and for all armed forces. "Lord, have mercy" (3 times).
> Again we pray for the people here present, who await from Thee great and abundant mercy, for those who have done charity for us, and for all orthodox Christians. "Lord, have mercy" (3 times).

Like every ektene, the triple ektene has its own silent prayer, which the priest recites before the ekphonesis. In the Greek and Russian Sluzhebnyks, the silent prayer follows the third ektene petition. However, its proper place is not between the ektene petitions but immediately before the invocation, which is the conclusion of the silent prayer of the priest. The whole content of the triple ektene is summarized in this silent prayer in which the priest appeals not to the merits of the people but to the mercy of God. Here he presents to God the supplications of the people. By his secret prayer, the priest intensifies the supplications:

> O Lord our God, accept this ardent supplication from Thy servants, and have mercy on us according to the abundance of Thy mercy; and send Thy compassion upon us and upon all Thy people who await from Thee great mercy. (*Ekphonesis*) For Thou art a merciful God and Lover of mankind, and we render glory to Thee, to the Father, and to the Son, and to the Holy Spirit, now and ever, and unto ages of ages. Amen.

The dominating theme is the "mercy" of God. Just as the theme of the Great Ektene was to implore God's peace and grace, so also the chief petition and motif of the triple ektene is His mercy. The words are relevantly taken from the 50th penitential Psalm of David (first line of Psalm) "Have mercy on us, O God, according to Thy great mercy," and from the penitential prayer of the Jewish King Manasses (2 Paral). Both these kings angered God by their grave sins, but returned to Him, expiated their sins and did not cease to call upon His mercy.

The triple ektene is a fervent, sincere supplication, a persistent appeal to, or invocation of, the mercy of God. Hence, it is aptly called the "insistent" ektene.

2. The Ektene for the Deceased

In the Liturgy for the deceased, between the triple ektene and the ektene of the catechumens, we have the ektene for the deceased. The Greek Liturgy does not contain this ektene, but both Greek and Russian Liturgikons commemorate the deceased in the triple ektene. However, Byzantine-Ukrainian Liturgy dedicates a special ektene to the deceased.

The ektene for the departed is borrowed from the burial services and the Parastas. This ektene is not an original part of the Liturgy, although praying for the dead is not new—the oldest Liturgies have prayers for the dead, not only in the form of an ektene of petition, but also in the form of a commemorative prayer like in the Anaphora.

The ektene for the departed, like other ektenes, has its own special petitions, petitions for the "repose of the deceased." The whole ektene revolves around this theme. This theme has other synonymous expressions and metaphors, as for example, the "peace of God", the salvation of the soul. In the ektene, we pray for peace for the departed souls, that peace which Christ brought to the world, which we have become partakers of through baptism, and which we shall enjoy in heaven while contemplating God in the Beatific Vision. Although the salvation of the souls of the living is the main concern of the Church, she sends up her petitions also for those who have gone to their eternal rest.

For a proper understanding of the character of the liturgical prayer for the deceased, we emphasize that the Church, in every prayer for the dead, recalls the moment when the soul departs from this world into everlasting life. It is to this moment that the liturgical prayer for the dead properly refers. The liturgical prayer for the departed is like a prayerful ransom which the Church, from its treasury of graces, offers for the deceased who must cross the threshold of eternity.

The ektene for the deceased is an appeal of the penitent David to the mercy of God:

> Have mercy on us, O God, according to Thy great mercy; we pray Thee, hear us and have mercy. "Lord, have mercy, Lord, have mercy, Lord have mercy."
> Again we pray for the repose of the souls of the departed servants of God N . . ., and that their every sin, voluntary and involuntary, may be pardoned. "Lord, have mercy, Lord, have mercy, Lord, have mercy."
> That the Lord God will establish their souls where the righteous repose. "Lord, have mercy, Lord, have mercy, Lord, have mercy."
> For the mercy of God, the kingdom of heaven, and the remission of their sins, we beseech Christ, King Immortal and our God. Grant it, O Lord. Let us pray to the Lord. Lord, have mercy.

Peace for the dead is the first petition of this ektene. We pray for the happy passage of the soul from this world into everlasting life. The actual meaning of the word "demise" (the Greek *anapausia*) is the happy departure from this life into eternity, the attainment of citizenship there and the right to reside there, as well as final repose, peace and contentment in the life beyond the grave. In other words, we pray for the final attainment of everlasting salvation for the departed. By the word "peace" we may understand that spiritual peace and freedom from sin which burdens the soul and prevents its entry into heaven. Therefore, to the prayer asking for "rest," the church adds the prayer for "forgiveness of sins," voluntary and involuntary, and for the "kingdom of God." For the sins of man prevent him from entering into the kingdom of heaven, where only those who are robed in the radiant and royal attire of God's grace are admitted.

The ektene for the deceased also has a secret prayer which the priest recites and which ends with the ekphonesis. Like the other prayers, it prolongs the theme of the ektene. This particular prayer is a classical example of liturgical prayer. It has three parts: a moment of reflection, the prayer itself and finally the doxology.

> O God of spirits and of every flesh, Who hast trampled down death, and overthrown the devil, and given life unto Thy world, do Thou, O Lord, give rest to the souls of Thy departed servants N . . ., in a place of brightness, in a place of repose, whence sickness, sorrow, and sighing have fled away. Pardon every transgression committed by them, by word, or deed, or thought, as a good God, and Lover of mankind; because there is no man who lives and sins not; for Thou alone art without sin; Thy righteousness is everlasting righteousness, and Thy word is truth. For Thou art the resurrection and the life and the repose of Thy departed servants N . . ., O Christ, our God, and unto Thee we render glory, together with Thy eternal Father, and Thy most holy and good and life-giving Spirit, now and ever, and unto ages of ages. Amen.

The prayer for the dead is one of the oldest prayers encountered in the divine services. In the last century one of the monuments discovered, i.e. burial stones in Egypt, had a prayer inscribed upon it in Greek which archeological examination revealed differed only slightly from our prayer for the dead. This prayer which was engraved on the grave stone of Father Shenudi, belongs according to some archeologists, to the fourth century (more accurately 344), before the Liturgies of St. Basil and St. John Chrysostom were composed. Hence, this prayer is to be considered one of the oldest.[1]

It expresses great confidence in God's mercy and goodness. God is the Lord of all "spirits and of every flesh"; He conquered death and gave life to the world; He can also give eternal "rest" to His departed servants. Not only can He transport them to the place of bliss and contentment where there iş no sickness, no care, no tears, but He does this because He is a "merciful God who is a lover of mankind." To this infinite mercy, Holy Church appeals, begging for the for-

---

[1] For this prayer see A. Khoynackij, *O proiskhodzhenii pogrebalnoy molitvi: "Bozhe dukhov i vsyakiya ploti,"* (Khrist, Cht., 1881, I, pp. 218–220). See also A. Dumont, *Fragment de l'office funebre de l'eglise grecque sur une inscription d'Egypt* (Bulletin de correspondance Hellenique, 1877, nos. VI–VII). Nikolskiy, F., *O molitvye za usopshikh*, Moskva, 1904. Silvester, epis., *Ob otnoshenii k usopshim*, (Tr. K.D.A., 1890, I, pp. 527–556). Sokolov, V. A., *Mozhno li i dolzhno nam molitsya v tserkvi za usopshikh-inoslavnikh?*, (Bogo, Vyes., 1906 I, pp. 1–31). Niechay, M., *Oratio liturgica pro defunctis in ecclesia Russa Orthodoxa, (exquisitio dogmatica)*, Lublini, 1933.

giveness of sins which weigh down the souls of the departed and close the gates of paradise. The Church reminds us that we are weak and sinful beings and that God alone is "holiness" and "truth." Fortified by her great confidence, the Church ends her prayer with an invocation glorifying God, the "resurrection, life and rest" of all His departed servants. Christ Himself said that He was the "resurrection and the life" and that whoever believes in Him, although he die, will live forever.

Thus this prayer ends with the same thought with which it began, namely, the mercy, goodness and omnipotence of God. In its content, form and style it is indeed a beautiful example of a liturgical prayer.

3. The Ektene for the Catechumens

The Liturgy of the Catechumens concludes with the *ektene for the catechumens*. Other Eastern Liturgies do not have supplications for the catechumens, at least in the form that exists in our Liturgy, nor does the Roman Liturgy. Only the Greek-Byzantine Divine Liturgy has retained the petition for this group of people.

The ektene for the catechumens is, certainly, a remnant of an ancient practice in the Church, namely, the catechumenate.

With its disappearance around the eighth century the other Liturgies ceased to commemorate the catechumens, but the Byzantine Liturgy has kept these prayers to the present day. When we, for example, compare the ektene for the catechumens with the supplications for the catechumens of St. John Chrysostom and the *Apostolic Constitutions,* we observe a literal similarity between the ancient texts and text of our own ektene.

The ektene for the catechumens, like the other ektenes, begins its supplications with an invitation to prayer: "Catechumens, let us pray to the Lord."

After this opening, the petitions follow:

Faithful, let us pray for the Catechumens, that the Lord have mercy on them.

Then come a series of supplications for the catechumens themselves:

That He reveal to them the gospel of righteousness.
That He unite them with His holy catholic and apostolic Church.
Save, have mercy, help and protect them, O God, by Thy grace.

To all these petitions the faithful respond: "Lord, have mercy." Then the priest asks the catechumens to bow their heads before God: "Catechumens, bow your heads to the Lord," after which he says the prayer for the catechumens:

Lord our God, Who dwellest on high and beholdest the humble, Who hast sent forth the salvation of the race of man, Thine Only-begotten Son and God, our Lord Jesus Christ, look down upon Thy servants the Catechumens, who have bowed their heads before Thee, and make them in due time worthy of the bath of regeneration, remission of sins and the robe of incorruptibility. Unite them unto Thy holy, catholic and apostolic Church, and number them among Thy chosen flock. That they also with us may glorify Thy most honorable and magnificent name, of the Father, and of the Son, and of the Holy Spirit, now and ever, and unto ages of ages. Amen.

As one can see, the content of the prayer for the catechumens is substantially the same as that of the ektene. Like the ektene, the prayer implores God for the grace of baptism for the catechumens, it asks that they persevere until the long desired hour when they will become full members of the Church.

After the invocation, the catechumens depart from the church:

All ye who are Catechumens depart: Catechumens depart. All ye who are Catechumens depart. Let no one of Catechumens remain. All we who are faithful, again and again, in peace let us pray to the Lord.

Long ago the Church was very strict in this matter. No catechumen was allowed to remain, and the deacon was commanded to stand at the door of the church to prevent any catechumens from entering. For this reason the church doors were closed as St. John Chrysostom and the *Apostolic Constitutions* testify. However, with the gradual disappearance of the catechumens, these strict rules lost their meaning. Since the catechumenate no longer exists, the dismissal from the church has ceased to exist.

A great number of liturgists regard the ektene for the catechumens as anachronistic and declare that it should be eliminated from our Liturgy, since the prayers for the catechumens have lost their original significance. With the disappearance of the catechumenate as a distince institution preparatory to Holy Baptism, they feel, the ektene should have also disappeared. Hence certain churches of the Byzantine Rite, although they have the ektene of the catechumens in their Sluzhebnyks, do, as a rule, omit it. There have also been those among the Russian liturgists and clergy who clamored for the removal of the ektene of the catechumens, but no final decision has been reached.[2]

The stand taken by these liturgists is certainly justified. But even in our modern Liturgy the prayers for the catechumens could still have their meaning, if not the original and proper meaning, at least a symbolic, metaphorical one. St. Maximos Confessor [3] and after him, Simeon of Thessalonica [4] compared the dismissal of the catechumens to the last judgment which is to take place at the end of the world. It will come, they remark, when the Gospel of Christ shall have been propagated throughout the world as a testimony to all nations. Then Christ will come with His angels to separate the saints and faithful from the sinners and infidels. The former will enter into everlasting happiness; the latter will be sentenced to everlasting suffering. This comparison is completely unsatisfactory, for here the catechumens are placed on a level with the reprobates or the

---

[2] Cf. Cyprian, *Evkharistiya,* Paris, 1947, pp. 188–190. He also quotes the names of those bishops who in Russia approved of eliminating the ektene of the catechumens from the Liturgy. Lectures on this are printed in "Otzivi eparkh. arkhiereev ko voprosu o tserk. reformye," Spb., 1906.

[3] Cf. Migne, PG, 91, 692–693.

[4] *Ibid.,* 155, 295.

eternally condemned. Just as we can be sure that not all the baptized will be saved, so also can we be sure that not all the unbaptized will be rejected and condemned. Hence, to compare the rite of dismissing the catechumens from the church to the condemnation of the reprobate at the Last Judgment is groundless.

If we wish to give a symbolic or metaphorical meaning to this rite today, then it should be in reference to the faithful, as with Gogol in his commentary on the Liturgy. At the beginning of the Liturgy of the Faithful, he makes the following beautiful remark: "Although we scarcely find unbaptized persons in the church today, i.e. Catechumens, neverthless, let everyone present (the faithful) be mindful that he is, in faith and deed, far from the faithful of ancient Christian times, who were admitted to the holy table of love." [5] Later on he compares the dismissal of the catechumens to the merchants and vendor who were driven and cast out of the temple by Christ: "Recalling the scene where Christ of Jerusalem drove out the idle vendors and shameful merchants, who converted His temple into a market place, let everyone present strive to drive out of his soul the carnal man, so that like the Catechumens (one who was not yet prepared to be admitted to the Holy Table) we may be worthy to approach the mysteries." [6]

This is the sort of meaning the ektene of the catechumens would have today. Thus it would be an invitation to sincere penance, to amendment of life, to return to God. Thus also it reminds us, with what heart and soul we should attend the Liturgy which is called the "Liturgy of the Faithful." Only with pure and innocent souls, pure hearts free from sin can we take part in the sacrifice of Christ, the eucharistic banquet. Renouncing all that is sinful, impure or unworthy, we should, like truly "faithful" and saintly members of Christ, offer to God the unbloody sacrifice of His Only-begotten Son and our Lord Jesus Christ.

SELECT BIBLIOGRAPHY

Dolotskiy, V., *Chin oglasheniya v drevney Tserkvi*, (Khrist. Cht., 1849, I, pp. 418–466).

Silchenkov, K., *K voprosu o proiskhozhdenii v drevne-khristiyanskoy tserkvi "Tainovodstvennaho Ucheniya,"* (Vyera i Razum, 1901, nos. 4, 5, 7, 20).

Zarin, S., *Katekhumenat*, (Pravo. Bog. Ents., Vol. IX (1908), p. 182–190).

Lukas, H., S.J., *The "Missa Catechumenorum" in Greek Liturgies*, (Dublin Review, Vol. CXII, (April 1893) pp. 268–292).

Thibaut, J., *L'initiation chretienne aux premiers siecles*, (Echos d'Orient, XXI., pp. 323–334).

De Puniet, P., *Catechumenat*, (DACL, II, cols. 2579–2621).

Funk, F. X., *Die Katechumenatshclassen des christlichen Altertums*, (Theol. Quartalschrift, 1883, 41–77; 1886, 355–390).

Corblet, Jules, *Du catechumenat*, Paris, 1881.

Probst, F., *Geschichte der katholischen Katechese*, Breslau, 1886; *Katechese und Predikt vom Anfang des 4. bis zum Ende des 6 Jahrhunderts*, Breslau, 1884.

Cellarius, B.—Druffel, J., *De catechumenis veteris Ecclesiae*, Helmstadii, 1657.

Mayer, J., *Geschichte des Katechumenats und der Katechese in den ersten sechs Jahrhunderten*, Kempten, 1868.

---

[5] Cf. Gogol, *Razmishleniya o Bozhestvennoy liturghii*, Jordanville, 1952, p. 22.
[6] *Ibid.*, p. 23.

Section 3, *THE LITURGY OF THE FAITHFUL*
(*The Liturgy of Sacrifice*)

Chapter I

PRELIMINARY REMARKS

This portion of the Liturgy differs substantially from the Liturgy of the Catechumens in character, content and purpose as well as in origin, structure and evolution. Although, together, they form one liturgy, nevertheless, they are actually two essentially distinct rites.

The division of the Divine Liturgy into the Liturgy of the Catechumens and the Liturgy of the Faithful (or Liturgy of the Word and Liturgy of Sacrifice) may, at first sight, seem anachronistic and archaic. Nonetheless, there is good reason for it. Before explaining each part of the Liturgy of the Faithful, it would help to point out the essential differences between it and the Liturgy of the Catechumens.

1. The first point of difference is in the name. This name can be fully understood only in the light of its historical background. The name "Liturgy of the Faithful," as opposed to the name "Liturgy of the Catechumens," has its justification in ancient Christian practice and discipline.

This name is usually explained by the fact that long ago, as we have seen, only the faithful were permitted to be present at this part of the Liturgy. Schismatics, Jews, heretics and catechumens were excluded from it. But this explanation is not totally adequate, for it omits giving any intrinsic reasons why these various classes of people should have been excluded. It must be remembered, too, that not even all the faithful—e.g., public sinners, the possessed, the penitents—were able to participate in this part of the Liturgy. Although baptized, they also like the catechumens had to leave the church when the Liturgy of the Faithful was about to begin.

The actual reason for this ancient Christian practice, which today may seem to have been too severe, was that long ago participation in the Liturgy was by far greater than it is today.

In the first centuries the faithful frequented the Sacrament in a body, that is, they took part not only in offering the sacrifice but also in its consumption (Holy Communion). Thus, not only catechumens, Jews, pagans, heretics and schismatics, but also sinners and penitents, could not participate in the Liturgy of the Faithful. These latter were excluded precisely because they could not receive Holy Communion; they were considered unworthy to approach the holy table, and therefore, were, to a degree, placed on an equal level with the cate-chumens and non-Christians.

With this in mind, one can understand why discipline in the early Church was so strict. The "faithful," in the ancient Christian concept, were not merely those who had received the sacrament of Baptism, but those who were permitted to receive the Body and Blood of Jesus Christ—those baptized persons who were not only members of the Church, but were in the state of grace and able to take part in the Eucharistic Banquet. Hence, the Liturgy of the Faithful is the Lit-urgy of the worthy, the holy, or in a word, the "Liturgy of the Faithful" in the full sense of the word.

2. *The principal and basic difference between the Liturgy of the Catechu-mens and the Liturgy of the Faithful lies in their distinct characters.* The Lit-urgy of the Catechumens, in its very nature and purpose, is homiletic-didactic or instructive; its purpose is to instruct and to teach. The Liturgy of the Faithful, on the other hand, does not have for its object the teaching of the faithful, but the offering to God of the eucharistic, Unbloody Sacrifice. In this we find its essential character—the offering of sacrifice, and this sacrificial character is what essentially distinguishes it from the Liturgy of the Catechumens.

In the Liturgy of the Faithful, a miraculous change of the eucharistic ele-ments, i.e., bread and wine, into the Body and Blood of Jesus Christ is effected. The Liturgy of the Faithful is actually the Liturgy proper, for during this Lit-urgy the mystical offering of Jesus Christ to God takes place. All that has been said in the historical introduction about the nature and purpose of the Divine Liturgy refers not so much to the Liturgy of the Catechumens as to the Liturgy of the faithful, which is the unbloody repetition, renewal and continuation of Christ's sacrifice on Calvary. It is a memorial to man's redemption, a living memory of Christ, a mystical and mysterious immolation of Christ for mankind.

Because of this fundamental and essential character of the Liturgy of the Faithful, it is also referred to as the Liturgy of Sacrifice, an expression even more suitable than the traditional name "Liturgy of the Faithful" because it reflects its character and nature. Precisely because this sacrificial offering tran-spires during the Liturgy for the faithful, it bears the name the Liturgy of the Faithful. It is also called by this name because it was during this part of the Liturgy that the eucharistic sacrifice was offered and consumed in Holy Com-munion in which only the faithful, i.e., the worthy, the irreproachable, those in the state of grace were permitted to participate.

Because the Liturgy of the Faithful is in essence the Liturgy of Sacrifice, it is here that the priest fulfills his greatest function. In the Liturgy of the Cate-chumens, the priest, as we have before emphasized, had a small role. Only in the Liturgy of the Faithful does he begin to perform his proper function. He stands at the holy table, i.e., altar, not only to render God "His due adoration and glorification" [1] as in the Liturgy of the Catechumens, but to "offer the unbloody sacrifice for all people," [2] in other words, "to consecrate the holy and most pure Body and precious Blood." [3] It is in the Liturgy of the Faithful or Sacrifice that the priest begins to discharge that duty which pertains essentially and exclusively to the priesthood—to offer sacrifice. In behalf of the people and as a representative of Christ, he offers the sacrifice of the New Law.

3. Not only does the Liturgy of the Faithful have its own character but it also has its own content, by virtue of which the Liturgy of the Faithful differs essentially from that of the Catechumens. Unlike the Liturgy of the Catechumens, the dominant feature of the Liturgy of the Faithful is not instruction, supplication or glorification of the Trinity, but the Eucharistic Prayer, within the framework of which the Eucharistic Sacrifice takes place. It is true, however, that during the Liturgy of the Faithful, the faithful do not cease to make their prayers known to God and to glorify Him, but these prayers and praises play a secondary role. They are intrinsically woven into the Eucharistic Prayer, wherein the motif is the transubstantiation of the holy gifts; not until later does the prayer of petition begin and conclude with the glorification or doxology. In this part the principal theme of the Liturgy of the Catechumens, i.e., the homiletic-didactic theme, has no place.

4. Another distinctive characteristic of the Liturgy of the Faithful, one flowing from its sacrificial character, is its purpose and aim. The aim of the Liturgy of the Catechumens is the word or doctrine of God; that of the Liturgy of the Faithful is not to preach the word of God or to impart instruction, not to read Sacred Scripture, but to actualize the redemptive act—to change the eucharistic species into the Body and Blood of Jesus Christ, and consequently, to have the faithful participate in the sacrifice. Christ speaks to the faithful through the Gospels in the Liturgy of the Catechumens, but in the Liturgy of the Faithful, He appears to the faithful in order to "sacrifice and give Himself as food."[4] Christ, the Second Person of the Divine Trinity, again, so to speak, "becomes flesh" and dwells among men. He assumes the eucharistic appearances in order to be with man, to give Himself to man as food, in order to unite Himself to man. In the Liturgy of the Faithful, man is a partaker of even greater graces than during the Liturgy of the Catechumens, for his food is not the word of God, but Christ Himself who preached the word of God to him. It is He who comes in order to sacrifice Himself for man and to enter into mystical union with him. Union with God, therefore, is the purpose and the aim of offering and consuming the sacrifice. This is the purpose of the Liturgy of the Faithful.

5. There is also another difference between the Liturgy of the Faithful and the Liturgy of the Catechumens, i.e., origin.

---

[1] See the prayer of the *Trisagion*.
[2] See the first prayer for the Faithful.
[3] See the prayer of the Great Entrance.
[4] The words are taken from "Let all flesh be silent . . ." which is sung on Holy Saturday instead of the *Cherubikon*.

The Liturgy of the Catechumens, as we know, is of apostolic origin. It was introduced into the rite of the eucharistic sacrifice under the influence of the Jewish synagogue. It is an imitation of the Saturday synagogue services; a Christian version or modification of the Jewish Sabbath gathering.

The Liturgy of the Faithful has a distinct origin. It comes to us not from the Apostles but from Christ Himself. Christ instituted the rite of eucharistic sacrifice at the Last Supper, and thus endowed the Liturgy of the Faithful with its sacrificial character. According to the will of Christ, therefore, the Liturgy of the Faithful in its fundamental and essential elements is the rite of offering the sacrifice, the rite of consecration and the rite of consuming the elements of sacrifice in Holy Communion. This will be discussed later in the explanation of the Anaphora.

We have already remarked that the Liturgy of the Catechumens was based on the synagogue services. Does the Liturgy of the Faithful or Sacrifice have an example or model after which it was patterned? The answer is the Jewish Passover. Christ instituted the eucharistic sacrifice within the framework of the Jewish Paschal supper. Liturgists point to a series of similarities and parallels between the Anaphora (the most important part of the Liturgy of the Faithful) and the rite of consuming the Paschal Lamb. A careful examination of these similarities will be made later in the explanation of the Anaphora.

6. The distinct origins of both Liturgies had their influence on their separate historical evolutions.

To avoid details which will be discussed later, one can say in general that the Liturgy of the Faithful, comparatively speaking, does not have as long a history of development of either texts or rites as the Liturgy of the Catechumens. The Liturgy of the Faithful has hardly undergone any evolution, especially in its essential part (the Anaphora) where it has retained the same outline and scheme that Christ followed at the Last Supper. In examining the oldest monuments and sources of the Byzantine present-day Anaphora, such as the testimony of St. Justin, and Anaphora of St. Hippolytus, the Liturgy of the *Apostolic Constitutions,* the description of the Liturgy by St. Cyril of Jerusalem, the so-called Anaphora of Serapion, one can affirm that it has remained almost totally unaltered in its scheme, structure, and component elements. Only small and insignificant changes appear through the course of centuries. Certain modifications and insertions, present today in the Byzantine Anaphora, were introduced also into the anaphoras of all the other Liturgies, so that one is not aware of them as later additions. This can apply to the interpolations in the primitive eucharistic Anaphora, as for example, the epiklesis, the commemorations, the hymn *"Sanctus"*, and the "Our Father." The anaphoras of all the Liturgies reveal great similarity in the structure and order of each separate part, as well as in ritual sequence and arrangement. This indicates that the Apostles and the various Churches in formulating the Eucharistic Sacrifice, adhered faithfully to the scheme and structure by which Christ instituted the sacrifice of the New Law.

That is not to say, however, that all the constituent parts of the Liturgy of the Faithful reveal the same process of historical development. While the Anaphora has remained in almost the same form since the fourth and fifth centuries, the other parts of the Liturgy of the Faithful underwent a greater evolution. This is true of the rite of consuming the sacrificial gifts (Holy Communion), and especially of that part which comes before the Anaphora, that is, the preparation for the Eucharistic Sacrifice, where the Great Entrance reveals the longest evolution in text and rite.

7. The Liturgy of the Faithful, with a few exceptions, remains the same, unchanged throughout the whole ecclesiastical or liturgical year. This means that the liturgical year with its festive cycles exercises very little influence on it. The Liturgy of the Faithful, then, is also distinguished from the Liturgy of the Catechumens in that the latter has variable parts, i.e., parts that change (e.g. the *troparion,* antiphons, Epistles and Gospels, etc.) according to the various themes of the holydays.

8. A few words must be said about the symbolism of the Liturgy of the Faithful, for this part reveals frequent symbolic allusions. This does not mean, however, that every rite or text, even the most insignificant, has a symbolic meaning. Hyperbolic symbolism cannot be ascribed to the Liturgy itself, but only to the interpreters who in their interpretations go beyond the limits of the true and real sense. Ample opportunity to be convinced of this has already been given in the course of this commentary. Furthermore, it must be remembered that the Liturgy of the Faithful, being by nature the Eucharistic Sacrifice, is a *real* memorial of the death of Christ on Golgotha. It is not, therefore, a symbolic, but a real (though mystical) repetition, continuation and renewal of the Sacrifice on the Cross, with this difference of course, that on the cross Christ offered Himself up as a sacrifice in a bloody manner, while in the Liturgy He offers Himself in an unbloody manner. Hence, the Eucharistic Sacrifice is the real sacrifice of the New Law, and not a mere symbolic rite.

The Eucharistic Sacrifice, by nature, is a renewal and continuation of the work of redemption which Christ completed and sealed with His death on Golgotha. Yet, it does not follow that every part that precedes or follows the Eucharistic Sacrifice must necessarily refer to the events that preceded and followed Christ's death. In other words: The Divine Liturgy is not a symbolic chronology of the life of Jesus Christ. This has already been discussed and must be stressed again so that in interpreting the texts and rites of the Liturgy of the Faithful one will avoid and guard against the hyperbolism of the symbolic method of interpretation.

In regard to the use of symbolism in the Divine Liturgy, the following principle must be followed: Do not look for symbolism where it does not exist. In our opinion, the historical-critical method is by far more conducive to a better understanding of the liturgical texts and rites than the purely symbolic method.

The historical-critical method of interpretation, to its credit, is based on the texts and rites, whereas the symbolic method is based on the subjective and unbalanced views of the interpreter.

9. The Liturgy of the Faithful is divided into three parts. This division is based upon the structure itself of the Liturgy of the Faithful and, therefore, is well-founded.

The first portion is the preparation for the Eucharistic Sacrifice. It embraces prayers for the faithful, the rite of the Great Entrance, the ektene of offertory and the Symbol of Faith. The characteristic of this part of the Liturgy is that it is well developed—in some respects, even overly developed. This preparatory part has known many modifications.

The second part of the Liturgy of the Faithful is the Eucharistic Sacrifice, known also as the "Canon," the "Anaphora," or the "Eucharistic Prayer." The components of this part are: the eucharistic dialogue, the prayer of thanksgiving, the hymn called the Hagiology, the words of the Eucharistic Consecration, the Anamnesis, the Epiklesis and the commemoration of the saints, living and dead. Not only is this the oldest, but it is the most significant, part of the Liturgy of the Faithful and of the entire Divine Liturgy. Here the sacrifice of the Divine Liturgy reaches its completion, its highest point, its climax. It is the core, the center, the heart of the entire Divine Liturgy.

The third part of the Liturgy of the Faithful is the consuming of the sacred gifts or the rite of the Eucharistic Banquet (Holy Communion). This part is comprised of the following component elements: the prayers preparing for Holy Communion, the ektene of supplication the "Our Father," the rite of Holy Communion, the prayers of thanksgiving after Holy Communion, the consuming of the Holy Gifts and finally the dismissal of the faithful. This final part of the Liturgy of the Faithful is a natural complement to the Eucharistic Sacrifice.

Consideration of its different parts leads to the conclusion that the Liturgy of the Faithful differs essentially from the Liturgy of the Catechumens. Today, of course, these differences are often not apparent since the Liturgy is viewed as an inseparable unit, an integral whole, and the line of demarcation between the two parts is often not seen. Hence it may be difficult to understand and appreciate the strictness of the early Church in excluding all unworthy people from participation in the Liturgy of the Faithful. Today it is not easy to understand the great solicitude of the primitive Church in safeguarding the Holy Eucharist against desecration and irreverence. No longer does the custom of corporate Communion, i.e., participation of *all* the faithful in the eucharistic feast, exist. But it was this which was responsible for the strict discipline in the early Church.

Although catechumens do not exist in our day, and anyone, without discrimination, may be present at the Liturgy of the Faithful, and although the Church does not draw a distinction between the two Liturgies, the significance of this Liturgy and its meaning for us should not be forgotten. The dismissal of the catechumens from the church, indeed, belongs to the past; yet, the beginning of the Liturgy of the Faithful should serve as a constant reminder that a new and important phase of the Liturgy is about to begin. Our hearts, therefore, should be prepared for this important moment. The dismissal of the catechumens, which was preserved in the Liturgy until recently, if nothing else, should remind the faithful that they, at the beginning of every Liturgy of the Faithful, are entering the sanctuary which only the holy, the irreproachable and the pure are permitted to enter.

Chapter II

PREPARATION FOR THE EUCHARISTIC SACRIFICE

The First Part of the Liturgy of the Faithful

The first part of the Liturgy of the Faithful is the preparation for the Eucharistic Sacrifice.

In the Divine Liturgy there are two other rites of preparation for the sacrifice—the Liturgy of the Catechumens and especially the rite of Proskomide. These however, are remote, indirect and mediate preparations. The proximate, direct, immediate and actual preparation for the Eucharistic Sacrifice is that portion of the Liturgy of the Faithful that precedes the Anaphora. It consists of: 1. the prayer for the faithful; 2. the Great Entrance or procession with the holy gifts; 3. the ektene of supplication (or offertory); 4. the prayer of oblation; 5. the Kiss of Peace; and 6. the Symbol of Faith. All these liturgical components, though of different origin, have but one end, i.e., to prepare the priest and the faithful for a worthy sacrifice.

Historically, this preparatory part is the most recent part of the Liturgy of the Faithful. Its present form is the product of a long evolution. In the early Liturgy of the Faithful, the part preparatory to the Anaphora was not as fully developed as it is today. It did not embrace, for instance, the Symbol of Faith or the Great Entrance; it began with the Kiss of Peace, which was followed by the gift-offering of bread and wine and then immediately by the Eucharistic Prayer. According to St. Justin, the Liturgy of the Faithful began with the Kiss of Peace as did also the Liturgy of Sacrifice of St. Hippolytus. In the Liturgy of St. Cyril of Jerusalem, the washing of the hands and the Kiss of Peace preceded the Eucharistic Sacrifice. The Liturgies of St. James, the *Apostolic Constitutions,* the liturgical descriptions in the works of St. John Chrysostom and of Pseudo-Dionysius—all have a similar beginning.

Our modern-day preparatory part of the Liturgy of the Faithful, in its constituent elements, began to take form between the fifth and eighth centuries. It evolved more completely in the succeeding centuries. The longest and most elaborate evolution was that of the Great Entrance.

1. The Prayer of the Faithful

(The Beginning of the Liturgy of the Faithful)

The Liturgy of the Faithful begins with the words:

All we who are faithful, again and again, in peace let us pray to the Lord.

As the priest says these words he unfolds the eileton. Then follows the prayer of the priest or the first prayer for the faithful, the acclamation:

Help, save, have mercy and protect us, O God, by Thy grace,

and the invocation of glorification:

For to Thee is due all glory, honor and adoration, to the Father, and to the Son and to the Holy Spirit, now and ever, and unto ages of ages.

After this comes the Little Ektene and the second prayer for the faithful followed by the doxology: "That ever protected by Thy might."

Not only the prayers of the faithful but the rite of unfolding the *eileton*, performed during the first prayer for the faithful, merits attention. Few attach great importance to this rite, but its placement at the beginning of the Liturgy of the Faithful has deep significance. It actually marks the beginning of the Liturgy of the Faithful, and for this reason, it should be examined more closely.

The rite of unfolding the *eileton* at the beginning of the Liturgy of the Faithful is found in the oldest liturgical manuscript, i.e., the Barberini Codex (eighth century). In this ancient manuscript, the first prayer for the faithful is called "the first prayer of the faithful after the unfolding of the eileton." [1] The oldest Byzantine liturgical commentary, that of Pseudo-Herman,, also mentions the *eileton,* and says that it "signifies those linens, in which the Body of Christ was wrapped after being taken down from the cross" [2]—an interpretation that was adopted by all the Liturgies. It was perhaps under the influence of this interpretation that the *antimension* developed. This is a sacred cloth which itself is an eileton with part of a relic sewn into it, on which Christ's burial is usually represented. [3]

What meaning, therefore, does the rite of unfolding the *eileton* be the beginning of the Liturgy of the Faithful have? Why does the priest unfold it immediately after the dismissal of the Catechumens from the church? The unfolding has its own beautiful meaning. It is a sign that marks the beginning of the Liturgy of the Sacrifice. Although the holy gifts have not yet been carried to and placed on the altar, the priest, nevertheless, unfolds the *eileton* to indicate that the Eucharistic Sacrifice is about to begin. The unfolding of the

---

[1] It is interesting to note that the Ambrosian Rite has the prayer of the eileton at the beginning of the Liturgy of the Faithful, i.e. the so-called *oratio super sindonem.* (See S. Salaville, *Liturgies orientales,* II, La messe, Paris 1942, p. 94)).

[2] Migne, PG, 98, 417.

[3] Cf. literature on the eileton, or the antimension: A. Petrovskiy, *Iliton*, (Pravo. Bogoslov. Ents., 5 (1904), pp. 854–855); *Antimins,* (Pravo. Bogoslov. Ents., 1 (1900), pp. 797–809); D.M., *Antimension,* (Triskeutike khristiyanike Ents., 1, pp. 1176–1178) .

eileton is a symbolic act which introduces a new part in the Divine Liturgy. Up until this point, the priest stood and prayed at the altar and all his actions were performed *before* the altar and not upon the altar. The unfolding of the *eileton*, or *antimension*,[4] indicates that an action is being performed upon the altar itself, namely, the offering of the sacrifice.

This rite of the eileton has a purpose and meaning similar to that of the raising of the gospel book aloft at the beginning of the Liturgy of the Catechumens. At the invocation, "Blessed be the kingdom . . . ," the priest raises aloft the book of Gospels and with it makes a sign of the cross over the altar. This rite at the beginning of the Divine Liturgy indicates the purpose of the Liturgy of the Catechumens which is to teach the word of God, the symbol of which is the Gospel. Analogically speaking, the rite of unfolding the eileton expresses exactly the same meaning; it is a sign that the sacrifical part of the Divine Liturgy is about to begin. The rite stresses the sacrificial character of the Liturgy of the Faithful. Both, the raising of the gospel book aloft at the beginning of the Liturgy of the Catechumens and the unfolding of the eileton at the beginning of the Liturgy of the Faithful, have their own character and content. They both have their reason and meaning, although liturgical commentators do not give much attention to it and fail to see a deeper reason for the beautiful parallelism that exists between the two rites.

That a new part of the Liturgy of the Faithful is about to commence with the unfolding of the *eileton* is expressed by the prayers for the faithful. These are the two secret prayers which the priest says immediately after the dismissal of the catechumens. Their history is still uncertain. They are found as early as the eighth century,[5] although liturgists do refer to a canon of the Synod of Laodicaea (fourth century), wherein the prayers of the faithful are mentioned.[6] This Synod prescribed three prayers of the faithful after the departure of the Catechumens and penitents from the church; one silent and two with the ekphonesis. Whether the Synod had the silent prayers for the faithful in mind is not known for certain. St. Basil and St. John Chrysostom [7] mention prayers for the faithful in their works, although, again, one cannot be sure that they are referring to *the* prayers for the faithful. It is probable that the prayers of the ektene are here referred to rather than the silent prayers of the priest for the faithful. Already in the liturgical descriptions of St. Justin, common prayers for the faithful which were said after the reading of the Gospel, are mentioned. Unfortunately, there are no extant sources which supply information on the silent prayers of the priest. Only in the Liturgy of the *Apostolic Constitutions* is found a prayer which is similar in content to, and reminiscent of, the prayers for the faithful.

---

4 The Russian Synodal Rite prescribes here the unfolding of the antimension which ordinarily rests on top and not under the altar cloth.

5 Cf. the Barberini Codex.

6 Mansi, 2, 567.

7 Migne, PG, 32, 612 and 613 (St. Basil) ; and 48, 725 (St. John Chrysostom) .

The content of the prayers for the faithful deserves particular consideration. It differs greatly from previous secret prayers of the priest. In all the prayers thus far analyzed in the commentary on the Liturgy of the Catechumens, there is no reference to the Eucharistic Sacrifice, a fact that is not surprising since the Liturgy of the Catechumens had nothing in common with sacrifice. But it is different with the prayers in the Liturgy of the Faithful; the concept of sacrifice appears at the very beginning of these prayers and becomes their dominant theme.

The prayers are similar to each other and both share almost the same theme. In both the same thoughts and the same petitions dominate; both are a sincere plea that God will grant the priest and all the faithful grace to offer the Unbloody Sacrifice worthily and to derive spiritual benefit from it. These are prayers which appear at first sight not to be prayers *for* the faithful, as their title would suggest, for in them the priest prays first of all for himself and for those who assist him, and, last, for the faithful. In any case, the prayers speak for themselves.

The text of the first prayer is:

We give thanks unto Thee, O Lord God of powers, Who hast vouchsafed us to stand even now before Thy holy altar, and to fall down before Thy compassion for our sins and ignorance of the people. Accept, O God, our supplication; make us be worthy to offer unto Thee supplications and prayers, and unbloody sacrifices for all Thy people. And enable us, whom Thou hast placed in this Thy ministry, by the power of Thy Holy Spirit without blame and without offense, in testimony of a pure conscience to call upon Thee at every time and place; that hearing us, Thou mayest be merciful to us, according to the abundance of Thy goodness. For to Thee is due all glory, honor and adoration, to the Father, and to the Son, and to the Holy Spirit, now and ever, and unto ages of ages.

The second prayer is similar in content, to the first:

Again and oftentimes we fall down before Thee and beseech Thee, O good One and Lover of men, that Thou mayest regard our supplication, cleanse our souls and bodies from every defilement of flesh and spirit; and give us that we stand blameless and without condemnation before Thy holy altar. Grant also, O God, unto those who are praying with us betterment of life and faith and spiritual understanding. Give that they may serve Thee always with fear and love, and that they may blamelessly and without condemnation partake of Thy holy mysteries, and become worthy of Thy heavenly kingdom. That ever protected by Thy might, we may render glory to Thee, to the Father, and to the Son, and to the Holy Spirit, now and ever, and unto ages of ages.

The same thoughts are found in the silent prayers of St. Basil's Liturgy of the Faithful. There the priest also implores God to send His Holy Spirit to "strengthen" him with His grace for the celebration of the Unbloody Sacrifice. From this it can be seen that the main theme of all these prayers for the faithful at the beginning of the Liturgy of the Faithful is the desire to offer worthily to

God the Unbloody Sacrifice. It has already been remarked that, although called "prayers for the faithful," they are not prayers for the various needs of the people present at the Divine Liturgy, but rather prayers for a worthy celebration of the Unbloody Sacrifice on the part of the priest and a worthy participation of the faithful in the eucharistic banquet. The name given the prayers must be understood, then, not in the sense that they are prayers for the faithful, but that they are to be understood as the first prayers of the Liturgy of the Faithful.

Between the first and the second prayer is a small ektene—a remnant of the ancient Great Ektene which was repeated frequently in the beginning of the Liturgy of the Faithful. That the position of the Great Ektene was once at the beginning of the Liturgy of the Faithful is proved by certain Sluzhebnyks in which the reiteration of five petitions of the Great Ektene is prescribed. The reason for this repetition was to fill in the pause which occurred when the priest recited the silent prayers. The *Diataxis* of Patriarch Philotheus (fourteenth century) prescribes that the deacon recite the petitions of the Great Ektene until the priest finishes his silent prayers. As soon as he notices the priest finishing, he stops reciting the petitions of the ektene and with the acclamation, "Wisdom" introduces the ekphonesis.[8] Thus, the usage of the acclamation "Wisdom" before the ekphonesis of the first and second prayer is easily explained. We come across this acclamation in the Liturgy of the Catechumens in the rite of reading the Scriptures. There the priest reads the Scriptures after this invocation for attention. Here the word "Wisdom" has the same meaning. It is a sign conveyed by the deacon to the priest to begin the ekphonesis.

This is the explanation which the context offers. Therefore, the explanation of the word "Wisdom" by T. Mishkovskiy is not the correct one. This word, according to him, admonishes the faithful after the departure of the catechumens—that this wisdom was hidden from the catechumens and was communicated only to the faithful, i.e., the wisdom that is revealed in the institution of the New Testament Unbloody Sacrifice. Mishkovskiy even sees in this word "an allusion to the hypostatic Wisdom—Jesus Christ—God," to that Wisdom which we read about in the Old Testament (Wis. 9.1.) as building a temple, erecting an altar and preparing a tabernacle. In other words, "Wisdom" is an allusion to Jesus Christ, who is divine, eternal Wisdom (Sophia). This "hidden meaning"[9] of the word "Wisdom," as Mishkovskiy explains it, has no basis in the liturgical text. His interpretation is too strained and artificial.

The unfolding of the eileton and the prayers of the faithful, therefore, mark the beginning of the Liturgy of the Faithful. Both ritual and text are in perfect harmony. Together they introduce a new part of the Liturgy and indicate its character and purpose as the Unbloody Sacrifice. Hence, the rite of unfolding the eileton and the two prayers of the faithful are a beautiful prologue to the Liturgy of the Sacrifice, i.e., to the eucharistic sacrifice.

[8] Krasnoselstev, *Materialy dlya istorii chinoposlyedovaniya liturghii sv. I. Zlatoustaho,* Kazan, 1889, pp. 58, 107.

[9] Cf. Mishkovskiy, *Izlozhenie tsaregrad. liturghii,* p. 85.

2. The Great Entrance

In the strict sense, the Great Entrance, is understood as the rite of transferring the holy gifts from the Table of Prothesis to the altar. In a wider, more extensive meaning, it comprises all those prayers and rites which either precede the transfer of the holy gifts or which complete it.

The whole congregation takes part in the Great Entrance, i.e., the priest, the deacon and the people or choir. The participation of the faithful is indicated by the singing of the *Cherubikon* immediately after the ekphonesis of the second prayer of the faithful. During the singing the deacon incenses the altar, the sanctuary, the Table of Prothesis, the iconostasis and the people, while the priest recites privately the prayer of the Great Entrance, "No one who is bound unto carnal desires . . ." After the priest finishes the prayer, he and the deacon recite the Cherubic Hymn *(Cherubikon)* three times and execute three metanias before the altar. Then the actual rite of the Great Entrance begins, i.e., the procession with the holy gifts from the Table of Prothesis to the altar. The priest and deacon go to the Table of Prothesis to honor the holy gifts by incensing them. The priest then gives the diskos with the holy gifts on it to the deacon, and taking the chalice with the wine, he begins the procession with the holy gifts (offertory procession).[1] Meanwhile the people interrupt the singing of the Cherubic Hymn, and after the priest commemorates the Church hierarchy, civil authorities, founders, benefactors of the church and all the faithful present, the people than resume singing the final part of the Cherubic Hymn: "That we may receive the King of all invisibly escorted by the angelic hosts. Alleluia, alleluia, alleluia." The priest and the deacon then enter the sanctuary through the Royal Doors and place the holy gifts on the altar. As this is done the priest says the accompanying prayers: "Noble Joseph" and "Do good, O Lord, in Thy benevolence to Sion." He then incenses the gifts, and finally gives his blessing to the deacon to continue the Liturgy.

A. Character and Origin of the Great Entrance

The Great Entrance is one of the most complicated and solemn rites of the Divine Liturgy. In solemnity it excels all other rites not only in the Liturgy of the Faithful but also in the Liturgy taken as a whole.

From a comparative point of view, the Great Entrance very much recalls the rite of the Little Entrance in the Liturgy of the Catechumens. The two entrances are similar. During the Little Entrance there is the procession with the Gospel, whereas in the Great Entrance there is the procession with the holy

---

[1] When the Divine Liturgy is celebrated without the deacon, the priest himself performs the rite of incensation and the rite of transferring the holy gifts; consequently the subsequent dialogue between the priest and deacon before the beginning of the ektene of supplication is omitted.

gifts. Both entrances reveal their essential meaning: The Little Entrance with the Gospel indicates the homiletic-didactic or instructive character, while the Great Entrance with the holy gifts emphasizes the nature and character of the Liturgy of the Faithful, i.e., its Eucharistic, sacrificial character. Just as the symbol of the Liturgy of the Catechumens is the Gospel, so too the Eucharistic Elements or the holy gifts are the symbol of the Liturgy of the Faithful.

The resemblance between the Great and Little Entrances is not confirmed only to their external solemnity. They are similar also from the standpoint of their historical development. As mentioned earlier, the Little Entrance signified historically not the entrance of the celebrant into the sanctuary but the actual beginning of the Liturgy. The same must be said of the Great Entrance; it too did not originally have the same meaning and role that it has today. The Great Entrance began not as a solemn transferring of the holy gifts to the altar; *rather it was the moment when the Christian faithful brought their gift-offerings.*

This has already been mentioned in our commentary on the Proskomide. There, in speaking of the historical development of the Proskomide, we noted that its original place was at the beginning of the Liturgy of the Faithful. The rite of gift-offering or the Proskomide began after the dismissal of the catechumens and was the immediate introduction to the Eucharistic Sacrifice. The oldest liturgical documents [2] as well as the Liturgies of other Rites, which still retain the original place of the rite of the Proskomide i.e., at the beginning of the Liturgy of the Faithful,[3] are witnesses to this fact.

The gift-offering at the beginning of the Liturgy of the Faithful, i.e., where the Great Entrance is today, was preserved until about the seventh or eighth centuries. In the eighth century, the rite of gift-offering was moved to the beginning of the Divine Liturgy, and since that time the Great Entrance has lost its original meaning and character. From the rite of gift-offering, it became the rite of transferring the holy gifts, and this character it preserves to this day.[4]

Keeping in mind the origin and original character of the Great Entrance, one can better understand its present-day structure. Reference is made here to the striking structural similarity between the Great Entrance and the Proskom-

---

[2] According to the testimony of St. Justin, the rite of offertory or gift-offering had its place immediately before the Eucharistic Prayer (See *Apol.*, I, 65 and 67). In the *Apostolic Constitutions* it occupies the same place. After the departure of the catechumens from the church the deacons brought bread and wine to the altar and the bishop recited a prayer of oblation over them, and then he began the Eucharistic Prayer. (Cf. 8th book, Chapter 12 of the *Apostolic Constitutions*; Funk, *Const. Ap.*, I, p. 494–496).

[3] The present-day Roman Mass has the proskomide in the Liturgy of the Faithful, as does the Chaldean Liturgy (of the Eastern Rite). All other Eastern Liturgies moved the rite of gift-offering to the beginning of the Divine Liturgy after the example of the Byzantine-Greek Liturgy.

[4] The oldest witnesses to the Great Entrance are of the sixth century: Eutychius, Patriarch of Constantinople (552–565) in his *A word on the Pasch and the Eucharist,* (Migne, PG, 86, 2400–2401), Pseudo-Dionysius (Migne PG, 3, 425), St. Maximos Confessor (Migne, PG, 91, 693). The following commentators describe and explain symbolically the Great Entrance: Pseudo-Herman (Migne, PG, 98, 420–424), Pseudo-Sophronius (Migne, PG, 87, 4000–4001), Theodore Andides, (Migne, PG, 140, 441–444), Nicholas Cabasilas (Migne, PG, 155, 295).

ide, a similarity to which liturgical commentators fail to give much consideration. They are generally concerned with the symbolic interpretation of the Great
Entrance to the neglect of its origin and original meaning and purpose. An analysis of the internal structure of the Great Entrance and of the similarities so
evident in both the Great Entrance and the Proskomide is in order.

These points of similarity can be reduced to six.[5] 1.) First of all, there is a
similarity in the introductory-preparatory prayers. The prayer of the Great
Entrance: "No one who is bound . . . " is nothing but an amplification or elaboration of the prayer before the entrance into the sanctuary: "Lord, stretch forth
Thy hand . . . ." both being a petition to celebrate worthily the Unbloody Sacrifice. Both inspire the same spirit, both express the same unworthiness of the
priest to approach the altar of God. 2.) Before the Proskomide there is the rite
of washing the hands. In the thirteenth century this rite was performed during
the Great Entrance, i.e., before the priest transferred the holy gifts to the altar,
he washed his hands. Today only the bishop during the Pontifical Liturgy
washes his hands before the Great Entrance. 3.) The rite of preparing the sacrificial elements at the Proskomide corresponds to the transfer of the same sacrificial elements to the altar during the Great Entrance. In the Pontifical Liturgy
the bishop even today cuts the particles, not during the Proskomide, but during
the Great Entrance, immediately before the transfer of the holy gifts. 4.) During
both rites there are almost the same commemorations. 5.) The rite of incensing
is carried out in both functions, during which Psalm 50 is recited. 6.) Finally,
just as during the Proskomide, so also during the Great Entrance there is the
prayer of prothesis or oblation. This prayer completes the rite of Proskomide,
but in the rite of the Great Entrance, the prayer of prothesis is recited during
the ektene of supplication immediately following the Great Entrance.

These similarities in the Proskomide and the Great Entrance are not simply
fortuitous or coincidental. They are clear proof that the two rites once formed
but one. Even after transferring the rite of the gift-offering to the beginning of
the Liturgy, the Great Entrance retained the scheme and structure of the Proskomide. It may, indeed, be considered an imitation of the Proskomide.

The original character of the Great Entrance may still be seen in the Pontifical Liturgy. As was previously mentioned, the bishop washes his hands before
the Great Entrance, then at the Table of Prothesis he cuts out the particles and,
placing them on the diskos, he commemorates the living and the dead, incenses
the holy gifts, recites the offertory prayer, in a word—the bishop completes the
rite of Proskomide during the Great Entrance, just as was done in the eighth
century. The place of the rite of the Pontifical Proskomide at the Great Entrance
is therefore, a remnant of the ancient rite of gift-offering. For liturgists it is the
key to a plausible understanding and interpretation of the sense and meaning of
the Great Entrance.

---

[5] The Russian liturgist Muretov gives a more extensive treatment of the subject: *Istoricheskiy obzor chinoposlyedovaniya proskomidiy do "Ustava liturghii", Konstantonopolskaho
patriarkha Filofeya,* Moskva, 1895, (pp. 11–59).

After these general observations regarding the origin and character of the Great Entrance, one can now examine each integral part of the Great Entrance —the Cherubic Hymn, the silent prayer of the priest, the rite of incensing, the transfer of (or procession with) the holy gifts, the commemorations and finally the rite of placing the holy gifts on the altar.

B. *Cherubikon or The Cherubic Hymn*

The *Cherubikon* is without question one of the most beautiful hymns of the Liturgy. Its marvelous and profound theme has always inspired Church composers to set it to music. They try to give it as much triumphant expression as possible. Besides the *Monogenes* and the *"Holy, Holy, Holy"* (*"Sanctus"*), the *Cherubikon* is exceptionally adaptable to choral music.

Unfortunately, we do not know the composer of the *Cherubikon*. In all probability it originated in the sixth century. The Byzantine historian Cedrin (eleventh century) relates that Emperor Justin II (565–578) ordered the hymn to be sung in the Liturgy.[6] Cedrin, however, does not mention whether the emperor himself or someone else was its author.[7] First to mention the singing of the *Cherubikon* during the Great Entrance was Eutychius, Patriarch of Constantinople (sixth century.)[8] According to Cherkasov, the *Cherubikon* is probably an excerpt from a sermon of some Church Father or writer. He also remarked that it was introduced into the Liturgy because it was brief and full of meaning.[9]

The Cherubic Hymn, as its contents discloses, is a hymn that accompanies the offertory procession and the preparation of the faithful for the Eucharistic Sacrifice. It is evident that it originated at a time when the gift-offering was part of the Great Entrance. According to the prescription of the typikon, the entire Cherubic Hymn is not sung as a whole, but is divided into two parts: the first part, up to the words, "let us now lay aside every earthly care . . ." is sung before the procession with the holy gifts begins; the second part is sung from the words, "That we may receive the King . . ." to the end, after the procession ends. However, the two parts form an inseparable grammatical and stylistic unit as can be readily observed. In English it can be rendered as follows:

> We who mystically represent the Cherubim, and who sing the thrice-holy hymn to the life-giving Trinity, let us now lay aside every earthly care.

---

[6] Cf. Cedrin, *Historiarum compendium,* Migne, PG, 121, 748.

[7] A. Mikita, in his typikon "Rukovodstvo v tserkovniy tipikon," Ungvar, 1901, p. 188, writes: "Pyesn kheruvimsku sostavil vyeroyatno sv. Yustin Muchenik." S. Sabov also assigns the Cherubic Hymn to Justin, *"Expositio S. S. Liturgiae S. Johannis Chrysostomi historica, dogmatica, et moralis,"* Ungvar, 1901, p. 204. Our opinion is that both authors erroneously identify Emperor Justin, who introduced the Cherubic Hymn, with St. Justin the Martyr. Actually no liturgist so far has credited the composition of the Cherubic Hymn to the latter because of lack of evidence.

[8] Cf. his "A Word on the Pasch and The Eucharist; Migne, PG, 86, 2400–2401.

[9] Cf. Cherkasov, V., Bogosl. Vyestnik, 26 (1917), Fevral-Mart, pp. 305–316.

That we may receive the King of all, invisibly escorted by the angelic hosts. Alleluia, alleluia, alleluia.

The first and foremost thought of the hymn is, therefore, that the people represent the Cherubim. This same thought is found in the silent prayer of the Little Entrance, and is a favorite, recurring thought of the Liturgy. In this way the Liturgy wishes to remind the faithful of the part they play in the Divine Liturgy. On earth they represent the choir of the Cherubim who incessantly sing praise before the throne of God. The Liturgy is, therefore, an imitation and reflection of the heavenly, angelic liturgy.

This being the case, the faithful should dismiss "all worldly care." By "worldly care" the Liturgy refers to undue anxiety for bodily needs, for material cares, for a worldly life, in a word, all that binds a Christian to earth and prevents him from thinking about God and caring for his eternal salvation. A true Christian should be free from the vain and undue solicitude about the body, conveniences and pleasures, which Christ condemned. He taught His disciples to "seek first the kingdom of heaven." (Luke 12:31) and not to be overly anxious or troubled about their physical needs. If the Christian is to be always free of all "earthly care," then how much more must his soul be free of such cares during the Divine Liturgy which is an imitation and reflection of the eternal service rendered by the angels before the throne of God.

Actually the real reason why Christians must be free from every kind of worldly care is because they are "receiving the King of all." This last phrase requires clarification. What does it mean? What kind of "receiving" is understood here? Usually these last words are improperly translated, and consequently misconstrued. The Old-Slavonic words *"Yako da Carya vsy podyemem . . ."* are usually translated "that we may lift up the King . . .,"[10] and the word, *"dorynosyma"* is translated "who is carried. . . ." Thus this last part of the song is translated as meaning that the faithful are to lift up Christ the King, who at the moment of the procession with the holy gifts is carried by the angelic hosts. According to the traditional explanation, the ancient Roman military custom of electing and proclaiming a new Emperor must be recalled. Among the Romans it was the custom for the soldiers to lift up the newly-elected Emperor on a shield which was held on high by their spears. They then carried him in procession throughout the military encampment to be hailed and accorded homage by the whole army.

Almost every liturgical commentator, when explaining the Cherubic Hymn, alludes to this military custom and applies it to the procession with the holy gifts. Here the priest and the deacon carry Christ, symbolized in the holy gifts, to the altar, thus imitating the example of the angels, who invisibly bear "the

---

[10] See the Ukrainian translation of archbishop Hilarion Ohienko. (*The Liturgy of our father Saint John Chrysostom*, Kohlm 1942, 42) in which he translates the Old Slavonic word *podimem* into the Ukrainian word *pidnyaty* which means to lift up: "*Shchob tsarya vsich pidnyaty yakoho nevydymo nesut chyny Anhelski. Allyluya.*" Rev. J. Lewitsky also translates *podimem* as *pidniaty*, which means to lift up. (Sluzhba Bozha sv. Yoanna Zol., Lviv, 1927, 25).

King of all" and carry Him, as it were, on their shields.[11] This explanation, however beautiful and suitable it may seem, is based on a misunderstanding of the text of the *Cherubikon*. The word *podyemem* [12] does not mean "to lift up" or to "raise," but "to receive." Likewise the word *dorynosyma* [13] does not denote "he who is borne aloft on spears," but "he who is accompanied" or "escorted by, etc." Hence, the explanation of these words is inaccurate, and obscures the proper meaning of the *Cherubikon* which actually does not refer to the lifting up of Christ (during the procession of the holy gifts) but to the receiving of fied Gifts. It also makes reference to Holy Communion:

The Russian liturgist, I. Karabinov, examining critically the words of the Cherubic Hymn, concludes that the word *podyemem* is a technical term denoting the reception of Holy Communion, to which, wherever the word is encountered in the Divine Liturgy, it always refers. "To *podyemity* the King of all" means, therefore, to receive Christ the King in Holy Communion.[14] The very purpose of the Offertory or of the rite of transfer, during which this hymn is sung, is eventually the receiving of the Holy Eucharist. The Cherubic Hymn receives its proper sense and meaning only in such an explanation. The *Cherubikon* is, therefore, an exhortation to set aside all earthly care and to receive Christ the King in Holy Communion worthily.

The best proof that the Cherubic Hymn refers to Holy Communion and not to the procession with the holy gifts, is the hymn which is sung in its stead on Holy Saturday. This hymn is presented as proof because it serves as a commentary to the Cherubic Hymn. It reads:

> Let all mankind be silent, and let it stand with fear and trembling, and let it not think of anything worldly, for the King of kings and the Lord of lords comes to be slain and to be offered as food for the faithful. Before Him go the legions of angels with all authority and power, the many-eyed Cherubim and the six-winged Seraphim, with covered faces singing Alleluia.

There is an evident similarity of the Holy Saturday hymn to the *Cherubikon*. In both hymns are found the same thoughts and even the same expressions. In both, the leading thought is the receiving of Jesus Christ in Holy Communion. In both the exhortation is to discard and detach oneself from "every earthly care" in order to receive Christ, who comes to offer Himself as food for the faithful. As further confirmation of this interpretation, reference can be made to a hymn that is sung during the Great Entrance in the Liturgy of the Pre-sanctified Gifts. It also makes reference to Holy Communion:

---

[11] Cf. for example, the interpretation of the Cherubic Hymn by Pelesh, (*Pastir. Bogosl. Liturghika*, pp. 490–491), Gogol (*Razmishleniya o Bozh. liturg.*, Maltsev, pp. 58–59) and other commentators (Dmitrevskiy, Malinovskiy, Vissarion, Muravyev, Sabov, etc.).

[12] In the Greek text we have the word *hypodexomenoi* which means, not "to lift up" as the Old Slavonic has it, but to "receive."

[13] The Greek *doriphorumenos* does not mean "he, who is carried or borne on spears," but "he, who is gloriously escorted," i.e., by the military retinue.

[14] Cf. J. Karabinov, *Lektsii po liturghikye*, SPB. 1914, pp. 138–139.

Today the heavenly powers render service with us, for the King of glory makes His entrance. The mysterious and perfect sacrifice is now being borne in triumph. Therefore, let us approach with faith and love, so that we may become partakers of everlasting life. Alleluia.

The *Cherubikon* is, therefore, a mystical invocation for a worthy participation in the eucharistic feast. It anticipates the moment of Holy Communion and forewarns the faithful to dispel from the soul all that is carnal, vain and ephemeral, and to imitate the angels whom they represent during the Divine Liturgy, so that when it is time to partake of the eucharistic banquet, they can with hearts pure and free of all worldly troubles "receive the King of all" into their souls.[15]

C. The Silent Prayer of the Great Entrance

During the singing of the *Cherubikon* the priest silently recites the prayer, *"No one who is bound unto carnal desire. . . ."* In the older Greek liturgical manuscripts this prayer is called "the prayer in which the priest prays for himself, while making the entrance with the holy gifts."[16] It is, therefore, the personal, private prayer of the priest asking for help from above to celebrate worthily the Unbloody Sacrifice. The priest uses the singular and not the plural number as he usually does in the silent prayers of the Liturgy; in his own name, he prays for himself exclusively.

The authorship of this prayer is not known for certain. It is usually ascribed to St. Basil the Great,[17] probably because in the oldest liturgical manuscripts it is found in the formularies of the Liturgy of St. Basil. It is found, however, in those of the Liturgy of St. John Chrysostom.[18] Hence, it may be surmised that this prayer found its way into the Liturgy of St. John Chrysostom from the Liturgy of St. Basil. It is also interesting to note that the same prayer is found in most of the Eastern Liturgies, for example, in the Syrian Liturgy of St. James, in the Armenian Liturgy, and in the Alexandrine Liturgy of Gregory the Theologian. It is difficult to determine from which Liturgy the others originally received it. Most probably the Syrian, Armenian and Alexandrine Liturgies took it from the liturgical formula of St. Basil. This, of course, does not prove St.

---

[15] The hymn chanted during the Great Entrance on Holy Thursday also refers to Holy Communion: "O Son of God, let me today partake of Your mystical supper, for I will not reveal Your mystery to Your enemies, nor give You a kiss like Judas, but like the thief I confess to You: Remember me, O Lord, when You come into Your kingdom. Alleluia." It is worth noting here that Pseudo-Herman relates the words of the Cherubic Hymn to the moment of Holy Communion and not to the moment of the solemn procession with the Holy Gifts, which, according to him, typifies or portrays the triumphal entry of Christ into Jerusalem. (Cf. Migne, PG, 98. 420).

[16] Cf. the Barberini Codex (eighth century) and the Sevastiyanov Codex (tenth-eleventh centuries).

[17] Se Dmitrevskiy, *Istor., dogmat., i tainstvennoe uzyasnenie na liturhiyu*, Moskva, 1894.

[18] The *Porphyrian* (eighth-ninth century) and the *Rozanivskiy Codices* (eleventh-twelfth centuries) do not have our prayer; the *Barberini* and *Sevastiyanov Codices* have it only in the Liturgy of St. Basil.

Basil to have been its author, although it does bear the mark of his style. S. Muretov assumes that the prayer comes from the time when the Proskomide was performed during the Great Entrance. [19] Dr. Mishkovskiy on the basis of an analysis of the dogmatic terms used in this prayer, supposes that it originated before the Council of Chalcedon (451), i.e., before the sixth century.[20]

The prayer, "No one who is bound . . ." can without hesitation be categorized as classical. It is one of the most beautiful prayers of the Liturgy and, in the opinion of many, it is also the most characteristic and most outstanding prayer of the Divine Liturgy. Hence, Bennigzen calls it the "most beautiful prayer." [21] One who examines it more closely and delves into its meaning must admit that it is distinguished from the other silent prayers by its remarkable beauty.[22] It is especially remarkable for its dogmatic content; it expresses in short but meaningful words the dogma of the eternal priesthood of Christ and its continuation in the priesthood of the New Testament. Nowhere in the other prayers of either the Eastern or the Western Liturgies is the sacrificial theme of the Eucharist and Christ the true High Priest so distinctly crystalized as here.[23]

In this prayer one can discern certain thoughts which are logically and stylistically interwoven and which converge into one idea, i.e., that Christ is the actual priest offering the Divine Liturgy.

The introductory sentence expresses in general the thought that no man is worthy to offer sacrifice to God:

> No one who is bound unto carnal desires and pleasures is worthy to approach or to draw near, or to minister to Thee, O King of glory: For to serve Thee is great and dreadful even to the heavenly powers themselves.

If the angels—holy and pure spirits—serve God with fear and trembling, then how much more must man, who is fragile, weak and sinful, feel his unworthiness to appear before God and to offer Him the Unbloody Sacrifice. Of himself man is not capable of performing such a sublime service for it exceeds all his power.

Nevertheless, God in His inscrutable ways chose from among men certain persons upon whom He conferred the power and authority to offer the Unbloody Sacrifice:

> And yet, because of Thine ineffable and boundless love of man, Thou didst become man unchangeably and immutably, and didst become our High Priest, and hast given unto us the sacerdotal ministry of this liturgical and unbloody sacrifice, as Master of all. For Thou alone, O Lord our God,

---

[19] Cf. Muretov, *Istor. obzor chinoslye. proskom. do "Ustavu liturghii,"* Konstant. patr. Filofeya, p. 23. This assumption in our opinion has its foundation in the text of the prayer, where it is presupposed that the *Holy Gifts are already on the Altar.*

[20] Cf. T. Mishkovskiy, *Izlozhenie tsaregrad, liturghii,* pp. 94–95 (footnote).

[21] Cf. H. Bennigzen ("Katolicheskiy Vremenik", 3, Paris, 1929, p. 154).

[22] "In general this prayer is remarkable for its content and sublimity; it belongs to the most touching and fondest prayers of the Divine Liturgy," T. Mishkovskiy, *Izlozhen. tsaregrad. lit.,* p. 91.

[23] See H. Bennigzen, *O Liturghiakh Vostochnoy i Zapadonoy,* pp. 154–155.

rulest over those in heaven and on earth; Thou art borne on the Cherubic throne; Thou art Lord of the Seraphim and King of Israel (Is 44:6); Thou alone art holy and restest in the holies (Is 57:2).

Here the prayer alludes to the institution of the New Testament priesthood. The Lord of the universe, of all the angels, the Holiest of the Holy, did not despise sinful and passionate man. On the contrary, He elevated him, conferring upon him the power to offer the Unbloody Sacrifice and making him a partaker of His eternal priesthood. It was not enough that He became man and died on the cross; He instituted the new priesthood which, by His will and power, renews His sacrifice of redemption in an unbloody manner.

Man, although he was chosen to share in Christ's priesthood, nevertheless remains weak and sinful. The grace of God's calling to the holy priesthood does not necessarily render him immune to sin; it does not automatically make him holy and impeccable. Hence, the priest before performing every Liturgy should be mindful of his unworthiness, wretchedness and shortcomings. This prayer was designed, therefore, to remind him to humble himself and to recall his unworthiness:

> Therefore do I entreat Thee, Who alone art good and gracious: Look down upon me, Thy sinful and worthless servant, and cleanse my soul and heart from an evil conscience; and by the power of the Holy Spirit enable me, endued with the grace of the priesthood, to stand before this Thy holy table and to consecrate Thy holy and most pure Body and precious Blood. For unto Thee do I approach, bowing my head, and beseech Thee: turn not Thy face from me, nor reject me from among Thy children; but vouchsafe that these gifts may be offered unto Thee by me, Thy sinful and unworthy servant.

With these words the priest begs for the grace of the Holy Spirit to begin the Unbloody Sacrifice.

The highest point of the prayer are these very beautiful words which conclude the prayer:

> For Thou dost offer and art offered, and dost receive and art received, O Christ our God; and we render glory unto Thee with Thy eternal Father, and Thy most holy and good and lifegiving Spirit, now and ever, and unto ages of ages. Amen.

These last words are described as "very beautiful" because they so succinctly express the profound dogmatic truth concerning Christ's priesthood. They teach men about the role Christ plays in offering the Unbloody Sacrifice, i.e., that He is the actual and principal priest. Christ is first of all the "Offerer," the One who offers *(prospheron)*, because Christ, and not the priest, is the first minister of the Liturgy. In every Liturgy, He performs His office of eternal High Priest and the human priest is only a visible instrument of the invisible priest—Christ, or, in theological terminology: Christ is the "principal minister," while the priest is the "secondary minister."

Again, Christ is the "offered," the one who is offered *(prospheromenos)*, i.e., He is the sacrifice, for that which is sacrificed in the Liturgy is His most holy Body and most precious Blood. But even this is not all. Christ is not only the minister and the sacrifice, but also the *"receiver of the sacrifice" (prosdekho-menos)*, i.e., the one who receives this sacrifice. According to the teaching of the Church, Christ offers Himself up as a sacrifice to the heavenly Father for all mankind. At the same time, however, being one with and equal to the Father and the Holy Spirit, He receives His own sacrifice. Just as He became man for our salvation, never ceasing for one moment to be God, so too in the Divine Liturgy He offers Himself to the Holy Trinity for all mankind, and at the same time, as "one of the Blessed Trinity" He receives His sacrifice. Like the mysteries of the Trinity, incarnation and redemption, this profound mystery is impossible to grasp.[24]

Finally, the prayer calls Christ "the one who art received" *(diadidomenos)*, i.e., One who gives Himself as food in the eucharistic banquet.

The content of the prayer "No one who is bound . . ." recalls very much the two prayers for the faithful and the prayer which the priest recites before entering the sanctuary prior to Proskomide, "Lord, stretch forth Thy hand." The theme of all these prayers is the petition to celebrate the Unbloody Sacrifice worthily. The most beautiful of them all is, undoubtedly, the prayer of the *Cherubikon*. The latter is the most appropriate one to prepare the priest for the sacrifice of the Holy Eucharist; it motivates him to predispose himself for a worthy celebration of the Unbloody Sacrifice.

D. The Procession with the Holy Gifts

The principal rite of the Great Entrance is the transfer of, i.e., the solemn procession with, the holy gifts, from the Table of Prothesis to the altar. The rite of incensing precedes the act of transferring the holy gifts. The deacon usually performs this rite while the priest prays silently. According to the present-day Typikon or Order of Celebration, the deacon, or the priest (if the deacon is not

---

[24] The words *prosdekhomenos-priyemlyay* were responsible for a controversy which arose in the twelfth century among the Byzantine Theologians. The whole crux of the controversy was the question of how the words were to be understood, and whether they could apply to Jesus Christ. One of the deacons of Constantinople affirmed that, if applied to Jesus Christ, they would be heretical, for Christ only offers the sacrifice; it is the Father and the Holy Spirit that receive it. The Unbloody Sacrifice cannot be offered to Jesus Christ, but only to God the Father and Holy Spirit. This statement gave rise to inflammatory theological controversies. Espousing the deacon's theory were bishops Soterix Panteugenes, Patriarch-nominate of Antioch, Eustachius of Dirrachion (the present day Durazzo) and Michael of Salonika. To settle the controversy a Synod convened in Constantinople in January, 1156. The Synod, under the direction of the Patriarch of Constantinople, Luke Chrisobergos, condemned the deacon and his partisans, and sanctioned the use of the words *prosdekhomenos-priyemlyay* as referring to Christ, and forbade the omission of the words in the Divine Liturgy (Card. Mai, *Specilegium Romanum*, X, Romae, 1844; pp. 16–93). Cf. Jugie, *Theologia Dogmatica . . .*, III, Parisiis, 1930, pp. 317–320.

present) incenses the altar, sanctuary, Table of Prothesis, iconostasis and the people.[25] The incensing here has the same connotation as in other parts of the Liturgy, namely, purification and sanctification. Long ago, as we mentioned earlier, the rite of washing the hands immediately preceded the transfer of the holy gifts. This ritual fell into disuse, more or less, about the thirteenth or fourteenth centuries and has been preserved only in the Pontifical Divine Liturgy.[26] The washing of the hands is a survival of the ancient rite of gift-offering which once took place during the Great Entrance.[27]

In the present-day Liturgy, the rite of transferring the holy gifts is a very solemn one. In a Pontifical Liturgy or a concelebrated Liturgy it is even more solemn. This was always the case since the solemnity of the rite of the Great Entrance developed gradually. Long ago, when the Proskomide was performed during the Great Entrance, the rite of transferring the holy gifts was very simple. It was not performed by the priest but by the deacon, or rather by the deacons. The priest did not go to the Table of Prothesis but remained at the altar where he accepted the holy gifts from the deacon. This practice was followed up to the thirteenth and fourteenth centuries, and it was not until after the thirteenth century that the priest began to take a more active part in this rite. Today he accompanies the deacon to the Table of Prothesis and together they transfer the holy gifts.[28]

The Liturgy of the Pre-Sanctified Gifts had its influence on the development of the solemnity of the procession with the holy gifts. In this Liturgy during the Great Entrance, the consecrated gifts are solemnly transferred to the altar. Under the influence of the rite of transferring the consecrated gifts, the solemn procession with the unconsecrated gifts in the Liturgy of St. John Chrysostom developed. The unpretentious and simple people of the East, unaware of the difference between the two rites, showed the same latreutic signs of deference and reverence for the unconsecrated gifts in the Liturgy of St. John Chrysostom as they did for the consecrated gifts in the Liturgy of the Pre-Sanctified Gifts. Hence, the custom in the East (which existed perhaps as early as the sixth

---

[25] At first only the holy gifts on the Prothesis and sometimes the altar were incensed. (Cf. Krasnoseltsev, *Materiali dlya istorii chinoposlyedovaniya liturghii sv. I. Zlatoustaho*, Kazan, 1889, pp, 25, 107; *Svyedyeniya o nyekotorykh liturghichekikh rukouisakh vatikanskoy biblioteki*, Kazan, 1885, pp. 134, 215); A. Dmitrievskiy, *Opisanie liturghicheskikh rukopisey, khranyash-chikhsya v bibliotekakh pravoslavnaho vostoka*, II. Evkhologhia, Kiev. p. 141. The *Diataxis* of Philotheus (fourteenth century) prescribed also the incensing of the people and the sanctuary. The recitation of Psalm 50 during the rite of incensing we find practiced in the fifteenth-sixteenth century (in the Greek manuscripts, see Krasnoseltsev, *Svyedeniya . . .*, pp. 134, 215) and in the Slavonic manuscripts a little earlier (thirteenth century). Cf. Petrovskiy, A., *Istoria slavyanskoy redaktsii liturghii I. Zlatoustaho*, (Chrysostomika, Rome, 1908, p. 875).

[26] While the priest washed his hands he recited Paslm 25: "I wash my hands . . . ," vid. A. Petrovskiy, *Istoria . . .*, pp. 875, 873; *Vkhod v oltar, velikiy i maliy*, Pravoslav. Bogosl. Ents., III, (1902), pp. 1064–1075.

[27] The rite of washing the hands was retained in the same place in all the Liturgies of the East and in the Roman Liturgy, with the exception of the Byzantine Liturgy.

[28] Cf. De Meester, *Les origines . . .*, p. 332; also A. Dmitrievskiy, *Opisanie.*, Eukhologhia, pp. 141, 173, 205.

century of kneeling during the Great Entrance in adoration of the holy gifts. Both Eastern and Western liturgists and clergy objected to the custom.[29] In the fourteenth century, Nicholas Cavasilas [30] opposed it. There were some however, who preserved it and emphasized its significance, as for instance, Simeon of Thessalonica [31] and the Metropolitan of Philadelphia, Gabriel Severos. [32] In the seventeenth century in the West, the custom was opposed by Peter Arkudius.[33] Goar [34] and Pope Benedict XIV [35] voiced a more mitigated opposition to it. In the Ukraine, the custom of kneeling was forbidden by the Synod of Zamost in the year 1720,[36] but it is still retained by the Greek and Russian Orthodox churches.

The fact that the deacon and the priest make their commemorations during the rite of transferring the holy gifts contributed to its solemnity. The commemoration of the deacon is short and general:

> May the Lord God remember all your orthodox Christians in His kingdom, always, now and ever, and unto ages of ages.

The formula of commemoration which the priest recites is longer and more detailed. He commemorates the hierarchy (the Pope, the Metropolitan, the bishops), the clergy (priests, deacons and religious), higher authorities, founders and benefactors of the church, and ends like the deacon remembering the faithful present in the church.

Prior to the fifteenth century the commemorations during the Great Entrance were very simple and were made silently.[37] They developed under the influence of the eucharistic and proskomide commemorations, and are to be considered a remnant of the ancient liturgical custom of the reading of the dip-

---

[29] Cf. Migne, PG, 86, 2400–2401. Patriarch Eutychius clearly states that until the Eucharistic Prayer has been said over the holy gifts, they are not consecrated.

[30] Cf. Migne, PG, 150–420.

[31] Cf. Migne, PG, 155, 728–729. According to Simeon, the holy gifts should be accorded reverence even though they are not consecrated, because they are the symbol of Christ, and if we show respect toward the holy icons then even more so should we respect the holy gifts, which, according to the expression of St. Basil, are the prefiguration of Christ.

[32] He wrote a small book in 1604 in defense of the Byzantine custom of adoring the holy gifts kneeling, while they were being transferred to the altar. Richard Simon published his book after his death: *Fides Ecclesiae orientalis seu Gabrielis metr. Philadelphiensis opuscula*, Parisiis, 1671.

[33] Cf. the work of Arkudius: *Libri VII de concordia Ecclesiae occidentalis et orientalis in septem sacramentorum administratione*, Parisiis, 1626, pp. 220–239.

[34] Cf. Goar, *Euchologion sive Rituale Graecorum*, Parisiis, 1647, pp. 131–132.

[35] In the constitution *"Ex quo primum tempore,"* although he did not forbid this custom, he instructed the bishops and the priests to inform the people that the holy gifts which were being transferred were not consecrated. Cf. Mikulas who treats of this extensively in his *Liturgiae S. I. Chrys. interpretatio*, M. Varadini, 1903, pp. 111–112.

[36] *Synodus Prov. Ruthenorum habita in civitate Zamosciae 1720*, (ed. 3), Romae, 1883, p. 73.

[37] A. Petrovskiy, *Vkhod v oltar, velikiy ta maliy*, Pravo. Bogo. Ents . . ., III, (1903), p. 1073.

tychs, i.e., commemorations.[38] As a point of information, the Greeks and the Russian old ritual traditionalists have retained the original short formula.[39] The longest rite of commemoration is to be found in the Russian-Synodal Sluzheb-nyks; they have a system of commemorations which is composed of more formulas.[40]

Concluding the commemorations, the priest together with the deacon enters the sanctuary through the Royal Doors and places the holy gifts on the altar. While placing them on the alter and covering them with the *aër* the priest recites the accompanying prayer: "Noble Joseph. . . ." Then he incenses the holy gifts, reciting the last two verses of Psalm 50: "Do good, O Lord, in Thy benevolence to Sion."

The *troparion* "Noble Joseph . . . ," taken from the Good Friday service, is commemorative of the burial of Christ. It was introduced into the Liturgy in the fourteenth century.[41] The incensing of the holy gifts on the altar is not an old custom for it also dates back only to the thirteenth-fourteenth centuries.[42] The same can be said of the recitation of the last two verses of the 50th Psalm: "Do good. . . ." Originally this Psalm was said by the deacon during the rite of incensing which took place before the Great Entrance. The priest recited it while placing and incensing the holy gifts on the altar. Liturgical commentators, forgetting the original purpose of the 50th Psalm, give it a fabricated meaning.

---

[38] In ancient times the **Diptychs** were tablets upon which were instribed the names of those to be commemorated in the Liturgy. The term "diptych" is derived from the Greek word *dis* (twice) and *ptisso* (put together—for the diptychs consisted of two tablets joined together in such a way as to allow them to be opened and closed like covers of a book. The inside of the tablets was coated with soft wax on which the names of those to be commemorated during the Liturgy were inscribed with a stylus. It was very easy to erase the names inscribed and write in new ones. The exterior of the diptychs was decorated. Diptychs were known to exist even in the pagan world, e.g., the diptychs of the Roman consuls, in which were recorded in chronological order the names of the governing consuls and the important dates of their rule. In the third-fourth centuries these diptychs were accepted into the Christian divine services. The names of donors and benefactors of the Church, bishops, saints and baptized, the dead, martyrs, etc. were entered into these diptychs. Liturgical commemoration in the diptychs was regarded as a special honor, hence only those who devoutly and generously offered their services to the Church were inscribed there. The Church excluded from the diptychs all those who had renounced their faith and become heretics, or by sin had tarnished their Christian name. The diptychs were frequently called the "book of life." Anyone inscribed in this book was (esteemed) a saint. To obliterate (expunge) one's name from the ditychs meant to excommunicate him from the Church community, to condemn, anathematize him. (Here we may mention St. John Chrysostom whose name was unjustly erased from the diptychs by his enemies).

Pseudo-Dionysius is the oldest witness to the reading of the diptychs during the Liturgy (Migne, PG, 3, 425) around the fifth century and the Acts of Synod of Constantinople in the year 536 (Cf. Mansi, 8, 1066).

[39] They only know our deacon's formula of commemoration "And all you . . .," they do not mention the hierarchy, civil authority nor the founders or benefactors of the Church.

[40] Archimandrite Cyprian explicitly complains about the over-elaboration and amplification of the commemorative formulas in the Russian-Orthodox Rite: "In developing the commemoration formulas we have gone to extremes and *variety* . . . and created a whole system and hierarchy of commemorations." Cf. *Eukharistiya*, Paris, 1947, p. 198.

[41] That is with the *Diataxis* of Patriarch Philotheus.

[42] Cf. Krasnoseltsev, *Materiali . . .*, p. 25.

Thus, for example, Bishop Bessarion asserts that the priest while reciting the words of the Psalmist "Do good . . . ," is praying for the Christian Church in Jerusalem. When the priest places the holy gifts on the altar, his thoughts go back to Our Lord's grave which was in the hands of the infidels. Therefore, he prays to God to revive the Orthodox Church in Jerusalem, to renew its ancient power and glory which it once had during the times of the Apostles, so that, wherever desolation reigns, the Eucharistic Sacrifice may be offered.[43] S. Sabov affirms that the word "Sion" in the first verse of the Psalm signifies Christ's Church, and that the "walls of Jerusalem" signifies the bishops and priest who protect the Church from its visible and invisible enemies, and finally that the words "the sacrifice of righteousness, with oblation and holocaust . . . " in the second and last verse are the prophecies pertaining to the sacrifice of Jesus Christ and the Divine Liturgy.[44]

After placing the holy gifts on the altar, a short dialogue between the priest and deacon ensues, which, though different from that at the beginning of the Liturgy, is similar in content. The dialogue is as follows: First, the priest asks the deacon: "Remember me, brother and fellow-minister," and the deacon responds: "May the Lord God remember thy priesthood in His kingdom." The priest: "Pray for me, my fellow-minister." The deacon: "May the Holy Spirit come upon thee and the power of the Most High overshadow thee." The priest: "May the same Spirit minister with us all the days of our life." The deacon: "Remember me, venerable Master." The priest: "May the Lord God remember Thee in His kingdom, always, now and ever and unto ages of ages." The deacon: "Amen." This dialogue marks the conclusion of the commemorations of the Great Entrance. It is already found in texts of the eleventh-twelfth centuries, such, for example, as the Latin translation of St. John Chrysostom's Liturgy by Leo Tuscus (twelfth century).[45]

E. Symbolism of the Great Entrance

An examination of the prayers and of the ritual ceremonies of the Great Entrance can scarcely overlook its symbolism. On the contrary, the symbolic element deserves special attention, because it contributed, to a very great extent, to the development of rite and was responsible for its becoming the most solemn moment in the Divine Liturgy.

The first symbolic interpretation of the Great Entrance was given by St. Maximos Confessor (+662). According to him, the entrance with the holy gifts signifies the beginning of the life of glorification in heaven and the revelation of the salvation of God.[46] This interpretation is somewhat obscure and nebulous,

---

[43] *Tolkovanie na lit.*, pp. 191–192.
[44] *Expositio S. S. Liturgiae . . .*, p. 204.
[45] De Meester, *Les Liturgies . . .*, p. 333.
[46] Migne, **PG**, 91, 693.

and it was not adopted by the commentators of the Byzantine Liturgy. A more fortunate symbolic interpretation was that of Pseudo-Herman [47] who saw in the Great Entrance a portrayal and imitation of Christ's triumphal entry into Jerusalem. This interpretation has become classical; it was adopted by almost all the commentators of the Byzantine Liturgy, such as Pseudo-Sophronius,[48] Theodore Andides,[49] Nicholas Cabasilas,[50] and others. Simeon of Thessalonica [51] sees in the Great Entrance the dramatic representation of Christ's Second Coming at the end of the world to judge the living and the dead. This interpretation refers only to the entrance with the holy gifts; the placing of the gifts on the altar is usually interpreted differently. Pseudo-Herman, Pseudo-Sophronius and other later commentators see in tht rite of placing the offertory gifts upon the altar the symbol of Christ's burial.[52]

These interpretations had their effect on the formation of the ritual functions and prayers of the Great Entrance. The symbolic representation of Christ's triumphal entrance into Jerusalem influenced the rite of the Entrance with the holy gifts by adding greater solemnity to it. Again, under the inspiration of the same symbolic interpretation of placing the holy gifts on the altar, the following *troparia* were introduced into the Liturgy: "Noble Joseph . . . " and two others: "In the grave with the body . . . " and "As life-giving. . . ." Although these two are not in the old Liturgicons, nevertheless, they do appear in the Greek Liturgikons and Old-Slavonic Synodal Sluzhebnyks.[53]

Two critical remarks are in order at this point. First of all, we must affirm that the allusion of the procession with the holy gifts to Christ's entrance into Jerusalem is based merely on a remote analogy. The analogy in itself is not enough to warrant the explanation that the procession with the holy gifts is symbolic of Christ's triumphal entrance into Jerusalem. Besides, not one word in the liturgical texts alludes to Christ's entry into Jerusalem. As a matter of fact the hymn (Hagiology) "Holy, Holy, Holy," would seem to serve as a more suitable analogy, seeing that it ends with the words "Blessed is He who comes in the name of the Lord, Hosanna in the Highest" with which the people greeted Christ upon His solemn entry into Jerusalem. Moreover, immediately after this hymn the institution of the Holy Eucharist and the words of consecration are mentioned. Therefore, it is only a beautiful continuation of the chronology of events in the life of Christ. There is no reason, then, why we should accept this symbolic interpretation of the Great Entrance since it is not based on the practi-

---

[47] *Ibid.*, 98, 419.

[48] *Ibid.*, 87, 4001.

[49] *Ibid.*, 140, 441–444.

[50] *Ibid.*, 150, 420.

[51] *Ibid.*, 155, 295.

[52] Cf. Pseudo-Herman, Pseudo-Sophronius. See also Simeon of Thessalonica, Migne, PG, 155, 728; K. Nikolskiy, *Posobie k izucheniyu Ustava Bogosluzheniya prav. Tserkvi*, SPB., 1907, p. 422.

[53] The *troparia* "In the grave . . ." and "As the lifegiver . . ." are found in the Slavonic Sluzhebnyks of the seventeenth century, i.e., in the Kievan editions. (Cf. Sluzhebnyks of 1620, 1629 and 1639).

cal nature and purpose of rite. The purpose of the Great Entrance is to transfer the sacrificial elements, i.e., the holy gifts, from the Table of Prothesis to the altar for consecration. In this lies its main and true meaning.

If the entrance with the holy gifts suggests, at least, a remote analogy with the solemn entrance of Jesus into Jerusalem, the rite of placing the holy gifts on the altar suggests no analogy at all with His burial. What parallel is there between the rite of placing the offertory gifts on the altar and the placing of Christ's body in the grave? Furthermore, there is an evident inconsistency in making these holy gifts a symbol of the Christ who entered Jerusalem, and at the same time of the Christ who was placed in the tomb. The triumphal entry of Christ into Jerusalem was a moment of joy and festivity, while His burial was one of sorrow. How could one and the same rite symbolize two such antithetic events?

From this one can see in general how far-fetched, fanciful and unfounded some of these symbolic interpretations of the rites of the Divine Liturgy are, and how unrelated they are to the ceremonies and functions themselves. Yet these interpretations have been accepted as an explanation of the Divine Liturgy, and have even been responsible for the addition of prayers, which, in turn, served to sanction and confirm the symbolic interpretations. This can be said of the first, second and third *troparia* which were not in the Liturgy until the fourteenth century. It was under the influence of the symbolic interpretation that the placing of the holy gifts on the altar came to represent Christ's burial, and that these prayers were inserted into the Liturgy. Their content gives the rite a meaning which of itself it neither does nor could possess.[54]

It would be interesting to know where this symbolism of Christ's burial originated and what foundation and justification it has. According to Muretov,[55] its origin derives from the symbolic interpretation of the altar. The altar, according to Pseudo-Herman and Pseudo-Sophronius, is a symbol of Christ's sepulcher and, therefore, the placing of the gifts on the altar symbolizes the laying of Christ's body into the tomb. Hence, the explanation of the Great Entrance as the symbol of Christ's burial. Why symbolists prefer to associate the altar with Christ's tomb rather than with the table of the Last Supper where Christ first offered Himself up as the Unbloody Sacrifice, is difficult to comprehend. There is a by far greater resemblance and a more suitable analogy between the altar and the table on which the first Unbloody Sacrifice was offered than with the tomb in which our Lord was laid.

---

[54] All three *troparia* are taken from the services of Passion Week and all allude to Christ's burial. ("The noble Joseph, when he had taken down your spotless body from the tree, wrapped it in fine linen and spices, and *sorrowing placed it in a new tomb.*" "*In the grave with the body,* but in Hades with the soul, as God; in Paradise with the Thief, and on the Throne with the Father and the Spirit were You, O Christ, filling all things, *thyself* uncircumscribed." "As giving life, as more splendid than Paradise, and more radiant than any appeal chamber, O Christ, is shown forth *Your tomb,* the fountain of our resurrection.")

[55] Cf. Muretov, *Istorichestk, obzor . . .,* pp. 63–65.

Leaving aside all these incongruous and unwarranted symbolic interpretations, it must be affirmed that The Great Entrance was encumbered with later accretions and additions from the textual as well as from the ritual point of view. These additions altered the original meaning of the Great Entrance and enhanced its solemnity to a point of exaggeration. Thus, the Great Entrance may at times detract from the most important part of the Divine Liturgy, namely, the sacrifice itself. This, undoubtedly, is no asset to the Liturgy; it promotes confusion.

3. The Ektene of Supplication

The ektene of supplication is a link connecting the Great Entrance with the rites that immediately precede the Anaphora, that is, with the rites of the Kiss of Peace and the Symbol of Faith.

Its first petition "Let us fulfill our prayers to the Lord" indicates that it is a complement to the previous ektene supplication, especially the Great and the triple ektenes. The natural place of the ektene of supplication in many Eastern Liturgies is not after the Great Entrance, but after the reading of the Scriptures.[1] The place it now occupies between the Great Entrance and the Anaphora was due to a later insertion or interpolation. However, the ektene itself, or at least some of its petitions, are of ancient origin. They are found already in the Liturgical documents of the fourth and fifth centuries.[2]

The first petitions of the ektene of supplication are drawn from the Great Ektene,

> For this holy church and for all those who enter therein with faith, devotion and fear of God, let us pray to the Lord,
> That we may be delivered from every affliction, wrath, and want, let us pray to the Lord,
>
> Help, save, have mercy and protect us, O God, by Thy grace.

Only the second petition is a special one, namely:

> For the precious gifts placed here, let us pray to the Lord.

This is the petition for the consecration of the gifts, which is about to be performed during the Anaphora.

The actual petitions of the ektene are the six short supplications to which

---

[1] The Armenian and Malabar Liturgies and the Liturgy of St. Jacob, have the ektene of supplication after the Gospel. (Cf. Skabalanovich, M., *Ektenii*, (Trud. K.D.A., 1912, no. 7, pp. 195–201).

[2] Cf. the Liturgy of the *Apostolic Constitutions* (eighth book) and the Liturgy which St. John Chrysostom describes in his homilies, especially the homily on the Second Epistle of St. Paul to the Corinthians (Migne, PG, 61, 404). Here St. John quotes petitions which are almost identical to those of our ektene of supplication. These petitions were addressed to God by the faithful immediately after the reading of Holy Scripture, i.e., after the dismissal of the catechumens. From this we may conclude that the ektene supplications, which are suitably interspersed throughout the whole Liturgy, at one time followed the reading of the Holy Scripture.

the people respond: *"Grant it, O Lord."* If all these petitions were to be reduced to one, it would be simply a petition for a happy life here on earth. Just as the leading though of the Great Ektene is *"peace"* in all forms and implications, so the leading theme of the ektene of supplication is *a holy, sinless life* here on earth and consequently, a happy passage into eternity.

Each petition deserves examination. In the first one grace to pass the day happily is the quest of the Christian:

> That this whole day be perfect, holy, peaceful and sinless, let us beseech the Lord.

Here, one prays, first of all, for the holy and sinless passing of the day. By the word "day" is understood man's whole life. This is evident in the second petition:

> For an angel of peace, a faithful guide, a guardian of our souls and bodies, let us beseech the Lord.

Here God is asked to give man a guardian angel not only for a day but for life. This petition is really a continuation of the first, for with the help of a guardian angel, the custodian of soul and body and a faithful guide, the faithful will be able to spend their entire lives in holiness and sinlessness. This petition evidences the belief of the primitive Church in the existence of guardian angels which are assigned to every Christian for protection from the dangers that imperil soul and body.

The third petition directs attention to the principal enemy that prevents man from passing the day in holiness, namely, "sin," which is the greatest obstacle to the Christian in his pursuit of holiness and perfection. Where there is sin, there is no holiness; there can be no room for "a perfect, holy, peaceful day." Hence, the Christian asks God for "pardon and forgiveness of our sins and offenses," thus, renouncing sin and promising to wage war against the greatest enemy of sanctity and perfection.

But even this is not entirely sufficient. To advance in perfection man needs God's grace for without it his efforts will be futile. Hence, the fourth petition asks God for

> what is good and beneficial to our souls and for peace in the world.

In this short, general formula are included all the graces needed for a holy and sinless life here on earth.

The fifth petition asks for final perseverance in God's grace:

> For the remaining time of our life to be spent in peace and repentance, let us beseech the Lord.

Man's eternal fate will depend on this perseverance. Perseverance in the grace of God to the last hour is one of God's greatest gifts; hence the Liturgy urges Christians to ask for it.

The last petition of the ektene is a prayer for a happy death. A happy and holy death is the culminating point of a holy life. Thus, God is petitioned to grant the faithful a holy, Christian death:

> For a Christian end to our life—painless, blameless, peaceful—and a good account at the dread tribunal of Christ, let us beseech the Lord.

First of all, a Christian's end should be a *Christian* one, i.e., the death of a just man who considers death as passage into and the beginning of eternal life and who, unlike the mundane, sinful man, exhibits no fear of death. Further, God is petitioned to grant a death "without pain," for excessive pain in the last hour has proved to be the cause of many falling into despondency. A "shameless," death, i.e., a death without reproach, fear or shame before the judgment seat of God is also the object of this petition. Finally, the Christian begs for a "peaceful death" so that he may die reconciled to God and with the consoling thought that God has forgiven him his sins which he has expiated with sorrow and penance. It is, therefore, natural that after such a holy death the Christian need not fear Christ's judgment. The judgment of God is not terrifying to the Christian who passes his day without sin, for he is filled with hope in God's mercy and knows that he will receive a reward for his life on earth. He is confident that Christ will welcome him with the words, "Well done, good and faithful servant: because thou hast been faithful over a few things, I will place three over many things: enter thou into the joy of thy Lord." (Mt 25:23)

The ektene of supplication is inspired by two leading thoughts; a holy Christian life and a holy death. In other words, the theme of the petitions is the salvation of the soul through the sanctification of every day of man's entire life. In this respect, it reduces ultimately to the fundamental petition of the Great Ektene—for the peace of God, for the salvation of man's immortal soul and the attainment of his last end here on earth.[3] Just as in the Great Ektene the prayers conclude with the commending of one's self to the Savior, so too, in this ektene, Christians place all their petitions for a happy life at the feet of Christ. They commend themselves, their fellowmen and their whole life to Him in the firm conviction and hope that one day they will obtain that for which they prayed so ardently, and that after a holy life and a holy death they will receive from Him everlasting life in heaven.

---

[3] The basic thought of the ektene of supplication not only recalls the predominant theme of the Great Ektene which is "peace" but it presents this word in a variety of applications. For in the ektene of supplication we encounter the word five times—each time with a different application or connotation. "That this day be *peaceful;*" For an angel of *peace*"; "For *peace* in the world;" "That we may spend the rest of our life in *peace*"; "For a *peaceful* end." Hence, we can see how fond the Liturgy is of using this word and what great importance it attaches to it. The word "peace" recurs in our Liturgy thirty-six times, which indicates that it is one of the favorite words of the Liturgy. M. Tarchnishvili wrote about this word "peace" in our Liturgy in his article, *Die Idee des christlichen Friedens in der byzantinischen Liturgie,* Das Wort in der Zeit, 6, 1937, pp. 219–226).

4. The Prayer of Oblation

The ektene of supplication, like all other ektenes, has its own secret prayer. It precedes the fifth petition: "Help, save, have mercy. . . ." Actually, this prayer should be placed before the invocation:

> By the mercies of Thine only-begotten Son, with whom Thou art blessed together with Thy most holy and good and life-giving Spirit now and ever, and unto ages of ages,

because it completes the prayer of Oblation.

The prayer of Oblation has no connection with the petitions of the ektene. In content and original purpose it is not the concomitant prayer of the ektene of supplication, but of the Proskomide. This is indicated by the title of the prayer. In the liturgikons it is called the "prayer of Prothesis," [1] or the "prayer of Oblation after placing the holy gifts on the holy altar." Its natural place, then, is in the Great Entrance when the priest places the holy gifts on the altar. Long ago when the rite of gift-offering was still customary during the Great Entrance, this prayer was in conclusion, i.e., the "prayer of Prothesis" in the full sense of the word. When the Proskomide was moved to the beginning of the Liturgy, the prayer lost its original meaning and purpose, and became the attendant prayer of the rite of placing the holy gifts on the altar. In the present-day Liturgy it has lost even this purpose, for in its place are found the *troparia* "Noble Joseph . . ." and "Do good, O Lord. . . ." These two additions separated the prayer of Oblation from the Great Entrance and from the act of the placing of the holy gifts on the altar, and as a result, it lost its immediate connection with the gifts.

From these historical observations it can be seen how additions and interpolations can alter and complicate the original structure of the Divine Liturgy, destroying the harmony and arrangement of the rites and introducing into the Liturgy unnecessary exaggerations and superfluities, as for example, the symbolic allusion to Christ's burial which has been examined above.[2]

In the prayer of Oblation, the petition found in the prayers of the faithful and in the prayer of the Great Entrance is repeated. Now the priest again begs God to make him worthy to celebrate the Liturgy. Like the previous prayers, the prayer of Oblation also prepares him for the sacrifice. Its text is as follows:

> Lord almighty God, Who alone art holy, Who dost accept the sacrifice of praise from those who call upon Thee with their whole heart, accept also the prayer of us sinners, and bring it to Thy holy altar. And enable us to

---

[1] This is the name given to our prayer in the oldest liturgical manuscript, the eighth-century Barberini Codex.

[2] Our Liturgy has more of these later insertions and additions which interrupt the logic and the natural train of liturgical thought. They may be compared to "digressions" commonly found in narrations, which only tend to prolong the narration and to divert one's attention from the central thought.

offer Thee gifts and spiritual sacrifice for our sins and for the ignorance of the people. And deign that we may find grace before Thee; that our sacrifice may be acceptable unto Thee; and may the Good Spirit of Thy grace rest upon us, and upon these gifts placed here, and upon all Thy people.

Similar in content to the above is the prayer of Oblation in the Liturgy of St. Basil. Here the priest also asks God that he may offer a worthy sacrifice, that it be pleasing to Him, that He send the grace of His Holy Spirit and that He accept the sacrifice from his hands, as He had graciously accepted sacrifice from the hands of Abel, Noah, Abraham, Moses, Samuel and the Apostles.[3] There is one petition in this prayer, however, that is outstanding, i.e., that God send His Holy Spirit upon the priest, upon the holy gifts and upon the faithful. The priest needs the grace of the Holy Spirit so that he may celebrate the Liturgy worthily. It is through the operation of the Holy Spirit that the holy gifts are converted into the Body and Blood of Jesus Christ. Finally, the help of the Holy Spirit is invoked for the faithful, that through His help they may obtain an abundance of graces and derive benefit from the sacrifice. Hence, with the liturgists, one can justly call this prayer of Oblation an *anticipatory Epiklesis,* i.e., an epiklesis that anticipates the words of consecration and the epiklesis which follows this consecration. This anticipatory or antecedent epiklesis is found not only in the Liturgy of St. John Chrysostom, but also in the Liturgy of St. Basil and many others.[4]

5. The Eirenikon or the Kiss of Peace

After the invocation: "By the mercies of Thy Only-begotten Son . . ." the priest turns to the people and salutes them with the words: "Peace be to all." The deacon sings or recites: "Let us love one another, that with one mind we may confess." Then the people respond: "The Father and the Son and the Holy Spirit, the Trinity consubstantial and undivided." The Kiss of Peace follows. The priest first executes three metanias or bows before the holy gifts on the altar, repeating after each metania a verse from Psalm 17: 2–3:

I will love Thee, O Lord, my strength: the Lord is my fortress and my refuge.

Then he kisses the holy gifts which are veiled; first he kisses the diskos, then the chalice and finally the altar. When more than one priest celebrate the Liturgy, they perform the same rituals as the first priest. The priests then kiss each other on the shoulders and the older priest says: "Christ is amidst us" and the younger one replies: "He is and always will be."

---

[3] Similar expressions are found in the Liturgy of the *Apostolic Constitutions,* the Liturgy of St. James, the Roman Liturgy and others. It must be remarked that the text does not place the sacrifices of Abel, Abraham, Melchisedech and others on an equal level with the sacrifice of the Divine Liturgy; it only asks God to accept the sacrifice of the priest as He did their sacrifices.

[4] For example, the Coptic Liturgy of St. Cyril, the Liturgies of St. Mark, St. Gregory and even the Roman Liturgy contain this preventive or antecedent epiklesis. (Cf. M. Jugie, *De forma Eucharistiae,* De epiclesibus eucharisticis, Romae, 1943, pp. 15–24.

The Kiss of Peace is one of the oldest of all liturgical customs. St. Paul frequently encourages the Christians to kiss one another as a token of mutual love and peace.[1] The private custom of kissing which is common to all peoples now becomes a public rite of the Liturgy. This custom probably originated in the Apostolic Period. St. Justin, in his description of the Liturgy, mentions this Kiss of Peace [2] with which, according to his testimony, the Liturgy of the sacrifice commences. Origen [3] is a witness to the Kiss of Peace in the third century. St. Cyril of Jerusalem,[4] St. John Chrysostom,[5] and the Synod of Laodicaea [6] in the fourth century, and Pseudo-Dionysius [7] refers to it in the fifth century. The Liturgy of the *Apostolic Constitutions,* the Liturgies of St. James, St. Mark, and many other ancient liturgies have the Kiss of Peace.

In ancient times, not only the celebrants, but also the faithful kissed one another—the men kissed the men and the women, the women. Later the Kiss of Peace among the faithful went out of practice, probably at the time when "the custom of corporate communion of all those present at the Liturgy" also ceased to be a practice.[8] Community participation in the Eucharistic Banquet was one of the more important reasons why the Kiss of Peace was introduced into the Liturgy. Now only the Kiss among the celebrants remains.

There is no need to expatiate on the meaning of the Kiss of Peace. A kiss is a natural manifestation of love and friendship, and in the Liturgy it retains the same meaning; it is an expression of mutual love, of the spirit of friendship and of the peace of Christ among those who profess the Christian faith. The motive for introducing the Kiss of Peace into the Liturgy was, without doubt, the words of Christ: "So, then, if you are bringing your offering to the altar and there remember that your brother has something against you, leave your offering there before the altar, go and be reconciled with your brother first, and then come back and present your offering." (Mt 5:23–25) This explains why the Kiss of Peace precedes the Eucharistic Sacrifice.[9] The Christians recalled the words of the Savior: "And, when you stand in prayer, forgive whatever you have against anybody, so that your Father in heaven may forgive your failings too." (Mk 11:25)

Although the custom of actually kissing one another in the Liturgy has been discontinued, nevertheless, the idea of the Kiss of Peace remains as expressed in the acclamation:

Let us love one another that with one mind we may confess the Father and the Son and the Holy Spirit, the Trinity consubstantial and undivided.

---

[1] Cf. Rom 16: 16; 1 Cor 16:19; 2 Cor 13:11–12; 1 Thess 5:26; Phillip 4:21; Tit 3:15.
[2] *Apol.,* 1:65.
[3] Migne, PG, 14, 1282–1283.
[4] *Ibid.,* 33, 1112.
[5] *Ibid.,* 47, 398; 49, 382; 61, 606–607.
[6] Mansi, 2, 567.
[7] Migne, PG, 3, 425.
[8] Cf. Bishop Bessarion, *Tolkovanie na bozh. lit.,* p. 200.
[9] The Roman Mass has the Kiss of Peace immediately before Holy Communion.

This, therefore, is an exhortation to mutual, forgiving love, which is the chief commandment of Christians. Without this love our sacrifice cannot be pleasing and acceptable to God. Love is assumed to be the distinctive characteristic of Christ's followers (Jn 13:35); it is by this mutual love that the world recognizes the true servants of Christ who "confess with one mind the Father and the Son and the Holy Spirit." [10]

The rite of the Kiss of Peace has still another meaning. Not only does it exhort the faithful to love one another, but it also inculcates symbolically the foundation upon which this mutual love rests, i.e., love of God. Love of neighbor must spring from the love of God for these two commandments are inseparably bound to each other (Mt. 22:34–50). This love is beautifully expressed in the rite of kissing the holy gifts and the altar which the celebrants perform before they kiss each other. Therefore, they kiss first of all the Christ-God Himself whom the holy gifts and altar symbolize. Only after the symbolic kiss given to Christ, do they kiss one another on the shoulders and recite the words: "Christ is amidst us . . . ," "He is and always will be." They do this as if to remind each other that the source of brotherly love is the love of God, and that Christ is the bond of mutual love among Christians. In this lies the profound and beautiful significance of the Kiss of Peace.[11]

6. The Symbol of Faith

The Kiss of Peace is followed by the Symbol of Faith. The deacon exclaims: "The doors, the doors! In wisdom let us attend," and the lector or the people recite the Symbol of Faith aloud. Meanwhile the priest holds the large veil aloft in his hands and waves it gently over the holy gifts. Toward the conclusion of the Symbol of Faith, he folds the veil and kissing it places it at the right of the chalice.

The words: "The doors, the doors! " are an elliptical or incomplete exclamation. They are used in the accusative or objective case without a transitive verb and must be complemented to read:

"GUARD the doors!" "WATCH the doors!" or "CLOSE the doors!"

---

[10] The words "That with one mind we may confess: the Father and the Son and the Holy Spirit . . ." appear in the text of the Liturgy at quite a later date. They are an insertion of the fourteenth century. The *Diataxis* of the Patriarch Philotheus was responsible for its being introduced into the Liturgy (Cf. De Meester, *Les origines* . . ., p. 336).

[11] T. Mishkovskiy is of the opinion that the words "I will love you O Lord . . ." are not only an addition to the rite of kissing the holy gifts and altar, but that the main emphasis should be laid on the words and not on the rite of kissing. (Cf. his *"Izlozhenie tasaregrad. lit.,* pp. 102–103, footnote). In our opinion, the direct opposite is true. The words of the Psalm are only a prayer attending the rite of kissing the holy gifts, therefore, emphasis is to be placed on the rite rather than on the words. The kissing of the holy gifts and the altar is the main rite of the Kiss of Peace, and the words of the Psalm are only a beautiful prayer accompanying this rite thus investing it with meaning.

Similar exclamations are found in other Eastern Liturgies.[1] Once these words were taken literally as a command to the doorkeeper to close the doors of the church, or to guard the doors which were already closed. They are, therefore, a carry-over from the times when the catechumenate still prevailed, and are a continuation of the dismissal of the catechumens from the church. Because the Eucharistic Sacrifice was imminent, a last warning was given that no catechumen, infidel, heretic, or anyone who was not entitled, dare be present for this.

Obviously by the words "the doors, the doors!" have lost their original meaning, for today we have neither catechumens nor the prescription to close the church doors before the sacrifice begins. They can, however, have a symbolic meaning. They can be construed as being the last appeal to the faithful to close the doors of their hearts to the external world, its cares and its troubles, to dismiss from the heart "every earthly care," and rivet their whole attention on the impending sacrifice. Bishop Bessarion offers a beautiful commentary on the words "the doors, the doors! " in his liturgical commentary. They should, he says, remind the faithful to reflect whether they are worthy to remain in the church for the sacrifice. They should ask themselves whether they are better, holier, worthier than the unfaithful, the heretics, or the catechumens, or, on the contrary, whether they are only nominal believers.[2] In our present-day Liturgy, therefore, the words have the same meaning as in the rite of the dismissal of the catechumens: they warn the faithful against being spiritual catechumens during the Eucharistic Sacrifice.[3]

Although the Symbol of Faith was not an original part of the Liturgy, nevertheless it has made its way into all Liturgies, both Eastern and Western. It is not necessary here to go into the history of the Symbol of Faith, its origin, its development and its crystallization into its present form. This belongs to the history of dogma. It is enough to say that it was not an original part of the Liturgy, but a borrowing from the sacrament of Baptism.

The dogmatic disputes of the fifth and sixth centuries were the cause of its introduction into the Liturgy. The first to incorporate it was the Monophysite Patriarch of Antioch, Peter the Fullo (+471). Following his example the Patriarch of Constantinople, Timothy (510–518), ordered the Nicene Creed to be

---

[1] Cf. e.g., the Liturgy of St. James or the Syrian-Jacobite Liturgy which was edited by Renaudot. There we find the expression "Close the doors" (E. Renaudot, *Liturgiarum Orientalium Collectio*, II, Francofurti ad Maenum, 1847, p. 10). In the Armenian Liturgy there is a similar, though more developed acclamation: "Watch the doors! The doors! With the greatest attention and caution."

[2] Cf. *Tolkovanie na bozh.*, p. 201.

[3] N. Cabasilas explains the words "The Doors! The Doors!" as exhorting the faithful to open the doors of their souls so that they may hear and accept the Symbol of Faith. Such a symbolic interpretation robs these words completely of their original meaning. Cabasilas completely forgets that the words refer not to the opening of the doors but conversely, to their closing. This proves only one thing, that interpreters of the liturgical texts and rites, in neglecting to give due attention to historical origin and evaluation, thus fail to give the proper interpretation of the Liturgy.

recited at every Liturgy.[4] Emperor Justin II (567–578) ordered that the Constantinopolitan Symbol of Faith, which we use to this day, be used instead of the shorter Nicene Creed.[5] The Western churches followed the example of tht Eastern churches. In the West, the Spanish Church at the Synod of Toledo (589) introduced the recitation of the Symbol of Faith into the Liturgy. In the second canon the Fathers of the Synod referred to the practice of the Eastern Church of professing the faith during the Liturgy.[6] In the seventh and eighth centuries, the Churches of France and Germany adopted this practice, but it was not until the year 1014 that Pope Benedict VIII officially introduced it into the Roman Liturgy.[7]

The Symbol of Faith appears at various points in various Liturgies. The Roman, Armenian and Malabar Liturgies place it immediately after the reading of the Gospel, thus associating it with the Liturgy of the Catechumens, i.e., with the didactic part of the Liturgy. The other Liturgies have it before the sacrifice, i.e., before the Kiss of Peace.[8] The Byzantine Liturgy is the only one that has moved the Symbol of Faith from its original place and placed it, not before, but after the Kiss of Peace.

No precise information is had on the position the Symbol of Faith occupied immediately after it was incorporated into the Liturgy. According to the testimony of the historian, John of Biclara, it appeared before the "Our Father." The Synod of Toledo ordered it to be recited before the "Our Father." However, John of Biclara probably made a mistake in referring to this as the original position of the Symbol in the Liturgy, for all the other Eastern liturgical documents have it, not preceding the "Our Father," but before or after the Kiss of Peace.[9] Maximos the Confessor, who lived in the sevnth century, bears witness to the fact that its position in today's Liturgy is the same as in his time.[10]

What meaning does the Symbol of Faith have in the Liturgy? It was noted before that in some Liturgies it was recited after the reading of the Gospel. In this position, the Symbol is considered to be a complement to the Gospel for it is a resumé of the truths of the faith, the source of which is the Gospel of Christ. But in other Liturgies the Symbol, with its position immediately before the sacrifice, indicates that faith is a prerequisite or a necessary condition for participation in the Eucharistic Sacrifice. Between faith and sacrifice, between dogma and cult and between theory and practice there exists an intrinsic relation. Man's composite nature, consisting of both body and soul, tends to seek external mani-

---

[4] Cf. the Byzantine historian Theodore Lector (sixth century); Migne, PG, 86, 201.

[5] Cf. the testimony of John of Biclara (Spain, seventh century) , "*Chronicle*"; see Theodore Momsen. *Monumenta Germaniae historica, XI, Cronica minora*, II, p. 211.

[6] Mansi, 9, 990.

[7] Cf. Brinktrine, *La Santa messa*, Roma, 1945, p. 108.

[8] Cf. St. James', the Syrian-Jacobite, Maronite, Chaldean, Coptic and Ethiopian Liturgies.

[9] In the Chronicle of John of Biclara an error must have been made or an inadvertence, at least such is the opinion of the liturgist M. Hanssens: *Inst. lit.*, III, 300.

[10] Migne, PG, 91, 695.

festation of itself. Cult with its element of sacrifice is based on faith and is the best expression of faith.

The Symbol of Faith has the same meaning in the Liturgy as it does in the rite of Baptism where, before the grace of a new life or spiritual regeneration is given to the soul, the Christian, through the lips of his godparents has to renounce "the devil, all his works, his service and his pomps," and to declare his faith in Christ and in the truths of the Christian religion. The Symbol of Faith in the rite of Baptism was, therefore, a solemn proclamation of faith and allegiance to Christ. In the Divine Liturgy it has the same meaning; it is a solemn declaration of faith in Christ. In the Liturgy the baptismal promise and pledge of allegiance to Christ is renewed; once again the devil and his works are renounced, and the promise is made of an unwavering faith in Christ, in His holy doctrine, in fact, in all that the Church commands man to believe. Hence, the Symbol of Faith is a very beautiful and meaningful act preparatory to the Eucharistic Sacrifice. Christ gives Himself totally to man in the Holy Eucharist, and man gives himself to Him entirely in his act or protestation of faith. Hence, we are justified in feeling that, although the Symbol of Faith is a later interpolation, it is a suitable and appropriate one. So interwoven into the Liturgy is the Symbol that today we are not conscious of it as a relatively late insertion.[11]

In discussing the Symbol of Faith, one must not overlook the rite that accompanies the recitation of this prayer, the waving of the veil over the holy gifts. There is scarcely a rite in the Liturgy that claims such a variety of interpretations as this one, a clear indication that its original purpose, whatever it may have been, is unknown to commentators today.

This rite is usually interpreted symbolically—very frequently as representing the descent of the Holy Spirit upon the holy gifts.[12] Why it should represent the advent of the Holy Spirit during the Symbol of Faith, and not, for example, during the Consecration or after the Consecration or during the Epiklesis, is difficult to understand. Others give it a different meaning: the raising of the veil during the Symbol of Faith was to signify the sublimity of the truths of the faith, and the waving of the veil, the earthquake which occurred when the angel rolled away the stone from the grave at Christ's resurrection for, according to them, the veil or *aër* symbolizes that stone.[13] Still others think that the waving of the aer typifies the Holy Spirit that moved over the great void during the creation of the world.[14] Bishop Bessarion sees in this rite the symbol of Christ's pro-

[11] The introduction of the Symbol of Faith into the Liturgy "did not in any way disrupt the arrangement of the Byzantine Liturgy, but . . . conversly, it blended in so well with the stream of liturgical thought that one is completely unaware of its being a later interpolation. It seems that it was inserted during the pristine formative years of the Liturgy." (Cf. T. Mishkovskiy, *Izlozhenie tsaregrad. lit.,* p. 104).

[12] De Meester, *La divina liturgia del n. P.S.G. Crisostomo,* 1925, p. 129.

[13] Cf. Dmitrevskiy, *Isto. dogm. tainstv. izlozh. na lit.,* p. 66. See also K. Nikolskiy, *Posobie k izucheniyu Ustava Bogosluzheniya Pravoslavnoy Tserkvi,* (7 izd.) SPB., 1907, p. 428.

[14] Cf. Dmitrevskiy, *op. cit.,* p. 66.

tection of the faithful. The raising of the veil over the holy gifts signifies Christ who, like a bird protecting its young ones by flapping its wings, thereby repelling all danger, protects the faithful. Thus, during the Proskomide the priest, when covering the holy gifts, begs Christ:

> Shelter us with the sheltering of your wings, drive away from us every foe and adversary.[15]

J. Pelesh gives still another interpretation. According to him, "the priest holding the veil between himself and the holy gifts, declares that we, in professing our faith, staunchly and steadfastly cling to our holy faith and believe in all the mysteries, even though before the eyes of our body and mind they are hidden and incomprehensible." [16] Myshkovskiy gives the same interpretation saying that during "the Symbol of Faith the holy gifts are unveiled, and the priest holds the veil over the holy gifts. This signifies the revelation of God's doctrine as was given to us in the New Testament." [17]

These interpretations make clear how obscure the rite of the raising and the waving of the veil during the Symbol of Faith is. To them should be added a few remarks about the original and true meaning of these two rites.

The raising of the veil aloft has, first of all, a practical purpose rather than a symbolical one. Since the Anaphora—during which the consecration of the holy gifts takes place—is about to begin, the gifts must be uncovered and exposed. Hence, every Eastern Liturgy contains a more-or-less solemn unveiling of the holy gifts before the Anaphora.[18] Some even have a separate prayer accompanying this rite which they call the Prayer of the Veil or Aer.[19] The unveiling of the holy gifts is a sign to the people that the Anaphora is about to begin. The priest customarily lifted the veil aloft, not during the Symbol of Faith but while saying the words "Let us stand well . . ."[20] i.e., *after* the Symbol. In the liturgical manuscripts up to the fourteenth and fifteenth centuries inclusively there are nowhere found rubrics for raising and waving the veil over the holy gifts during the Symbol of Faith.[21] Hence, it can be concluded that this rite was introduced into the Liturgy at a later date.

The rite of waving the veil over the holy gifts, has another practical purpose as well. It was an old custom to wave the ripidion (fan) over the holy gifts

---

[15] Cf. Bishop Bessarion, *Tolkov. na bozh. lit.*, p. 210.

[16] Cf. *Pastirsk. Bohoslovie, Liturghika,* p. 494.

[17] *Izlozhenie tsaregrad. lit.*, p. 103.

[18] Hanssens, *Inst. Litur.*, III, pp. 333–335.

[19] *Ibid.*, 331–333. In some rites (Maronite and Syrian), the *aër* is called the "anaphora" because it is unfolded before the Anaphora, cf. Hanssens, pp. 332, 334, 338.

[20] Cf. the manuscript of Isidore Pyromalos (tenth-eleventh centuries) in Goar's *Euchologion*, 183. Cf. also the Latin interpretation of the Liturgy of St. John Chrysostom by Leo Tuscus (twelfth century), Hanssens, p. 336.

[21] In the manuscripts of the fourteenth-fifteenth centuries, i.e., after the liturgical reform of Patriarch Philotheus, the rubrics direct the priest to uncover the holy gifts only after the Symbol of Faith, during the recitation of the words "Let us stand well." They mention nothing about the waving of the *aër* over the gifts. Cf. Krasnoseltsev, *Materiali . . .*, pp. 64, 90, 109.

so that nothing would fall into the chalice or on the bread. This can be proved by a rubric which is still contained in the Russian-Orthodox Sluzhebnyks and in the Ukrainian Sluzhebnyk published in Rome in 1941. There, after the words, "Stand well," is found the prescription: "The priest removes the veil from the holy gifts and kissing it, he places it on the right of the chalice and says: The grace of our Lord Jesus Christ. . . ." The deacon, making a metania, goes to the altar, takes the ripidion and waves it devoutly over the holy gifts. And if there should be no ripidion, then he uses one of the veils." From this it may be concluded that the waving of the aer over the holy gifts had for its purpose the protection of the holy gifts, so that nothing would fall on them and contaminate them.[22] This was at one time the function of the deacon and it took place only after the recitation of the Symbol of Faith. When, about the fifteenth century, the practice of unveiling the holy gifts during the Symbol of Faith was introduced, the waving of the aer over the holy gifts during the Symbol of Faith began. Therefore, liturgists and liturgical commentators who interpret this rite symbolically and give no attention to its original and true purpose, do not give a satisfactory explanation. With their strained and exaggerated symbolism, they not only fail to explain it, but, on the contrary, they obscure it and render it unintelligible.[23]

SELECT BIBLIOGRAPHY

Fortescue, A., *Cheroubicon*, (Dictionarire d'Archeol. e. Liturg. chret., III, (1913), cols. 1281–1286).

Cherkasov, V., *Kherumiskaya pyesn v osvyeshchenii liturghiynim tekstom*, (Bog. Vyest., 26 (1917), Fevral-Mart, pp. 305–316).

Karabinov, J., *Lektsii po Liturghikye*, SPB., 1914, pp. 138–139.

N. M., *Diptikhi*, Pravo. Bogo. Ents., IV, (1903), pp. 1059–1060; Bishop E., *The diptychs*.

Connolly, R. H., *The liturgical homilies of Narsai*, Texts and Studies, III, (1909), pp. 101–114, Appendix III.

Cabrol, F., *Diptiques* (Liturgie), DACL, IV, 1, (1916), cols. 1045–1094.

Leclerq, H., *Diptiques* (Archeologie), DACL, IV, 1 (1916) cols. 1094–1170.

Delbrueck, R., *Die Konsular-Dyptichen*, 1929.

---

[22] K. Nikolskiy, *Posobiye* . . ., p. 428.

[23] As an example of how affected and far-fetched an interpretation of the rites of the Liturgy could be, it suffices to adduce an excerpt from Pseudo-Herman. According to him, the covering of the holy gifts (during the Great Entrance) signifies the night when Christ was betrayed and delivered up to Annas and Caiphas, as well as the testimony of the false witnesses who testified against Christ and His being struck on the face. The covering is called the *aër* for no other reason than that it symbolizes the air of that dark night when Peter denied Christ. Again the removal of the *aër* from the holy gifts and its being placed aside symbolizes that morning when Christ was delivered to Pilate. (Cf. Migne, PG, 98, 425) .

Chapter III

THE EUCHARISTIC SACRIFICE

(The Second Part of the Liturgy of the Faithful)

The preparation for the Eucharistic Sacrifice concludes with the Symbol of Faith. All the rites and prayers of the first part of the Liturgy of the Faithful have a preparatory character, i.e., they have for their purpose to make the priest and the faithful ready for a worthy offering of the sacrifice. The prayers for the Faithful, the Cherubic Hymn, the prayer of the Great Entrance, the Kiss of Peace and the Symbol of Faith, all are intended as preparation of priest and people for the most important part of the Liturgy, the Eucharistic Sacrifice.

Finally comes the climax of the Liturgy—the Eucharistic Sacrifice. The Eucharistic Sacrifice of the New Testament is offered here in commemoration of the redemption by virtue of a miraculous change of the elements of bread and wine into the Body and Blood of Jesus Christ. Here is the culminating point of the entire Liturgy. If the Liturgy can be considered a mystical drama, then the Anaphora is the climax of dramatic suspense. If the Liturgy were to be compared to a magnificent basilica, then the Eucharistic Sacrifice would be the sanctuary, "The Holy of Holies."

1. Anaphora of the Byzantine Liturgy

There is no need to explain all the various names used to designate the Eucharist Sacrifice, because they are in themselves clear. In the Western Church, this central part of the Divine Liturgy is usually called the "Canon" or "Liturgical Canon"; in the Eastern Church, it is called "an offering," "offering of sacrifice," "Eucharist," "Eucharistic Prayer," or the "Anaphora." [1] In this commentary the name Anaphora will be used.

Like all the rites and prayers of the Divine Liturgy, those of the Sacrifice can best be understood in the light of their historical background. History affords us the key to understanding why this scheme and structure of the Anaphora was chosen and not another. How and where did it originate? What factors influ-

---

[1] The word "anaphora" in its extended sense is understood by liturgists to mean not only the Eucharistic Canon, but also the whole formula of the Divine Liturgy which encompasses all the prayers of the priest from the Kiss of Peace to the dismissal of the faithful. The "anaphora," in the nomenclature of the liturgist means, therefore, "the formulary of the eucharistic part of the Liturgy or the Liturgy of the Faithful."

enced the present-day form? What were its basic and underlying thoughts and ideas? How did it develop throughout the centuries? What is each integral element meant to express? In brief: What is the origin and historical development of the Anaphora?

These are among the most important and most investigated questions in the history of the Liturgy, owing to the fact that the Anaphora, after the Bible, is considered to be the most precious text which the Church has preserved in her deposit of faith. Many liturgists and scholars have striven and are still striving to shed some light on the origin and evolution of the Anaphora, its prayers, its component parts and its ritual function. Certain matters are still not completely clarified, as for example, the question of the origin and meaning of the Epiklesis. However, in general it can be said that recent investigations into the texts of old liturgical documents have produced wonderful results and have contributed much to a better understanding of the structure, plan, inherent logic and meaning of the Anaphora.

The limited space of this book does not allow for an exhaustive and detailed discussion of the origin and historical development of the Anaphora. Hence, reference will be made only to the most significant data.

1. *Origin of the Anaphora*. The Anaphora fundamentally owes its origin to Jesus Christ as has been mentioned in Part One of this book. The Divine Liturgy was instituted by Christ, and the Anaphora is the kernel, core and essence of this Liturgy. Therefore, the Anaphora derives from Christ. But Our Lord did not give the Anaphora in the form it has today; He gave only the essentials from which the Anaphora, or the Canons of the various Liturgies, evolved. This evolution was brought about by various external factors. Consequently, not all the elements of today's Anaphora derive their origin directly from Christ and the Last Supper.

Today's Anaphora is divided into eight component parts: 1. the eucharistic dialogue, 2. prayer of praise and thanksgiving, 3. the Seraphic Hymn ("Holy, Holy, Holy, etc."), 4. the Eucharistic Prayer (Consecration), 5. the prayer of the Anamnesis, 6. the Epiklesis, 7. the eucharistic commemorations, and 8. finally the doxology. Of all these elements only two come directly from Christ, i.e., the prayer of praise and thanksgiving, and the Eucharistic Consecration. The other parts are later additions and complements introduced by the Church.

The evangelists and St. Paul have recorded the consecratory words of Jesus Christ: "Take and Eat, THIS IS MY BODY," and "Drink of this all, THIS IS MY BLOOD OF THE NEW TESTAMENT."[2] They did not, however, give an accurate account of the contents of the prayer of praise and thanksgiving which Our Lord said immediately before the consecration of bread and wine. They only mention the fact that Christ "gave thanks" and "blessed" before He changed the bread and wine into His Body and Blood. These words denote

---

[2] Cf. Mt 26:26; Mrk 14:22; Lk 22:19; 1 Cor 11:24.

praise and thanksgiving. What the exact contents of this original prayer were is not known, but it is known that it contained the same thoughts as those in the other prayers of praise and thanksgiving which are found in the Liturgies. Parts of this prayer are found in Christ's "priestly prayer" which was recorded by St. John the Evangelist in his narrative of the Last Supper (Ch. 17). Christ certainly must have expressed His gratitude to His Father for all the great deeds He had performed for the Chosen People and especially for the redemption of mankind by His death on the cross. Liturgists emphasize that Christ instituted the Divine Liturgy within the framework of the Old Testament Paschal Supper during which the head of the family—the paterfamilias—recited the prayer of praise and thanksgiving for the liberation of the Jewish people from Egyptian bondage. Christ, the Head of the new People of God, adhering to the Jewish ritual, turns to the Heavenly Father with words of praise and thanksgiving for the great works He performed for mankind. Thus, from the very beginning of the Anaphora one can detect influences of the Jewish services. Christ in instituting the Holy Eucharist and in formulating its prayers according to the Old Testament patterns gave the Apostles and their successors a foundation upon which to formulate the Anaphora. Besides the prayers of the Paschal Supper they could have used other prayers, especially those prescribed before eating, i.e., those said everyday at the table. According to liturgists, these prayers also served as a model for the Anaphora. In its plan, structure and principal theme the Anaphora is simply an imitation and a modification of the various Jewish ritual prayers, especially the prayer of the Paschal Supper.[3]

The Anaphora, therefore, derives from the Last Supper. The development of its integral elements were greatly influenced by Jewish ritual. These two facts must be kept in mind when treating of this part of the Divine Liturgy.

2. Historical development of the Anaphora. The first phase of development *is the Apostolic Period* (the end of the first and the beginning of the second century). The Apostles and their successors imitated Christ in offering the Eucharistic Sacrifice. Remembering Christ's command: "Do this in commemoration of Me," they, like Him, began the Sacrifice with a prayer of praise and thanksgiving, in which they thanked God for the work of redemption. Then they pronounced the words of consecration over the bread and wine. The Anamnesis was probably added to these two constituent parts of the Anaphora in the Apostolic age; the Apostles, recalling the command of Christ during the Anaph-

---

[3] The question of the derivation of the Anaphora from the Jewish prayer types are discussed especially by such scholars as Bickell, Probst, Moreau, Leclerque, Cabrol, Goltz and others. We shall cite their works in regard to this question in the bibliography presented at the end of this chapter. While Bickell derives the origin of the Anaphora from the ritual of the Jewish Passover, Goltz points out especially the similarity between the Anaphora and the Psalms, prayers of thanksgiving and domestic table prayers of the Jews. However, as J. Karabinov rightfully remarks (*Ekhariticheskaya molitva*, p. 20), some scholars place too much emphasis on the derivation of the Christian services from the Jewish services forgetting at the same time that Christian services had their own peculiar sources for the composition (formulation) of liturgical prayers.

ora, also recalled His death and resurrection. Proof of this is found in the words of St. Paul in his First Letter to the Corinthians (11:23).

Liturgists are of the opinion that the Anamnesis entered into the composition of the Anaphora sooner than the other parts. Therefore, it would follow that the Anaphora of the Apostolic Period already had the three most important parts of the present-day Anaphora: 1. The prayer of praise and thanksgiving, 2. the Consecration and 3. the Anamnesis.

It can be said with certainty that the Anaphora of the *Doctrine of the Twelve Apostles,* or *Didache* belongs to the Apostolic Period. Although not all scholars consider these prayers to be fragments of the Anaphora of the Apostles, they are nevertheless, of great importance in understanding their development. Of course, these prayers are not ordinary prayers recited at table; they are prayers connected with the Eucharistic Sacrifice, even though they do not contain Christ's words of consecration.[4]

The other phase of development is given in St. Justin's description of the Liturgy (second century), in which he speaks briefly of the Anaphora: "Bread and the chalice with wine and water are presented to the one presiding over the congregation, and, he taking these gifts, gives praise to the Father of all, through the Son and Holy Spirit, and fervently gives thanks for these gifts, which He deigned to bestow upon us. When he concludes the prayers of praise and thanksgiving, the congregation exclaims: 'Amen.' "[5]

From these words, general though they are, it can be ascertained that the prayer of praise and thanksgiving recited by the president of the assembly was directed to God the Father, "through the Son and Holy Spirit." The Trinitarian character of this prayer was preserved in the prayer of the Anaphora. Another important fact which St. Justin mentions in his *Apologies* is that at that time the Anaphora was not as yet fixed, but that the minister improvised as he went along.[6]

The third stage of development is found in the *Apostolic Tradition* of St. Hippolytus.[7] Here is the first and oldest formula of the Anaphora. Besides the component parts which thus far have been found in the Anaphora, i.e., the prayers of praise and thanksgiving, the prayers of the consecration and anamnesis, there are other elements, such as the Eucharistic dialogue, the epiklesis and the concluding doxology. The Anaphora of St. Hippolytus has, therefore, six integral parts: 1. The Eucharistic dialogue, 2. the prayer of praise and thanksgiving,

---

[4] Literature on the *Didache* is quite extensive. What commands the interest of the liturgists most are the "eucharistic prayers" in the ninth and tenth chapters of the *Didache.* Some scholars consider them table prayers of the first Christians, others, prayers of the repast of love (agape) and still others the eucharistic prayers themselves.

[5] Cf. the 65th Chapter of the *Apology* in Otto's, *Corpus Apologetarum,* I., p. 180.

[6] Cf. Chapter 67 *Apology, ibid.,* p. 184.

[7] It comes from the first half of the third century. For the anaphora of St. Hippolytus: E. Hauler, *Didascaliae Apostolorum Fragmenta Veronensia latina . . .,* Lipsiae, 1900, pp. 106–107.

3. the words of consecration, 4. the Anamnesis, 5. the Epiklesis and 6. the concluding doxology. All these elements are distingusihed for their classical brevity and unity.

The fourth century marks the fourth and last stage of development of the Anaphora. The liturgical sources of this period are: the description of the Liturgy by St. Cyril of Jerusalem,[8] the Liturgy of the *Apostolic Constitutions*,[9] the Anaphora of Serapion,[10] and the liturgical fragment of Der-Balizeh.[11] All these documents already possess all the elements of the present-day Anaphora. Two new elements are added to the former ones: the hymn of the Seraphim ("Holy, Holy, etc.") and the Eucharistic commemorations of the living and the dead. Thus, in the fourth century, the Anaphora reaches its zenith of development. Some elements, as for example, the prayer of praise and thanksgiving and the triple commemoration, acquire greater dimensions. This can be clearly seen in the Liturgy of the *Apostolic Constitutions*,[12] which, perhaps is very similar to the Anaphora of the Liturgies of St. John Chrysostom and St. Basil the Great.

Generally speaking, nothing certain can be said about the development of these last-mentioned Anaphoras because their original manuscripts did not survive to modern times. Between the fourth and eighth centuries, there are no manuscripts of the Liturgy of St. John Chrysostom or St. Basil the Great. Hence, it is difficult for liturgists to reproduce or to reconstruct the complete Liturgy of that time. The oldest manuscripts of the Byzantine Anaphora come from the eighth and ninth centuries (the Codex Barberini, and the Porphyrian manuscripts). Comparing the text of the Anaphora contained in these manuscripts with the present-day text, one observes only slight differences.

When reviewing the historical development of the Anaphora, one more important fact claims attention, i.e., that in ancient times the Anaphora was not recited silently, as it is today. Today the priest recites aloud only certain parts of it, but the greater part of the prayer is said silently while the people sing the hymn, "Holy, Holy, Holy, etc.," and "Meet it is indeed to bless Thee, Mother of God." According to the testimony of St. Justin, in the first centuries the whole Anaphora was said aloud. Liturgists cannot determine the exact time when the audible recitation of the Anaphora was superseded by its silent recitation, but in all probability it occurred between the sixth and eighth centuries.[13] It happened

---

[8] Migne, PG, 33, 1109–1128.

[9] F. X. Funk, *Didascalia et Const. Apostolorum,* I, Paderborn, 1905, pp. 476–520.

[10] *Ibid.,* II, pp. 158–181.

[11] T. Shermann, *Der Liturgische Papyrus von Der-Balizeh* (Texte und Unters., 36, 1913).

[12] Probably the Liturgy of the *Apostolic Constitutions* was never used, and is only a compilation of various eucharistic prayers of some unknown (anonymous) author. Liturgist call it the "ideal" formulary since practically speaking it was never used. (Cf. Hanssens, *Inst. liturg. de ritibus orientalibus,* III, 642–643).

[13] For literature on the history of the silent recitation of the Anaphora, see A. P. Golubtsov, *O prichinakh i vremeni zmyeni glasnaho chteniya liturghiynikh molitv tainimi,* (Bog. Vyestnik, 1905, sentyabr, pp. 68–77); A. Jungmann, *Praefatio und stiller Kanon,* (Zeitschr., f. kathol. Theol., 53 (1929), pp. 66–94, 247–271); E. De Moreau, S. J., *Recitation du Canon de la Messe a voix basse,* Nouvelle Revue Theologique, 51 (1924), 65–94.

gradually, not rapidly, for liturgical development does not admit of rapid change.

From a novel of the Emperor Justinian (527–565) it is learned that the custom of reciting the Anaphora silently was already widespread in those times. Justinian opposed the custom and strongly forbade its practice. Here is an excerpt from this novel: "I order all the bishops and priests to pronounce the Anaphora not silently but aloud, in order that the faithful might hear it and be inspired with piety and glorify God. Therefore, it is necessary that the bishops and the priests offer aloud the holy sacrifice and the other prayers to our Lord Jesus Christ Who is with the Father and Holy Spirit." [14]

Justinian's ordinance, however, was ineffective and did not do away with the custom which began to root itself more and more in the East and in the West. Finally, it was adopted by all Churches and Rites. In the Byzantine-Ukrainian Rite only the words of consecration and certain acclamations are pronounced aloud ("Singing, crying, calling aloud . . ." "Especially for our most holy . . .", "Among the first remember," "And grant us with one mouth . . . ", "And may the mercies. . . ."). In certain Liturgies, as for example, in the Roman or Latin Rite Liturgy, the whole Canon including the words of consecration was recited silently until Vatican Council II ordained otherwise.

The reason for introducing the silent or secret reading of the Eucharistic Canon was perhaps the desire to emphasize its mysterious and sacred character. Moreover, the tendency to shorten the Divine Liturgy because of the indifference of the faithful also played a great role. It must be remarked that the majority of faithful do not have a proper idea of the course or contents of the Anaphora. The few acclamations do not help much because, divorced as they are from their context, they have lost their meaning. The aim of the liturgical commentaries is precisely to direct attention to these silent prayers and to show the logical relationship existing between the prayers of the Anaphora.

2. The Eucharistic Dialogue

The first component element of the Anaphora is the "Eucharistic dialogue." By this name the liturgists refer to the brief exchange carried on between priest and people immediately before the beginning of the Eucharistic offering. The dialogue is called "Eucharistic," because it is an introduction to the Anaphora.

This dialogue consists of the following acclamations of the deacon and the priest and the responses of the faithful:

Deacon: Let us stand well; let us stand with fear; let us attend to offer the holy oblation in peace.

People: The mercy of peace, the sacrifice of praise.

---

[14] Cf. *Corpus Juris civilis*, (ed. R. Scholl—W. Kroll), Berolini, 1899, Vol. III, Novellae, 137-novella, pp. 699–700.

Priest: The grace of our Lord Jesus Christ, and the love of God and the Father, and the communion of the Holy Spirit, be with you all.

People: And with thy spirit.

Priest: Let us lift up our hearts.

People: We have lifted them to the Lord.

Priest: Let us give thanks to the Lord.

People: Meet and right it is to adore the Father and the Son and the Holy Spirit, Trinity consubstantial and undivided.

History of the Eucharistic Dialogue. All Liturgies, Eastern and Western, have an introductory dialogue between the priest and the people before the beginning of the Anaphora. In many Liturgies the content is exactly the same— convincing proof that the dialogue had a common origin. The oldest witness to the eucharistic dialogue is the *Apostolic Tradition* of St. Hippolytus [1] (the first half of the third century). It contains the oldest formula of the Anaphora and the dialogue in it is almost identical with that found in the Liturgy today. The eucharistic dialogue is probably older, although St. Justin (second century) does not mention it in his description of the Liturgy of his time. Furthermore, apart from the reference of St. Hippolytus, this dialogue is found in all the oldest liturgical documents, i.e., in the Liturgy of the *Apostolic Constitutions* [2] and in the descriptions of the Liturgy found in the works of St. Cyril of Jerusalem and St. John Chrysostom. The oldest commentary on the Eucharistic dialogue was left by St. Cyprian in the West (third century) and St. Cyril of Jerusalem in the East (fourth century).

Significance of the Dialogue. It was said earlier that the Eucharistic dialogue is an introduction to the Anaphora. It is also a final exhortation of the Church to celebrate the Eucharistic Sacrifice worthily.

The words: "Let us stand well; let us stand with fear; let us attend to offer the holy oblation in peace," alert the faithful to begin the Eucharistic Sacrifice with fear and attentiveness. Here the Liturgy admonishes the faithful, just as Christ admonished His Apostles in the Garden of Olives before His passion: "Watch ye, and pray that ye enter not into temptation. The spirit indeed is willing, but the flesh weak." (Mt. 26:41) St. John Chrysostom explains how these words are to be understood: "The deacon does not pointlessly alert all with the words 'Attention! Let us stand well . . .,' but urges that we lift up our souls which are earthbound, that we overcome all weaknesses caused by worldly cares, that we stand before God irreproachable. To 'stand well' actually means to stand before God with fear and confidence." [3]

---

[1] Hauler, *Didasc. Apostolorum . . .*, p. 106.
[2] Funk, *Didasc. et Const. Apost . . .*, I, p. 496.
[3] Migne, PG, 48, 734 (fourth discourse on the inscrutable God).

In the Syrian Liturgy the deacon addresses the faithful at the beginning of the Anaphora: "Let us stand with faith, let us stand with fear, let us stand in purity, modesty, and holiness of heart! Let us stand, Brothers, in true faith, in fear before God and let us consider this terrible and holy sacrifice, which is about to take place and which is about to be offered for us to the Father, the Lord of the Universe, by the hands of the priest, for our salvation and as a sacrifice of praise." [4] These words are a beautiful commentary on the first section of the Eucharistic dialogue.

To this warning of the deacon, to offer the holy sacrifice with attention, the people respond: "The mercy of peace, the sacrifice of praise." These words must be understood as a continuation and an explanation of the words: "the holy oblation." With these words the people solemnly express their attitude toward the "holy oblation." Through this oblation the faithful receive "the mercy of peace," i.e., reconciliation with God, and God receives "the sacrifice of praise." The Eucharistic Sacrifice has two main purposes: first, to give God praise and, second, to solicit forgiveness for man's transgressions and reconciliation with God. In these words of the dialogue, therefore, lies the essence of the Eucharistic Sacrifice.

After the deacon's exhortatory acclamation inviting all to approach the holy sacrifice worthily and with attention, the priest greets the people and blesses them:

> The grace of our Lord Jesus Christ, and the love of God and the Father and the communion of the Holy Spirit, be with you all.

These words which are taken verbatim from the second epistle of St. Paul to the Corinthians,[5] are also found in the other Eastern Liturgies.[6] With them the priest begs God's blessings for the faithful from each Person of the Blessed Trinity. From God the Father, love; from God the Son, grace; and from God the Holy Spirit, unity. The Son of God, by dying on the cross, obtained grace for us. That is why the priest asks Him for graces. God the Father "so loved the world, as to give his only begotten Son: that whoever believeth in Him may not perish, but may have life everlasting." (Jn 3:16) Therefore, the priest asks Him for love. Finally, the Holy Spirit with His cooperation completed the work of redemption and still continues His work through His gifts; hence, the priest asks for unity with Him, i.e., participation in His heavenly gifts.[7]

The people, answering the priest with the words "And with Thy spirit," wish him the same blessings which he implores from the Blessed Trinity for them. They are blessings especially indispensable to the priest who is the representative of God.

---

[4] Hanssens, *Institutiones liturgicae de ritibus orientalibus*, III, (1932) p. 339; M., v. Sachsen, *Missa syro-antiochena*, p. 25.

[5] 2 Cor, 13:13; cf: Engberding, H., *Der Gruss des Priesters zu Beginn der "Eucharistia" im oestl. Liturgien*, Jhb. f. Liturgiewissenschaft 9, 1929, pp. 138–143.

[6] For example, in the Liturgies of St. James, *Apostolic Constitutions*, and others.

[7] Cf. the liturgical commentary of N. Cabasilas; Migne, PG, 150, 424.

The priest then exclaims, "Let us lift up our hearts." He calls upon the people as once did Jeremias; "Let us lift our hearts with our hands to the Lord in the heavens." (Lament 3:41.) The words recall those of the Apostle Paul: "Mind the things that are above, not the things that are upon the earth." (Col 3:2) In other words, the Liturgy admonishes the people once more, as it did during the Cherubic Hymn, to forget all that is earthly, to raise their thoughts above earthly thoughts, to recall heavenly things, and to lay aside all temporal cares and anxieties. The heart of the Christian should be raised aloft because the Eucharistic Sacrifice is about to begin. Hence, St. Cyprian says: "When we pray, we should be confident and give our whole heart to it. Let all carnal and worldly thoughts leave us, and let our soul think of nothing but that which it prays for. Hence, the priest prepares the souls of the faithful by saying: Let us lift up our hearts. As a result, the people when answering him "We have them lifted to the Lord, think only of the Lord."[8]

The congregation, answering the priest "We have them lifted to the Lord," asserts that their thoughts are directed toward heaven just as the holy sacrifice requires. "At this terrible moment," says St. Cyril of Jerusalem, "the soul truly must have its heart orientated toward God and not toward earthly cares. The priest instructs all to discard their worldly cares and to lift their hearts up to a God who truly loves mankind. Let there be no one among those present, who would say with their lips: 'We have them lifted to God,' and have their thoughts occupied with the anxieties of this life. We must at all times think of God and, if this be impossible because of human frailty, then we must at least at this moment strive to think of him." [9]

The last exhortation of the priest is: "Let us give thanks to the Lord." He does not call upon the faithful to express just ordinary gratitude to God for blessings received, but to express gratitude and thanksgiving through the offering of the Eucharistic Sacrifice. "To thank God" means, therefore, to offer Him the Eucharistic Sacrifice in thanksgiving for salvation. In the Greek original, the word *eucharistein* is used, which later became the technical term indicating the sacrifice of the New Testament, i.e., a Eucharistic sacrifice—a sacrifice of thanksgiving.[10]

The assembly declares its willingness and readiness to offer God a sacrifice of thanksgiving: "Meet and right it is to adore the Father and the Son and the Holy Spirit, Trinity consubstantial and undivided." God is truly worthy of our praise, homage and thanksgiving. "We should, indeed, thank God for bestowing upon us unworthy servants such a great grace. Although we were His enemies,[11] He reconciled us, giving us the grace to become His adopted sons through the Holy Spirit. Therefore, we are justified and right in giving God thanks." [12]

---

[8] St. Cyprian *De dominica oratione*, c. 31, (Migne, PL, 4, 539).

[9] Migne, PG, 33, 1112–1113.

[10] For the meaning of the word *eucharistein* see Th. Chermann's *Philologus*, 69 (1910), 375–410.

[11] A. Baumstark, *Trisagion und Queduscha* (*Jahrb. f. Liturgiewissenschaft*, 1923, pp. 18–32).

[12] The words of St. Cyril of Jerusalem; Migne, PG, 33, 1113.

3. Prayer of Praise and Thanksgiving

The Eucharistic dialogue introduces the first prayer of the Anaphora which is called the *prayer of praise and thanksgiving,* so called because of its theme.[1] It is a continuation of the words of the Eucharistic dialogue "Meet and right it is . . . " and stresses that God is deserving of our praise and thanksgiving for His own sake, i.e., for the sake of His nature and attributes. He also deserves our praise and gratitude for the manifold blessings we have received from Him, especially for accepting the service of human beings, even though the heavenly choirs are constantly singing to Him a hymn of praise. The prayer of praise and thanksgiving is as follows:

Meet and right it is to praise Thee, to bless Thee, to glorify Thee, to give thanks unto Thee, to adore Thee in every place of Thy dominion: for Thou art God ineffable, inconceivable, invisible, incomprehensible, existing forever, being the same, Thou and Thine Only-begotten Son, and Thy Holy Spirit. Thou didst bring us out of nothingness into being; and Thou didst raise the fallen again; and Thou hast not ceased doing everything until Thou hast drawn us to heaven, and granted Thy kingdom to come. For all these things we give thanks to Thee, and to Thine only-begotten Son, and to Thy Holy Spirit for all benefits which we know and which we know not, manifest and concealed, that have come upon us. We give Thee thanks for this ministry which Thou dost deign to accept from our hands, even though by Thee stand thousands of archangels and myriads of angels, cherubim and seraphim, six-winged, many-eyed, soaring aloft on their wings, singing, crying, calling aloud, and saying the triumphant song: Holy, holy, holy . . .

History of the prayer of praise and thanksgiving. All Liturgies, without exception, have a prayer of praise and thanksgiving at the beginning of the Anaphora. St. Justin mentions such a prayer in his description of the Liturgy; the oldest text of Anaphora of St. Hippolytus and all other later anaphoras also refer to it. The prayer of praise and thanksgiving, as before mentioned, is the earliest element of the Anaphora, for Christ, before instituting the Holy Eucharist at the Last Supper, offered to His Father such a prayer.

Earlier we pointed out that the prototype of the prayer of praise and thanksgiving which Christ offered at the Last Supper was the prayer, which, according to the Old Testament ritual precription, the master (or father) of the house recited during the Paschal Supper. He was obliged to explain to the family why God had commanded the Chosen People to consume the Paschal Lamb each year. Recalling how the Lord had miraculously liberated their ancestors from Egyptian bondage and other blessings, the paterfamilias offered the prayer of praise and thanksgiving.

Christ's prayer was very similar to the one said at the Paschal Supper. The theme was God's goodness shown throughout the history of the Chosen People.

---

[1] Some call this a "theological" prayer, ("*oratio theologica,*" cf. Hanssens' *Inst. litur.,* III, p. 347, 380–390) and rightly so, for it is distinguished for its theological depth. In the Roman liturgy this prayer goes by the name *"praefatio"* because it is a "preface or prelude" to the Eucharistic Canon.

Undoubtedly Christ added the note of gratitude for the work of redemption. From these origins the prayers of thanksgiving and praise of the various anaphoras developed. Liturgists rightly emphasize the influence the Old Testment formulas had upon the content and composition of the present-day prayer. Besides these Paschal prayers of praise and thanksgiving, the Old Testament prayers said at the table [2] also had great influence on the composition of the Christian prayer of the Anaphora or Eucharistic prayers. For example, one sees the influences of the prayers: Shema, Shemoneezre and Kiddush. This last can be called the prototype of the Eucharistic prayer of praise and thanksgiving.[3] This explains why the prayer of praise and thanksgiving of the various Liturgies reveals the same composition, content and motives.

Significance of the prayer. Comparing the prayers of praise and thanksgiving of the various Liturgies, one can discern three principal motives: 1. God's incomparable majesty and power, 2. the work of creation and 3. the redemption of mankind. Others are added at times, such as praise and thanksgiving for various blessings and for the institution of the Holy Eucharist.

In the Liturgy of St. John Chrysostom, the prayer of praise and thanksgiving is short and general. It emphasizes, first, that God is deserving of praise, thanksgiving and homage. His nature and divine attributes are the first motives which induce man to praise Him and to thank Him, for He is an "ineffable, inconceivable, invisible, inscrutable, eternal, immutable" God. Man should praise Him, not for what He does for him but because of His infinite majesty alone.

Another reason for praising and thanking Him is His work of creation. This motive affects man directly, for God "created him from nothing." The motive of redemption which He brought about through His Only-begotten Son deserves particular attention. God graciously extended His almighty hand to fallen man. He again "raised us up and does not cease doing everything until He has drawn us to heaven" which we had lost through original sin. We also praise and thank Him for other graces "which we know and know not about, manifest and concealed," especially for giving us the Holy Eucharist. He wants to "accept our services," though He has legions of angels who are forever singing praises to Him.

In the prayer of thanksgiving and praise the priest pours out his heart and soul in thanks to God for all the blessings conferred upon mankind. Hence, the sublime, solemn nature of the prayer. It abounds in epithets which the Fathers

---

[2] "The Eucharistic prayers of the first Christians undoubtedly evolved from the Jewish table-prayers," (*Karabinov, Evkharisticheskaya molitva,* p. 19) ; "The Jewish prayers said at the table left a deep mark on the divine services of the first Christians. The schema of the synagogue and paschal (prayers) 'keddusha' were adopted by the Apostles without any exceptional changes. They were only given a new Christian coloring." (Archimandrite Cyprian, *Eucharistiya,* p. 222).

[3] For the texts of these Jewish prayers, see Moreau, *Les liturgies eucharistiques,* Bruxelles. 1924, pp. 192–194; also Archimandrite Cyprian, *op. cit.,* pp. 220–221.

of the Church fondly employed in describing God's nature. The Liturgy of St. Basil is noted for these epithets, as witness the following prayer: "Lord of all creation, Lord of heaven and earth and of all creatures visible and invisible, who sits on the throne of glory and beholds the depths, without beginning, invisible, inaccessible, indescribable, immutable, Father of our Lord Jesus Christ, the great God and Savior, who is our hope, the image of Thy goodness, the perfect seal which signifies Thee God, the Father who is the living Word, the true God, Eternal Wisdom, Life, sanctity, power, true light. Through Him the Holy Spirit, the Spirit of Truth, the gift of adoption, guarantee of future goods, the beginning of eternal bliss, life-giving power, spring of sanctity, was revealed. . . ." But words are too weak and inadequate to describe properly the majesty of God: "who is capable of describing Thy power, declaring Thy glory, or of expressing all Thy wonderful works?" Hence we wish, with all the angels and all creation, first of all, to render God homage, to praise and thank Him. Man, as a rational being and the epitome or microcosmic counterpart of God's creation, is called upon in this prayer to give homage to God for all other creatures irrational, rational and inanimate. This thought inspired the Fathers and all those who composed liturgical prayers: man does not pray in his own name only, but as a representative of the whole rational, irrational and inanimate world. Man is the masterpiece and crown of God's creatures. He speaks for all creation, visible and invisible; he has become the priest of the universe. His calling is the "service of God." In this and through this service the entire universe joins in a symphony of praise and thanksgiving. The eternal God, though possessing an infinite number of heavenly powers that incessantly sing praise to Him, wishes that man, the crown of His creation, also sing Him a hymn of praise.

The prayer of praise and thanksgiving is, therefore, an invitation to serve God joyfully, disinterestedly and enthusiastically throughout our entire life. It is a special invitation to thank God for all blessings, great or small, conscious or unconscious, hidden or known, especially for the graces of creation and redemption. In this lies the content and significance of the prayer of praise and thanksgiving in the beginning of the Anaphora.

4. Seraphic Hymn ("Holy, Holy, Holy")

The prayer of praise and thanksgiving ends with the Seraphic Hymn. The priest, who recites this prayer silently, pronounces aloud the last few words: "Singing, crying, etc . . . ," and the people in reply sing the hymn:

Holy, holy, holy Lord of Sabaoth, full is heaven and earth of Thy glory. Hosanna in the highest. Blessed is he that cometh in the name of the Lord. Hosanna in the highest.

History of the Seraphic Hymn. All present Liturgies end the prayer of praise and thanksgiving with the Seraphic Hymn. In the Liturgy it is called the "hymn of triumph," that is, the hymn of the victory of God. It was introduced into the Anaphora at the end of the third or the beginning of the fourth century. The oldest description of the Liturgy by St. Justin (second century) and the oldest formulary of the eucharistic Anaphora of St. Hippolytus (third century) do not know the Seraphic Hymn. St. Cyril of Jerusalem [1] and St. John Chrysostom [2] in the fourth century are the first witnesses to it. It first appeared in the Anaphora of Serapion (mid-fourth century) and in the Liturgy of the *Apostolic Constitutions* (end of the fourth century). From this one can infer that it was incorporated into the Liturgy between the middle of the third and the middle of the fourth centuries.

The hymn was introduced under the influence of the synagogue service. According to the opinion of such scholars as Baumstark,[3] Lietzman,[4] and Moreau [5] the prayer Keddusha, which we mentioned earlier, influenced the introduction of this hymn into the Liturgy. That the hymn is of Jewish origin is evident from the hebraisms ("Sabaoth," "Hosanna") which appear in it and which in ancient times no one dared translate into the vernacular because of their sacred character. Thus they remain in the Liturgy to this day, like the other frequently used hebraisms, "Alleluia" and "Amen."

Meaning of the Seraphic Hymn. According to its contents the hymn is divided into two parts which differ in origin and significance.

The first portion, "Holy, holy, holy, etc.," is taken from the well-known vision of Isaias [6] in which he saw God sitting upon an exalted throne. The seraphim moved about Him each having six wings—two wings covering the face, two, the legs, and two moving about—and one after the other exclaimed: "Holy, holy, holy, the Lord God of hosts; all the earth is full of his glory." (Is 6:3) The first part of the hymn generally refers to the Blessed Trinity, hence the reason for the thrice repeated word "holy."

The second part begins with the words: "Hosanna in the highest; blessed is He who comes in the name of the Lord! Hosanna in the highest," taken from the Gospel.[7] These are the words with which the crowd greeted Jesus when He entered Jerusalem. Thinking that Christ, the promised one, was going to restore the throne of David and Himself become the King of the Jews, they greeted Him as a victor: "And the multitudes that went before and that followed, cried, saying: 'Hosanna to the son of David: Blessed is He that cometh in the name of

[1] Migne, PG, 33, 1113 (Fifth Mystagogical Catechesis).

[2] *Ibid.,* 49, 370; 61, 627; 62, 105.

[3] See Archimandrite Cyprian for these Jewish prayers, *op. cit.,* pp. 220–221.

[4] H. Lietzmann, *Messe und Herrenmahl,* Bonn, 1926, p. 130.

[5] F. Moreau, *Les liturgies eucharistiques,* Bruxelles, 1924, pp. 192–194. An example showing the similarity existing between the Seraphic Hymn and the second prayer of the Keddusha, is the text of that prayer: "We bless You and declare Your glory as the holy Seraphim bless You with their holy, sweet, and mystical voices, for it is written by Your prophet: "One after another sing: Holy, Holy, Holy Lord of the Sabaoth. The earth is full of thy glory . . ." (See Archimandrite Cyprian, *Evkharistiya* p. 221).

[6] 6: 1–5. See other parallel quotations, e.g. Daniel 7:10 and Revelation, 4:6–8.

[7] See Mt 21:9; Mk 11:9–10; Lk 19:38; Jn 12:13.

the Lord: Hosanna in the highest.' " (Mt 21:9). The second part of the Seraphic Hymn, therefore, refers exclusively to Christ and not to the Blessed Trinity; hence, it can hardly be called the Seraphic Hymn in the strict sense. However, both parts formed one whole, so that we do not perceive their different
origins and their two-fold reference.

Although the hymn of the Seraphim is a later introduction into the Liturgy,
nevertheless, it harmonizes intrinsically with the foregoing prayer of praise and
thanksgiving, and has found its proper place before the consecration. In this
prayer heaven (the angels) and earth (the faithful) join in singing a hymn of
praise to God. The celestial and terrestial hierarchy merge into one choir—one
symphony to honor God's name, to glorify Him, to give Him homage, thanksgiving and praise. St. John Chrysostom beautifully remarks: "At the moment
this hymn is being sung, you should put aside all worldly cares and forget that
you are still on earth and that you are among people. One would have to be
made of stone, to think at this moment of wordly things and forget that the
angels are also in the choir with him." [8]

The final words of the hymn are a salutation in honor of Christ, who mysteriously enters the new Jerusalem as the Lamb of God, and who is about to offer
Himself again to the Heavenly Father for His people. In a few moments the
eucharistic gifts will become His Body and Blood. The Church welcomes Christ
as the crowd once did at His entrance into the city of Jerusalem. Every Liturgy,
every consecration, is a new manifestation, a new coming of Christ, "a new par-
ousia." He comes in the name of the Lord, according to the eternal decree of
God dictated by God's love, to dwell among men and to offer Himself for them.
The Seraphic Hymn is a triumphant march whose resounding sounds announce
the immediate coming of Christ; it marks the most solemn and holy moment of
the Divine Liturgy.[9]

5. The Eucharistic Prayer (Consecration)

As the Seraphic Hymn is being sung the priest silently recites the prayer
which comes immediately before the consecration of the Holy Gifts. It is called

---

[8] Migne, PG, 62, 105 (24th homily on the Epistle to the Ephesians).

[9] It is strange that commentators, who are always searching for some symbolic-mystical
meaning in the texts and rites of the Divine Liturgy, fail to refer the words of the Seraphic
Hymn to Christ's entry into Jerusalem, even though the very words of the hymn warrant such
an interpretation. They see rather a symbolic portrayal of the solemn entry of Christ into Jerusalem in the Great Entrance which, actually, does not recall this event. Symbolists are very
fond of interpreting the words, *"Singing, crying, calling aloud the hymn of victory, and saying,"*
mystically, i.e., the last words of the latreutic-eucharistic prayer, which precedes the Seraphic
Hymn. In these words they, together with Pseudo-Herman (Migne, PG, 98, 429–432), see symbols of the four evangelists; "singing" alludes to the eagle, the symbol of the evangelist John;
"crying" to Luke, who is symbolized by the ox; "calling aloud" to St. Mark who is represented
by a lion; "saying" to Matthew who is typified by a man. Symbolists forget that these expressions are synonyms alluding to the "song of victory" which is sung not by the eagle, ox, lion or
man but by "thousands of Angels, Archangels, Seraphim and Cherubim." Here we are dealing
with a subjective search for symbols which in no way at all indicate any reference to the
liturgical text.

"eucharistic" because there is an allusion to the institution of the Holy Eucharist and the very words Christ used in instituting it.[1] As the priest says the prayer which is, so to speak, a continuation of the Seraphic Hymn, in spirit he joins the millions of heavenly powers who in heaven sing before God the triumphal hymn:

> With these blessed powers we also, O Master, Lover of men, cry and say: Holy and most holy art Thou and Thine Only-begotten Son, and Thy Holy Spirit. Holy and most holy art Thou and magnificent is Thy glory. Who hast so loved Thy world as to even give Thine Only-begotten Son, that whosoever believeth in Him shall not perish, but shall have everlasting life; Who came and fulfilled the whole dispensation in regard to us, and in the night wherein He was delivered, or rather, when He surrendered Himself for the life of the world, having taken bread into His holy and most pure and immaculate hands, gave thanks and blessed, (he blesses once and does not take the diskos into his hands, nor elevate it) sanctified and broke it, He gave it to His holy disciples and apostles, saying: "Take, eat, THIS IS My BODY, which is broken for you for the remission of sins." (*People:* Amen!) In like manner (blesses once) also the chalice, after the supper, saying: "Drink of this all, THIS IS MY BLOOD OF THE NEW TESTAMENT, which is shed for you and for many for the remission of sins." (*People:* Amen!)

Meaning of the Eucharistic Prayer. We need not mention here the origin and history of the prayer that precedes the Consecration for it was discussed earlier. The Eucharistic Prayer is a continuation or amplification of the foregoing prayer of praise and thanksgiving. They form one whole in content and origin.

Praise and thanksgiving characterize the Eucharistic Prayer also, but it differs from the preceding prayer in that its motives for praising and thanking God are different. In the former the chief motives of praise and thanksgiving were God's majesty in itself, the work of creation and His graces. In the Eucharistic Prayer the outstanding motive is *the work of redemption.*[2]

In the work of redemption God the Father is mentioned. He manifested His infinite love for mankind not only by creating the world and man from nothing but also by sending His Only-begotten Son into the world to save man: "For God so loved the world, as to give his only begotten Son; that whosoever believeth in him, may not perish, but may have life everlasting. For God sent not his Son into the world, to judge the world, but that the world may be saved by Him." (Jn 3:16, 17).

All that the Son of God had wrought for our redemption is expressed in one sentence of the liturgical prayer of St. John Chrysostom, "He came and fulfilled His mission—our redemption." While the Eucharistic Prayer of St. John Chrysostom is known for its laconic expressions, that of St. Basil is known for its

---

[1] Orthodox liturgist as Karabinov (*Eukharisticheskaya molitva*) very frequently understand the "Eucharistic Prayer" to be the entire Anaphora or Eucharistic Canon of the Liturgy.

[2] Thus liturgists call our prayer before consecration a "Christological prayer," for it summarizes all that Christ has done for the salvation of mankind. (cf. Hanssens, *Inst. liturg.,* III, pp. 404–442).

sublimity, embellishment, and amplification. It describes dramatically the whole history of the redemption, from the fall of man to the death, resurrrection and ascension into heaven of Jesus Christ. It gives a detailed account of how God prepared mankind for the redemption and how He did not reject sinful man, "He did not forget the work of His hand, but visited him in manifold ways: He sent the prophets, wrought miracles through His saints . . . He spoke to us through the lips of the prophets, predicted our salvation, which was to come, He gave the Law to help us, and the angels for custodians . . . " When the "fulness of time" came, the eternal God appears on earth, the Only-begotten Son, who humbled Himself by assuming the form of a servant, and became like us in order to make us like Himself . . . He brought with Him true knowledge of God, He conquered sin, made mankind His chosen people, gave Himself up to die only to rise again thus showing man the way to a new life . . ." In like manner the redemption is described in the Anaphora of the *Apostolic Constitutions*.[3] All this detailed account of what Christ did for our salvation is recalled before the Consecration in order to awaken within the priest fear before the mystery that is about to take place before his eyes and through his instrumentality.

The second motif of the Eucharistic Prayer is the memory of the institution of the Holy Eucharist at the Last Supper. This theme is found in all Liturgies. It is one of the essential motifs of the Eucharistic Prayers. However, Eucharistic Prayer is not merely an historical account of the institution of the Eucharist at the Last Supper now to be simply commemorated, for according to the teaching of the Church, the priest in commemorating the Institution of the Holy Eucharist repeats Christ's words of Consecration and in doing so performs the same miracle which Christ performed at the Last Supper, that of changing the holy gifts into the Body and Blood of Jesus Christ. In other words, the words of Christ have the power of consecration.

The priest pronounces the words of consecration in the first person as if he were Christ, the High Priest, Himself. At this holy moment Christ, the Eternal Priest, who is at the same time the "one who is offered, and the one offering, the one receiving the offering and the one distributing the offering," speaks through the mouth of the priest. The priest is only the instrument of Christ. As His representative he pronounces the words of consecration "in the person of Christ." The priest is, as St. Maximos [4] says, "the image of God Himself," or in the words of Hesychius of Jerusalem (+451): "the lips of Christ." [5]

Even the rubrics confirm this for they direct the priest at the moment of the words of consecration to bless the holy gifts (the bread and then the chalice) and to point to them with his hand as Christ did at the Last Supper.[6] At the

---

[3] Funk, *Didasc. et Const. Ap.*, I, pp. 506–509.

[4] Migne, PG, 4, 140.

[5] M. Jugie, *De formia Eucharistiae, De epiclesibus eucharisticis*, Romae, 1943, p. 101.

[6] For the historical evolution of these rubrics and their meaning read the extensive dissertation of S. Vandik, *De Apparatu liturgico circa verba et epiclesim in Anaphora byzantina; Explicatio rubricarum*, Romae, 1945, p. 97, 117.

moment of consecration the priest withdraws into the background, or rather, the person of the priest becomes one with Christ the Eternal Priest. St. John Chrysostom beautifully remarks: "It is not man that converts the holy gifts into the Body and Blood of Christ, but Christ Himself, who gave Himself to be crucified. The priest, who utters these words, is only an image of Christ but the power and grace are from God. He says: This is My Body. These words change the sacrificial elements. Just as the words: Increase and multiply and fill the earth (Gen 1:28) although spoken once, gave our nature the permanent power of procreation, so also these words once pronounced, are effective on all the altars from that time until now and will be to His second coming."[7]

Chrysostom's comparison of the mystery of transubstantiation with the natural process of procreation illustrates beautifully the consecratory power of Christ's words and the participation of the priest in the consecration. Nevertheless, the comparison remains a comparison, and the mystery a mystery. The transubstantiation is one of the greatest mysteries of our faith which no human mind can completely fathom. Here one of God's greatest miracles takes place on the altar wholly unobserved. To our eyes the holy gifts appear unchanged, only faith dictates that a mysterious change has truly taken place.

The moment of Consecration, namely, the consecratory words of Christ, is indicated by the priest saying them aloud. The rubrics prescribe that, after each consecration, he make a profound bow expressing his faith in the real presence of Christ under the Eucharistic species and reverence toward the Consecrated Gifts.

To each separate formula of consecration, the congregation responds: "Amen." This word has its own special significance. First of all it is a solemn reaffirmation or confirmation of the Eucharistic transubstantiation on the part of the people. For "Amen" literally means: "So it is", "So be it." By this word the faithful declare their faith in the veracity of the words of consecration and that after their utterance bread and wine are no longer bread and wine but the Body and Blood of Jesus Christ. The word "Amen" is also an expression of the people's participation in the Eucharistic offering. Through their "Amen" the people express assent to what has taken place; they unite with the priest and together with him and through him they offer up to God the Unbloody Sacrifice.[8]

6. The Anamnesis

After the words of consecration follows the Anamnesis, that is, a prayer in which the priest recalls Christ's command that the Unbloody Sacrifice be

---

7 See Migne, PG, 49, 380 (First homily on the betrayal of Judas, Chapter 6).

8 For the "Amen" after the Eucharistic Prayer see St. Justin's description of the Liturgy. (Cf. his *Apology*, nos. 65 and 67, in De Otto's edition, *Corpus Apologetarum*, I (Jena, 1847), pp. 180, 184).

repeated in His everlasting memory.¹ Hence the name "anamnesis," which in Greek means the prayer of commemoration.

The priest finishing the words of consecration and giving due honor to the Consecrated Gifts, prays silently:

> Remembering therefore this salutary commandment, and all that has been done for us: the cross, the sepulcher, the resurrection on the third day, the ascension into the heavens, the sitting at the right hand, the second and glorious coming again: Thine own of Thine own, we offer Thee, in behalf of all, and for all.

> *People:* We praise Thee, we bless Thee, we give thanks unto Thee, O Lord, and we pray to Thee, our God!

History of the Anamnesis. The Anamnesis, as was earlier mentioned, was introduced into the Liturgy in the Apostolic Age. By nature it is a development and a complement to the words of consecration. After consecrating the bread and wine Christ immediately added the words: "Do this in commemoration of me." (Lk 22:19.) Therefore, the Church, in obedience to this command, recalls Christ's mandate directly after the consecration, and offers up the consecrated gifts to God in commemoration of all that Christ has wrought for our salvation. All Liturgies have the Anamnesis in one form or another.

Significance of the Anamnesis. Two things are to be distinguished in the Anamnesis: 1. the act of commemorating the redemption, and 2. the act of offering sacrifice in commemoration of the redemption.

By commemorating the redemption, the Liturgy wishes to express officially its redemptive aspect and reveal the nature of the Eucharistic Sacrifice as a commemoration of Christ and His work of redemption. It was Christ's desire that the memory of all He had accomplished for our salvation should not perish. Hence, He wished that His Bloody Sacrifice on the cross be repeated on all alters in an unbloody manner, that it continue always "until he comes," (1 Corin 11:26), that is, until the end of the world. Every Liturgy is, therefore, a second coming of Christ into the world, a new Golgotha, a new resurrection from the dead, a new ascension into heaven. The characteristic note of the Eucharistic Sacrifice according to the context of the Anamnesis is that it is not only a repetition of Christ's sacrifice on the cross, but of His resurrection, "His sitting on the right of the Heavenly Father," and even His second coming for the Last Judgment. The Eucharistic Sacrifice is, therefore, a commemoration *of the work of redemption in the full and complete sense of the word.*

Here the Liturgy reveals its nature; it is inseparably connected with the work of redemption. However, it must be noted that this repetition or continuation of Christ's redemption in the Liturgy does not occur before or after the Consecration but at the very moment of consecration itself, for it is the consecration of the holy gifts and not any other act that precedes or follows the Consecration that is the renewal or repetition of Christ's death on Golgotha, His resurrection and ascension, or in general of the whole work of redemption.

---

¹ Lk, 22:19; "Do this in commemoration of me."

From what has been said it must be evident how far the Liturgy is from being all symbolic, and especially from being a chronology of events in the life of Christ from His birth to His ascension into heaven. We have stressed this fact over and over, in this commentary, and the liturgical texts themselves confirm our opinion that the Divine Liturgy cannot be a mystical-symbolic chronology of Christ's life and the entire work of redemption. The Liturgy is indeed a drama of the redemption, but each individual rite and prayer in the Liturgy does not necessarily represent an individual event in the Life of Christ. The Liturgy unites all the events of redemption in the one act of eucharistic consecration, i.e., this one act of consecration sums up the whole work of redemption; it is, then, the hinge, or the center of gravity, of the whole Liturgy. The Anamnesis refers the commemoration of the work of redemption to the Consecration. We, therefore, should not ascribe this commemoration to some other rite in the Divine Liturgy nor should subjective symbolism divest the Consecration of its essential property, namely, sacrificial commemoration, repetition and the re-en-actment of Christ's work of redemption.

The themes of Christ's sitting at the right hand of the Father and the par-ousia i.e., His second coming at the end of the world, give the Eucharistic Sacri-fice timeless meaning and value. Past, present and future merge in that one moment of the Eucharistic Sacrifice. Christ, for whom there are no boundaries of time or space, appears on the altar—the same Christ that was, is and will be the Lamb, who gave Himself to be killed; the "man of suffering," who died on the gibbet of shame; who was anointed at His burial; who conquered death by death, returns to heaven, and sits on the right of the Father. Finally, this Christ is the King and the Judge, who will come again to judge the living and the dead. The Liturgy, then, is a living memorial of the timeless Christ and His timeless redemption.

Not only is the Anamnesis a commemoration of Christ and His work of redemption, but it is also *on the part of the Church a formal act of offering the Body and Blood of Jesus Christ to God.* We say, "on the part of the Church" for the formal act of offering sacrifice on the part of Christ is the consecration of the eucharistic gifts. This must be kept in mind if we are to understand prop-erly the Liturgy and its rites. Although Christ's sacrifice is included formally in the act of consecration itself, and although in the act of consecration the mysti-cal conversion of the holy gifts takes place and the work of our redemption is repreated, the Liturgy is incapable of expressing all these moments in just the few words of consecration alone. It feels the need to express these thoughts immediately after the Consecration so that the Church too may take formal part in offering up the Body and Blood of Jesus Christ.

This formal participation of the Church is expressed by the last words of the Anamnesis. The priest, recalling the cross, the grave, the resurrection and so forth, takes in his hands the Holy Gifts, raises them aloft, and offers them to the Heavenly Father in the name of the faithful. At the same time he says aloud the beautiful words:

Thine own of Thine own, we offer Thee, in behalf of all, and for all.

These words formally conclude the act of offering on the part of the Church. Just as the priest, who is the instrument and "lips" of Christ, represents Christ when pronouncing the words of consecration, so too, he represents the whole Church when offering to the Heavenly Father the Consecrated Gifts.

We must stop here briefly to explain the contents of these last words since they are frequently misinterpreted. The misinterpretation stems from a translation of the Old-Slavonic text that is faulty because it fails to take into consideration the Greek original text. The Greek text has the words: *"ta sa ek ton son soi prospheromen kata' panta kai dia panta,"* which means literally "we offer to You Yours of Your own in behalf of all and for all." These words reveal the Church's participation in the act of offering sacrifice and the priest's role of representing the Church. J. Pelesh renders this text improperly: "The priest raises aloft the holy gifts and says: 'Thine' (i.e., Thy Gifts) from Thine own (i.e., servants) we offer to Thee for all (i.e., all the faithful) and because of all (i.e., blessings received)' ".[2]

The first error lies in the words: "Thine from Thine own" being translated: "Your Gifts from Your servants (faithful)." The Greek text has a different meaning, for the proposition *ek* in Greek does not mean "from" but "of." Therefore, *"ek ton son"* does not mean "from your own" but "of your own." The meaning of the words becomes clearer when we add the nouns to the pronouns. In this way "Thine from (or "of") Thine own" means: "We offer to you, O God, Your Gifts of Your Gifts" (or "Your own Gifts").

The second error is found in the words: "for all the faithful and for all blessings (received)" *("kata' panta kai dia panta")*. This certainly does not mean "for all" ("for all" here does not refer to people) for the Greek word *kata* does not have this meaning. If "for all" referred to all the people, as Pelesh explains, then the following word in the Greek text would not have been *"panta"* (which is the neuter gender), but *"pantes!"* Hence, the words "for all" have no reference to people. "For all" then, must apply to the graces of the redemption mentioned in the Anamnesis. "For all" means, therefore: "because of all blessings." These last words can be paraphrased as follows: "We offer to You, O God, Your own Gifts in behalf of all that Christ had wrought for our salvation and in gratitude for all that we have received."

The words we have just analyzed are biblical in origin, being taken from the first book of Chronicles where King David was said to have blessed God after building the temple: "Everything is from You, O Lord, we have given You that which we have received from you." (Chron 29:14).

Similar formulas of offering sacrifice are also found in other Liturgies. In the Alexandrine Liturgy of St. Mark, we have these words: "Before You we have placed Your own Gifts." [3] On the altar in the church of St. Sophia in Constanti-

---

[2] Cf. *Pastirskoe Bogoslovie*, II, Liturghika, p. 497.

[3] Brightman, *Liturgies Eastern and Western*, I, 133.

nople, there was the inscription: "Your servants, O Christ, Justinian and Theodora, offer to You Your Gifts of Your own Gifts." [4] The Canon of the Roman Liturgy contains similar words. [5]

The final words of the Anamnesis are, therefore, the formal act of offering the Consecrated Gifts to God. A more valuable gift than these the Church could not have offered to God. They are the ransom for our salvation and the guarantee of life everlasting. Man does not have, nor could have, a better way of thanking God for all blessings than by offering the Unbloody Sacrifice. There is nothing we can call our own that we can offer up to God in gratitude for His love. Therefore, not having anything of our own to offer, we offer up to Him His own gifts, the Body and Blood of the Only-begotten Son.

The continuation of the words: "Thine own of Thine own" are the words of a song which the congregation sings after offering the sacrifice: "We praise Thee, we bless Thee, we give thanks unto Thee, O Lord, and we pray to Thee, our God." Thus the people show their gratitude to God for His graces. Bishop D. Nyarady beautifully comments on these words: "These are Your Gifts, O God—Father; You have given us bread and wine to sustain our life. Your Only-begotten Son of all Your innumerable gifts chose bread and wine under the species of which He offers His Body and Blood at the Last Supper as a sacrifice of the New Law. Following His command we too now offer the consecrated gifts of the Body and Blood of Jesus Christ as a sacrifice of thanksgiving for the Cross, the Burial, the Resurrection, the Ascension, His sitting at the right side of the Father, and His Second Coming into the world. Heavenly Father! After all these gifts *(kata panta)* we thank You, and glorify You, the Supreme and most perfect Being, with hymns, we glorify You as the all-wise and all-powerful Creator and Lord of all creatures. We thank You, Lord, most merciful Benefactor, for offering up Your Only-begotten Son for our salvation. We pray to You . . ." [6]

7. The Epiklesis

Liturgists define the Epiklesis as a prayer in the Anaphora in which the Holy Spirit is entreated to descend upon the Holy Gifts. In this wider sense the Epiklesis is a common liturgical phenomenon, for almost all Liturgies have an invocation of the Holy Spirit upon the gifts, some before, others after the words of Christ (i.e. the words of Consecration). We also find this appeal to the Holy Spirit to come down and sanctify both the priest and the holy gifts in other portions of the Liturgy. It so happens that one and the same Liturgy (e.g., of St. John Chrysostom) has more appeals or invocations to the Holy Spirit, or, to put it technically—more Epikleses. [1]

---

[4] De Meester, *Les Origines . . .*, 340.

[5] "Unde et memores . . . offerimus praeclarae maiestati tuae de tuis donis ac datis hostiam puram . . ."

[6] Nyarady, D., *Sluzhba Bozha abo Liturghiya*, Dyakovo, 1932, pp. 106–107.

[1] We shall treat of this a little later.

However, when speaking of the Epiklesis in the strict sense of the word, we usually have in mind that invocation of the Holy Spirit which appears 1. in the Anaphora, 2. after the Consecration, 3. and has as its purpose the consecration of the Holy Gifts. It is in this last sense that we consider the Epiklesis in the Liturgy of St. John Chrysostom.

The epiklesis presents a most difficult dogmatic-liturgical problem. Proof of this is the extensive treatment and particular attention it has been accorded in dogma, Liturgy, history, philology, etc.[2] Much has been and is still being written on the subject, its origin, significance, necessity and its interpretation. It is one of the important points of controversy among Western-Catholic and Eastern-Orthodox theologians. The Eastern Orthodox maintain that the power of consecration lies in the Epiklesis independently of Christ's words of institution or in both the Epiklesis and the words of institution, while the Catholic theologians hold that the Epiklesis does not possess this power.

This problem can scarcely be overlooked in our commentary. Because the Epiklesis can be viewed from various aspects, we shall restrict ourselves only to *its liturgical-historical aspect*. First of all, we will examine the text of the Epiklesis in St. John Chrystostom's Liturgy, its origin and historical development. Then we shall try to explain its significance and role in relation to the Anaphora.

A. The Text of the Epiklesis in the Liturgy of St. John Chrysostom

The invocation of the Holy Spirit occurs frequently in the Liturgy of St. John Chrysostom. In the prayer of the Great Entrance the priest implores God to make him "by the power of the Holy Spirit" worthy to stand before the holy altar to "discharge his priestly functions," especially those pertaining to the Unbloody Sacrifice. After the Great Entrance the priest asks in the "prayer of Oblation" or Prothesis:

> deign that we may find grace before Thee, that our sacrifice may be acceptable unto Thee, and may the Good Spirit of Thy grace rest upon us, and upon these gifts placed here, and upon all Thy people.

These two prayers we may call the antecedent or anticipatory or preconsecratory epikleses, for the real Epiklesis with which we are mainly concerned here is the one directly connected with the Anamnesis. The text is as follows:

> Again we offer to Thee this reasonable and unbloody worship, and we entreat, and pray, and humbly beseech Thee, send down Thy Holy Spirit upon us, and upon these presented gifts.

Now the priest makes three metanias and continues:

> And make this Bread the Precious Body of Thy Christ. And that which is in this chalice, the Precious Blood of Thy Christ. Changing them by Thy

---

[2] See bibliography at the end of this chapter.

Holy Spirit. That to those who partake thereof they may be unto soberness of soul, unto the remission of sins, unto the communion of Thy Holy Spirit, unto the fulfilling of the kingdom of heaven, unto confidence towards Thee; not unto judgment, nor unto condemnation.

In this prayer we can distinguish three parts, namely: 1. an appeal to the Holy Spirit to come down upon the Holy Gifts; 2. to change them into the Body and Blood of Jesus Christ; and 3. to produce sanctifying effects within the souls of the recipients of these gifts.

The first and third parts of the prayer present no problem. It is the second part that is difficult, for here the priest calls upon the Holy Spirit to "change" tht gifts and "make" the bread into the "Body" of Christ and the wine into the "Blood" of Christ, changes which have been already effected by virtue of the consecratory words of Christ: If the eucharistic elements have been already changed, why call upon the Holy Spirit to change them? To answer this question properly, especially that part dealing with the "consecration of the holy gifts," we must first inquire into the origin and historical background of the Epiklesis. This will, to a certain extent, offer us a key to the solution of the problem.

B. Origin and Historical Development of the Epiklesis

Almost all the Eastern Liturgies contain this prayer of the eucharistic Epiklesis [3] which occurs immediately after the words of Christ. The question is: When and how did the prayer find its way into these Liturgies? Is it of primitive origin or is it a later addition?

There are basically two answers to the question of the origin of the Epiklesis. Some theologians, predominantly non-catholics, consider it to be of Apostolic origin and trace it to the works of the earliest Fathers and Church writers. Such is the opinion of I. Dmitrievsky,[4] L. Mirkovich,[5] Archimandrite Cyprian,[6] and other Orthodox theologians and liturgists.

Their opinion, however, lacks the support of the oldest liturgical documents and writings of the Apostolic period (first and second centuries). Hence, Catholic scholars deny the Apostolic origin of the Epiklesis, especially the part where the Holy Spirit is invoked to change the holy gifts. According to the opinion of the learned liturgists, Cabrol, Baumstark, Sallaville,[7] the prayer comes from the

---

[3] For the texts of the epiklesis in the various Liturgies see M. Jugie, *De forma Eucharistiae. De Epicl. euch.*, pp. 15–35; *Dict. theol. cath.* V, 194 ss; Russnak, *Epiklizis*, Pryashev, 1926, pp. 24–54.

[4] *Ist. dogm. i tainstv. izyasnenie na lit.*, M. 1804, p. 204.

[5] Mirkovich, appealing to the testimony of Pseudo-Proclus (Migne, PG, 65, 849), considers the invocation of the Holy Spirit to be of Apostolic origin. In the testimony of Pseudo-Proclus it is related that the Apostles were waiting for the advent of the Holy Spirit (Pentecost) and were celebrating the Divine Liturgy (offering the sacrifice) at the same time waiting for the Holy Spirit to come down upon the Gifts to change them into the Body and Blood of Our Lord. (Cf. *Pravoslavna Liturghika*, II, Sremski Karlovtsi, 1920, p. 101).

[6] Cyprian, *Evkharistiya*, pp. 245, 261–263.

[7] See the works of the above mentioned scholars in the literature at the end of the chapter.

post-apostolic period, specifically, the third and fourth centuries.

In his *Apology*, where he describes the Liturgy, St. Justin [8] does not mention an invocation of the Holy Spirit, although he does mention a prayer of "thanksgiving" said over the Holy Gifts. But he is referring here to the whole Anaphora for in this description neither the words of Christ, nor still less, the Epiklesis, are mentioned.[9]

The oldest document in which we find the Epiklesis is the *Apostolic Tradition* of St. Hippolytus. In this third-century liturgical document, the Anamnesis occurs immediately after the words of Christ, and directly following the Anamnesis there is the prayer:

> We implore Thee to send down Thy Holy Spirit upon the sacrifice of the holy Church. Gathering it into one body give to all the saints who receive this sacrifice, the fullness of the Holy Spirit, in order to strengthen them in faith and truth, and in order to praise and glorify Thee through Thy Son Jesus Christ.[10]

We shall not analyze this prayer, which is, according to scholars, the oldest formula of the Epiklesis. However, it must be noted that there is no explicit appeal or invocation of the Holy Spirit to "change" or "sanctify" the gifts. Altogether another reason is given for the Holy Spirit's descent upon the holy gifts namely, that the communicants derive from them spiritual benefit.

In the liturgical documents of the fourth century the Epiklesis appears in the anaphoras of the *Apostolic Constitutions*,[11] the Liturgy of St. James, the descriptions and commentaries of the Liturgy of St. Cyril of Jerusalem, the so-called *Euchologion of Serapion*, and in the fragmentary papyrus of Der-Balyzeh.[12] In these documents we explicitly find in the Epiklesis as the purpose of the descent of the Holy Spirit, to consecrate the offertory Gifts and sanctify the communicants. In other words: by the fourth century the Epiklesis finally assumes its present day form and significance. It has three parts: 1. the descent of the Holy Spirit upon the Gifts; 2. consecration of the Gifts; and 3. the sanctification of the faithful. Although the words vary in the different liturgical documents, the sense of the prayer is everywhere the same.

With such evidence as our basis, we may conclude that the Epiklesis, though not of Apostolic origin, is, nevertheless, one of the oldest elements in the Anaphora. It is older than the Seraphic Hymn, "Holy, Holy, Holy . . ." and as we shall see, it is a natural prolongation of the Eucharistic Prayer, of Christ's words of institution and the Anamnesis. Small wonder, then, that it appears in one form or other in almost all Liturgies of both East and West. Even the Latin Liturgy, which, as we know, does not have the Epiklesis in the strict sense of the

---

[8] Otto, *Corpus Apolog* . . ., I, 177–180, 184–188.

[9] S. Salaville, *La Liturgie decrite par S. Justine et l'epiclese:* E. d'Or. XI (1909), p. 226.

[10] Hauler, *Didascalia Apost* . . ., p. 107.

[11] Funk, *Didascalia et Const.*, I, 510.

[12] Jugie, *op. cit.*, 27–30.

word, probably had it in earlier centuries. So the scholars Cabrol,[13] Rauschen,[14] Sallaville [15] and others affirm.

What, therefore, inspired or influenced the introduction of the Epiklesis into the Liturgy and what was its original form? Was the appeal to the Holy Spirit to come down upon the gifts the original prayer, or conversely, did it develop from the invocation to sanctify the faithful in Communion? We still have no satisfactory answer to this question because we lack pertinent documents from the first centuries. All extant liturgical documents are unable to supply us with the key to the complete solution of this problem. Scholars are left with only conjecture and hypothesis.

The Orthodox scholars and liturgists who maintain that the Epiklesis is the consecratory or co-consecratory formula are inclined to ascribe the origin of the prayer to Apostolic institution.[16] Catholic scholars, on the other hand, assert that the original petition of the Epiklesis was not to the Holy Spirit to come down upon the holy gifts to consecrate them, but to produce beneficial effects in the souls of those who received them in Holy Communion,[17] that from this latter petition the petition to consecrate the holy gifts developed. The truth of this assertion is evidenced in the oldest text of the Epiklesis so far known, namely, the *Apostolic Tradition* of St. Hippolytus, which we have quoted earlier. There-fore, an evolution must have occurred in the Epiklesis. But, supposing that an evolution did take place, the question still remains: Why did the evolution pursue the same course in the majority of Eastern Liturgies, i.e., why was the invocation to consecrate the holy gifts added to the invocation for the spiritual benefits of Holy Communion? Whatever the case may be, the question remains the same: What signification does the invocation of the Holy Spirit to descend upon and sanctify the holy gifts have?

In the opinion of Karabinov the Epiklesis developed from a personal or pri-vate petition of the priest in which he asked the Holy Spirit to purify him. In other words, from what was originally a private prayer in which the priest invoked the Holy Spirit to render him worthy and pure to offer the Eucharistic sacrifice, the Epiklesis, taken in the strict sense as a prayer to the Holy Spirit to consecrate the holy gifts, gradually developed. Karabinov corroborates his assumption with the help of the texts from various Liturgies, especially St. John Chrysostom's where in the prayer of the Epiklesis the Holy Spirit is asked to descend "upon us," and finally "upon all the gifts before us."[18] But even this hypothesis does not solve the mystery surrounding the question of the Epiklesis and its pristine form and significance.

Our opinion is that the origin and development of the Epiklesis can best be explained by the organic or intrinsic development of the Anaphora. The Epik-

---

13 Cabrol, *La messe en Occident*, p. 77.
14 Rauschen, *Eucharistie u. Bussakrament* . . ., p. 86.
15 Salaville, *L'Epiclesis dans le canon romain* . . ., Revue aug., 1909, pp. 303–378.
16 Cyprian, Arch., *Evkharistiya*, p. 284.
17 Cabrol, *Epiclese* . . ., p. 174.
18 See his *Evkharisticheskaya molitva*, pp. 115–116.

lesis, like the Anamnesis, developed from the Eucharistic Prayer and the words of Christ; it is the completion and amplification of the words of Christ's institution. We shall discuss this more in detail when treating of the significance and sense of the Epiklesis.

Although the history of the origin and development of the Epiklesis is not yet satisfactorily clarified, it is not its historical aspect that presents a problem but its dogmatic-liturgical aspect, for the chief difficulty lies in its explanation.

C. *Explanation of the Epiklesis*

Orthodox theologians and liturgists solve the problem of the Epiklesis by assigning to it alone or to it with the words of Christ's institution the power of consecration.[19] We here refer to the doctrine of recent Orthodox theologians and liturgists, for in the seventeenth century many leaned toward the Western Catholic doctrine which held that the words of Christ alone possess the power of consecration.[20]

It must be said that the opinion of the Orthodox theologians not only lacks any basis in the writings of the Fathers,[21] but is also extremely vulnerable from a purely liturgical point of view. One who attributes the consecratory power exclusively to the Epiklesis must, by the same token, reduce Christ's words to a mere historical account. But this theory is refuted in the writings of the Fathers who ascribe the consecratory power to the words of institution [22] and in the spirit and structure of the Liturgies of both East and West. In all these Liturgies the words of Christ are the central point; the Epiklesis plays only a secondary role. In the Liturgies of St. John Chrysostom and St. Basil, Christ's words are pronounced aloud by the priest, whereas the prayer of the Epiklesis is recited silently. This of itself convinces us that Christ's words were accorded a distinctive place in the Liturgy.[23]

Equally unsatisfactory is the argument presented by those who attribute the power of consecration to both the Epiklesis and the words of Christ's institution.[24] According to this theory the changing of the bread and wine into the Body and Blood of Jesus Christ would have to take place gradually and not

---

[19] Russnak presents the doctrine of the Orthodox theologians, *Epiklizis*, pp. 58–94.

[20] Especially the theologians of the "Kievan school" defended this doctrine. These were well-known Ukrainian theologians as Mohyla, L. Baranovych, I. Galiatovsky, I. Gizel, T. Safonovich, S. Polotsky, Dymytry Rostovsky-Tuptalo, and especially S. Medvedev, who was executed in 1691 for upholding this theory.

[21] See Russnak, *Epikl.*, pp. 138–154 and Spacil, *Doctrina Theologiae orientis separati*, II (1929), pp. 41–58.

[22] See the testimonies of the Fathers presented by Russnak (pp. 138–154) and Spacil (41–58).

[23] The Chaldean Liturgy of the Holy Apostles does not have Christ's words, but this is the only exception in the history of the Liturgy.

[24] This theory was defended by Cabasilas in the fourteenth century and later by A. Maltsev (*Liturgikon*, Berlin, 1902, p. 427) and (*De vestigiis epicleseos in Missa Romana*, Acta II, Conv. Velehrad., 1910, p. 135).

instantaneously. The concept of such a "gradual consecration" of the eucharistic elements, if not contradictory, at least presents philosophical and scientific difficulties. The transubstantiation can hardly be explained as a gradual process, for between the bread and wine, on one hand, and the Body and Blood on the other, a middle or intermediary entity, is inconceivable. The process of transubstantiation is of its very nature "indivisible," hence it does not admit of graduality or succession. Although the Fathers did not treat of the time or exact instant the consecration took place during the Anaphora and did not pinpoint this moment,[25] it does not follow that no such time or exact moment exists, or that the Eucharistic change must take place gradually.[26]

Appeal to the writings of the Fathers and theologians who attribute the power of consecration to the Holy Spirit [27] helps but little, for the question of the Epiklesis is not concerned with whether the Holy Spirit is the cause of this change or not. Catholic theologians also ascribe the consecration to the operation of the Holy Spirit, since the Holy Spirit, equal to God the Father and God the Word, also takes part in the transubstantiation. There is no Catholic theologian who would deny this. The real question is whether the transubstantiation takes place during the Epiklesis or during the words of institution. These are two entirely different questions which should not be identified. It is true that the Fathers ascribe the transubstantiation to the Holy Spirit but that does not prove that they *ipso facto* ascribe the power of consecration to the Epiklesis. On the contrary, the Fathers, especially the Eastern Fathers, assign the power of consecration to the words of Christ.

If the Epiklesis constituted the exclusive formula of consecration, then all those Liturgies that do not have the Epiklesis, as the Latin Liturgy, or those that only have an anticipatory, antecedent or pre-consecratory Epiklesis, would have no consecration. In other words, the eucharistic consecration in those Liturgies that do not possess the Epiklesis would be invalid. However, even the Orthodox theologians do not concur with this conclusion. They admit the validity of consecration in these Liturgies which do not have the Epiklesis in the strict sense of the word.

Other dogmatic proofs advanced by those who affirm that the power of consecration does not die in the Epiklesis can be found in any textbook of Dogmatics, so we need not treat of them here. Laying aside the improper theory of the Epiklesis, we will focus our attention on the various Catholic explanations of its significance and role. Not all these explanations, it must be said, give us a satisfactory solution nor are they persuasive.

First of all we must reject *the "historical theory"* or *the theory of historical evolution.* Some theologians such as Probst [28] and Heller [29] strove to prove that

---

[25] F. Cabrol, *Epiclese* . . ., 174; Salaville, *Epicl. euch* . . ., 201, 224.

[26] Cyprian, *Evkharistiya*, pp. 264–265. This theory of gradual consecration was maintained also by G. Kostelnyk, *Spir pro epiklezu*, pp. 130–131.

[27] See Cyprian, *op. cit.*, 239–245.

[28] *Liturgie des 4 Jahr. und deren Reform*, Muenster, 1893, p. 14.

[29] *Die Epiklese* . . ., p. 109.

the text of the Epiklesis underwent an evolution. Originally, they hold, there were no words in the text such as "make," "convert," but only: "show." Later the word "show" was replaced by the expressions "make," "convert" and thus the problem arose.

This theory still does not resolve the problem. To begin with, the assumption regarding the "distortion" of the original words of the Epiklesis is not based on solid grounds. It would be difficult to believe that such distortion could have found its way into so many Liturgies unnoticed. The authors forget too that in liturgical usage the words "make," "convert" and "show" have the same meaning. They are synonymous with the modern term "transubstantiation." Therefore, to take the words "to show" in the metaphorical sense would be to force the liturgical text. The theory of historical development is, therefore, unsatisfactory, for it evades the issue, giving the words of the Epiklesis an improper meaning.

A similar theory is that of Holy Communion. According to this theory the Epiklesis is an invocation of the Holy Spirit to render effective *and beneficial the fruits of the Consecrated Gifts within the souls of the communicants.* The prayer does not call on the Holy Spirit to change the bread and wine into the Body and Blood of Christ, but to sanctify the faithful through the gifts consecrated by virtue of the words of Christ. This explanation is given by many of the ancient theologians, like Bessarion, Arkudius, Allatius, Bellarmine, Suarez, Torquemada,[30] as well as by some of the recent ones.[31]

This theory is not conclusive either, although it explains well the last part of the Epiklesis in which the priest prays that the holy gifts be for the faithful,

> unto soberness of soul, unto the remission of sins, unto the communion of Thy Holy Spirit, unto the fulfilling of the kingdom of heaven, unto confidence towards Thee; not unto judgment, nor unto condemnation.

Yet it does not offer *the* solution, for it overlooks the most important aspect of our problem: why besides the petition for the beneficial effects of Holy Communion, does the petition that the gifts be consecrated occur as the main theme of the prayer? This theory does not consider the essential point in the question of the Epiklesis, and it gives the words of the Epiklesis an improper meaning.

Therefore, we must look for an explanation that will not, on the one hand, force the text, distort it or give it an incorrect meaning, and on the other hand, will not ascribe the time or exact instant of consecration to the Epiklesis instead of to Christ's words of institution. Such an explanation is given by the *"Liturgical Theory"* espoused by many Catholic theologians.[32] This theory offers perhaps the best solution to this complicated problem; its argument is based on the nature of the liturgical prayers.[33]

---

30 Cf. Spacil, *op. cit.,* pp. 60–69.
31 Russnak, *Epiklizis,* p. 132, and other places.
32 See list of these theologians in Spacil, *op. cit.,* p. 69.
33 Sallaville also draws his attention to it, *op. cit.,* col. 279.

Character of liturgical prayers and actions. Liturgical prayers have a tendency to unfold and to develop the main rite or prayer. This means that the Liturgy does not rest with only the main and essential rite in a given service, but develops it, adding new prayer formulas and a variety of expressions.

As in the Liturgy, so too, in the rites of the sacraments and various blessings, the Liturgy again and again reverts to the main theme or principal thought, treating it from a variety of aspects, in order to exhaust its content. For example, in the rite of baptism, extreme unction, or holy orders the Church is not satisfied with only the essential formula of the sacrament. On the contrary, she repeats the formula in various ways, develops the principal thought of the rite in manifold prayers, which either precede or follow upon the essential rite. A classical example is the sacrament of the priesthood in the Byzantine-Ukrainian Rite, where after the essential formula or ordination, the help and descent of the Holy Spirit is again invoked upon the one receiving the sacrament, as if he had not yet received it.

This characteristic of liturgical prayer is psychologically sound. Human speech is incapable of expressing in two or more words all that in contained, implied, or hidden in a rite which is simple by nature. The natural order of things requires that in expressing our thoughts, which are in themselves simple and abstract, we use more than one word. Only then does our thought find relatively full expression and becomes more intelligible.[34]

So it is with liturgical prayer. The Liturgy, in order to express the main rite, requires a great variety of expression. It is forced to expound in many ways that which happens in one moment. Grace comes and acts instantly (as for example at the Consecration, the sacrament of the priesthood, etc.), and the Liturgy, according to our manner of conceiving things, reveals this in various prayers and rites. According to the laws of human psychology, the Liturgy portrays that which occurs in its rites and ceremonies, gradually and piecemeal. It returns, again and again to the same thought, expressing it in various ways, uncovering new aspects and nuances of the same priestly function. It unfolds the semantics of the rite. In other words, the rites and prayers of the Liturgy reveal a tendency to bring out the semantics of each rite or to make explicit that which is implicit. They reveal a tendency toward verbal "dramatization."

The prayer of the Epiklesis serves as a classical example and application of this characteristic so peculiar to the Liturgy. It implores the Holy Spirit to descend upon the Gifts to sanctify them immediately after the Consecration,

---

[34] An idea is the intellectual representation of a thing. Because of the limited power and capacity of our intellect, we are incapable of grasping the full reality of an object within the content of a single idea. In consequence of this, the intellect turns its attention first to this, then to that property or attribute, and makes a separate concept for each one. In nature, the thing is actually undivided and one, but potentially divisible and many; in the intellect, the concepts of the thing are actually divided and many, but potentially undivided and one. The intellect recognizes this fact. None of these ideas represents the full reality, but each represents an aspect, a phase, a portion of it.

which, according to the doctrine of Catholic theologians [35] has already taken place by virtue of pronouncing the words of Christ.

This invocation of the Holy Spirit to descend upon the Gifts and consecrate them after they have already been consecrated may, at first glance, seem illogical, superfluous and meaningless. Nevertheless, this invocation conforms to the spirit of liturgical prayer, hence, there is no inconsistency or lack of logic.

Let us examine it closely. The focal point of the Anaphora and the Divine Liturgy as a whole are Christ's words of consecration. The consecration performs God [36] by means of Christ's words procounced by the priest "in the person of Christ." After the pronouncement of both consecratory formulas, there no longer exists bread and wine on the altar but the Body and Blood of Jesus Christ. But the act of consecration, though simple in itself and occurring at one moment, embraces implicitly other various moments and aspects which the Liturgy wishes to express more clearly and accurately: 1. The Consecration is, first of all, a miraculous changing of the bread and wine into the Body and Blood of Jesus Christ. By virtue of this consecration Christ becomes present under the appearances of bread and wine. He takes the place of the substance of bread and wine. 2. However, the same Consecration is *a sacrificial offering,* namely, the act, whereby Christ offers Himself up as a sacrifice for the people. 3. Furthermore, this sacrifice of Christ is *analogous* to the sacrifice of Christ on Golgotha. 4. This sacrifice is a repetition and realization of the sacrifice on the cross. Like the sacrifice on the cross, it is a sacrifice of reconciliation, praise, thanksgiving and petition.

As we can see, all these aspects are implicit in the one act of consecration. The moment of consecration is at one and the same time the realization of Christ's presence under the species of bread and wine, the New Testament sacrifice and the renewal of the work of redemption. However, the Church, pronouncing the words of consecration, cannot express all these aspects implicit in the act; therefore, it uses various prayerful formulas, in order to bring out into high relief and express each aspect of the Consecration. Before the Consecration itself, i.e., in the prayer of praise and thanksgiving, it expresses one of the aspects of te Eucharistic sacrifice, namely, that it is a thanksgiving to God for countless blessings (creation, redemption, etc.). Immediately after the Consecration (in the prayers of the Anamnesis) the Sacrifice is revealed as a commemora-

---

[35] The doctrine that the power of consecration lies in Christ's words is not yet a defined dogma of faith (*de fide definita*), but is a common doctrine of Catholic theologians. See Spacil, *o.c.,* p. 10.

[36] When we say "God" we mean the Blessed Trinity, for the Consecration is an act shared by all Three Divine Persons. However, the Eucharistic Consecration is ascribed in a very special manner to the Holy Spirit, for according to the teachings of Catholic theologians. He is the principle and source of all sanctification. Hence, the objection that the Catholic Church denies to the Holy Spirit the Consecration of the holy gifts has no foundation whatsoever. Catholic theologians deny that the power of Consecration lies in the epiklesis but they do not deny that the Holy Spirit consummates the Consecration. These two facts Orthodox theologians do not distinguish, and in their failure to do so they confuse the issue.

tion of the redemption. In the words "Thine own of Thine own" the Church formally offers the Body and Blood of Jesus Christ "in behalf of all, and for all." Like the eucharistic prayer of praise and thanksgiving, the Anamnesis and the act of offering also refer to the act of Consecration. With these prayerful formulas the Liturgy expresses that which could not be expressed in the act of Consecration itself.

The Epiklesis has the same purpose. As in the Anamnesis, so here the Church expresses what in one simple act of consecration she could not. In the Epiklesis new aspects are expressed which have not yet been expressed by the Liturgy.

First of all, *the prayer of the Epiklesis is an expression of the belief of the Church that the Eucharistic consecration is performed not by man but by God.* The words of consecration were not the Church's but Christ's words. They, by virtue of God's power, effect the Consecration of the gifts. However, the Church wishes to emphasize this very important moment, and therefore turns to God with the petition that the Holy Spirit sanctify the gifts. It is in this prayer of the Epiklesis that *the Church formally asks that the gifts be consecrated.* The Epiklesis is, therefore, a manifestation of the faith of the Church in the exclusive power of God over the holy gifts. Although the prayer imploring God to sanctify the gifts, follows the Consecration itself of the gifts, nevertheless, it refers to the moment of Consecration, namely, to Christ's words, or to put it in other words, it possesses a *retroactive function.*

This is not all. The Epiklesis has still another very important moment. It is not only a formal admission of the Church that God is the cause of the Consecration, but also a *formal entreaty of the Church that God condescend to accept the Eucharistic Sacrifice from her hands.* Imploring God to send the Holy Spirit upon the gifts, to sanctify and change them, means nothing else *but that God accept the Unbloody Sacrifice* and that, consequently, this Sacrifice prove beneficial to the members of the Church. In this lies the correct and true meaning of the Epiklesis.[37]

The Anamnesis, as we have seen, was a commemoration of the work of the redemption and a formal act of offering sacrifice on the part of the Church: "Thine own of Thine own, we offer Thee, in behalf of all, and for all." In the Epiklesis, the Church prays that God accept the sacrifice of the New Testament from the hands of the faithful, although it is at the time of the Eucharistic Sacrifice that God accepts this sacrifice. In fact the Church asks for that which has already taken place. It is the same with the prayer of the Anamnesis. The Church here formally offers to God the Body and Blood of Christ, although this act of offering has already taken place during Consecration. Hence, the Anamnesis, like the Epiklesis, refers to the act of Consecration. These prayers essentially do not add to the Consecration; they only prolong that which has already taken place at the Consecration. The Epiklesis, like the Anamnesis, is *a natural devel-*

---

[37] Theologians rarely if ever give attention to this aspect of the Epiklesis which in our opinion is the key to its understanding.

opment of the act of consecration and refers to the act of Consecration. In the Anamnesis and the Epiklesis the Church "wishes to express" that which could not be expressed with the words of Consecration.

One might object: If the epiklesis is by nature a formal entreaty of the Church that God accept the Unbloody Sacrifice, then why is it expressed in terms that seem to imply that the Consecration has not yet taken place? For in the Epiklesis we do not pray: "Accept this sacrifice, this Body and this Blood," but rather: "make this Bread the Precious Body of Thy Christ and that which is in this Chalice, the Precious Blood of Thy Christ, changing (them) by Thy Holy Spirit." Why, then, do we use such terms as "make" and "convert" instead of the term "accept?" The answer is simple. The Church uses the words "make" and "convert" instead of "accept" *because for God to accept sacrifice is nothing else but its "conversion," its consecration.* God accepts the Eucharistic Sacrifice only when the Eucharistic elements i.e., bread and wine, are consecrated, when they are converted into the Body and Blood of Jesus Christ. The Consecration on the part of God is at the same time the acceptance of the sacrifice of the New Testament. Hence, by asking God to accept the holy gifts, the Church uses the words: "make," "convert," i.e., the Church asks that God consecrate the Holy Gifts.

This prayer *to accept and sanctify the holy gifts* occurs in the Byzantine Liturgy not before but after the Consecration. *The psychological reason* for it is this. The bread and wine are on the altar for the Consecration; the Church could ask God to accept these offertory gifts even before the Consecration,[38] but the gifts are not yet consecrated. After the Consecration the situation is different. By virtue of Christ's words of institution, the gifts have been changed into His Body and Blood, and therefore, the Church can now offer them to God (Anamnesis) and ask that God receive them (Epiklesis); asking God to sanctify the gifts is the same as asking Him to accept them.[39]

It becomes clear from our discussion why the Epiklesis is found in one form or other in all Liturgies. For since there is question here of asking that the gifts be accepted, it would be impossible to imagine a Liturgy without it. Every Liturgy that does not have the Epiklesis after the Consecration, at least has the antecedent Epiklesis. *Both subsequent and antecedent Epikleses are prayers*

---

[38] As in the Coptic Liturgies of St. Basil and St. Gregory, and the Alexandrian (Greek) Liturgies of St. Mark and St. Gregory, which have the Epiklesis before the Consecration, i.e. the antecedent or prevenient Epiklesis. See M. Jugie, *De forma Eucharistiae*, pp. 21–24).

[39] "La supplica di accetazione si concreta nel chiedere la transsubstanziazione del pane e del vino nel Corpo e nel Sangue di Cristo. Essa in realta e gia avvenuta, ma per una figura di posticipazione usata qui dai greci e leggitima tanto quanto quella di anticipazione che adoperiamo noi latini nell' Offertorio, offrendo a Dio il pane eil vino. In tale azione noi adoperiamo espressioni-ostia immacolata, calice di salvezza—che rispecchiano evidentemente non il pane e il vino, ma Cristo, come se fosse gia presente sotto le specie eucaristiche, mentre in realta non e. La ragione si e che spesse volte nella preghiera noi poniamo la mente non nella situazione reale del momento, in cui ci troviamo, ma in una determinata situazione psicologica, che puo rispecchiare tanto il passato quanto il futuro, invece del presente." (P. Albrigi, *Sacra liturgia*, II. *Il sacrificio cristiano*, pag. 89–99).

asking God to consecrate and accept the gifts.

The Roman Liturgy serves as an example. It does not have the Epiklesis after the Consecration as do the Liturgy of St. John and other Eastern Liturgies. Nevertheless, the arrangement, the train of thought and the content of the prayer after the Consecration of the gifts is the same in the Roman Liturgy as in ours. In the Roman Liturgy immediately after the Consecration, the work of redemption is mentioned (Anamnesis),[40] then later the act of offering sacrifice by the Church which correspond to the words of our Liturgy: "Thine own of Thine own." [41] Then follows *The prayer asking God to accept the sacrific.*[42] This petition corresponds with that part of the prayer of the Epiklesis in which we ask the consecration of the gifts. Finally, the Roman Liturgy immediately petitions that the effects or fruits of Holy Communion be beneficial to the soul,[43] which petition corresponds to the last part of Epiklesis in the Byzantine Liturgy.

From this it follows that *the Epiklesis has the character of a petition that God accept the sacrifice offered by the Church.* Analogically, it has the same meaning as the sending of fire by God upon the sacrifices of the Old Testament. We know that by sending fire down to consume the sacrifice offered by the people, God indicated that the sacrifice was pleasing to Him and that He accepted it.[44] In the Epiklesis the Church asks God to send the "fire" upon His sacrifice, namely, His Holy Spirit "the heavenly, spiritual fire" [45] upon the already consecrated gifts.

The prayer of the epiklesis emphasizes still another aspect, that is, *the role of the Holy Spirit in the Liturgy,* especially in relation to the Consecration. St. Gregory of Nyssa says that "every work created by God comes from the Father, through the Son and is completed by the Holy Spirit." [46] In analyzing the prayer of praise and thanksgiving and the Eucharistic Prayer, we saw how the Liturgy confirms this truth. It begins the Anaphora with the glorification of the Holy Trinity which means that the Three Divine Persons in the Holy Trinity take part in the Unbloody Sacrifice just as in the work of redemption and creation.

---

[40] "Unde et memores, Domine, nos servi tui, sed et plebs tua sancta, eiusdem Christi filli tui, Domini nostri, tam beatae passionis, necnon et ab inferis resurrectionis, sed et in coelos gloriosae ascensionis: offerimus praeclarae majestati tuae de tuis donis ac datis . . ."

[41] " . . . offerimus praeclarae majestati tuae de tuis donis ac datis hostiam puram, hostiam sanctam, hostiam immaculatam, Panem sanctu vitae aeternae et Calicem salutis perpetuae."

[42] "Supra quae propitio ac sereno vultu respicere digneris: et accepta habere . . . sanctum sacrificium, immaculatam hostiam."

[43] "Supplies te rogamus, omnipotens Deus . . . ut, quotquot ex hac altaris participatione sacrosanctum Filii tui Corpus et Sanguinem sumpserimus, omni benedictione caelesti et gratia repleamur."

[44] From the Old Testament we know that God sent fire down upon the sacrifices of Abraham, Aaron and Elias wich fire consumed them. This was a sign that God was pleased with the sacrifices and that He accepted them.

[45] See the writings of St. Gregory of Nyssa in which the Holy Spirit is called the heavenly fire. Migne, PG, 46, 805 (sermon on St. Basil) and *ibid.*, 46, 845 (sermon on St. Ephrem).

[46] Cf. Migne, PG, 45, 125.

From glorification of the Blessed Trinity, the Liturgy in the Eucharistic prayer passes over to glorification of the Father who out of love for mankind, sent His only Son into the world. The Liturgy then goes on to mention all that the Son of God did for the salvation of man (words of consecration, Anamnesis). Finally and naturally the Liturgy mentions the Holy Spirit—asking God to send the Holy Spirit upon the gifts to consecrate them and to sanctify those about to receive them.

The Epiklesis is, therefore, a new descent of the Holy Spirit upon the gifts and the faithful. As the descent of the Holy Spirit upon the Apostles in the day of the Pentecost was the completion of the work of redemption, so also the coming of the Holy Spirit during the Anaphora, so to speak, completes the Eucharistic Sacrifice. The coming of the Holy Spirit upon the Apostles in the form of fiery tongues made them courageous men, full of faith and determination, sowers of the word of God and Christ's doctrine. The Holy Spirit gave them strength to "renew the universe," to carry the light of Christ's doctrine into the world.[47] A similar miracle is performed by the Holy Spirit in the Liturgy. The Church asks God to send the Holy Spirit in order to "renew the face of the earth," [48] and to instill into the hearts of the faithful, by means of the consecrated gifts, courage to destroy their sins, to confer upon them abundant graces, to enkindle within them an unshakeable hope in God and to save them from eternal damnation.

This is the meaning of the Epiklesis. To understand it properly, dogmatic speculation is not enough. Theologians who have treated the question of the Epiklesis at times viewed it too subjectively. In considering it from the dogmatic viewpoint they divorced it from its liturgical context and its contextual relation to the Anamnesis and the words of Christ. Theologians have frequently disregarded the peculiar structure of the eucharistic prayers and their character. Small wonder, therefore, that they became entangled in difficulty when the question concerning the sense of the words "make" and "convert" in the Epiklesis, emerged. Misunderstanding of the character of liturgical prayer led to the distortion of the original and true meaning of the words of the Epiklesis; there have even been theologians who, in order to remove all "dogmatic difficulties," advocated the elimination of the Epiklesis from the Anaphora.[49]

We have intentionally devoted a great deal of space to the Epiklesis in order to show the profound meaning of this prayer and to seek a key to its proper understanding. Further liturgical research will, we are sure, one day clarify difficult points and help rectify certain views which have been voiced so far concerning the problem.

---

[47] See the troparion of the Pentecost: "Blessed art Thou, O Christ our God, Who hast *made Thy apostles into wise fishermen* by sending down upon them the Holy Spirit and *through them winning the whole world:* O Thou Who lovest men, glory to Thee."

[48] Ps 103: 31.

[49] Cf. Rauschen, *Eucharistie und Bussakrament . . .*, p. 126.

D. Additions in the Epiklesis

This treatment of the Epiklesis would be incomplete if we overlooked certain textual and rubrical additions made in the prayers of the Epiklesis. Setting aside modifications of secondary significance, we shall concentrate on the well known *troparion* of the Third Hour, introduced into the Liturgy:

> Lord, who at the third hour didst send down upon thine Apostles Thy Holy Spirit: Take not the same from us, O Good One, but renew Him in us who make our supplications unto Thee.

We cannot determine the exact time when this *troparion* appeared in the Epiklesis. De Meester assumes that it was introduced into the Liturgy about the twelfth or thirteenth centuries.[50] Porphyrius Uspenskiy asserts that it was during the liturgical reform of the Patriarch Philotheus (fourteenth century).[51] However, the well known Russian Liturgist A. Dmitrievsky, on the basis of manuscripts, proved that this *troparion*, although it did appear here and there in the fourteenth century, made its way into the liturgikons only in the sixteenth century.[52] It found a place in the Slavic sluzhebnyks and was retained in both the Catholic and Orthodox editions. The Greeks also introduced it; however, starting with mid-nineteenth century, they began to eliminate it in the publications of the liturgikons.[53] In the Ukrainian Catholic Church this *troparion* was first omitted in the Lviv publication of the Sluzhebnyk of 1929–1930, and finally from in the Roman publication of 1941.

The reason for the introduction of this *troparion* was undoubtedly the desire to give the Epiklesis more solemnity and "power," thus emphasizing that the consecration of the holy gifts takes place during the Epiklesis. The innovation was, therefore, the result of the disputes concerning the consecratory power of the Epiklesis.

The polemic against the "Latin" position that the Consecration takes place at the pronouncement of Christ's words and not during the Epiklesis brought about this innovation. The dispute dates back to the fourteenth century and the time of Nicholas Cabasilas,[54] who was the first to carry on argument with the "Latins" ascribing the consecratory power to the Epiklesis and the words of Christ inclusively.

But aside even from its causes, the insertion of this *troparion* into the Epiklesis was in itself bad. The Orthodox themselves are aware of this. The inser-

---

[50] As for example the acclamation of the deacon: "Master, Bless this holy bread, etc." This dialogue was introduced into the epiklesis about the sixteenth century. See S. Vandik, *De apparatu liturgico . . .*, Romae, 1945.

[51] *Les origines et le develop.*, p. 341.

[52] *"Istoriya Atona"*, III, 2, pp. 491–495.

[53] Dmitrievskiy, *Bogosluzhenie v russkoy tserkvi v XVI v.*, Kazan, 1894, I, p. 121.

[54] Already in the eighteenth century the Greeks opposed the interpolation of the *troparion*: "O Lord who at the third hour . . ." P. Uspensky, (*Istoriya Atona*, III, 2, pp. 470–483) refers to the treatise written by an anonymous Greek author at the close of the eighteenth century who sharply condemned this interpolation.

tion, as one of the Orthodox authors put it: "is an illiterate innovation from the theological and liturgical viewpoint." [55] It "violates grammatical coherency and consequently, the sense of the Epiklesis." [56] This is evident, especially in the Liturgy of St. Basil, were the *troparion* interrupts the prayer in violation of all rules of grammar and logic. In the Liturgy of St. John Chrysostom it causes disharmony. While the whole prayer of the Epiklesis appeals to God the Father, the inserted *troparion* appeals to the Son, thus interrupting the train of thought and causing disorder in the text. In one word, it "causes" disharmony in the whole structure of the Anaphora, and not only the Epiklesis; [57] its existence alone and its recitation in the prayer of the Epiklesis "contradicts the syntactic and theological sense of the Liturgy." [58] The Greeks, as well as our own recent publications of the Sluzhebnyks, therefore, were entirely justified in rejecting this *troparion;* only the Russian Synodal Sluzhebnyks preserved it.

There is still another innovation which was connected with a controversy with the "Latins." In 1702 the Orthodox Patriarch of Alexandria, Gerasimos II Pallados, ordered that the consecratory words of Christ be recited silently and the Epiklesis aloud, thus indicating that the consecratory power is not contained in the words of Christ but in the Epiklesis. The Patriarch of Constantinople, Gabriel III (1702–1707), however, denounced this change and severely reprimanded Gerasimos and ordered that traditionbe preserved.[59]

In summation, we affirm that the Epiklesis, although not the consecratory formula of the Eucharist, nevertheless, does occupy an important place in the Anaphora: *being a prolongation or natural development of the Consecration, it is a formal petition that God accept the sacrifice offered to Him by the Church.* In this lies its significance.

8. The Eucharistic Commemorations

The Epiklesis is followed by the commemoration of the saints, the deceased and the living. Liturgists call this new portion of the Anaphora the "prayer of intercession" or "mediation." [1] It is organically united to the preceding prayers, i.e., the prayers of the Epiklesis and Anamnesis. The final words of the Epiklesis implore the fruits of the sacrifice for the faithful. In the prayer of commemoration the Church expresses *the intention* for which the Eucharistic Sacrifice is

---

[55] Migne, PG, 150, 428–440.

[56] Archimandrite Cyprian also condemns the interpolation of the Troparion. (*Evkharistiya,* p. 281.)

[57] *Ibid.,* p. 281.

[58] *Ibid.,* p. 285.

[59] S. Salaville, *Une innovation liturgique a Alexandrie en 1702,* (Echos d'Orient, XIV (1911), pp. 268–270).

[1] Archimandrite Cyprian (*Evkharistiya,* p. 286), calls the Eucharistic commemorations "khodataystvenyya molitvi" (prayers of intercession), Hanssens (*Inst. litur.,* III, 464), "oratio intercessionis," and De Meester (*Les origines . . .,* 342) "intercessio."

being offered. Like the two preceding prayers the prayer of commemoration is a natural development and enlargement upon the Eucharistic Prayer and Christ's words of institution.

A. History of the Eucharistic Commemorations

The triple commemoration: of the saints, the deceased and the living found its way into all the Liturgies of the East and the West. It became a component part of the Anaphora back in the formative period of liturgical types, that is, in the fourth century. Although we find vestiges of these commemorations in the oldest liturgical documents, the actual system of the triple commemoration in the Anaphora derives from the fourth century.

Although the Apostle Paul exhorted his disciple Timothy: "that supplications, prayers, intercessions, and thanksgivings be made for all men." (1 Tim 2:1), one cannot conclude that the triple commemoration existed in the Liturgy of the Apostolic Age. Certain allusions to prayers for the Church are found in the *Didache* [2] and St. Justin,[3] but these are not yet the Eucharistic commemorations in the present-day meaning of the word. There are no Eucharistic commemorations in the Anaphora of St. Hippolytus either (third century), although we have trustworthy witnesses in the liturgical documents of the fourth century, in the commentary of Liturgy of St. Cyril of Jerusalem,[4] the descriptions of Liturgy by St. John Chrysostom [5] and the *Apostolic Constitutions.*[6]

The Liturgy of St. John Chrysostom has commemorations in other parts of the Liturgy, as in the Proskomide, the ektenes and the Great Entrance. However, those in the Anaphora have a special meaning and distinct character, i.e., a *sacrificial* character—is an application of the Eucharistic Sacrifice to the various categories of people.

The purpose of Christ's sacrificing Himself on the cross was *to redeem mankind.* Christ's death reconciled mankind to God and secured grace for man. The Eucharistic Sacrifice has the same purpose; it is a sacrifice for the people. The Lamb of God is mystically slain "for the remission of the sins" of mankind. Hence, it is not surprising that, after the Consecration, the commemoration of the redemption in the Anamnesis, and the acceptance of the Eucharistic Sacrifice by God in the Epiklesis, the Church interceeds for all the members of the Mystical Body of Christ. At this moment the Church does not pray alone, but with Her also prays the Lamb of God who, having been mystically slain, is present on the altar. Hence, the Eucharistic commemoration, as we have said, has a sacrificial character which makes it different from the other commemorations of the Liturgy, which have only the character of supplication and petition.

---

2 See Chapter 10, 5; Tosti, La *"Didache"*, pp. 84–85.

3 Cf. 65th chapter of the *Apology.*

4 Migne, PG, 33, 1116–1117, (5th *Mystagogical Catechesis*).

5 *Ibid.*, 48, 680–681; 50, 602; 61, 361.

6 Cf. VIII book, 12th chapter (Funk, *Didascalia et Const.* Ap., I, pp. 510–515).

The Eucharistic commemorations are indeed the primitive commemorations. They served as a model for the commemorations of the Proskomide and the Great Entrance. Most likely the diptychs were read during the Anaphora in the first centuries. This is evident from the rubrics in our Liturgy which after the acclamation: "Among the first remember" prescribe that the deacon commemorate the living.[7]

B. The Commemoration of the Saints

When comparing the commemoration of the saints, in the Anaphora with that of the Proskomide, we find that the former as opposed to the latter, does not enumerate the names of individual Saints, but only mentions the various categories or classes of Saints. This general form of commemoration in the Anaphora is proof that it is of earlier date than those of the Proskomide. Only the Blessed Virgin Mary, St. John the Baptist and the saint of the day are individually named in the Anaphora. The text of the commemoration of Saints is as follows:

> Again we offer Thee this reasonable worship for those who have departed in the faith, forefathers, fathers, patriarchs, prophets, apostles, preachers, evangelists, martyrs, confessors, ascetics, and for every righteous spirit who hath died in the faith. Especially four our most holy, most pure, most blessed, glorious Lady, Mother of God and ever-virgin Mary. For holy John, the Prophet, Forerunner and Baptist; for the holy, glorious and all laudable Apostles; for Saint N . . . whose memory we commemorate; and all Thy Saints; through whose prayers look down upon us, O God.

From among the host of saints, "who died in the faith" namely, those who have been saved through faith, the Church singles out the Blessed Virgin Mary, John the Baptist and the Apostles. The Blessed Virgin Mary is set apart from the rest, because of her great role in the redemption.[8] The priest reads here name aloud. After the Blessed Virgin Mary comes St. John the Baptist who was the precursor of the Savior and the greatest saint of the Old Testament, and then the Apostles who preached Christ's doctrine throughout the world. The Blessed Virgin Mary, John the Baptist and the Apostles were connected in a very special way with Christ and the work of salvation; for this reason they are deserving of special place and mention in the Sacrifice of the Holy Eucharist.[9]

What is the character of the commemoration of the saints? Why are they commemorated in the Anaphora?

---

[7] Cf. the 1940 Roman edition of the Sluzhebnyk.

[8] Here the people sing the Mariological hymn: "Dostoyno yest . . .," or another Marian hymn suitable to the holyday. The hymn is a glorification of the Blessed Virgin Mary, of her part in the work of redemption. This hymn is also sung to give the priest ample time to continue the silent prayer of commemoration and to fill in the pause.

[9] The icon of supplication (intercession) or "deisis" originated from this liturgical commemoration of the Blessed Virgin Mary, the Precursor and the Apostles; this icon is commonly found on the iconastasis and it portrays Christ on the throne with the Blessed Virgin Mary on His right, St. John the Baptist and the Apostles on the left, all interceding for mankind.

The assertion of certain Orthodox theologians that the Church prays for the saints in order that God may increase their glory and holiness can hardly be accepted.[10] The Liturgy cannot pray for the sanctification of those who already possess God and live in a state of perfection and sanctity. Since they are already contemplating God, such a prayer would be superfluous and pointless. The Church commemorates the saints in the Anaphora, to thank God for their holiness, for the graces which He bestowed upon them. The Church also commemorates them in order that "through their prayers God may look down upon us." The commemoration of the saints is therefore, 1. *a prayer of thanksgiving* for the success of Christ's sacrifice as manifested in the salvation and sanctification of the saints, and at the same time 2. *a petition* that the work of redemption be actualized, that it find its realization in us.

C. The Commemoration of the Dead

Following the commemoration of the saints is the commemoration of the dead. Although the two commemorations are component parts of the same prayer, the Liturgy draws a distinctive line between them:

> And remember all those who have departed in the hope of resurrection to life eternal.[11]—And give them rest where shines the light of Thy countenance.

The commemoration of the saints differs from that of the deceased in that the saints are called "those departed in faith" while the dead are called "those departed in the hope of resurrection to life eternal." In other words, the Liturgy remembers the saints, who have already obtained eternal life through faith, who already are contemplating God and who are in the position to intercede to God for us. But as for the departed souls, the Liturgy prays for them as for those who have not yet been admitted to the beatific contemplation of God, who are not yet in the kingdom of heaven, who have not joined the countless cast of the happy souls. Hence, the Liturgy prays to God to give them "eternal rest" or to open to them the gates of heaven after they have been cleansed of their sins.

From the words of the Liturgy we find an unequivocal belief in the existence of life beyond the grave, with an intermediary state between that of the saints and that of the reprobates, i.e., *purgatory*, where, according to the doctrine of the Catholic Church, souls are purified by expiating their sins in order that they can be admitted into heaven pure and undefiled to contemplate God face to face.

D. The Commemoration of the Living

Of the Eucharistic commemorations, the commemoration of the living is the longest. The commemoration of the Church hierarchy throughout the world

---

[10] Cf. *Simeon of Thessalonica;* Migne, PG, 155, 282.

[11] Here the priest remembers by name the deceased if he so desires.

occupies first place. Then follows the prayer for the universal Church and civil authority. The head of the universal Church and the local hierarchy are mentioned aloud by the priest. Finally he remembers the particular locality and the different needs of the people:

> Again we beseech Thee, remember, O Lord, every episcopacy of the orthodox rightly dispensing the word of Thy truth; every priesthood, the diaconate in Christ, and every sacerdotal order.[12]

The hierarchy occupies first place in the diptychs of the living because it constitutes Christ's teaching Church which continues the work Christ entrusted to His Apostles, that is, the work of preaching the Gospel throughout the world. The phrase "dispensing the word" is taken from St. Paul, who exhorted Timothy, to strive to "be the workman that needeth not to be ashamed, rightly handling the word of truth"[13] in his apostolic work.

The commemoration goes on to remember Christ's entire Church:

> Again we offer Thee this reasonable worship for the whole world, for the holy, catholic and apostolic church, for those who lead a chaste and honorable life. . . .

Here the Liturgy intercedes for all members of the Mystical Body of Christ. The monastic state is mentioned separately, namely, those who have dedicated their lives to God "in chastity and righteousness." The prayer for the Church perhaps is the oldest of all commemorations. We find it in the *Didache*:[14]

> Remember, Lord, Thy Church, deliver it from all evil. Perfect it in Thy love, gather her from the four corners of the world,[15] into your kingdom, which Thou have prepared for her.

To the prayer for the Church is added the prayer for civil authority:

> for our God-protected Sovereign (or King) N . . ., and for all the reigning house; for our government and for all the armed forces. Grant (him) them, O Lord, a peaceful reign, that we also in (his) their peace may lead a quiet and tranquil life in all piety and honesty.

These are words taken from St. Paul.[16] They unveil the true and original meaning of the prayer for civil authorities. The Church prays for those who are the rulers of the country, that they may promote the well-being of the Church and not persecute it.

Immediately after the commemoration of the civil authorities, the priest mentions the Head of the Church and the local hierarchy aloud:

> Among the first remember, O Lord, our holy, universal Supreme Pontiff N . . ., Pope of Rome, our most reverend Archbishop and Metropolitan N . . .,

---

12 That is, the entire clergy or those belonging to the religious state.
13 2 Tim, 2:15.
14 Tosti, (*La "Didache"*), pp. 84–85.
15 This means: "from the four corners of the earth."
16 1. Tim. 2:2.

our God-loving Bishop N . . .; preserve them for Thy holy Churches in peace, in safety, in honor, in health, in length of days, rightly dispensing the word of Thy truth.[17]

While saying the words "in peace" and "in safety" we recall the severe persecutions the Church suffered in the first centuries of Christianity and is still suffering. These words will always be pertinent, for the Church, according to the prediction of Her Divine Founder, will never be free of persecutions by the "powers of the world."

Finally, the different types of needy people are remembered:

Remember, O Lord, this city, wherein we dwell, (or this village, wherein we dwell, or this monastery, wherein we dwell), and every city and country, and those who with faith dwell therein. Remember, O Lord, the voyaging, the traveling, the sick, the suffering, the imprisoned, and their salvation. Remember, O Lord, those who offer fruits and do good in Thy holy churches, and those who remember the poor; and upon all of us send down Thy mercies.

The last supplications recall the petitions of the Great Ektene, which perhaps developed from the individual commemorations of the Anaphora. The antiquity of this prayer is evident from the words: "Remember, O Lord, those who offer fruits and do good in Thy holy churches . . . " which point to an origin during the time when the custom of gift offering in the churches prevailed. The faithful brought to church the fruits of the earth for the support of the clergy and the indigent.

The prayers for various needs and different classes of people are eloquent especially in the Liturgy of St. Basil. Here the priest prays that God bestow upon the faithful abundant graces:

Fill their treasuries with every good thing; maintain their marriage-bond in peace and concord; rear the infants; guide the young; support the aged; encourage the faint-hearted. Collect the scattered, and turn them from their wandering astray, and unite them to Thy Holy Catholic and Apostolic Church. Set at liberty those who are vexed by unclean spirits; voyage with those who voyage, journey with those who journey; defend the widows; protect the orphans; free the captives; heal the sick. Remember, O God, those who are under trial, and in the mines, and in prison, and in bitter labors, and in all affliction, distress and tribulations;

Remember, O God, all those who invoke Thy great loving-kindness; those also who loved us, and those who hate us, and those who have enjoined us, unworthy though we are, that we should pray for them; and all Thy people, O Lord our God: and upon them all pour out Thy rich mercy,

---

[17] Here the people respond, "i vsikh i vsya" *(kai panton kai pason)*, i.e. "all (men) and all (women)." These words do not refer to the last words of the commemoration of the Church hierarchy, for it is composed of men only, but it must be considered rather the conclusion of the diptychs, which once were read here. The priest (or deacon) read from the diptychs the names of various people, and the faithful would add "all (men) and all (women)" whom they wished to commend to God.

granting unto all such of their petitions as are unto salvation. And those whom we, through ignorance, or forgetfulness, or the multitude of names, have not remembered, do Thou Thyself call to mind, O God, who knowest the age and the name of each, and knowest every man even from his mother's womb. For Thou, O Lord, art the Helper of the helpless, the Hope of the hopeless, the Savior of the storm-tossed, the Haven of the voyager, the Healer of the sick. Be Thyself all things unto all men, O Thou who knowest every man, his petition, his abode, and his need. Deliver, O Lord, this city, and every city and land from famine, plague, earthquake, flood, fire, sword, the invasion of enemies, and from civil war.[18]

The Church does not overlook anyone. Offering the Body and Blood of Jesus Christ the Church cannot overlook anyone. She mentions the daily adversities and needs of the people and sanctifies them by prayer. She encompasses in her prayers the sufferings of the people, the supplications of the poor and needy, the aged, youth, children, vows of virgins, the prayers of widows and the injuries done to orphans;[19] all these needs and wants she places upon the altar and offers to God as a sacrifice, so that the blessing of God may flow upon all, so that they may unite with Christ's sacrifice and in this way attain perfection, and undergo a spiritual transformation and divinization.

The prayer of commemoration places before God all the various needs of mankind. The priest stands before the Lamb of God slaughtered upon the altar and surrounded by the countless saints, the departed and the living. This great assembly together with the priest forms one potent prayer. Heaven and earth unite in offering a prayer to God through the lips of the priest.

E. *"The Service of words"*

This phrase recurs three times during the Anaphora: once during the Epiklesis and twice during the Eucharistic Commemoration. How is this phrase to be understood? Why is the Eucharistic Sacrifice called "a verbal service?" or "the service of words?"

The Slavonic wording of this phrase is very misleading. The phrase *"Slovesnaya sluzhba"* is tantamount to the Greek phrase: *logike tisia*. The word *logikos* may be translated as either "verbal" or spiritual." The latter meaning is preferable because it alone is properly related to the Eucharistic Sacrifice.

Bishop Bessarion translates these words altogether incorrectly. He says: "We further offer Thee, Father, this verbal and Unbloody Service, i.e. the service of sacrifice, which is performed by virtue of mysterious words."[20] Bessarion follows Cabasilas who understood the words "verbal service" as " a service which is performed by virtue of priestly words." The sacrificial offering, according to Cabasilas, is called "verbal service" because the priest who offers it does not offer it by

[18] Cf. also the Eucharistic commemoration in the Liturgy of St. James, which is very similar in wording and style to the Liturgy of St. Basil.
[19] Cfr. Archimandrite Cyprian for the prayer of St. Ambrose, (*Evkharistiya*, pp. 28 and 290).
[20] See his *"Tolkovanie na bozh. Liturghiyu"*, p. 224.

an action or gesture but by uttering words, i.e., the words of consecration, for etiologically speaking God is responsible for the miracle of transubstantiation. The priest only pronounces words, hence, the phrase "verbal service," whereas, during the Proskomide, besides prayer, the offering of sacrifice is carried out by an act (i.e., an act of cutting out the Lamb). This first service Cabasilas calls "active service" (*"praktike latria,"* not a service involving only words, like prayer, but also action) which he places in opposition to the "verbal service" of Anaphora (service of prayer or word) [21] This interpretation, however, cannot withstand criticism. The words in the Anaphora are far older than the rite of Proskomide and the "active service" of the gift offering. There cannot be any question of the verbal sacrificial character of the consecration in contradistinction to the "active" character of the Proskomide. The Anaphora and "the verbal service" existed before the Proskomide or "active service" (for example, the cutting out of the Lamb and all the other related ritual functions). Although it is true that no ordinary man or priest is the cause of the Eucharistic change, nevertheless, it is not because of this that the Eucharistic Sacrifice is called a "verbal service."

"Verbal service" again does not mean the "service of the Word" or the sacrifice of the Only-begotten, the Word of God, for then in the Greek original it would have to be not *"logike latreia"* but *"latreia tou logou."*

"Verbal service" means nothing else but "rational, spiritual service." Even in the Roman Liturgy the sacrifice of the Body and Blood of Jesus Christ is called a "rational service." [22] The Unbloody service is called "rational" or "spiritual" to distinguish the Christian sacrifice of the Liturgy from the material sacrifices of the pagans and the Old Testament. The pagan and Jewish sacrifices were bloody and material; goats, calves, rams, oxen and other animals were offered to God in sacrifice. They were slaughtered and burnt. The sacrifice of the New Testament has nothing in common with these material and bloody sacrifices. In comparison to them it is a "pure" [23] sacrifice, not a material but a spiritual, divine sacrifice.

That the word "verbal" is to be translated as "rational and spiritual" is proven in the New Testament where the word *logikos* is used in the sense given above. Thus, St. Paul uses this word in his epistle to the Romans [24] and St. Peter in his,[25] both taking the word *logikos* as meaning "spiritual," "rational," "immaterial." This meaning of *logikos* is derived from Greek philosophy. Among the philosophers, *logos* signifies "reason," "soul," the spiritual element of the cosmos, "the soul of the universe." [26] Philo, the first-century Jewish philosopher, employs

[21] Migne, PG, 150, 485–486.

[22] "Oblatio rationabilis," See the articles of O. Casel in the bibliography.

[23] See the prophecy of Malachias, 1, 10, where the prophet called the Eucharistic sacrifice "a pure offering."

[24] Rom 12:1.

[25] Pet 2:2 and 2:5.

[26] E.g. the philosophy of the Stoics.

the word in this meaning, and it was taken in this sense in the Greek mystical-hermetic writings.[27] Therefore, it should not come as a surprise that the word with this same meaning found its way into the works of the Fathers, and finally, into the Liturgy.[28]

9. Conclusion of the Anaphora

The Anaphora closes, as in all the other Liturgies, with the doxology:

> And grant us with one mouth and one heart to glorify and praise Thy most honorable and magnificent name, of the Father, and of the Son, and of the Holy Spirit, now and ever, and unto ages of ages. Amen.

To this conclusion is added the final "peace greeting," and invocation of God's blessing:

> And may the mercies of the great God and our Savior Jesus Christ be with you all.

And the people respond: "And with Thy spirit."

This last part of the Anaphora is called by liturgists the "final doxology."[1] It probably comes from the Apostolic Age. All Liturgies have it. It undoubtedly had its origin in the injunction of St. Paul "to do all things for the greater glory of God." (1 Cor. 10:31) St. Paul always ended his letters, even the more important parts of the letter, with the doxology.[2] It was natural for the Christians to conclude the Eucharistic Sacrifice by glorifying God.

The doxology is a logical complement to the Anaphora in which the glorification of God was paramount. The glorification of God and thanksgiving was one of the themes of the Anaphora which the priest began with a hymn of praise, always mindful that the Eucharistic offering is a "sacrifice of praise."

The final "peace greeting" expresses well the character of the Eucharistic Sacrifice. It is not only a "sacrifice of praise," but also of the "mercy of peace" for the faithful which was mentioned in the Eucharistic dialogue. The theme of the Eucharistic Sacrifice is the revelation of God's mercy which was so clearly manifested in the love of God the Father who sent His Only-begotten Son into the world to save it from perdition. The Eucharistic Sacrifice is a memorial and renewal of the work of the redemption. His mercy revealed itself also in the sanctification of the Saints, as was mentioned in the prayer of commemoration. We find God's mercy manifested in the souls in purgatory and those living on earth, who are "awaiting the great and rich mercy of God."

---

[27] Lietzmann, H., *An die Roemer, Kommentar,* pp. 108–109.

[28] O. Casel, *Oblatio rationabilis,* (Tuebingen Theol. Quartal., 99 (1917–1918), pp. 429–439) ; ———, *Quam oblationem,* (Jahr. f. Liturgiewissenschaft, 2, (1922), pp. 98–101) ; ———, *Die "Logike tisia" der antiken Mystik in christlich-liturgischer Umdetung,* (Jahr, f. Liturgiewissenschaft, 4, (1924). pp. 37–47).

[1] Hanssens, *Inst. liturg.,* III, p. 481: *extrema doxologia.*

[2] See Rom, 11:36, and other places.

Thus to these concluding prayers of the Anaphora, converge all the purposes of Eucharistic Sacrifice which are called the fruits of the sacrifice. The Eucharistic Sacrifice is (1) a sacrifice of praise, (2) sacrifice of thanksgiving, (3) reconciliation, and (4) petition. The first two purposes are expressed with a doxological formula, and the last two with a blessing. The Eucharistic Sacrifice is, therefore, the best way to praise and to thank God; it is the most efficacious prayer of petition and contrition. Here the Lamb of God Himself praises, expresses thanks, asks for forgiveness and prays with us. He gives Himself up to be slaughtered on the altar as "the mercy of peace" and "sacrifice of praise."

The Anaphora is in itself a harmonious whole. Not only in significance and value is it the focal point of the whole Liturgy, but also in its structure which is remarkable for its harmony and consistency.

All the constituent parts of the Anaphora converge toward its center—the Eucharistic Prayer together with the words of consecration. The prologue to this masterpiece is the Eucharistic dialogue, which, after the fashion of a musical overture, leads both priest and faithful into the sphere of mystery. The prayer of praise and thanksgiving recalls the works of God (creation, redemption). The Anamnesis after the Consecration has the same purpose: It refers Christ's Sacrifice to the entire work of the redemption and is the formal sacrifice of thanksgiving for all God did for mankind. In the prayer of the Epiklesis the Liturgy begs God to accept the Unbloody Sacrifice for all those for whom it prays. Finally, it concludes with the glorification of God and an appeal to His mercy.

The Anaphora is a masterpiece which can scarcely be compared with any other part of the Byzantine Liturgy. On it is the imprint of ancient Greek genius so sensitive to beauty, harmony and art in general. Since the fourth century this masterpiece has been preserved practically unaltered to our day, and one must acknowledge with satisfaction that later insertions and changes have been so insignificant as not to mar its beauty and harmony, as happened with the other parts of the Liturgy. The masterpiece still remains a masterpiece!

SELECT BIBLIOGRAPHY

I. *Anaphora:*

Karabinov, J. A., *Evkharisticheskaya molitva (Anaphora)* , SPB., 1908.

Zhurakovskiy, A., *Liturghicheskiy kanon teper i prezhde.* (K voprosu o tserkovnoy reformye) (Khrist. Misl, Kiev 1917, September-October) .

Sove, B. J., *Evkharistiya v drevney tserkvi i sovremennaya praktika,* (Zhivoe Predanie, Paris, 1937, pp. 171–195).

Golubtsov, A. P., *Liturghiya v pervie vyeka khristiyanstva,* (Bog. Vyestnik, 1913, iyul, pp. 621–643; noyabr, pp. 332–356; dekabr, pp. 779–802).

Gumilevskiy, J., *Apostolskoe ponimanie bogosluzhebnaho china,* (Bog. Vyestnik, 1913, fevral, pp. 250–264).

Arnold, A., *Der Ursprung des christlichen Abendmahls,* Freiburg, 1937.

Bickell, G., *Messe und Pascha, Der apostolische Ursprung der Messliturgie und ihr genauer Anschluss an die Einsetzungsfeier der hl. Eucharistie durch Christus aus dem Pascharitus nachgewiesen,* Mainz, 1872.

———*Die Entstehung der Liturgie aus der Einsetzungsfeier,* (Zeitschrift fuer Kathol. Theologie, IV, 1880).

Goltz von Der, *Das Gebet in der aeltesten Christenheit.* Eine geschichtliche-Untersuchung, Leipzig, 1901.

———*Tischgebete und Abendmahlsgebete in der altchristlichen und in der griechischen Kirche,* Leipzig, 1905.

Goetz, K. G., *Die Abendmahlsfrage in ihrer geschichtlichen Entwicklung,* Leipzig, 1904.

Lietzmann, H., *Messe und Herrenmahl. Eine Studie zur Geschichte der Liturgie,* Bonn, 1926.

Barth, M., *Das Abendmahl—Paschmahl, Bundesmahl und Messiasmahl,* (Theol. Studien, Heft 18), Zuerich, 1945.

Berning, W., *Die Einsetzung der heiligen Eucharistie,* Muenster, 1901.

Cullmann, O., *Urchristentum und Gottesdienst,* (Abhandlungen zur Theol. des A. u. N. Testam., no. 3, 1944).

Dibelius, F., *Das Abendmahl,* Leipzig, 1911.

Hoffmann, J., *Das Abendmahl im Urchristentum,* Berlin, 1903.

Oesterley, W. O. E., *The Jewish Background of Christian Liturgy,* Oxford, 1925.

Dugmore, C. W., *The influence of the Synagogue upon the divine office,* London, 1945.

Holtzmann, O., *Das Abendmahl im Urchristentum,* Zeitschr. f. kath. Theol. V. (1904).

———*Der Hebraeerbrief und das Abendmahl,* (ibid., 1909).

Juelicher, *Zue Geschichte der Abendmahlsfeier in der aeltesten Kirche,* Freiburg in Br., 1892.

Spitta, *Die urchristliche Tradition ueber Ursprung des Abendmahls,* Goettingen, 1893.

Lohmeyer, E., *Vom urchristlichen Abendmahl,* (Theol. Rundschau, Neue Folge, 1937, pp. 168–207; 273–314; 1938, pp. 81–99).

Schweitzer, E., *Das Abendmahl eine Vergegenwaertigung des Todes Jesu oder ein eschatologishes Freudenmahl,* (Theol. Zeitschr. Univ. Basel, März-April 1946, pp. 81–101).

Skene, W. F., *The Lord's Supper and the passover ritual,* Edinburgh, 1891.

Andersen, *Das Abendmahl in den zwei ersten Jahrhunderten nach Christus,* Giessen, 1904.

Woolly, *The Liturgy of the primitive Church,* Cambridge, 1910.

Warren, *The Liturgy and the ritual of the antinicene Church,* London, 1904.

Probst, F., *Liturgie der drei ersten christlichen Jahrhunderten,* Tuebingen, 1870.

Cagin, Dom P., OSB, *L'Anaphore apostolique et ses temoins,* Paris, 1919, et *L'Eucharistia. Canon primitiv de la messe,* Rome, 1912.

Goguel, M., *L'Eucharistie des origines a Justin Martyr,* Paris, 1910.

Drews, P., *Untersuchungen ueber die sogenannte Clementinische Liturgie im VIII Buch der Ap. Konstitutionen,* Tuebingen, 1908.

Frere, W. F., *The Anaphora or great eucharistic Prayer,* London, 1938.

Dix, Dom Gr., *The shape of the liturgy,* London, 1945.

———*The Apostolic Tradition,* London, 1937.

Wordsworth, *Bishop Serapion's Prayerbooks,* London, 1910.

Engberding, P. H., *Das eucharistische Hochgebet der Basiliusliturgie,* Muenster, 1931.

Brightman, F. E., *The sacramentary of Serapion of Thmuis,* (Journal of theolog. Stud. 1899, Oct. 88–113; 1900, Jan., 247–277).

Schermann, T., *Der liturgische Papyrus von Deir-Balizeh,* Leipzig 1910;—*Fruehchristliche Liturgien,* Paderborn, 1915.

Ruecker, A., *Die syrische Jakobusanaphora nach der Rezension des Jaquobh von Edesse,* (Liturg. Forschungen, IV), Muenster, 1923.

Mercier, B., *La liturgie de saint Jaques,* (Ed. critique du texte grec avec traduction latine), (Patr. Or. (R. Graffin), Vol. XXVI, Fasc. 2), Paris, 1946.

II. *Epiklesis:*

The following are the works of Catholic, Orthodox and Protestant authors:

Atchley, C., *The epiclesis*, (Theology, 3, (1921), pp. 90–98).

Baurain, L., *L'Epiclese*, (Revue Augustinienne, I, Paris, 1902, 460 ss).

———, *A propos de l'epiclese* (ibid. IX (1906), 85 ss).

Batareith, *La forme consecratoire de l'eucharistie d'apres qualques manuscrits grecs*, (Revue de l'Orient chret., VIII, pp. 459–476).

Batiffol, B., *La question de l'epiclese eucharistique* (Revue du clerge français, LVI (Paris, 1908) 4, p. 641 ss).

———, *L'eucharistie, la presence reelle et la transubstantiation*, Paris, 1913.

———, *Lecons sur la Messe,* Paris 1919.

Baumstark, A., *Le liturgie orientali e le preghiere "Supra quae" e "Supplices" del Canone Romano*, Grottaferrata, 1913.

———, *Zu den Problemen der Epiklese und des roemischen Messkanons*, (Theol. Revue, XV (Muenster, 1916, 337 ss).

Berning, W. *Die Einsetzung der Eucharistie in ihrer urspruenglicher Form*, Muenster, 1901.

Bessarion, Card., *De sacramento Eucharistiae;* Migne PG, 161, 494 ss.

Bishop W. C., *The primitive form of the consecration of the holy Eucharist*, (Church Quarterly Revue, 66 (London, 1908), pp. 384–440).

Bougeant, *Traite theologique sur la forme de la consecration de l'eucharistie*, Lyon et Paris, 1729.

Brightman, F., *Invocation in the Holy Eucharist*, (Theology, 9 (1924), pp. 33–40).

Brinktrine, I., *Zur Entstehung der morgenlaendischen Epiklese*, (Zeitschrift fuer kath. Theologie, 42 (1918), 301 ss; 483 ss).

———, *De epiclesis eucharistiae origine et explicatione*, Romae, 1923.

Buchwald, A., *Die Epiklese in der roemischen Messe*, Wien, 1907.

Cabrol, F., *Epiclese*, (Dict. d'Archeol. chret. et de liturgie, V, col. 142–184).

———, *Eucharistie*, (Ibid. DACL, V. (1922), col. 686 ss).

Cagin, *L'Eucharistie*, Paris, 1912.

Casel Odo, *Zur Epiklese* (Jahrbuch f. Liturgiewissenschaft, III (1923), pp. 100–102).

———, *Neue Beitraege zur Epiklesenfrage* (Jahrb. f. Liturg., IV, (1924), pp. 169–178).

Connolly, R. H., *On the meaning of Epiclesis*, (The Downside Review, 1923, 28–43).

Cieplak, I., *De momento, quo Transsubstantiatio in augustissimo Missae sacrificio peragitur*, Petropoli, 1901.

Franz, I. T., *Die eucharistische Wandlung und die Epiklese der griechischen und orientalischen Liturgien*, 2 vol., Wuerzburg, 1880.

Goeken, B., *Die eucharistische Epiklesis in ihrem Verhaeltnis zu den Einsetzungsworten* (Zeitschr. f. kath. Theol. 21 (1897), 372 ss).

Grube, *De forma consecrationis eucharisticae*, Londini, 1721.

Halushchynsky, M., *De nova illustratione epicleseos ex liturgia ecclesiae orientalis, praecipue graecae et russicae petita* (Acta I, Conv. Velehr., Pragae, 1908, 56 ss).

Harapin, T., *Epikleza s povjesnog i teoloskog gledista*, (Bogoslovska Smotra, 13 (1925, Zagreb), 262 ss 395ss).

Henke, C., *Die katholische Lehre ueber die Konsekrationsworte der hl. Eucharistie*, Trier, 1850.

Hoeller, I., *Die Epiklese der griechisch-orientalischn Liturgien*, Wien, 1912.

———, *Die Stellung der Paepste zur Epiklese der griechisch-orientalischen Liturgien*, (Theol. praktische Qrartalschrift, 66 (Linz, 1913), 315 ss).

Hoppe, L. A., *Die Epiklesis der griechischen und orientalischen Liturgien*, Schaffhausen, 1864.

Hunkin, J. W., *The invocation of the Holy Spirit in the Prayer of the Consecration*, Cambridge, 1927.

Jugie, M., *Theologia dogmatica christianorum orientalium ab ecclesia catholica dissidentium*, III, vol., Parisiis, 1930.

———, *Considerations generals sur la question le l'epiclese,* (Echos d'Orient, 35, pp. 324–330).

———, *L'epiclese et le mot antivype dela messe de saint Basile,* (Echos d'Orient, 9, pp. 193–198) .

———, *De sensu epicleseos iuxta Germanum Constantinopolitanum,* (Slavorum litterae theologicae, IV, (Pragae 1908), 385 ss).

———, *De forma Eucharistiae. De epiclesibus eucharisticis,* Romae 1943.

Kostelnyk, H., *Spir pro epiklezu mizh Skhodom i Zakhodom,* Lviv, 1928, (vidbytka z "Nyvy").

Cyprian Arkhim, *Epikliza u alexandriskim liturghiyama,* ("Bogoslovlye"), Beograd, 1932.

———, *Epikliza u vizantiskim liturghiyama* ("Kh. Delo'), Skople, 1939.

———, *Epikliza u prvim kh. liturghiyama,* ("Bohoslovle"), Beograd, 1933.

Karabinov, J., *Evkharisticheskaya molitva* SPB., 1908.

Le Bachalet, *Consecration et l'epiclese,* (Etudes, 75, 1898).

Lingens, E., *Die eucharistische Consecrationsform,* (Zeitschr. f. kath. Theol., 1897, 51–106).

———, *Zur Erklaerung der eucharistischen Epiklese,* (Zeitschrift. f. kath. Theol., 1896, 743 ss.).

Lisowski, F., *Slowa ustanowienia najsw. sakramentu a epikleza,* Lwow, 1912.

Lotocky, I., *Der Heilige Geist in den byzantinischen Liturgie. Ein liturgischdogmatischer Versuch,* Wien, 1945, (Inaugural-Dissertation).

Malakhov, V., *Presushchestvlemye sv. Darov v tayinstyve Eckharistiyi,* (Bogosl. Vyestnik, VII (1898), 2, 298 ss; 3, 113 ss).

Maltsev, A., *Liturgikon,* Berlin, 1902, (418–438).

———, *De vestigiis epicleseos in missa Romana,* (Acta II, Conv. Velehr., Pragae 1910, 135 ss).

———, *O sledach prizyvaniya sv. Dukha v modlityve rimskoy liturghiyi: Iube haec preferri,* (Khrist. Chteniye, 90, (1910), 2, 1412–1428).

Markovich, I., *O eucharistiyi s osobitim obzirom na epiklezu,* Zagreb, 1893.

Marcus Eugenicus, *Quod non solum a voce dominicorum verborum sanctificatur divina dona,* (Graffin-Nau, Patrol. Orient., 17 (Parisiis, 1923, 463 ss).

Maximilianus de Saxonia, *Pensees sur la question de l'union des Eglises,* (Roma e l'Oriente, I, (Grottaferrata, 1910) 13 ss, 76 ss).

Merk, K. I., *Die Epiklese,* (Theol. Quartalschrift, 96 (Tuebigen, 1914), 367 ss).

Mihalyfi, A., *Epiklezis,* Budapest, 1908.

Mirkovich, G., *O vremeni presushchestvleniya sv. Darov,* Vilno, 1886.

Orsi, A., *Dissertatio theologica de invocatione Spiritus Sancti in liturgiis,* Mediolani, 1731.

Peterson, E., *Die Bedeutung von anadeiknymi in den griechischen Liturgien* (Festgabe f. Ad. Deissmann zum 60. Beburtstag, 320–326), Tuebingen, 1927.

Popovichu, N., *Epicleza eucharistica,* Sibiu, 1933.

Rauschen, G., *Eucharistie und Bussakrament,* Freiburg in Br., 1901.

Russnak, N., *Epiklezis,* Prjasev, 1926.

Safonovich, T., *Vyklad o tserkvi svyatoy,* Kiev, 1668.

Salaville, S., *Epiclese eucharistique,* (Dict. de Theol. catholique, V (Paris 1913), 194–300).

———, *Les fondements scripturaeires de l'epiclese,* (Echos d'Or., 12 (1909), 1 ss).

———, *La liturgie decrite par S. Justine et l'epiclese,* (Echos d'Or., 12 (1909), 129 ss., 222 ss).

———,*L'Epiclese d'apres saint Jean Chrysostome et la tradition occidental,* (Echos d'Or., 11 (1908), 101–112).

———, *La consecration eucharistique d'apres quelques auters grecs et syriens,* (Echos d'Or, 13 (1910), 321 ss).

———, *Consecration et epiclese d'apres Chosrov le Grand,* (Echos d'Or., 16 (1913), 10 ss).

———, *L'epiclese africaine,* (Echos d'Or., 39, pp. 268–282).

———, *La double epiclese des anaphores egyptiennes,* (Echos d'Or., 13 (1910), pp. 133–134).

———, *Consecration et epiclese dans L'eglise armenienne au XII, siecle,* (Echos d'Or., 16 (1913, 28–31).

———, *Doctrina de Spiritu S. ex Filio processione in quibusdam syriacis epicleseos formulis aliisque documentis,* (Slavorum litterae theologicae, V, Pragae, 1909) 165 ss).

———, *L'epiclesis dans le Canon Romain de la Messe,* (Revue augustinienne, 14 (Paris 1909), I, 303 ss).

Spacil, T., *Doctrina theologica Orientis separati de Ss. Eucharistia*, (2 vol.), Romae, 1928–1929, (Orient. Christiana, 48, 52).

———, *Lis de epiclesi*, (Orient. Christ., 16 (1929), 99–114).

Swiatkowski, Z., *Ojcowie kosciola i epikleza eucharystyczna*, Chicago, 1914.

Smolikowksi, *Epiklesis seu de invocatione Spiritus Sancti post consecrationem in liturgiis orientalibus*, (Analecta ecclesiastica, I, (Romae, 1893), 282 ss).

Tyrer, J. W., *The eucharistic epiclesis*, Liverpool, 1917.

Varaine, F., *L'Epiclese eucharistique*, Brignais, 1910.

Vandik, S., *De apparatu liturgico circa verba Domini et epiclesim in Anaphora Byzantina*, Romae, 1945 (Dissertatio ad Lauream).

Watterich, I., *Der Konsecrationsmoment im hl. Abendmahl und seine Geschichte*, Heidelberg, 1896.

———, *Der Streit um die Konsecrationsform auf dem Konzil zu Florenz*, (Revue intern. de Theologie, IV, (Berne, 1896), pp. 538 ss).

Chapter IV

THE CONSUMPTION OF
THE EUCHARISTIC SACRIFICE

(The Third Part of the Liturgy of the Faithful)

Introduction

The last part of the Liturgy of the Faithful is the rite of Holy Communion or the consumption of the Eucharistic Sacrifice. We call this part of the Liturgy of the Faithful "the consumption of the Eucharistic Sacrifice" because the sacrificial gifts, the Body and Blood of Jesus Christ, are consumed.

Holy Communion is the natural fulfillment and consummation of the Eucharistic Sacrifice—they are interrelated and mutual complements. From the very outset we must in our commentary on Holy Communion draw attention to the distinct character and historical evolution of the rite of consuming the sacrifice.

a) *The Character of the rite of consuming the sacrifice.* The consumption of the Sacrificial Gifts belongs by its very nature to the rite of the sacrifice. The consecration of the Eucharistic gifts, which takes place during the Anaphora, is a rite of the Unbloody Sacrifice of the New Testament. The moment the Eucharistic consecration occurs, the Unbloody Sacrifice is fulfilled and completed. The Liturgy, however, is not only a sacrifice, it is also a sacrament. The Holy Eucharist, according to the doctrine of the Church, is one of the seven sacraments instituted by Jesus Christ as a source of grace and divine life. Christ instituted the Holy Eucharist not only as a sacrifice of the New Testament but also as a sacrament whereby the faithful receive, under the appearance of bread and wine, the Body and Blood of Christ, thereby becoming partakers of the supernatural life of God.

Ordinarily we do not draw a distinction between the Holy Eucharist as a sacrifice and the Holy Eucharist as a sacrament because these different aspects are not so noticeable. For us the Liturgy is one priestly function where Christ offers Himself up as a sacrifice for us and gives His Body and Blood as food. From the theological point of view, however, there exists an essential distinction between the Holy Eucharist as a sacrifice and as a sacrament. This essential difference lies in their distinct characters.

According to the theologians, the Liturgy, taken as a sacrifice, is consummated during the Consecration. The moment the words of Consecration are pronounced and the bread and the wine are changed into the Body and Blood of Christ, the Eucharist as a sacrifice is completed. From this it follows that the rite of Holy Communion, or the rite of consuming the sacrifice, although necessary, does not belong to the very essence of sacrifice. This is a distinct liturgical rite, which does not enter into the general concept of sacrifice nor the Eucharistic Sacrifice in particular. Still it is a complement to or the consummation of the Eucharistic Sacrifice.[1]

Although the rite of Holy Communion is not an essential part of the Eucharistic Sacrifice, it does not follow that, in the Liturgy taken as a whole, it possesses secondary significance. Such a deduction would be incorrect, because the Liturgy, as we have mentioned earlier, beside being a sacrifice, is also a sacrament. Like every sacrament the Holy Eucharist is a visible sign of invisible grace. Not only do we have under the appearance of bread and wine "invisible grace," but we also have the very Giver of this grace, Jesus Christ. The Holy Eucharist is food for the soul, the heavenly manna which sustains our spiritual life. It is also the wellspring of supernatural life.

From this the distinction between the Eucharist as sacrifice and the Eucharist as sacrament becomes evident. Holy Communion is not an essential part of the Eucharistic Sacrifice; it is only its complement or integral part which, although being in nature a rite of the sacrament, has its own character which the rite of sacrifice does not possess. Nevertheless, there does exist an essential relation between these two rites and regardless of their distinct characters and purpose, one complements the other; they both have their own significance in the Liturgy. The Liturgy in its entirety embraces the concept of sacrifice and sacrament (Holy Communion). Both concepts taken together exhaust the essence of the Liturgy.

b) *Historical evolution of the rite of consuming the sacrifice.* At the Last Supper Christ instituted the Holy Eucharist as a sacrifice and as a sacrament. Since that time both the rite of offering sacrifice and the rite of consuming the sacrifice have undergone a long evolution before assuming their present form. Since we have already discussed the historical development of the Eucharistic Sacrifice, we shall confine ourselves here to the historical evolution of the rite of consuming the sacrifice.

The consumption of the sacrifice at the Last Supper was a little different from what it is today. Christ, according to the testimony of the evangelists, gave the Apostles first the consecrated bread, and then the consecrated wine. Giving the bread and wine separately indicates that He consecrated each element separately. From this we may conclude that the two rites, the *"consecration" (sacrifice) and "communion" (consumption of the sacrifice), formed one whole.* They were not separated as they are today. At the Last Supper the consecration of bread and wine was connected with their consumption. The Apostles sat with Christ at the same table [2] consuming the Holy Eucharist like any other food.

---

[1] Theologians call Holy Communion "an integral part" of the Eucharistic Sacrifice, but not an essential part: *"pars integralis, non vero essentialis."* See the extensive treatment of Filograssi I., *De Sanctissima Eucharistia*, 1940, pp. 293–299.

[2] Actually according to the custom of that time the Apostles did not sit at the table but ate in a reclining position.

The first Liturgy and the first Communion was, therefore, of the nature of a banquet or supper. As the rite of Holy Communion developed, this character gradually changed.

In regard to how the rite of Holy Communion looked in the times of the Apostles, we have only allusions. Probably it was no different from the Last Supper since the Apostles faithfully observed all that Christ did.

As early as the second century, however, a marked change took place in the rite of Holy Communion: *the consumption of the holy gifts became distinct from the rite of the consecration of the holy gifts.* The rite of Holy Communion was divorced from the Eucharistic Consecration and began to develop into a separate liturgical rite. In the oldest liturgical description of St. Justin (second century) we find the rite of Holy Communion distinct from the Consecration: Holy Communion is not connected with the Consecration of the bread and wine, but follows it: "when the president finishes the prayer of thanksgiving i.e., the Eucharistic prayer of consecration, and the assembly expresses its assent with Amen, then the deacon distributes to each of those present a portion of the bread, over which the Eucharist was pronounced, and wine with water for consumption."[3]

Although the rite of Holy Communion in the time of St. Justin was distinct from the rite of Consecration, nevertheless, it still had the character of a banquet similar to the Last Supper: the faithful participated with the presiding priest or bishop in the offering of the sacrifice, and after the Consecration the deacons distributed the holy gifts to the faithful for consumption.

In the Anaphora of St. Hippolytus (third century) the rite of Communion undergoes a further phase of development. The offering of Sacrifice here is not only distinct from Holy Communion, but it is a well developed rite from the textual and ritual point of view. Between the Consecration of the holy gifts and Holy Communion we find first of all preparatory prayers to Holy Communion. In the first prayer the bishop asks God that all the faithful receive the consecrated gifts worthily. Then follows a prayer recited with head bowed, the theme and expressions of which recall very much the prayer of the Liturgy of St. John Chrysostom before Holy Communion. Immediately before Holy Communion we have the deacon's acclamation: "Look up," and then that of the bishop: "Holy things for the holy," to which acclamation the faithful respond with the words: "One is holy, the Father, one is holy, the Son, one is holy, the Spirit! " Hippolytus also recalls the song of praise which the people sang immediately before Holy Communion. The rite of Holy Communion was carried out as follows: the faithful stood before the bishop and received the holy gifts from him. In the Anaphora of St. Hippolytus we also have a text of the thanksgiving prayer following Holy Communion and the prayer of dismissal.[4]

Comparing the rite of Holy Communion as described by St. Justin with that of St. Hippolytus, we notice two chief distinctions: First, according to Hippolytus, Holy Communion follows the preparatory prayers, which St. Justin does not

---

[3] See *Apology* Chapter 65 (Ed. Ott, p. 180).
[4] Hauler (*Didasc. Apostolorum . . .*) pp. 106–107.

mention, and it concludes with a prayer of thanksgiving. Second, in the Ana-phora of St. Hippolytus the consumption of the Sacrifice has lost its pristine character of a supper or meal: the deacons no longer distribute the holy gifts to the faithful, as St. Justin has them doing; on the contrary, the faithful walk up to the priest and receive Holy Communion from his hands. Thus we find that in the third century the rite of Holy Communion was similar to our present day rite, although not entirely identical, for the faithful received the Body and Blood of Christ separately and not under both species together as we receive them today.

A similar manner of Communion is recorded in the documents of the fourth century, namely, the *Apostolic Constitutions* and the *Catecheses* of St. Cyril of Jerusalem. According to the testimony of the *Apostolic Constitutions* both the clergy and faithful received the Holy Bread from the bishop separately and drank from the chalice, which was presented to them by the deacon.[5] St. Cyril accurately describes the rite of Holy Communion in his *Catecheses*: the faithful received the Holy Bread on the palm of their hands (as the deacon does today), and before consuming it they touched their eyes with it; after drinking from the chalice, they devoutly touched their lips still wet (from the consecrated wine) with their hands an dwith the last drops of the precious Blood they anointed their eyes, forehead and other senses.[6]

The new changes which occurred after the fourth century did not essentially affect the rite of Holy Communion. The only change which can be considered of marked importance is the manner of distributing Holy Communion. The custom of receiving the Holy Bread and Holy Wine separately survived to the eighth century. The original custom of distributing Holy Communion was grad-ually superseded by the custom of distributing it with a spoon.[7] Such a manner of distribution is found in the oldest manuscript of the Byzantine Liturgy, the Barberini Code.[8] This practice was universally accepted and prevails to this day.[9]

Again, from the viewpoint of the text, the rite of Holy Communion of the eighth century remained almost without any alterations. Some of the later changes and additions will be discussed when we investigate each component part of the rite.

After having considered in general the character and historical development of the rite of Holy Communion, we now come to a more detailed analysis of each constituent element. The structure of the rite of Holy Communion is divided into three parts: 1. the preparation for Holy Communion, 2. the rite of Holy Communion, and 3. the prayers of thanksgiving following Holy Commun-ion.

---

[5] Funk, *Didasc. et Const. Apost . . .* , I, 516–519.

[6] See Migne, PG, 33, 1124–1125. Although such a custom may seem to us shocking, even scandalous and desecrating, nevertheless, it bespeaks the profound faith of the first Christians in the sacramental efficacy of the Holy Gifts, which upon contact, sanctify all things.

[7] A. Petrovskiy, *Istoria prichashcheniya . . .* Khrist. Cht., 1900, I, P. 368.

[8] *Ibid.*, pp. 368–369.

[9] *Ibid.*

1. Preparation for Holy Communion

Holy Communion is, after the Consecration, the most significant and most sacred moment of the Divine Liturgy. Hence, it is understandable that the Liturgy should prepare us for this moment with a series of prayers. These preparatory prayers are composed of: a. the prayer of the ektene of supplications, b. the "Our Father," c. the prayer with bowed head, d. the prayer, "Hear us, O Lord Jesus Christ our God." Let us examine each prayer more closely.

a. *The Prayer of the Ektene of Supplication.* Immediately following the final ekphonesis of the Anaphora the deacon or the priest begins the impetratory ektene or *Ektene of Supplication,* which is to prepare for Holy Communion. This purpose is especially noticeable in the silent prayer of the priest during the ektene.

We have already examined the ektene of supplication earlier in the Liturgy. Here we shall advert only to the three petitions which are different from the previous ones. The first is an ordinary summons to prayer,

> Having commemorated all the saints, again and again in peace let us pray to the Lord.

This petition is directly related to the Anaphora, or more accurately, to the commemorations of the Anaphora, in which we have a general memento of "all the saints." Under the phrase "all the saints" the Liturgy embraces first of all those righteous and holy souls which occupy first place, that is, the Blessed Virgin Mary, St. John the Baptist, the Apostles, Prophets, Martyrs, and other Saints. But the word "saints" has a far wider meaning in the Liturgy embracing all deceased and living Christians. St. Paul used the word in this sense, as did Christian literature of the first centuries. Thus, "all the saints" are all those whom the Liturgy commemorates in the Anaphora.

The second and third petitions indicate the object and purpose of the ektene prayer. The object is the Consecrated Gifts:

> For the precious Gifts, offered and consecrated, let us pray to the Lord.

This petition, taken by itself apart from its context, could give rise to certain reservations. For the Consecrated Gifts, having already been changed into the Body and Blood of Christ, require no further prayers. Nevertheless, the following petition indicates the purpose of our prayer: why and in what sense we pray "for the offered and Consecrated Gifts":

> That our God, the Lover of men, having accepted them on His holy and super-celestial and spiritual altar as an odor of spiritual fragrance, may send down upon us in return His divine grace and the gift of the Holy Spirit.

It is not the Gifts themselves, nor their Consecration, as was indicated previously in the ektene of supplication following the Great Entrance, that is the object and aim of our prayers, but their beneficial effects, namely, the sanctification of the faithful by these Gifts.

The Divine Liturgy has two main purposes, the Consecration of the Eucharistic gifts and the sanctification of the faithful by consuming these Consecrated Gifts in Holy Communion. The Consecration of the holy gifts took place in the Anaphora; at that very moment God received them as the New Testament Unbloody Sacrifice "for all." This sacrifice was pleasing to Him, for the chief priest and the sacrifice or victim was His Only-begotten Son, God-Man, Jesus Christ. The Liturgy compares the acceptance of the Unbloody Sacrifice by God to the fragrance of incense! Just as a pleasant odor is naturally agreeable to us and satisfies the sense of smell, so also the Unbloody Sacrifice, by nature, gives infinite glory to the Heavenly Father and to man a full reconciliation with God.

The words "holy, super-celestial and spiritual altar," are an allusion to the altar so frequently mentioned in the Scriptures. According to St. Paul, Christ, by offering Himself on the cross as a bloody sacrifice, entered into heaven to continue interceding for us before His Father and to continue, so to speak, to sacrifice Himself: "But Christ, becoming a high priest of the good things to come . . . neither by the blood of goats, or of calves, but by His own blood, entered once into the holies, having obtained eternal redemption . . . For Jesus is not entered into the holies made with hands, the patterns of the true: but into heaven itself, that He may appear now in the presence of God for us." (Hebr 9:11–12; 24) There in heaven Christ does not cease to intercede for us, for His priesthood is everlasting. Therefore, he is able always to save those who come to God through Him, for He is ever ready to be their mediator.[1] Jesus Christ, who died and arose again, and who sits at the right hand of the Father, intercedes for us. (Rom 8:34) St. John the Evangelist describes in his vision "the heavenly altar," upon which he saw the Lamb "slaughtered." (Apoc 4:2; 5:5) Thus, in heaven Christ continues to sacrifice Himself in a glorified manner. By means of the wounds on His glorified Body He reminds God of us and He intercedes for us before God.

The aim of this intercession is "divine grace and the gift of the Holy Spirit," namely, the sanctifying effects and fruits of the Consecrated Gifts. In exchange for the holy Gifts, which we offer to God, we expect the fullness of God's grace and the gifts of the Holy Spirit. Those same Gifts which God accepted and sanctified, we receive in Holy Communion as a source of His grace and our sanctification.

The continuation and extension of the prayer for "the Consecrated Gifts" is the silent prayer of the priest which he says during the ektene of supplication. It explains clearly the significance of the Gifts:

> To Thee, O Master, and Lover of mankind, we commend our whole life and hope, and we beseech, and pray, and humbly entreat: make us worthy to partake of Thy heavenly and dread mysteries, of this holy and spiritual altar, with a pure conscience, for the forgiveness of sins, for the pardon of

---

[1] Hebr 7:25.

our offenses, for the communion of the Holy Spirit, for the inheritance of the kingdom of heaven, for confidence in Thee: not for judgment, nor for condemnation.

This is almost a literal repetition of the last part of the prayer of the Epiklesis, the main theme of which is a worthy Communion upon which depends the efficacy of the holy Gifts. Although the efficacy of the sacrament depends upon its nature,[2] the effects it produces in the soul depend a great deal on our preparation and disposition. Hence, the priest prays that God will make him and the faithful worthy to partake of the Consecrated Gifts, begging Him to remove from their souls all that might impede the work of the sacrament.

The silent prayer of the ektene of supplication is, therefore, a new invocation of the Holy Spirit upon the already consecrated Gifts that they may become beneficial to the partakers. Here we have another confirmation of the tendency so typical of the liturgical prayers—that of repeating and developing the same thought and petition. The Liturgy is not satisfied with asking once, but delights in expressing the same petition in many different ways.

b. *The Lord's Prayer, "Our Father."* Of the prayers of preparation for Holy Communion the Lord's Prayer occupies first place. All the Liturgies, both Eastern and Western, have it.

In all Liturgies, too, the "Our Father" has a solemn character. In our Liturgy the priest lifts up and extends his hands while reciting it. In other Liturgies various ceremonies are employed to give it distinction.[3] We see special reverence shown this prayer because its author was not the Church, but Christ Himself.[4]

History of the Lord's Prayer in the Liturgy. Where and when the Lord's Prayer was first introduced into the Liturgy is difficult to say. The oldest witnesses to its appearance in the Liturgy are St. Cyril of Jerusalem in the East and St. Augustine in the West.[5] Hence, it is safe to say that the second half of the fourth century saw the introduction of the Lord's Prayer into the Liturgy. Cyril's testimony also shows that when it was first introduced, it was in the same place it occupies today, i.e., before Holy Communion.

Probably it was the fourth petition "give us this day our daily bread" that influenced the introduction of the "Our Father" into the Liturgy, since this petition has been referred to the heavenly bread, i.e., to Holy Communion, by many of the Fathers and Church writers.[6]

The meaning of the Lord's Prayer. The Lord's Prayer, as we have said, is

---

[2] Theologians distinguish two types of effects produced by the Holy Sacraments—effects produced "ex opere operato" (i.e. those which flow from the very nature of the Sacrament) and those which depend upon the spiritual attitude or disposition of the soul, "ex opere operantis."

[3] As for example, in the Roman Mass the Lord's Prayer is sung by the priest according to a prescribed aria, but at a Low Mass he recites it aloud.

[4] Lk, 11:1–2; Mt, 6:7–13.

[5] Migne, PG, 38, 1101, 400–402. Only the Liturgy of the *Apostolic Constitutions* of the fourth century does not have the Lord's Prayer.

[6] P. Parsch, *Messerklaerung*, p. 292.

very solemn in nature. The Liturgy solemnly prefaces this prayer with the words:

> And make us worthy, O Master, to dare to call with confidence and without condemnation upon Thee, heavenly God, the Father, and to say.

We ask God that we may say this prayer "with confidence and without condemnation": "with confidence," for the Lord's Prayer more than any other prayer demands that we have complete confidence in God; and "without condemnation," for in the Lord's Prayer we ask that He forgive our transgressions in proportion to the manner in which we love our enemies: "And forgive us our debts, as we forgive our debtors." We know, of course, that in reality we do not always forgive those who have offended us. Therefore, when we recite the "Our Father" while at the same time harboring in our minds the offenses of our enemies, we compromise ourselves, knowing that God will not forgive us our offenses. Thus the Lord's Prayer is also a prayer of self-accusation and self-condemnation.

Commentators divide the Lord's Prayer into six parts or petitions. In the first place we express confidence in our Heavenly Father: "Our Father who art in heaven" The Old Testament did not know this expression. Even the most righteous men did not dare call God a "Father." To them God was a Lord and Judge and they, servants and slaves. We first find God being called "Father" in the New Testament. It was through the merits of our Lord Jesus Christ, our first brother, who redeemed us and reconciled us to God, that we became the children of God and received the "Spirit of adoption" (Rom 8:15), the grace of becoming His adopted chilren. It is by virtue of the sacrifice of Christ, the living memorial of which is the Divine Liturgy, that we dare call God our "Father."

The first petition of the Lord's Prayer *"hallowed be Thy Name"* indicates the aim and end of all creatures: God's glory, the glorification of His name. The Liturgy has the same end, to glorify God in the best manner possible.

The second petition, *"Thy kingdom come,"* follows upon the first. The kingdom of God is God reigning in the world and in the souls of His rational creatures and the realization of this kingdom is the glorification of God's Name.

The manner in which God's kingdom is realized is suggested by the third petition, *"Thy will be done on earth as it is in heaven."* It shows us how to realize the kingdom of God and how He is to be glorified here on earth—by fulfilling His will, which is expressed in the ten Commandments, the Church precepts, the duties of one's vocation, but most of all—in our conscience. The way to God, to heaven, to sanctity, to the realization of God's kingdom, is through the observance of His will.

These three petitions actually form one whole. They can all be summed up in the following words: the glory of God is the realization of the kingdom of God on earth through observance of His will. This is the highest or supreme end of man on earth.

The central petition of the Lord's Prayer is *"give us this day our daily bread."* The real meaning of this petition is that God provide for our daily physical needs—food, drink, clothing, shelter, etc. All these things are implied in the word "bread" which is the symbol of life. But, besides a body, man has an immortal soul which also needs spiritual food to survive, and this food is the Holy Eucharist, "For my flesh is meat indeed; and my blood is drink indeed." (Jn 6:56) Christ in the Holy Eucharist is the food for our souls for He said: "I am the living bread which came down from heaven. If any man eat of this bread, he shall live forever; and the bread that I will give, is my flesh, for the life of the world." (Jn 6:51–52 The Fathers refer this petition "for our daily bread" to the Holy Eucharist,[7] and this as we have seen, probably influenced the introduction of the Prayer into the Liturgy and its being placed before Holy Communion.

The heavenly bread which we ask for here sustains our spiritual life. With its help we are able to realize our purpose here on earth, which consists in the glorification of God and the realization of the kingdom of God by fulfilling His will. This bread from heaven is related also to the last petitions of the Lord's Prayer. This bread offers forgiveness of sins: *"and forgive us our debts."* Forgiveness of sins is the main objective of the Eucharistic Sacrifice. We know also that Holy Communion washes away our venial sins. Whoever receives this Heavenly Bread, can be sure that God will hear and fulfill the last petitions of the Lord's Prayer: *"and lead us not into temptation but deliver us from evil."* For Holy Communion, according to the teachings of the Church, is an effective means of protecting the soul from temptation, from future relapses into sin, from the enticements of the "evil" enemy of our souls.

Thus we can see how all the petitions of the Lord's Prayer apply to the Holy Eucharist, our spiritual bread which aids us in realizing and obtaining from God fulfillment of all these petitions. The Eucharist is the heavenly bread which God has given us to strengthen our spiritual life, to realize the kingdom of God on earth; to give God due glory through the fulfillment of His will. Through this bread we obtain forgiveness for our sins and by virtue of this bread we conquer evil within and around us. Understood in this way, the Lord's Prayer is truly a beautiful introduction and preparation for Holy Communion. It could even be called the table prayer of Christians who wish to receive Holy Communion. The Lord's Prayer is a "domestic family prayer of the community which initiates the holy Eucharistic Banquet."[8] In this prayer we ask God to give us "the Heavenly Bread, the nourishment of the whole world, our Lord and God, Jesus Christ,"[9] along with its sanctifying effects. The Lord's Prayer is,

---

[7] Here we may recall the testimony of the third century: "Christ is our bread; not everyone posseses this bread, only we, Christians. Christ is our bread, when we receive His Body." (St. Cyprian; Migne, PL, 4, 539). "By imploring God for our daily bread, we ask Him to make us always partakers of His Body and to never separate us from Him." (Tertullian; cf. Migne, PL, 1, 1160–1164).

[8] Cf. Brinktrine: *La santa messa . . .*, p. 222.

[9] Cf. the prayer of Proskomide.

therefore, a confident prayer of God's children before partaking of the eucharistic supper.[10]

c. *The Prayer with Bowed Head.* The next prayer, also a preparation for Holy Communion, is the "prayer with bowed head." It follows the Lord's Prayer after the doxology:

> For Thine is the kingdom and the power and glory of the Father, and of the Son and of the Holy Spirit, now and ever and unto ages of ages. Amen.

The priest turns to the people and blesses them: "Peace to all." Then the deacon exclaims: "Let us bow our heads unto the Lord." Then priest prays secretly:

> We give thanks to Thee, O King invisible, who by Thine immeasurable power hast made all things, and by the multitude of Thy mercy didst bring all things out of nothingness. Thyself, O Master, look down from heaven upon those who have bowed their heads to Thee, for they have not bowed unto flesh and blood, but unto Thee, awesome God.[11]

> Do Thou, therefore, O Master, equally distribute to all of us for our good (these gifts) here lying according to the needs of each one; sail with the voyaging, travel with the traveling, heal the sick, O Physician of our souls and bodies. (*Ekphonesis*) By the grace and the mercies and the love of mankind of Thine only-begotten Son, with Whom Thou art blessed, together with Thine most holy, good and life-giving Spirit, now and ever, and unto ages of ages. Amen.

The history of the prayer with bowed head. This prayer before Holy Communion with bowed head we find in the oldest liturgical formula, the Anaphora of St. Hippolytus (third century). It is also found in the Liturgy of the "Apostolic Constitutions," where we also find another prayer with bowed head before the dismissal of the Catechumens from the church. Besides the Divine Liturgy, these prayers are found in other divine services, as for example, matins and ves-

---

10 Cf. *Bibliography on the Lord's Prayer:*
Chase, *The Lord's Prayer in the early Church,* (Texts and Studies, I, fasc. 3), Cambridge, 1891.
Ehrhard, *Das Vaterunser,* Mainz, 1912.
Heusle, *Das Vaterunser, Text und Literatur-kritische Untersuchungen* Muenchen, 1914.
Brinktrine, J., *Das Vaterunser in den Messliturgien,* Theologie und Glaube, XIII (1921), pp. 275–280.
———, *Das Vaterunser als Konsekrationsgebet,* Theol. u. Glaube, IX (1917), pp. 152–154.
———, *Vaterunser und Glaubensbekenntnis in der roemischen und in der griechischen Messliturgie,* Theol. u. Glaube, XXVIII (1936), pp. 78–80.
Laubot, D.G., *Le Pater noster dans la liturgie apostolique d'apres saint Gregoire,* Revue benedictine, 42 (1930), pp. 265–269.
Jungmann, A. *Das Pater Noster im Kommunionstritus,* Zeitschrift fuer kath. Theologie, 1934, pp. 552–571.
Bock, P., *Die Brottbitte des Vaterunsers,* Paderborn, 1911.

11 Literally: "for not before the Body and Blood did they bow . . ." The words body and blood is a hebraism meaning man, who is composed of body and blood (the soul). Perhaps we are dealing here with a play on words: we bowed our heads not before the human body and blood, but before God, before the Divine Body and the Divine Blood!

pers. The custom of praying with head bowed is one of the oldest of customs and one frequently used, especially at the end of the services, when the deacon would summon the faithful to bow their heads before the Lord, and the bishop prayed over them, placed his hands upon them, blessed them and finally dismissed them.

Significance and meaning of the prayer with the head bowed. This prayer can be said to be an official petition for God's blessing before the reception of Holy Communion. It is addressed to God the Father, who is, so to speak, the master of the house who is preparing a holy supper for us. Approaching the table, we turn to Him with the petition that He bless us for this preparation. The bowed head during this prayer is an external expression of humility and submission to God, as well as of deep gratitude for preparing a holy banquet for us. The faithful bow their heads, knowing that they bow them not to "flesh and blood" of man, but to the Body and Blood of Jesus Christ, before that same God who created all things from nothing.

The object of this prayer is that God "distribute to all of us for our good these holy gifts," that He give to everyone according to his needs and the beneficial effects of Holy Communion. In the prayer travelers and the sick are specifically mentioned, namely, those who are personally unable to participate in and be present at the Eucharistic Banquet. In ancient times all those who took part in the Liturgy received Holy Communion, and to those who were absent Holy Communion was brought by deacons and the lower clergy. Those who traveled a long way took with themselves Holy Communion in order to partake of them during their journey. Although this custom is no longer practiced, nevertheless, the Church shows her deep solicitude for those who are unable to receive Holy Communion. The Church does not forget those who are hindered by traveling or those who are bedridden and cannot participate with the congregation in the Eucharistic Banquet. Hence, the Church remembers them immediately before the beginning of the Holy Banquet, imploring God, that He "travel with the traveling" and "heal the sick."

The theme of the prayer is clearly evident in the text of St. Basil's Liturgy, where the priest asks the Lord, "God of all good things and the Father of mercy," to sanctify those who bow their heads before Him, to strengthen them, and remove all evil that stands in their way and make them good, especially to make them worthy of partaking of the Blessed Sacrament for forgiveness of sins and union with the Holy Spirit.[12]

d. *The Prayer "Look Down."* The last preparatory prayer before Holy Communion begins with the words: "Look Down . . . " and is recited silently by the priest.

Look down, O Lord Jesus Christ, our God, from Thy holy dwelling-place, from the throne of glory of Thine Kingdom. Thou who are seated on high

---

[12] The prayer with bowed head is mentioned in the works of St. John Chrysostom. (Cf., for example, his second discourse on 2 Cor; Migne, PG, 61, 404).

with the Father, and are invisibly present with us, come to sanctify us and grant that from Thy almighty hand there be given us Thy spotless Body and precious Blood, and through us to all the people.

History of the prayer. This prayer is not an original one of St. John Chrysostom's Liturgy. Many older manuscripts do not have it, and in a few manuscripts [13] we have still another prayer. The authorship of this prayer is ascribed to St. Basil,[14] from whose Liturgy it probably found its way into the Liturgy of St. John Chrysostom. In the two liturgical formulas we find this prayer to be the same and located in the same place—directly before Holy Communion.

Meaning of the prayer. The prayer "Look down, O Lord . . . " which, unlike most of the liturgical prayers, is directed to Jesus Christ and not to God the Father, has a beautiful theme. In the preceding prayer, the priest asked God the Father to bless the Holy Banquet of the Body and Blood of Jesus Christ. Now he turns to Christ, the Lamb of God and "Heavenly Bread," and asks Him for His "blessing" to begin the Eucharistic Supper.

This prayer is very suitable because Christ is not only the High Priest in the Liturgy and the Victim itself, but He is also the One who is Distributor. In this prayer we find again the theme expressed in the prayer of the Great Entrance, namely, that Christ is at the same time the "one who offers, the one who is offered, the one who receives, and the one who is received." It is He who offers the Holy Sacrament Himself to the priest, and through the priest to the people. Although Christ "sits on high with the Father" on the throne of glory, nevertheless, He is at the same time "invisibly present with us." Therefore, the priest asks Him to come and give him the Blessed Sacrament and through him, to the people.

The purpose of this coming of Christ is our sanctification: "come to sanctify us." The cleansing of our souls of sin and worldly cares is also included in this coming of Christ, for only the "holy" are able to partake of the holy gifts, for "holy things are for the holy."

2. Holy Communion

Holy Communion, in its ritual functions and text, is one of the most developed parts of the Liturgy. The rite of consuming the Holy Species underwent a long evolution before finally taking on its present form. A general outline of this evolution was given in the beginning of this Chapter. Let us now examine more closely each function and prayer of Holy Communion, which is composed of *a*) the rite of raising aloft the Lamb, or the Elevation, *b*) the breaking, or fraction, of the Lamb, *c*) the mingling of both species, *d*) the communion of the priest, and *e*) the communion of the faithful.

---

[13] For instance, in the Porphyrian Codex of the ninth century.
[14] Migne, PG, 29, 301–302.

a. *The Lifting Aloft of the Amnos or Holy Lamb or the rite of Elevation.*
The rite of Holy Communion begins with the solemn elevation of the Holy
"Lamb". The priest bows three times before the altar and recites the prayer of
the publican:

O God, be merciful to me a sinner.

Then the deacon sings: "Let us attend," after which the priest raises the
"Lamb" aloft and recites aloud: "Holy things for the holy." The people responds:

One is holy, One is the Lord, Jesus Christ, for the glory of God the Father.
Amen.

The history of this rite. Although some commentators hold that the rite of
raising the Lamb aloft is of apostolic origin,[1] it was not until the fifth century
that it began to appear in liturgical documents. St. John Chrysostom does not
yet mention this rite of raising the Lamb while pronouncing the words "Holy
things for the Holy," but he does mention clearly that at that moment the priest
raised his hand as a sign of warning.[2] The first to testify to the rite of elevation
were Pseudo-Dionysius[3], then St. Maximos the Confessor (seventh century)[4],
and Anastasius of Sinai (eighth century).[5] The rite appears in the Barberini
Codex (eighth century).

The words "Holy things for the Holy" and the hymn "One is holy . . . "
have earlier and better witnesses, i.e., the oldest Anaphora, that of St. Hippolytus of the third century. Later we encounter them in the Liturgy of the *Apostolic Constitutions* and in almost all the Liturgies except the Roman.[6]

Significance and symbolism of the rite. "The raising of the Amnos or Lamb
aloft before Holy Communion was to alert the faithful for the moment of the
Holy Communion and in this way awaken within their souls corresponding sentiments"—so write Pseudo-Dionysius and St. Maximos the Confessor.[7] It is
wholly natural that we, when we wish to arouse the attention of others, raise
something aloft that all may see. This rite is gradually losing its original purpose and meaning; indeed, it loses it completely when the people cannot see the
rite being performed, because at that moment not only are the Royal Doors
closed, but even the curtains are drawn.[8]

The Byzantine commentators see in this rite the raising up of Christ on the
cross (the crucifixion). This is the interpretation of Pseudo-Herman: "The rais-

---

[1] Dmitrevskiy, *Ist. dogm. i tayinstv. izyasneniye na liturghiyu,* p. 230.

[2] Migne, PG, 63, 132–133.

[3] *Ibid.,* 3, 425.

[4] *Ibid.,* 90, 117.

[5] *Ibid.,* 89, 841.

[6] Cf. the Armenian, Syrian, Chaldean, Coptic and Ethiopian Liturgies all have the same or
a very similar phrase before Holy Communion.

[7] See Migne, PG, 3, 425; and 90, 117.

[8] The closing of the Royal Doors and the drawing of the curtains is of later origin. We
find no allusion to this in any of the ancient codices.

ing of the bread aloft typifies the raising up of Christ on the cross and His dying upon it."[9] Simeon of Thessalonica gives a similar interpretation.[10] Not only does such an interpretation have no basis in the liturgical text but it diverts our attention from the true meaning of the rite, which is eminently practical and not symbolic, namely, to draw the attention of the faithful to the moment of Holy Communion.

The following words: "Holy things for the holy" and "One is holy . . ." confirm this; they are premonitory words directed to those who wish to receive Holy Communion. With them the priest warns the faithful that only the holy, pure, those free from sin can partake of the Eucharistic Banquet. In the ancient Christian sense the word "holy" simply meant the faithful, excluding the unbaptized, i.e., the catechumens. But this meaning has now been lost, because not all the faithful receive Holy Communion. "Holy things for the holy" is a solemn reminder to those who wish to receive Communion. St. John Chrysostom, alluding to these words, says: "Whoever is not holy should not receive."[11]

To these words of warning the faithful respond with the beautiful hymn "One is holy, One is the Lord, Jesus Christ, for the glory of God the Father, Amen." These words, which are a paraphrase of a statement of St. Paul to the Phillipians[12], declared that only Christ is holy and without sin. He is holy by nature, but we "were conceived in inquities; and in sins did our mother conceive us" (Ps 50:7). Our holiness cannot be attributed to ourselves but only to our Lord Jesus Christ.

St. Cyril of Jerusalem has a beautiful explanation of this hymn: "That which is holy" he says, "are the gifts placed upon the altar, for they received their holiness through the Holy Spirit. You are also holy through the Holy Spirit, and, therefore, holy things should be for the holy.[13] Then you add: 'One is holy, one is the Lord, Jesus Christ,' for in reality only one is holy and that is by nature, and we too are holy, not by nature but by participation, by our good deeds and prayers."[14]

The Liturgy refers the hymn "One is holy" to Jesus Christ; in some other Liturgies it is not Christological but Trinitarian in essence.[15] In the Byzantine Liturgy the reference is more natural, for it is organically connected with the ritual function of the raising up of Christ, the Lamb. Therefore, "One is holy..." is an expression of the belief that our sanctity derives from Christ through

---

[9] Migne, PG, 98, 448.

[10] *Ibid.*, 155, 297 and 741.

[11] *Ibid.*, 63, 132–133 (Discourse 17 on Hebrews).

[12] Phil. 2:11.

[13] St. Cyril here was speaking to the newly baptized.

[14] Migne, PG, 33, 1124 (5. Mystagogical Catechesis).

[15] Cf. the Syriac Liturgy. (For the hymn: "One is Holy" see the following works:

Quasten, J., *Der aelteste Zeuge fuer die trinitarische Fassung der liturgischen "eis hagios."*

———, *Akklamation*, f. kath. Theol., 58 (1934), pp. 253–254).

Peterson, E., *"Eis Theos." Epigraphische, formgeschichtliche und religions-geschichtliche Untersuchungen.* (Forschungen zur Religion u. Literatur des A. u. N. Testamentes. Neue Folge, 24), Goettingen, 1926.

the merits of Christ, who as the Lamb of God offered Himself up for us in order to redeem and sanctify us. "No one accomplishes sanctification by himself, for it exceeds all human power, but from Christ and through Him. Just as many mirrors placed in the sunlight reflect the rays of the sun, thus making one believe that he sees many suns although in reality there is one sun shining in all the mirrors, similarly, that One who is holy manifests Himself in many souls, thus making them holy, but in reality He alone is Holy." (N. Cabasilas).

b) *The Fraction or the Breaking of the Lamb.* The rite of breaking the Lamb is directly connected with the rite of raising it aloft. In the present-day rite the priest breaks it into four parts which he places in the form of a cross on the diskos. While doing so he recites the beautiful formula:

> The Lamb of God is broken and distributed, broken but not divided, ever eaten and never consumed, sanctifying those that partake thereof.

Later the priest takes the upper part of the Lamb with the inscription IC, and making the sign of the cross over the chalice he drops it into the chalice saying: "The fullness of the Holy Spirit."

History of the rite. Although the fraction, or breaking, of the Lamb in its present form is of a later origin, the rite derives essentially from the Last Supper at which Christ "broke the bread" before giving it to His Apostles.[16] This "breaking of the bread" had a practical purpose—to give each of the Apostles a portion of the bread. The "breaking of bread" is a Jewish custom. Their bread was in the form of round flat cakes; they did not cut the cakes but simply broke them. From this the expression to "break bread" among Jews meant the same thing as "to eat bread."

The breaking of bread, usually joined with the prayer of blessing, took place among the Jews at each meal. To break the bread was the privilege of the master of the house or of a guest.[17] This custom was adhered to by our Lord at the Last Supper. He, as the Master of the house, "broke bread" and distributed it among His Apostles. That the Apostles and their immediate successors faithfully followed this example of Christ at their eucharistic gatherings is proven by the fact that the Holy Eucharist was commonly referred to as the *"fractio panis,"* the "breaking of the bread."[18]

The practice of breaking the consecrated bread was preserved in one form or another in all the Liturgies. In the Roman Liturgy the priest breaks the Lamb into three parts, in the Syrian, into two parts; in the Coptic [19] and Mozarabic Liturgies the Lamb is broken into nine parts.[20] In the Byzantine Liturgy at

---

[16] Cf. the Evangelist: Mark 14:22–24; Matt. 26:36; Luke 22:19, and St. Paul, I Cor., 11:24–25.

[17] St. Luke gives us an account of the beautiful episode, when Christ made Himself known to the two disciples by the "breaking of bread." They gave Christ the privilege, as a guest, to "break bread" and it was by this act of breaking bread they recognized Him. (Luke 24:30).

[18] Cfr. for instance, the Acts, 2:46; 20:7–11; I Cor., 10:16.

[19] G. Graf, *Die Zeremonien und Gebete bei der fractio panis und Kommunion in der koptischen Kirche,* Der Katholik, 18 (1916), p. 242.

[20] Brinktrine, *La Santa messa,* Roma 1945, p. 226 (t nota).

first there was no breaking of the Lamb as we have it today. We find this rite in the ninth-tenth centuries, but in certain Liturgies the rite of breaking the Lamb into three parts has been preserved.[21] Beginning with the eleventh century the custom of placing the broken Lamb in four parts on the diskos gradually prevails.[22]

Significance and symbolism of the rite. From the history of this rite we can gather that it originally had a practical purpose. The rite of Holy Communion required that the bread be broken so that it could be distributed to its partakers. However, the old commentators attached much greater importance to the symbolism of the rite. The Middle Ages, which ignored the historical evolution of liturgical rites while delighting in allegorical interpretations, saw in the breaking of the Lamb the passion and death of our Lord, and again in the immediately subsequent rite of mingling the Eucharistic species together, His Resurrection, in which the blood and soul of Christ were united with His Body.[23] Such is the symbolic interpretation of Simeon of Thessalonica for the breaking of the Lamb.[24]

The interpretation has some foundation. In the Eucharistic Sacrifice, Christ again offers Himself up as a sacrifice; again He offers His *"Body which is broken for the remission of sins"* and His Blood which is shed for the salvation of the world. The rite of breaking the Lamb is to a certain extent a representation of what takes place in the Consecration. At first, when the rite of consuming the sacrifice was interwoven with the Consecration, the breaking of the Lamb had a far deeper meaning than when it was performed apart from the Consecration and placed immediately before Holy Communion. Therefore, the breaking of the Lamb essentially belongs to the rite of Consecration, where we have the appropriate words "which is broken for you." There the symbolism of Christ's death would have a better application than before Holy Communion.[25]

The accompanying prayer does not allude to Christ dying on the cross, but to Holy Communion. Its theme concerns the nature of the Eucharistic species, reminding us that the holy Lamb is broken but at the same time "not divided," and that in every single particle of Bread even the minutest, the whole Christ is present—His Body, Soul and Divinity. On thousands upon thousands of altars He gives Himself to the faithful as food, although this Holy Bread is "never consumed." The miracle of the Eucharist surpasses by far Christ's miracle of the multiplication of loaves. The supply of this Heavenly Bread is never depleted. This Bread of God "sanctifies the partakers," for its purpose is to raise them up to the heavenly sphere, to transform, deify and sanctify them.

---

21 De Meester, *Les origines el les developpements,* p. 347.

22 Ibidem., p. 347.

23 In the Mozarabic Liturgy the nine parts of the Holy Lamb symbolize the most important events in the life of Christ: the incarnation, nativity, circumcision, Epiphany, passion, death, resurrection, glorification and eternal reign of Christ in heaven. Cfr. Brinktrine, op. cit., p. 226.

24 Migne, PG, 155, 741.

25 Myshkowskyj, *Ixlozhenie tsaregradskoj Iiturghiji,* p. 144.

These words, in dogmatic content and external form recall the words of the silent prayer of the Great Entrance:

for Thou dost offer and art offered, and dost receive and art received.

However, they were introduced into the rite of Holy Communion at a considerably later date. Many of the Slavonic manuscripts of our Liturgy, instead of the prayer we now have, have other similar prayers. One of the well known ones is: "They recognized the Lord when He broke bread," [26] which recalls the scene when the disciples journeyed to Emmaus. We still find this formula in the liturgical manuscripts of the thirteenth and fourteenth century.[27]

c) *Rite of Commixture (A Portion of the Holy Bread or Lamb is Dropped into the Chalice) and "Zeon".* One part of the Lamb the priest drops into the chalice while he says: "The fullness of the Holy Spirit."

History of the rite. This rite is found in all Liturgies, but its history is not yet clear nor is its origin and first meaning. It was perhaps first mentioned in the catechetical sermons of Theodore of Mopsuestia (+428), friend of St. John Chrysostom. From this some conclude that at the time the rite was also in the Liturgy of Constantinople. We come across it in the oldest codex, the Barberini Codex of the eighth century.[28] However, it is surprising that the old commentators on the Chrysostom Liturgy not only do not explain it, but do not even mention it.[29]

Significance and symbolism of the rite. Not only is this rite itself not yet explained, but neither is its meaning and significance. The Byzantine commentators left us no interpretation of it, perhaps because they made this rite one with the rite of the "zeon."[30] But even among the Western Liturgists there is no agreement as to the meaning of the "mixing" (*commixtio*). The theologians and the Liturgists of the Middle Ages, as we have seen, gave it a symbolic meaning, i.e., the uniting of the Body of Christ with His Blood in the chalice symbolically typifies Christ's resurrection, for it was then that the Body of Christ was reunited to His soul and blood.[31]

The Russian liturgist Dmitrievskiy gives us the same interpretation. After the breaking of the Lamb the priest *drops* one portion *and lets the* particles fall into the Holy Blood in order to represent the union of the Body of Christ with His Blood in the resurrection. And just as the separate consecration of the holy gifts, the bread and the wine, symbolized the death of Christ, i.e., the separation

---

[26] Luke 24:30.

[27] Muretov, *K materiyalam dlya istoriji chinoposlyedovaniya lit* . . . , Sergiev Posad 1895, pp. 93–94, 97, 99. (Rukopis ch. 518 Peterb. Dukh. Akademiyi z 12st. contains these words:

[28] Brinkstrine, *LaSanta messa*, pp. 230–231.

[29] Brightman, *Liturgies Eastern and Western*, I, p. 341.

[30] Simeon of Thessalonica mentions (Migne, PG, 155, 741), but does not interpret it.

[31] Cf. Brinktrine, *op. cit.*, pp. 230–234. Cf. also M. Andrieu, *Immixtio et consecratio. La consecration par contact dans les documents liturgiques du moyen age*, Paris, 1924.

of soul from body, so the union of both species in the chalice represents the union of Christ's soul with His body at the moment of His resurrection.[32]

The words accompanying the rite of "mixing"—"The fullness of the Holy Spirit"—are also not clear. We encounter these words in the Barberini Codex. Dmitrievskiy interprets them symbolically.[33] According to him the Holy Spirit is invoked because the mystery of the Holy Eucharist, like the incarnation, passion, death and resurrection, was consumated through the operation of the Holy Spirit.[34] In our opinion, however, this interpretation is strained and artificial. It were better if the words were referred not to the mystery of Christ's resurrection, but to the Holy Gifts themselves which are united in the chalice. The Holy Gifts are "the fullness of the Holy Spirit," that is, they contain the fullness of God's grace and the gifts of the Holy Spirit. The Holy Eucharist is the source and well-spring of God's grace. The song that follows immediately upon Holy Communion helps to confirm our interpretation: "We have seen the true light, we have received the Holy Spirit." Therefore, the words, "fullness of the Holy Spirit" allude to the effects of the consecrated gifts.

To the most obscure and unclarified rites not only of Holy Communion but of the Liturgy in general, belongs undoubtedly *the rite of the "zeon."* [35] By the "zeon" we understand the rite of pouring warm water into the chalice after both Eucharistic Species have been united. After the priest has dropped a part of the Lamb into the chalice, the deacon takes a vessel containing warm water and says: "Bless, Master, the warm water" and the priest blesses it, saying:

Blessed is the fervor of Thy saints, always, now and ever, and unto ages of ages. Amen.

Then the deacon pours some of the water into the chalice saying: "The fervor of faith, full of the Holy Spirit. Amen."

History of the "Zeon." "Zeon" is peculiar to the Byzantine Liturgy. It is completely foreign to other Eastern Liturgies as well as to the Roman Liturgy.

According to Lebrun [36] and Grondijs [37] the rite found its way into the Liturgy during the time of Justinian (527–565). The earliest mention of it occurs toward the end of the sixth century when the Emperor Mauricius (582–602), seeking reconciliation between the Byzantine and Armenian (monophysite) Churches, invited the Armenian "Catholikos," Patriarch Moses II (574–604), for a theological dialogue with the Byzantine theologians. But the head of the

---

[32] Brinktrine, *La santa messa*, p. 233.

[33] Dmitrevskiy, *Ist. dogm. tainstv . . .* , p. 234.

[34] *Ibid.*

[35] Although the "Zeon" rite is generally not in use, nevertheless, we cannot overlook it in our commentary because of its connection with the rite of "commixture" as well as with its symbolic meaning.

[36] Lebrun, *Explication litterale, historique et dogmatique des prieres et des ceremonies de la Messe,* Vol. IV, (Liege, 1778), pp. 412–413.

[37] L. H. Grondijs, *L'iconographie byzantine du Crucifie mort sur la Croix,* Bruxelles, p. 204.

Armenian Church declined with the words: I am not willing to cross the bordering river Azot and I do not wish to eat sour bread nor do I wish to drink warm water." [38] By these words Patriarch Moses wished to say that he was displeased with the liturgical practice of the Byzantine Church of using leavened bread and the "zeon."

In the biography of St. Theodore Sikeotes (seventh century) we find mention of an oven used to heat water during the Liturgy.[39] However, not all ancient manuscripts mention the rite of the "zeon." [40] It is referred to in the Latin translation of the Liturgy of St. John Chrysostom by Leo Tuscus (twelfth century) and the Byzantine commentators, Pseudo-Herman,[41] Theodore Andides,[42] Nicholas Cabasilas [43] and Simeon of Thessalonica.[44]

The usage of the "zeon", as we have noted, was a "stumbling block" for the Armenians who opposed it. At the Council of Florence (1439) it became a question among the Greek-Byzantine and Latin Catholic theologians. The Greeks explained why warm water was poured into the consecrated wine, but unfortunately we do not have the text of this explanation.[45] In any event, the practice was not rejected by the Catholic Church for Pope Benedict XIV acknowledged it and we find it in the Roman edition of the *Euchologion* for Catholics of the Greek-Byzantine Rite.[46]

In Ukraine the "zeon" began to disappear at the beginning of the seventeenth century.[47] Finally the Synod of Zamost (1720) did away with the practice completely.[48] Although the Roman edition of the 1940 Sluszhebnyk contains the rite of the "zeon," its practice is optional; it may be used or omitted according

---

[38] J. Pargoire, *L'Eglise byzantine,* (Paris, 1923), p. 102; Cf. Migne, PG, 132, 1248–1249.

[39] Cf. Archimandrite Cyprian, *Evkharistiya,* p. 308.

[40] The following codices do not mention the use of the "zeon": Barberini Codex (eighth century), Porphyrian Codex (ninth century), Rumyantsevskiy Codex (tenth-eleventh centuries). Also certain Slavonic codices of the twelfth-thirteenth centuries do not mention it. (Cf. A. Petrovskiy, *Ist. slav. redaktsiyi . . . . u "Khrisostomika"* pp. 870, 885).

[41] Migne, PG, 98, 449.

[42] *Ibid.,* 140, 464.

[43] *Ibid.,* 150, 449–452.

[44] *Ibid.,* 155, 742–744.

[45] Mansi, 31a, 1040–1041.

[46] This *Euchologion* was issued in Rome in 1754. We cite here the words of Benedict XIV taken from his Apostolic Constitution, "Allatae sunt" 26. Vii. 1775: "Cumque in congregationibus, quae pro correctione librorum ecclesiasticorum Ecclesiae orientalis habitae fuerunt . . . diu multumque disputatum fuisset, utrum interdicendus est ritus infundendi in calicem aquam tepidam post consecrationem . . . , responsum fuit die 1. Maji 1746 nihil esse innovandum, quod rescriptum a nobis deinde confirmatum fuit."

[47] J. Botsyan, *De modificationibus in textu slavico liturgiae s. J. Chrysostomi apud Ruthenos subintroductis,* Chrysostomika, Roma, 1908 pp. 961–962.

[48] Botsyan, *op. cit.,* 962. "Inhibet sancta Synodus gravem ob causam, et abrogat toleratum in orientali ecclesia consuetudinem ad consecratas calicis species aquam tepidam effundendi post consecrationem ante communionem." (Tit. III, a. IV). Unfortunately, the Synod of Zamost does not give this "serious reason" why it abandoned the use of the teplota or "Zeon". The reason may have been that it "scandalized the Latins" who considered the pouring of warm water into the chalice before Holy Communion an irregularity. This reason was given by the author of "Bohosloviya nravouchytelnaya," published in Pochaiv 1779, p. 21, (Cf. Botsyan *op. cit.,* p. 962, and footnote 3).

to the decree of the local Ordinary.[49] This rite is still practiced in the Orthodox Church, although not everywhere.

Significance and symbolism of the zeon. What is the meaning and sense of this seemingly strange rite so unknown to all other Liturgies? The prayer accompanying the rite does not give us a full answer. The priest in blessing the vessel containing the warm water calls it the "zeon of the holy." [50] The deacon, pouring the "zeon" into the chalice utters the words: "The fervor of faith, the fullness of the Holy Spirit. Amen." Both expressions would indicate, therefore, the *"fervor of the holy."* What the word "holy" means, we do not know. Besides, in both Greek and Slavonic Liturgical manuscripts,[51] the prayers that accompany the rite of the "zeon" vary greatly. It is difficult to decide which of the accompanying prayers is the oldest and most appropriate. In certain Slavonic manuscripts no mention at all is made of the "fervor of faith" or "the fervor of the holy"; instead the priest, while pouring the warm water, says:

> He shall come down like rain upon the fleece: and as showers falling gently upon the earth always. (Ps 71:6)

It is evident, then, that the text of the concomitant prayers do not help us much in explaining the significance and meaning of this rite. Even the Byzantine commentators give no satisfactory answer because they interpret the rite symbolically. Pseudo-Herman sees in the "zeon" a symbolic allusion to the piercing of Christ's side from which flowed blood and water. The rite is performed before Holy Communion to remind us that our life flowed from the side of Christ.[52] Theodore Andides offers the same interpretation.[53]

Nicholas Cabasilas interprets the rite quite differently. According to him, the "zeon" signifies the descent of the Holy Spirit upon the Apostles. This interpretation has its logic for, as Cabasilas remarks, the rites of the Liturgy are a representation of the work of redemption. In the Liturgy we have Christ's nativity, death and resurrection; therefore, it is expedient that the consummation of the work of redemption through the descent of the Holy Spirit upon the Apostles be, in final analysis, represented. The "zeon" precisely, according to Cabasilas, symbolizes the Holy Spirit and its warmness, the fiery tongues, under which appearance the Holy Spirit came down upon the Apostles. The "zeon" also symbolizes the Church which receives the Holy Spirit through the reception of the Holy Gifts in Holy Communion.[54]

---

49 Cf. *Svyashchennaya i Bozhestvennaya liturghiya izhe vo svyatikh otsta nasheho I. Zlatoustaho*, Rim, 1940, pp. 84–85 (the practice of using the teplota), and p. 112 (footnote).

50 "Blessed is the fervor of Your Saints . . ."

51 S. Muretov, *K materialam dlya istor. chinopos. lit . . .* , pp. 93–94. (These manuscripts come from the twelfth-fourteenth centuries).

52 Migne, PG, 98. 449.

53 *Ibid.,* 140, 464.

54 *Ibid.,* 150, 449–452.

Simeon of Thessalonica, in his commentary, is more or less inclined toward the view of Pseudo-Herman and Theodore Andides, seeing in the "zeon" a symbol of the warm blood and water that flowed from the side of Christ.[55] Dmitrievsky in his interpretation combines the ideas of both Pseudo-Herman and Cabasilas. The purpose of the "zeon" is to make the Body and Blood of Christ "warmth-giving" so that, when we receive Holy Communion, we will have the impression of drinking the same warm Blood of Christ which flowed from His side. Again "the mystery of pouring warm water into the chalice signifies the descent of the Holy Spirit upon the Church represented and symbolized by the holy gifts." [56] Bessarion takes a slightly different view. The "zeon" of faith, full of the Holy Spirit, signifies that in our souls there should be a live, ardent faith in the life-giving power of the Holy Gifts. For only then can Holy Communion be for us a saving force or a salutary rite.[57]

The foregoing commentaries may well convince one how enigmatic the rite of the "zeon" is. All these symbolic interpretations do not unravel the mystery surrounding the rite. It is hard to find any very plausible connection of the "zeon" with the descent of the Holy Spirit upon the Apostles or the piercing of the side of Jesus on the cross. In our opinion, the rite of the "zeon" once had a practical purpose and only after it lost its original objective did it begin to be interpreted symbolically. Unfortunately, because of the lack of evidence, it is difficult to offer anything certain regarding its purpose and sense. Therefore, the question still remains open to investigation.

So far as its symbolism is concerned, we believe that one can see in it a symbol of the love and ardent faith with which we should receive Holy Communion. The accompanying prayer alludes to the "zeon of faith" and the "zeon of the holy," and if the word "holy" retains its ancient Christian meaning, then the "zeon of the holy" is the symbol of ardent love and faith of the faithful who receive Holy Communion. If we accept this symbolic interpretation, then it is easy enough to see why the pouring of warm water into the chalice is prescribed immediately before Holy Communion. But regardless of the interpretation given it, it still remains an enigma, unusual and unique. The rite of the "zeon" still awaits its interpreter.

---

[55] Migne, PG, 155, 742–744. The polemical work of Nicetas Stetatos (eleventh century) on the *unleavened bread* of the Latins testifies to the popularity of this opinion. It was probably Nicetas who gave the first explanation of the *"Zeon"* as symbolizing the blood and water, which flowed from the side of our Lord. This interpretation found its way into some of the liturgical codices. In one thirteenth century codex we find the following explanation in a rubric stating: "hot water is poured . . . , in order to show the fervor of the Holy Spirit." Afterwards the author of the observation appeals to the *troparion* in the fourth song of the canon for the Pentecost (St. John Damascene), in which are found the words: "O Divine Word let fall upon me as rain a stream from Your incorruptible pierced side, sealing it by the fervor of the Holy Spirit." (See Dmitrevskiy, *Opisanie lit. rukopisej*, Vol. III, (Evkhologhiya), p. 174). The codex, in which this observation is found derives from the thirteenth century. Dmitrevskiy discovered it in Patmos.

[56] Dmitrevskiy, *Istor, dogm. tainstv.* . . . , pp. 235–236.

[57] Bessarion, *Tolkovanie na Bozhestv. lit.* . . . , p. 258.

d) Communion of the Priest. Immediately following the rite of the "zeon," we have the communion of the priest and his assistants or concelebrants. The communion of the clergy has been preserved in its ancient form, that is, the priest and his concelebrants partake of the Body and the Blood of Our Lord separately.

The priest, taking into his hands a part of the Lamb, recites the following prayer silently: "I believe, O Lord, and confess. . . ." Actually this prayer is composed of a number of prayers, very suitable to the rite of Holy Communion. They express the most important sentiments with which everyone should approach the holy table of the Lord.

First of all the priest declares his faith in Christ, the Son of God, hidden under the appearances of the Eucharistic Species:

> I believe, O Lord, and confess that Thou art indeed Christ the Son of the living God, who didst come into the world to save sinners, of whom I am the first.

In these few words we find St. Peter's ardent profession of faith [1] and the profound humility of St. Paul.[2] St. Peter acknowledged the divinity of Christ, and St. Paul in his humility did not forget that Christ came into the world to save sinners, of whom he was the greatest.

After the profession of faith and humility follows the fervent promise:

> Of Thy mystical supper this day, O son of God, accept me as a partaker, for I will not speak of Thy mystery to Thine enemies, nor will I, like Judas, give Thee a kiss, but like the thief, will I confess to Thee.

The priest recalls the crime of the wretched disciple Judas in order to awaken in his heart hatred toward the sin, infidelity and betrayal. He expresses his wish not to be like the traitor Apostle.

In his soul the humble petition of the thief on the cross is re-echoed:

> Remember me, O Lord, when Thou shalt come into Thy kingdom. Remember me, O Master, when Thou shalt come into Thy kingdom. Remember me, O Holy One, when Thou shalt come into Thy kingdom.[3]

To this petition of the good thief is joined the prayer for a worthy reception of the Holy Communion:

> Not for judgment, nor for condemnation, be for me the communion of Thy holy mysteries, O Lord, but for a healing of soul and body.

In this petition we have an echo of the words of St. Paul admonishing the Corinthians to approach the table of the Lord worthily, for "whosoever shall eat this bread, or drink the chalice of the Lord unworthily, eateth and drinketh

---

[1] Cf. the profession of the faith of St. Peter in the divinity of Christ at Caesarea Phillipi, Mt 16:16.

[2] 1 Tim 1:15.

[3] Lk 23:42.

judgment to himself not discerning the body of the Lord." (I Cor 11:27–29).
The priest concludes his prayer before Holy Communion with the prayer of the
publican:

> O God, be merciful to me a sinner. O God, cleanse my sins and have mercy
> on me. Innumerably have I sinned before Thee; O Lord, forgive me.

Preparing his soul with sentiments of faith, hope and humility, the priest
consumes a part of the Lamb "with fear and piety" as the Liturgy prescribes,
reciting at the same time the prayer:

> The precious and all-holy Body of Our Lord, and God, and Savior, Jesus
> Christ, is given to me, N . . ., priest, for the remission of sins and life-ever-
> lasting.

He then drinks the Precious Blood from the chalice, reciting beforehand the
prayers:

> The precious, holy and pure Blood of our Lord and God and Savior Jesus
> Christ is imparted to me, N . . ., a priest, unto the remission of my sins and
> life everlasting. Amen.

Afterwards, wiping his lips and the rim of the chalice with the purificator, he
says:

> This has touched my lips and shall take away my iniquities and cleanse my
> sins.[4]

Of these prayers, we can say that they are of relatively late origin.[5] The
oldest liturgical codices do not record any prayers before Holy Communion. At
the beginning the priest improvised. It was not until the eleventh and twelfth
centuries that various prayers began to appear in the Liturgy. Uniformity in the
selection of prayers was introduced by the *Diataxis* of the Patriarch Philotheus
(fourteenth century). In it we find almost all the present day prayers.[6]

Of a still later date are the *troparia* recited during Holy Communion:

> In that we have beheld the resurrection of Christ. . . .
> Shine, shine, O new Jerusalem. . . . and
> O Christ, passover, great and most Holy. . . .

which are found in the Orthodox Sluzhebnyks.[7] These *troparia* were introduced
into the Liturgy under the influence of the symbolic interpretation of Holy
Communion, which commentators related to the resurrection of Christ.

The prayer: "This has touched my lips," is taken from the well known
vision of Isaias in which one of the Seraphim took from the altar of God a
burning coal, and with it touched the lips of the prophet to indicate that his

---

4 Is 6:7.
5 Krasnoseltsev, *Materialy dlya istoriyi chinoposl. lit.* . . . , Kazan, 1889, p. 173. See also his
Svyedyeniya o nyekotorikh lit. rukop. Vatikanskoy biblioteki, p. 190.
6 We find these *troparia* appearing in the sixteenth century.
7 A. Petrovskiy, *Ist. slav. redaktsiy lit* . . . , *sv. I. Zlatoustaho*, (Khrisostomika, p. 871).

sins were purged away.[8] Repeating these words during Holy Communion, the priest professes his faith in the saving power of the Holy Gifts, which, like the burning coal, consumes the sins of man and purges his soul of all evil. This prayer appears in the liturgical codices of the twelfth century.[9]

The Kinonikon or Communion Hymn. During the rites of Holy Communion, which require a long time, the faithful sing the so-called *kinonikon* or Communion Hymn. It is a short versicle taken from the Psalms or from other books of the Bible. The theme of the *kinonikon* usually refers to Holy Communion,[10] although it quite frequently relates to the mystery of a given Feast-day or to some Saint.[11] The *kinonikon* belongs, therefore, to the variable hymns of our Liturgy like the *troparia, kondatakia* and *antiphons.*

The practice of singing a hymn during Holy Communion is mentioned in the Anaphora of St. Hippolytus (third century).[12] In the Liturgy of the *Apostolic Constitutions,* while the rite of Holy Communion was being performed, the 33rd Psalm was recited as prescribed: "I will bless the Lord at all times; His praise shall continually be on my lips." [13] St. Cyril of Jerusalem mentions that in Jerusalem during Holy Communion a versicle from a Psalm was sung: "Taste and see that the Lord is sweet." [14] The *kinonikon,* besides its original purpose, i.e., to predispose the souls of the participants for reception of the Eucharist, now has as its chief purpose to fill in the pause which occurs during the performance of the rite of Holy Communion, especially those actions of the priest at the altar, as the breaking of the Amnos, his own communion and the dropping of the Consecrated Gifts from the diskos into the chalice.

e) The Communion of the Faithful. After the priest and his concelebrants have communicated, the priest drops all the particles of the Holy Bread into the chalice. Then the deacon receives the chalice with the consecrated holy gifts from the hands of the priest and standing in the middle of the Royal Doors, invites the faithful to receive Holy Communion: "Approach with the fear of God, and with faith." To this invitation the faithful responds: "Blessed is He who comes in the name of the Lord; the God is Lord, and has revealed Himself to us." Distribution of Holy Communion to the faithful then follows.

History of the rite. The distributing of Holy Communion to the faithful differs from the manner in which it was practiced in both the Eastern and Western Churches throughout the first thousand years. As we mentioned earlier

---

[8] Is, 6:7.

[9] Cf. the Kinonikon for the Nativity: "Let you receive the body of Christ and the immortal spring taste" (Kinonikon for Easter) or "I will take the chalice of salvation and I will call upon the name of the Lord" (Kinonikon for Wednesday).

[10] Cf. the Kinonikon for Christmas: "He sent redemption to His people," or "The grace of God, our Savior had appeared to all men." (Tit, 2:11).

[11] Cf. the Kinonikon for the Apostles: "Their sound had gone forth into all the earth and their words unto the ends of the whole world." (Rom 10:18).

[12] Funk, *Didasc. et Const. Ap.,* I, 518. This Psalm is sung while the antidoron is being distributed.

[13] Migne, PG, 33, 1125. This versicle is taken from Psalm 33, verse 8.

[14] Migne, PG, 33, 1125.

in the Apostolic period Holy Communion had the character of a supper. The Liturgy was performed at a common table at which both clergy and faithful were seated. But this manner of offering sacrifice and receiving Holy Communion did not last long in the Church. In the third century the rite of Holy Communion lost the character of a spiritual banquet, i.e., it was not received by both the clergy and the faithful at a common table; instead everyone had to come up to the priest in order to receive the Holy Bread and Holy Wine from the chalice separately. The Bread was received by the faithful on the palm of the hand and the Blood was drunk from the chalice which the deacon held in his hands and presented to the faithful.[15]

This ancient Christian practice prevailed in both the East and the West for many centuries. It was not until the end of the first thousand years that new changes appeared in the practice of distributing Holy Communion. The latest witnesses of this ancient Christian practice of the communion of the faithful were the Synod of Trullo (691)[16] and St. John Damascene (eighth century).[17] In order that all the participants could receive Holy Communion, a larger number of breads were consecrated on more diskos and more wine was poured into the chalices.[18] Perhaps, because of the inconvenience and various other reasons, toward the end of the first thousand years (most likely in the eighth century)[19] a new custom was introduced, that of, distributing Holy Communion by a spoon. At first this practice was limited to the Byzantine Churches; it was not immediately accepted elsewhere—on the contrary, it met with criticism on the part of the Western theologians and Synods. In fact it was not even acknowledged by all in the East.[20] But, beginning with the tenth century, the new practice became generally accepted in the entire Byzantine Church. In the West, at that time, the custom of distributing Holy Communion under one species, namely, bread, gradually became general,[21] and by the thirteenth century this practice prevailed in the West.[22]

The significance of the Communion of the Faithful. We do not intend here to expound upon the doctrine of the Church concerning the value and significance of Holy Communion for the faithful. Instead we will direct our attention to the views of past centuries on Holy Communion which in some respects differ from the present-day view.

---

[15] This manner of receiving Holy Communion is recorded in the *Apostolic Constitutions* of the fourth century. (Funk, *Didasc. et Const.* Ap., I, 516–519).

[16] 101 Canon (Mansi, 12, 54).

[17] Migne, PG, 94, 1149.

[18] The Barberini Codex mentions not the chalice on the altar but chalices (plural) (Brightman, *Liturgies . . .*, I, 341).

[19] A. Petrovskiy, *Istoriya Prichashcheniya . . .*, pp. 368–369.

[20] *Ibid.*, pp. 368–369. In the West this byzantine practice was condemned at the Synod of London 1175 (16 canon) and by Bernold of Constance (d. 1100) and in the East by the nestorian church writer Jesuab of Nisibis in his work, *Liber demonstrationis de vera fide.*, c. I.

[21] L. Eisenhofer, *Handbuch der Liturgik*, II, Freiburg in Br., 1941, pp. 305–310.

[22] *Ibid.*, p. 310

For the modern Christian the frequent reception of the Holy Gifts, which was practiced by the Christians in the first centuries, has become a rare phenomenon and seems to be the "privilege" of the clergy and a few pious persons. In the first centuries of Christianity the faithful received Holy Communion at every Liturgy. In the *Apostolic Constitutions* it is mentioned that those who abstained from receiving Holy Communion without reason were excluded from the community. In the works of the Fathers and Church writers we have many allusions and witnesses to frequent Communion in ancient Christian times.[23] The first Christians considered it a natural obligation to communicate at every Liturgy. Holy Communion was considered a symbol of ecclesial or Church unity and a manifestation of one's incorporation into the Mystical Body of Christ. The Fathers and the first Christians were extremely conscious of the significance of Holy Communion. St. John Chrysostom, among others, clearly stresses this. To him the Communion of the Faithful was a sign of membership in the Church. He remarks that all Christians should receive Holy Communion, for by doing so they become partakers of the Body of Christ which is the Church, and that just as bread is composed of many grains of wheat, so too, the faithful who receive Holy Communion form one body.[24]

As early as the time of St. John Chrysostom the practice of frequent Communion was beginning to disappear. Chrysostom complained about the indifference and lukewarmness of the people in reference to the Holy Euchrist, a phenomenon that was noticable also in the West. Nothing helped, neither the admonishments of Church writers nor the resolutions of Synods. The practice of frequent Communion began gradually to fall into disuse.[25]

In the West the Holy Eucharist was surrounded with such great reverence that it began to lose its true purpose as spiritual food for the faithful. In the East, where no special cult of the Holy Eucharist was known,[26] there arose an estrangement from the practice of frequent Communion. The Orthodox themselves complained of this, calling it a "lack of the true Eucharistic life."[27] However, there is a practice called "hoviniye" which is, so to speak, a spiritual renewal before the reception of the Holy Communion. The faithful devote a few days to renew themselves by preparing for Holy Communion with fasting, prayer, spiritual reading, meditation on the Bible, recollection of spirit and confession.[28] This praiseworthy custom expresses the reverence shown the Holy Eucharist. But it would be more praiseworthy, if the ancient Christian custom of frequent Communion were renewed.

---

23 Cf. citations in Eisenhofer, *op. cit.* II, pp. 305–310; also Archimandrite Cyprian, *Evkharistiya*, pp. 323–324.

24 Migne, PG, 61, 200.

25 See Eisenhofer, *op. cit.*, p. 307.

26 See the pertinent remarks of T. Mishkovskiy in his book, *Izlozhenie tsaregrad. liturghii*, pp. 5–10–13.

27 Cf. Archimandrite Cyprian, *op. cit.*, p. 323.

28 Cf. the article of an unknown author: *O tsyeli govyeniya i poryadkye blagogoviynikh zanyatiy khristiyanina, prigotovlyayushchahosya ko sv. Prichashcheniyu*, (Khrist. Cht., 1833, I, pp. 185–270).

3. Prayers and Rites Following Holy Communion

The prayers and rites following Holy Communion refer first of all to Holy Communion, as for instance, the transfer of the holy gifts to the Table of Prothesis, the prayers of thanksgiving, and finally the conclusion of the whole Liturgy, namely, the prayer behind the Ambo and the dismissal.

a) The Transfer of the Holy Gifts to the Table of Prothesis. After the Communion of the faithful, the priest blesses the people with the chalice, saying: "Save, O Lord, Thy people and bless Thine inheritance." [1] These words here have a very profound meaning, for it was through the Blood of Christ that we became "God's people" [2] and received the right to inherit the Kingdom of Heaven. Every Holy Communion is a pledge of eternal life, our inheritance. Through Holy Communion we become God's people in the truest sense of the word, for we unite ourselves with the head of that people, Jesus Christ.

To the blessing of the priest, the faithful respond with a short hymn taken from the vesper services of the Pentecost:

> We have seen the true light, and received the heavenly Spirit. We have found the true faith, worshipping the undivided Trinity, which has saved me.

As this hymn is being sung, the priest incenses the Holy Gifts on the altar while saying:

> Thou hast ascended into heaven, O God, and Thy glory is manifest throughout the earth.

He then gives the diskos to the deacon, himself takes the chalice and turning to the people he says: "Blessed is our God," and then aloud, "Always, now, and ever, and unto ages of ages. Amen." After these words he takes the Holy Gifts and carries them to the Table of Prothesis where he places them.

Thy hymn: *"We have seen the true light . . ."* was introduced into the Liturgy probably under the influence of the symbolic interpretation of Holy Communion. Taken, as was remarked above, from the versicles in the vespers of the Pentecost, it seems to accord with the view that sees the rites of Holy Communion as representing and symbolizing the mysteries of Christ's resurrection and ascension into heaven, and the descent of the Holy Spirit upon the Apostles. [3] Under the influence of this interpretation the prayer also found its way into the post-communion prayers. According to Pseudo-Herman the transfering of the Holy Gifts to the Table of Prothesis symbolizes the ascension of our Lord into heaven. [4] Hence, under the influence of this interpretation we can see how easily this latter versicle was adopted into the Liturgy. Not until the eleventh and

---

[1] Ps 27:9.

[2] I Pet 2:9; 1:18–19.

[3] Cabasilas, Migne, PG, 150, 449–452, and Dmitrevskiy, *Ist. dogm. i tainstv. izyasn. na lit.*, p. 234.

[4] Migne, PG, 98, 452.

twelfth centuries did this versicle appear in the Greek liturgical codices.[5] We also find it in the Slavonic codices of the fourteenth century.[6]

Of a slightly earlier date was the incensing of the Holy Gifts before their transfer to the Table of Prothesis. It appears in the eleventh century[7] and according to Pseudo-Herman it symbolizes the grace of the Holy Spirit which was bestowed upon the Apostles after the ascension of our Lord.[8] Also the most recent commentators, as for example, Dmitrevkiy,[9] Mishkovskiy[10] and the Archimandrite Cyprian[11] refer the last blessing with the Holy Gifts to our Lord's ascension and the descent of the Holy Spirit.

The Holy Gifts are taken to the Table of Prothesis for the priest to consume, a custom found in the oldest liturgical codices. The consuming of the Holy Gifts follows the prayer behind the Ambo. The practice of consuming the Holy Gifts after Holy Communion varies with each Rite. The Roman, Maronite, Armenian and Coptic Liturgies have it immediately after Holy Communion and before the dismissal of the faithful; the Byzantine, Syrian, Chaldean and Ethiopian Liturgies have this rite after the dismissal of the faithful, at the end of the Divine Liturgy.

b) The Prayers of Thanksgiving. After the Holy Gifts have been moved to the Table of Prothesis, a "thanksgiving" follows. Those prayers are composed of the hymn: "Let our mouths be filled . . . ," the ektene of thanksgiving and the silent prayer of the priest.

History of the (Post-Communion) Prayers of Thanksgiving. To express gratitude for benefits received is a natural reaction, a spontaneous response of the human heart toward a benefactor. It is not surprising, then, to find in the Liturgy "prayers of gratitude" for the great gift of Holy Communion which God has given us. As our hearts turn to God in thanksgiving at every meal, so should they turn to Him after the reception of the Heavenly Food at the table of the Lord.

Christ gave us an example of a thanksgiving prayer, for according to the Gospels, before leaving the cenacle where He instituted the Holy Eucharist and first gave Holy Communion to the Apostles, He sang a hymn of praise with them.[12] This hymn was prescribed by the ritual of the Old Testament Paschal supper and consisted of Psalms 115–118.[13] The oldest example of a thanksgiving after Holy Communion is found in the *Didache* (first century). Here we encounter the main thoughts found in the paryers of St. John Chrysostom's

---

[5] De Meester, *op. cit.,* p. 352.
[6] Petrovskiy, *Istoriya slav. redaktsii lit., sv. I. Zlatoustaho* (Khrisostomika, p. 878, 912).
[7] De Meester, *op. cit.,* p. 352.
[8] Migne, PG, 98, 452.
[9] Dmitrevskiy, op. cit., p.245.
[10] Mishkovskiy, *Izlozhenie tsaregrad. lit.,* p. 149.
[11] Archimandrite Cyprian, *Evkharistiya,* p. 331.
[12] Mt 26:30: "Having sung a hymn they went up to the Mount of Olives."
[13] That is, the Hallel-Psalms, from hallel-yah (Alleluia-Praise the Lord)".

Liturgy.[14] Similar prayers are also to be found in the Anaphora of St. Hippolytus[15] and in the *Apostolic Constitutions.,*[16] as well as in St. Cyril of Jerusalem,[17] Pseudo-Dionysius [18] and Eutychius, Patriarch of Constantinople.[19] The present-day prayers of St. John Chrysostom can be traced back to the oldest liturgical codices.

Content of the "Prayers of Thanksgiving." The first prayer is the hymn: "We have seen the true light" which the faithful sing during the blessing with the Holy Gifts, thus giving "the undivided Trinity" praise, homage and thanksgiving for the great graces bestowed upon them in the Eucharist. Through Holy Communion we have received the Gifts of the Holy Spirit ("We have received the Heavenly Spirit") and true enlightenment ("and the true light"). Holy Communion with its sanctifying effects can be compared to the descent of the Holy Spirit upon the Apostles in the form of fiery tongues, changing them into men of God, men of fortitude and faith. A similar descent of the Holy Spirit upon the faithful takes place at the moment of Holy Communion. It transforms, sanctifies and deifies man who is naturally weak and sinful.

The hymn of thanksgiving: "Let our mouths be filled" has a solemn festive character. It was incorporated into the Liturgy by the Patriarch of Constantinople Sergius, around the year 624.[20] In the first words we ask God that He teach us to thank Him: "Let our mouths be filled with Thy praise, O Lord,[21] that we may sing Thy glory, for Thou hast deigned to make us partakers of Thy holy, divine, immortal and lifegiving mysteries." These words imply that all the faithful have received Holy Communion, otherwise they have no meaning. The hymn ends with the sincere petition: "Preserve us in Thy holiness [22] that all the day long we may meditate upon Thy righteousness. Alleluia, Alleluia, Alleluia." With these words the faithful ask that, with the help of God's grace, they may remain in that state of sanctity bestowed upon them in Holy Communion, i.e., that they may avoid sin, lukewarmness in serving God and imitation of His jus-

---

[14] "We thank You, O Holy Father, for the sake of Your Holy Name, by virtue of which You deigned to dwell in our hearts, and for knowledge, faith, and immortality, which You have revealed to us through Your Son Jesus. Glory be to You forever. You, O Lord and Sustainer of all things, created all things for the sake of Your Name. You have given to us food and drink, in order that we may taste it and give You thanks, and You have given us spiritual food and drink, and eternal life through Your Son . . . Remember, O Lord, Your Church and liberate it from all evil and perfect her in Your love. Gather her from the four corners of the world into Your kingdom, which You have prepared for her, for Your glory is forever. Let grace come and let the world pass." Hosanna to the God of David." (Tosti, *Didache,* 83–86).

[15] P.Parsch,*Messerklaerung,* 271–272.
[16] Funk, *Didascalia et Const. Ap. . .,* I, 518–521.
[17] Migne, PG, 33, 1125.
[18] *Ibid.,* 3, 469.
[19] *Ibid.,* 86, 2396.
[20] *Ibid.,* 92, 1001.
[21] Ps. 70:8.
[22] Cf. Brightman, *Op. cit.,* p. 342. *"Hagiasma"* (in Slavonic "Svyatynya") means "holiness".

tice and holiness. In other words: the faithful ask that the effects of Holy Communion be lasting, that they remain with them everyday of their life.[23]

After this hymn the deacon begins the ektene in which he calls upon the faithful to express their gratitude toward God: "Upright having partaken of the divine, holy, pure, immortal, heavenly and life-giving, awesome mysteries of Christ, let us worthily give thanks to the Lord." Characteristic of this prayer are the epithets applied to the Holy Gifts; *"divine"* because they contain God and make us partakers of His life; *"holy"* because they sanctify us; *"most pure"* because they purify the soul; *"immortal"* for "this is the bread which cometh down from heaven, that if any man eat of it, he may not die." [24]; *"lifegiving"* because Holy Communion sustains our spiritual life; *"heavenly"* [25] because this bread, like the manna of the Old Testament, came from heaven; and finally *"awesome,"* for whoever receives the Holy Sacrament unworthily commits the grave sin of sacrilege.

The deacon then implores God's grace: "Help, save, have mercy and protect us, O God, by Thy grace," and summons all the faithful to "commend each other and their whole life" to Christ our God. While the deacon is singing the ektene, the priest recites the silent prayer:

> We give thanks to Thee, O Master, Lover of mankind, Benefactor of our souls, that even this present day Thou hast made us worthy of Thy heavenly and immortal mysteries. Make straight our path, strengthen us all in Thy fear, preserve our life, make secure our steps, by the prayers and supplications of the glorious Mother of God and ever-virgin Mary, and of all Thy saints. (Ekphonesis) For Thou art our sanctification, and unto Thee we render glory, to the Father, and to the Son and to the Holy Spirit, now and ever and unto ages of ages. Amen.

The priest asks that the Holy Gifts which have been received be effective and the source of a holy, irreproachable life. Holy Communion has to be for Christians a food which sustains them in their daily life and in the battle against sin and the devil, in which they often become weak and lose courage. The purpose of Holy Communion is precisely to strengthen us in our endeavor to become just and righteous, "to safeguard our life" against any deviation from God's commandments. Such is the sense and meaning of all these metaphorical expressions found in the silent prayer of thanksgiving.[26]

---

[23] This hymn has not been sung by the Greeks probably since the fifteenth century. Cf. Moreau, *Les origines liturgies eucharistiques,* p. 158, no. 4.

[24] Jn 6:50–51.

[25] Ibid.

[26] The silent prayer in St. Basil's Liturgy contains the same thoughts: "Do You, O Lord of all, grant that the communion of the holy Body and Blood of Your Christ may be for us unto faith which cannot be put to confusion, unto love unfeigned, unto increase of wisdom, unto the healing of soul and body, unto the turning aside of every adversary, unto the fulfillment of Your commandments, unto an acceptable defense at the dread judgment Seat of Your Christ."

c) The Prayer Behind the Ambo. After the prayers of thanksgiving, the priest says the prayer behind the Ambo,[27] which at one time was the final prayer of the Divine Liturgy. It has the nature of a dismissal prayer. It begins with the invitation of the deacon: "In peace let us go forth," to which the people reply: "In the name of the Lord."[28] Then the priest goes out of the sanctuary, reciting the prayer aloud.

The prayer behind the Ambo is the actual ending and the proper "dismissal" of the Divine Liturgy. It is the conclusion of the liturgical prayers and it is found in the oldest liturgical codices. This prayer was at one time a variable part of the Divine Liturgy, changing according to the feast days of the church year. Proof of this is the Porphyrian Codex [29] which contains not one but many prayers behind the Ambo. In the early days the bishop, during the reading of this last prayer, placed his hands upon the faithful, imparted a blessing and dismissed them. This prayer, is, therefore, a farewell prayer, an official conclusion of the liturgical meeting. Hence, the people during this prayer bowed their heads [30] so that the final blessing of the priest would flow upon them.[31]

The meaning of the prayer. Pseudo-Herman calls this the "seal of all the prayers." [32] It is indeed a short recapitulation of the most important petitions. The prayer behind the Ambo is especially remarkable for its universal spirit. Again for the last time the priest places the needs of the community before the altar of God's mercy.

The prayer begins with an appeal to God's mercy:

O Lord, Who blessest them that bless Thee,[33] and sanctifiest them that trust in Thee, save Thy people and bless Thine inheritance. Protect the fullness of Thy Church, sanctify those who love the beauty of Thy house. Do Thou honor them by Thy divine power; and forsake us not who hope in Thee. Give peace to Thy world, to Thy churches, to the priests, to our (Emperor or King) government, and to all Thy people. For every good giving and every perfect gift is from above, coming down from Thee, the Father of lights (Jac 1:17), and to Thee we render glory, and thanksgiving, and ado-

---

[27] So called because the priest recites it standing in the middle of the church (behind the ambo).

[28] Some see in these words an allusion to Christ's words: "Rise up: let us go: behold he that will betray me is at hand." (Mk 14:42) For example, Malinovskiy (*Izyasnenie na bozh . . . lit.*, p. 206). But this symbolism has no foundation! For how can there exist a similarity between the departure of the faithful from the church and Christ's voluntary embarkment upon His passion.

[29] Archimandrite Cyprian, *Evkharistiya*, p. 335. Besides the Porphyrian Codex, there are others of the ninth-eleventh centuries that contain various prayers behind the Ambo. Cf. De Meester, *op. cit.*, p. 354.

[30] Cf. Bessarion, *Tolkov. na bozh. lit.*, p. 278.

[31] In the Roman Liturgy the counterpart of our prayer behind the ambo is the so-called "post-communion" prayer.

[32] Migne, PG, 98, 452.

[33] Here "to bless" (*eulogein*) possesses a double meaning, the first meaning is to "bestow upon someone a blessing," and the second meaning is "to praise, glorify or to speak well of someone."

ration, to the Father, and to the Son, and to the Holy Spirit, now and ever, and unto ages of ages. Amen.

Almost every petition of the prayer behind the Ambo has appeared in one form or another throughout the Divine Liturgy. Here again we find the petitions for peace which the Liturgy solicits so frequently. The prayer concludes with an appeal to God's mercy, from whom we receive every assistance, grace and blessing. After the prayer behind the Ambo, the people, in gratitude for all the blessings conferred upon them, sing the hymn: "Blessed be the name of the Lord from now and unto ages."

d) *The Prayer Accompanying the Consumption of the Holy Gifts.* After the prayer behind the Ambo, we have the consumption of the Holy Gifts which have been carried from the altar to the Table of Prothesis. According to the testimony of the various Liturgies and ancient documents, the deacon performed this rite.[34] The prayer accompanying the consumption of the remains of the Sacred Species: 'Christ our God . . .," is called in the oldest liturgical codices "the prayer for the consumption of the holy gifts." [35] In essence it is a prayer of thanksgiving directed to our Lord Jesus Christ:

> Christ our God, who art Thyself the fulfillment of the law and the prophets, who didst fulfill all the Father's dispensation, fill our hearts with joy and gladness, always, now and ever, and unto ages of ages. Amen.

These words refer to the whole Divine Liturgy which is a commemoration of our redemption, that is, of all that Christ did for us. The Divine Liturgy is indeed the "fulfillment" of the Law and the Prophets, the fulfillment of God's promises and of the expectations and craving of the Old Testament for a perfect and true sacrifice and man's union with God.

St. Basil develops the thoughts so beautifully expressed in the prayer of the Liturgy of St. John Chrysostom. Here the priest prays:

> The mystery of Thy love, Christ our God, has been completed and perfected as far as in us lay. We have the memory of Thy death, we have seen the figure of Thy resurrection, we have been filled with Thine endless life; we have enjoyed Thy delights which cannot be made empty, of which also is the life to come: deign to count us worthy of Thy benevolence. Through the grace of the Father, who has no beginning, and of Thine all-holy, all-good and life-creating Spirit, now and always and forever and ever. Amen.

While the deacon consumes the Holy Gifts, the priest distributes to the people the so-called *"Antidoron"* namely, the remains from the prosphora, out of which the Lamb and the particles were cut. The custom is no longer in practice, for the rite of "the cutting out of the Lamb" and the particles from the prosphora no longer exists. Certain commentators see in the antidoron a symbol of the virgin body of the Blessed Virgin Mary, from which the Holy Spirit formed

---

[34] Hanssens, *Inst. lit.,* III, 527–533.
[35] Brightman, *op. cit.,* 344.

the Body of Christ.[36] This custom is a remnant of the agape or Meal of Love practiced in the first centuries of Christianity. In the Old Testament after the sacrifices of thanksgiving in the vestibule of the temple or outside the temple a banquet was prepared from the remains of the sacrificial offerings,[37] in which the Levites and the servants of the temple took part. The banquet of love, the agape, was practiced in the first centuries, but because of abuses it was eventually forbidden and eliminated.[38]

e) *The Apolysis or the Conclusion of the Divine Liturgy.* In the present-day Liturgy the prayer behind the Ambo and distribution of the antidoron is followed by the Apolysis. It was inserted into the Liturgy at a later date—we find it in the fourteenth and fifteenth centuries,[39] and it came from the other Church services. The real dismissal and conclusion of the Liturgy is, as we have said, the prayer behind the Ambo. The priest, before dismissing the faithful, blesses them:

> The blessing of the Lord be upon you, by His grace and love of men, always, now and ever, and unto ages of ages.

Then he gives praise to Christ:

> Glory be to Thee, Christ O God, our hope, glory be to Thee.

The people reply "Glory be to the Father, and to the Son, and to the Holy Spirit, and now and ever, and unto ages of ages, Amen. Lord have mercy, Lord, have mercy. Lord, have mercy. Bless us." Then commemorating the Blessed Virgin Mary and other saints, the priest begs Christ, "the Lover of Mankind," to have mercy on us and save us.

After concluding the dismissal, the priest closes the Royal Doors and leaves the altar. The Sluzhebnyk directs the priest, as he leaves the altar, to recite the prayer "Now Thou dost dismiss Thy servant, O Lord." A better and more appropriate prayer could not be found. This prayer of the venerable Simeon is most suitable as a farewell prayer. The sentiments of Simeon which were awakened when he held in his arms the Savior of the world naturally take expression in the soul of the priest at this moment. He repeats with Simeon the words of thanksgiving for the great gift and grace of the priesthood of the New Law, for he has been granted the grace to hold in his hands the Divine Savior and to be an instrument of the Eternal High Priest in the Unbloody Sacrifice.

The words of the hymn: "Now Thou dost dismiss Thy servant, O Lord" tells us what the Liturgy as a whole actually is. It is the "salvation" which the

---

[36] See the commentary of *Pseudo-Herman* (Migne, PG, 98, 452–453) and *Theodore Andides* (Migne, PG, 140, 465).

[37] Cf. Deuteronomy 12:7; 14:23; 16:10; 26:11.

[38] The Synod of Laodicea (fourth century), 28 canon; The Synod of Carthage (411) in Canon 41, and the Synod of Trullo (692) in Canon 74, Mansi, 2, 579.

[39] De Meester, *Les origines . . .*, p. 355.

Lord prepared for mankind; it is a memorial to our redemption. In the Divine Liturgy Christ does manifest Himself as the "light of revelation to the gentiles" and for the glory of the new chosen people. The Divine Liturgy is the new revelation of God's love, benevolence and mercy to mankind. It is the new coming of Christ into the world with the messianic graces. Here He enlightens us with His doctrine, here He speaks to us, here He sacrifices Himself and dies mystically, here He gives Himself to us as food and unites Himself with us in order that we "may have life and may have it more abudantly." [40] All this He does to insure our eternal salvation, which He has brought about by shedding His Blood. How, then, can one leave the altar and not recall with a thankful heart all that God has done for His children?

In the Greek Liturgikon [41] the priest is directed to kiss the altar before leaving the sanctuary, a custom that is practiced in some churches of the Byzantine-Ukrainian Rite.[42] This rite has a symbolic meaning which corresponds to the kissing of the altar upon entering the sanctuary before the Divine Liturgy begins. The final kiss bestowed upon the altar, which is the symbol of Christ, is the final expression of gratitude and love of the priest for his Eternal High Priest. It is a farewell kiss bestowed upon Christ, the Heavenly Bridegroom, by the Church.[43]

---

[40] Jn 10:10.

[41] De Meester, *La divina liturgia del nostro P.S.G. Crisostomo.* (testo greco e traduzione italiana), Roma, 1925, p. 104, 133.

[42] This practice is prescribed in the new *"Order of Celebration,"* published in Rome. Cfr. *Ordo Celebrationis,* p. 5 (a. 11, a).

[43] The Syrian Liturgy prescribes a very touching prayer accompanying the rite of bestowing a final kiss upon the Altar: "Remain in peace, holy altar of the Lord; I know not if I shall return to you or not. May the Lord grant that I shall see you amidst the assembly of the first-born into Heaven: in that covenant I put my trust. Remain in peace, holy and atoning altar: may the holy Body and the atoning Blood that I have received from you be for the forgiveness of my misdoings, the remission of my sins and my safeguard when I stand before the judgement-seat of our Lord, the ever-living God. Remain in peace, holy altar, table of life, pleading for me before our Lord Jesus Christ that I may always have Him in mind, henceforth and for ever. Amen." (Cf. Hanssens, *Institutiones liturgicae,* III, p. 533).

SELECT BIBLIOGRAPHY

Petrovskiy, A., *Istoriya china prichashcheniya v Vostochnoy i Zapadnoy Tserkvi*, (Khrist. Cht., 1900, I, pp. 362–371).

Muretov, S., *Poslyedovanie proskomidiyi, Velikaho Vkhoda v slaviano-russkilch sluzhebnikakh XII–XIVvv.* (Cht. v imp. obshch. Ist. i dr. rus., 1897, 2, pp. 1–43).

————, *K materialam dlya istorii chinoposlyedovaniya liturghiyi*, Sergiev Posad, 1895, p. 93 ff; (Anonymous), *O tsyeli govyeniya i poryadkye blagogovoynikh zanyatiy khristiyanina, prigotovlya-yushchahosa ko sv. Prichashcheniyu*, (Khrist. Cht., 1833, I, pp. 185–270).

Probst, F., *Verwaltung der Eucharistie als Sakrament*, Tuebingen, 1851.

Kleinschmidt, *Zur Geschichte des Kommunionritus*, (Theol.-prakt. Quartalschrift, 1906, 95 ff).

Funk, X., *Der Kommunionritus: Kirchegeschichtl. Abhandlungen und Untersuchungen*, I, Paderborn, 1897.

Schmitz, *Der Empfang der heiligen Sakramente gegen Ende des Mittelalters*, (Stimmen aus Maria-Laach, 1890, 540 ff.).

Rauschen, *Eucharistie und Buss-sakrament in den ersten 6 Jahr hunderten der Kirche*. Freiburg in Br., 1901.

Browe, *Die oeftere Kommunion der Laien im Mittelalter*, (Bonner Zeitschrift fuer Theologie und Seelsorge, 1929, 1–28).

Hoffmann, *Geschichte der Laienkommunion bis zum Tridentinum*, Speyer, 1891.

Smend, *Kelchversagung und Kelchspendung in der Abendlaendischen Kirche*, Goettingen, 1898.

Browe, P., *De frequenti communione in Ecclesia occidentali usque ad annum c. 1000*, Roma, 1932.

Kramp, J., *Eucharistia, Von ihrem Wesen und ihrem Kult.*, Freiburg in Br., 1926.

INDEX

(The reader will observe that in this English translation the foreign names, authors, book titles and certain terms are offered in different spellings and orthographic inconsistency. However, some of the double spellings are marked here in parenthesis.)

Abel, 243
Abraham Bar Liphen, 94
Abraham, patriarch, 243, 283
Acacius of Constantinople, 185
Acts of the Apostles, 29, 30
Adaptation (ritual), 43
Adoration, 22, 131, 148, 198
Aër, 108, 129, 248, 249, 250
African (Liturgy), 39
Agape (repast of love), 29–30, 103, 111, 332
Albanian (Rite), 48
Albrigi, P., 282
Alexandria, 42, 44, 45, 192, 286
Alexandrine (Liturgy, Rite), 39, 44, 229, 270
Alexandrian School, 78
Alexius, czar, 64
Alfonso, P., 162
Alkhimovich, I., 85
Allatius Leo, 71, 278
Alleluia, 198–9, 227, 263, 328
Altaner, B., 78
Altar, (holy Table), 106, 115, 121, 142, 145, 176, 184, 212, 220, 221, 223, 232, 242, 288, 322, 333
Amalarius, 94, 165
Ambrose, St., 39, 79, 164, 292
Ambrosian (Rite), 43, 87
Ambo (prayer of A.), 173, 202, 326, 327, 330–1, 332
Amen, 147–8, 254, 263, 265, 267, 294, 313
Amnos (or Lamb of God), 107, 323
Anamnesis, 216, 252, 253, 255, 267–71, 281–2, 284, 287, 295
Anaphora, 36, 38, 40, 46, 47, 49, 51, 86, 105, 154, 158, 206, 214, 215, 218, 239, 251–6, 260, 266, 271, 274–5, 277, 284, 286, 287, 288, 289, 291, 294–5, 302, 309, 312, 323, 328
Anastasius, Emperor, 186
Anastasius, Librarian, 71
Anastasius Sinaiticus, 70, 312
Andersen, K., 31, 296
Anthony, the Roman, 56
Antidoron, 331–333
Antimension, 82, 219
Antioch, (Liturgy, Rite, Church), 39, 44, 57, 164, 186
Antiphons, 49, 55, 139, 163–171, 172, 176–7, 185, 188, 196, 323
Antonov, A., 84
Apolysis (dismissal), 332–3
Apostles, 18, 19, 21, 23, 28, 29, 41, 42, 44, 126, 136, 182, 192, 197, 202, 214, 243, 253,

257, 273, 284, 288, 290, 294, 301, 319, 323, 326, 327, 328
Apostolic (age, period, times), 29–33, 44, 103, 136, 253, 254, 268, 273–4, 287
Apostolic Constitutions, 39–40, 87, 119, 150, 156, 158, 177, 189, 192, 208, 214, 218, 220, 239, 243, 244, 255, 257, 266, 274, 287, 303, 309, 312, 323, 328
Apostolic Tradition, 35–6, 39, 254, 257, 274, 275
Arius, (Arianism), 32, 33
Arkudius Peter, 81, 234, 278
Armed forces, (prayer for), 155
Armenian (Liturgy, Rite, Church), 43, 45, 50, 72, 139, 149, 190, 191, 201, 229, 247, 312, 317–8, 327
Arnold, A., 28, 295
Arnt, A., 37, 41
Arsenius of Kiev, 84
Arsenius Sukhanov, 39, 44, 71
Asia Minor, 42, 43, 44, 45, 52, 83, 164
Asteriskos, 106, 108, 129
Athanasius, St., 39, 44, 71
Athens, 59
Athos, Mt., 57
Atchley, G., 134, 297
"Attention", 194–6
Augustine, St., 39, 112, 148, 164, 306

Balaban, G., 61, 62
Banquet (divine, eucharistic, spiritual), 23, 103, 104, 209, 212, 216, 222, 229, 244, 308, 310, 313, 324
Baptism, sacrament of B., 23, 55, 88, 112, 135, 138, 209, 212, 246, 247, 248, 279
Baranovich, L., 80, 276
Barberini (Codex), 50, 55, 105, 106, 184, 192, 219, 220, 229, 242, 255, 303, 312, 317, 318, 324
Bardenhewer, O., 50
Barlaam Khutynsky, 56
Barth, M., 28, 296
Basil, St., (Liturgy of St. B.), 39, 44, 46–7, 49, 50, 51–2, 55, 71, 93, 126, 150, 164, 173, 179, 189, 198, 207, 220, 221, 229, 234, 243, 255, 262, 265, 276, 282, 286, 291, 292, 311, 329, 331
Batiffol, P., 26, 30, 34, 297
Baumgartner, L., 30, 34
Baumstark, A., 31, 32, 33, 37, 40, 41, 50, 52, 54, 149, 158, 160, 203, 259, 263, 273, 297
Bazylovych, I., 87

335